Mesoamerican Plazas

Mesoamerican Plazas

Arenas of Community and Power

Edited by
KENICHIRO TSUKAMOTO
and TAKESHI INOMATA

THE UNIVERSITY OF ARIZONA PRESS

TUCSON

The University of Arizona Press
www.uapress.arizona.edu

 Published 2014
First paperback edition 2016

Printed in the United States of America
21 20 19 18 17 16 7 6 5 4 3 2

ISBN-13: 978-0-8165-3058-8 (cloth)
ISBN-13: 978-0-8165-3246-9 (paper)

Cover designed by Leigh McDonald
Cover photo: Maya archaeological site of Palenque, Mexico, by Kenichiro Tsukamoto

A subvention for the publication of this book was provided by an Alphawood Foundation grant.

Library of Congress Cataloging-in-Publication Data
Mesoamerican plazas : arenas of community and power / edited by Kenichiro Tsukamoto and Takeshi Inomata.
pages cm.
Includes bibliographical references and index.
ISBN 978-0-8165-3058-8 (cloth : alk. paper)
1. Maya architecture—Mexico. 2. Maya architecture—Central America. 3. Indian architecture—Mexico. 4. Indian architecture—Central America. 5. Plazas—Mexico. 6. Plazas—Central America. 7. Mexico—Antiquities. 8. Central America—Antiquities. I. Tsukamoto, Kenichiro, 1973– II. Inomata, Takeshi, 1961–
F1435.3.A6M49 2014
711'.550972—dc23
2013039490

♾ This paper meets the requirements of ANSI/NISO Z39.48-1992 (Permanence of Paper).

CONTENTS

Mesoamerican Plazas

INTRODUCTION

Gathering in an Open Space

Introduction to Mesoamerican Plazas

TAKESHI INOMATA AND KENICHIRO TSUKAMOTO

Plazas are focal points of Mesoamerican public life. Throughout Mesoamerican history, plazas have been essential components of the site layouts of cities, towns, and even small villages. The integration of formal plazas into public spaces dates back to the Early Formative period (ca. 1650 BC) in Mesoamerica (Clark 2004), and plaza-centered designs continue today in many Latin American cities (Low 2000; Richardson 2003; Wagner et al. 2013). Despite this ubiquity and long historical tradition, archaeological and historical studies of ancient Mesoamerican plazas have been limited in contrast to those of surrounding monumental architecture such as pyramidal temples and palaces. The scarcity of studies examining plazas results from two problems. First, many scholars assumed that prehispanic Mesoamericans invested much labor, wealth, and symbolic value in pyramids and other prominent buildings and viewed plazas as remaining empty spaces of lesser cultural and social import. Second, even when researchers recognized the potential value of plazas, they thought that these vacant spaces offered few clues about their use and meaning (Holley et al. 1993:306).

The goal of this volume is to challenge these perceptions. The authors set plazas as central foci of their inquiry and examine their social significance in various parts of Mesoamerica (figure I.1). We recognize that plazas do not represent the only type of public space in most parts of Mesoamerica. There were most likely other kinds of space, ranging from broad causeways to unmarked open spaces outside of settlements, where a large number of people could interact. Nonetheless, plazas stand out as clearly recognizable and marked spaces. The high visibility of plazas is probably not unrelated to the social significance that people invested in those spaces. The chapters in this volume show that the study of plazas concern the broad issues of lived experiences of people and the political processes that they participated in.

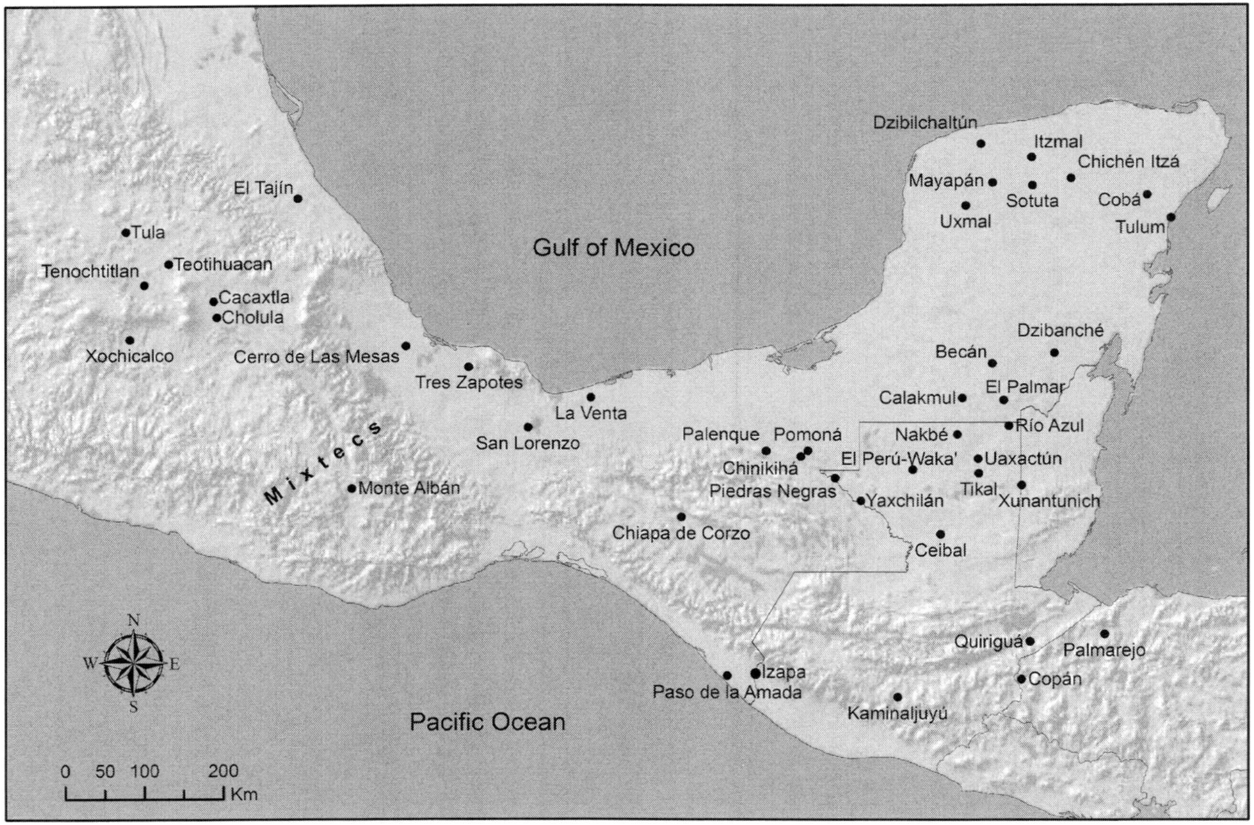

FIGURE I.1. Map showing the location of sites discussed in this volume.

Politics of Public Spaces

Our interest in plazas derives from theoretical perspectives that emphasize the importance of bodily actions set in specific historical and material settings in the creation and negotiation of social relations and values, as outlined by practice theory (Bourdieu 1977; Giddens 1979, 1984; Ortner 1984) and performance theory (Coben and Inomata 2006; Schechner 1985; Turner 1982). These theories direct our attention to the interplay between power relations and embodied practices mediated by material culture and historically shaped perceptions of meanings. The central point is that physical interactions among people are not mere masks or outcomes of political machinations held behind the scene, but they are the political processes in which people create, negotiate, and subvert social realities. If so, spacious plazas that were arguably designed for interactions among a large number of individuals must have provided a critical arena for the constitution and transformation of society (Foucault 1977, 1984; Geertz 1980; Houston 1998; Inomata 2006a; Inomata and Lawrence 2006; Rabinow 2003; Schechner 1985; Scott 1998; Turner 1982). Moreover, any society necessitates interactions among individuals based on their sensory perceptions to produce and reproduce collective identities (Geertz 1980; Inomata 2006a). In premodern societies that lacked print and communication technologies, which facilitated such interactions across distance, physical gatherings of many individuals in large spaces could contribute significantly to this process. The centrality of large plazas in most Mesoamerican settlements suggests that their residents consciously or unconsciously recognized the necessity of such gatherings and that plazas formed essential elements in historically ingrained forms of political discourse and interaction in this area.

More specifically, the study of plazas concerns the central issues in archaeology including the negotiation of power relations, community-making, and the constitution of political authorities. It addresses both Foucault's version of power rooted in social relations and collectivity and Weber's version, which is possessed and executed by certain individuals, groups, and institutions. As to the former, many Mesoamerican plazas appear to provide classic examples for the technology of power based on spectacles that Foucault (1977) saw prevailing in premodern societies. As dramatic events were witnessed by many individuals, the authority and value of society were created and reconstituted. Foucault argued that in modern European society this form of power was replaced by disciplinary power that created docile bodies through physical and perceived interactions set in certain spatial devices. However, as many critics have noted, we probably do not have to assume such a strict division. Public events held in Mesoamerican plazas doubtless distributed individual bodies in a certain order and controlled their movements through social norms, historical conventions, and the physical constraints of the spaces; they created a specific type of political subject that conformed, at least to a certain degree, to the norms of society (Foucault 2007; Rabinow 2003; Scott 1998).

As Foucault has noted, the effects of power are not always negative; it makes society. Mesoamerican plazas as stages of public gatherings probably facilitated the process of community-making. Plazas located in the centers of many

Mesoamerican cities were often large enough to accommodate a substantial number of individuals, and during the Contact and Colonial periods, plazas from central Mexico to the Maya lowlands were indeed used for mass gatherings. These events allowed participants to witness the bodily presence of other community members and share common experiences. They gave participants opportunities to act out and comment on ideas and values associated with the community.

In terms of Weber's version of power, spaces are integral parts of political processes involving the naturalization and contestation of dominant regimes (Lefebvre 1991; Smith 2003). The stake is particularly high for plazas as prominent public spaces. In some cases, ruling elites may have tried to manipulate these spaces and public events to promote their agendas. This issue has been an important concern for scholars, particularly in the study of prehispanic Mesoamerica, where the construction of central plazas was typically sponsored by the ruling elites and these public spaces were often filled with images and monuments of rulers (Lucero 2003). Historical documents from the Contact and Colonial periods show that public events in various parts of Mesoamerica highlighted the centrality of rulers and other elites, their ancestral genealogies, their ability to mediate communications with supernaturals, and their achievements in political and military affairs. It is likely that these patterns had deep historical roots. Nonelite participants in these events became, whether willingly or unwillingly, accomplices in the creation and maintenance of the dominant regime.

These effects of power, both in Foucault's and Weber's senses, never work one-directionally because public spaces and events inevitably allow a substantial degree of appropriation and reinterpretation by different individuals. De Certeau (1984), in particular, has emphasized the ability of individuals to resist the disciplinary forces of totalizing spatial schemes by transforming spatial signifiers through their practices. Centrally designed spaces emphasize consistent legibility and normalization, but individuals who visit them may improvise diverse reactions. In this sense, public spaces are arenas of constant negotiations and contestations (Lefebvre 1991). Likewise, public events offer participants opportunities to re-create and transform meanings and memories associated with plazas and to internalize them in diverse ways; in this process, rulers' claims on the places and their relations to the community are also evaluated. Thus, it is necessary to examine not only the strategies of ruling elites and the disciplinary effects of power reflected in spatial settings, but also the possibility of their reinterpretations and appropriation by various individuals.

We should note that many plazas, in addition to serving elite-sponsored mass spectacles, most likely served multiple purposes. It is probable that visitors of plazas on different occasions underwent distinct experiences of the spaces. One such use might have been the marketplace. Although the archaeological identification of marketplaces is challenging (see Dahlin et al. 2007), such use is amply documented in contact- and colonial-period Mesoamerica. Ringle (chapter 10) points out that Nahuatl *tianquiztli/tianquizco*, Yukatek *k'iuik*, and Mixtec *yahui* mean both plaza and market. These uses of plazas would imply a set of social conventions and rules different from elite-sponsored rituals.

All the chapters in this volume address the issue of power relations, but those by Murakami and by Tsukamoto most specifically examine the intertwined nature of disciplinary power and the technology of power based on spectacle, as well as the strategies of the ruling elite and other social groups tied to the politics of identity. Murakami's (chapter 2) analysis of plazas at Teotihuacan after the urban renewal shows the strong initiatives of the elite and the state in the establishment of standardized architectural styles and orientations throughout the city. However, he also sees that the variation among apartment compound layouts reflects the importance of decision-making at the neighborhood level. Tsukamoto (chapter 3) examines various plazas at the Maya center of El Palmar and finds that the power of the ruling elite increased from the Preclassic to Classic periods, which is reflected in the designs of public and exclusive plazas. At the same time, his excavation of an outlying group shows that the second-tier elites were able to establish this group and its hieroglyphic stairway through the interreliance and competition with the dynasty. In examining the Preclassic Maya center of Ceibal, Inomata (chapter 1) more strongly emphasizes the process of community-making through plaza construction and public events. While recognizing the role of the emerging elite and the possibility of dissent by various community members, he suggests that the plaza construction effort during the Preclassic period, which was more substantial than that of the Classic times, contributed to the creation of group identity and value for the newly established sedentary community. All these studies use the strength of archaeological studies in tracing diachronic patterns and in examining people's involvements and strategies reflected in construction volumes and materials.

Physicality of Plazas

In the examination of these social processes tied to plazas, one critical issue is the interplay between the physical and practical aspect of plazas and the abstract and ideational aspect. The former concerns physical characteristics of spaces in relation to human practices and perceptions, whereas the latter is about meanings and memories associated with plazas. If we are to follow the framework of practice theory, we should not view these two aspects as separate or distinct ones, with one reducible to the other. We need to address their inseparable, recursive relations. In his commentary, Moore (chapter 12) raises a similar point, referring primarily to Eric Wolf's (1999) concept of structural power, which is deployed in two directions: empirical effects of mobilizing labors and controlling resources; and symbolic ones shaping people's ideas.

In the study of the physical characteristics of space and human perception, an influential theory is called proxemics and was developed by Edward Hall (1968, 1990 [1966], 2003). Proxemics explores visual and auditory effects and potentials of human interactions defined by specific spatial parameters. Another approach is the notion of space syntax developed by Bill Hillier and Julienne Hanson (1984), which analyzes the patterns and degree of visibility and access among spaces to examine their social effects. Jerry Moore (1996b) has applied these methods to archaeological remains in coastal Peru and has explored possible patterns of interaction in ritual and perceptual effects of ceremonial architecture. Barbara Mills (2007) has also applied proxemics to examine the correlation between the visual prominence of ceramics and the performance of ritual feasting conducted in plazas in the Mogollon rim region of the American Southwest.

Another important aspect of the physical property of plazas is the issue of inclusiveness and exclusiveness shaped by their accessibility and size (Cooper 1993; Joyce 2004, 2009; Kolb 1994; Low 1995, 2000; Ringle and Bey III 2001; Sanchez 2005). Arthur Joyce (2004), for example, has examined diachronic changes in spatial organization at the Main Plaza of Monte Albán. This plaza was originally used as an arena for large-scale public ceremonies during the Terminal Formative period (100 BC–AD 200), but during the Classic period (AD 200–800) elite architectural complexes with carved monuments were built around the plaza, effectively restricting access. Joyce has concluded that the plaza during the Classic period became a locus of elite-focused ceremonies and their domestic activities, increasingly excluding commoners. Cyphers and Murtha (chapter 4) address the question of inclusivity and exclusivity through the sizes, layouts, and locations of plazas at the Early Preclassic Olmec center of San Lorenzo, estimated through a systematic coring program. The central plaza became more restricted to the ruling elite during the apogee period than the previous era, but unlike later Mesoamerican centers many stone monuments were placed outside the core area. They go on to argue that these monuments, along with ones placed in outlying communities, strengthened regional integration through the creation of broadly distributed sculptural scenes associated with ritual displays.

Estimated capacities of plazas based on their sizes provide baseline information with which to examine who participated in events held there and what kind of interactions might have been possible. Moore (1996b) has examined plaza capacities in the Andean region, and Inomata (2006a) has applied this approach to Classic Maya cases. However, capacities of plazas may vary significantly depending on specific ways of positioning participants. Moore's study has showed little consistency in estimated capacities, which has suggested that Andean plazas were used in diverse ways. Thus, such estimates should be used cautiously and only in heuristic manners. To mitigate this problem, Inomata has combined estimated capacities with the history of additions of plazas and causeways at Tikal and has suspected that Maya city plans were geared significantly toward the inclusion of substantial parts of community members in public events held in plazas.

Despite the ambiguity involved in capacity estimates, it is important to note that many plazas in Mesoamerica, including those of the Maya lowlands (Inomata 2006a) and the Ciudadela and the Great Compound of Teotihuacan (Cowgill 1983), are large enough to accommodate nearly entire communities. These data, along with eye-witness accounts from the Colonial period, provide strong evidence for the centrality of communal gatherings in Mesoamerican political processes. This interpretation accords with the finding presented by Liendo Stuardo, López Mejía, and Campiani (chapter 6) in their study of the western Maya lowlands. According to them, the major centers of Palenque and Chinikihá dwarfed other centers in terms of their size, but the general spatial patterns of palace complexes were replicated throughout the region. In most cases, estimated plaza capacities exceeded the surrounding populations, and there is a strong correlation between plaza capacities and population sizes. These data indicate that nonelite populations probably attended ceremonies held in plazas of centers, although, as commented by Moore (chapter 12), it is necessary to examine divergent patterns, including the proportionally smaller sizes of plazas at Palenque and Chinikihá in relation to their surrounding populations.

The chapters by Stoll and by Ossa also show that the analysis of plaza capacities is particularly illuminating when compared to the population sizes of the surrounding areas. Stoll (chapter 5) specifically applies proxemics to examine communicative potentials of interactions in plazas in Mixteca Alta. Her survey data show that the number of plazas in the region is relatively low and their sizes constantly small. These data suggest to her that plazas were used mainly for exclusive elite rituals. Her finding contrasts to the common pattern in other parts of Mesoamerica defined by the presence of large plazas for communal gatherings; Mixteca Alta possibly had a mechanism of social integration somewhat different from other parts of Mesoamerica. This observation reminds us of the importance of examining regional variations and local contexts. Ossa (chapter 8) examines plaza areas and access patterns in relation to broader settlement data in south-central Veracruz. During the Classic period when standardized spatial plans spread throughout the region, complexes having plazas with restricted access tended to have a large number of residential settlements around them. This finding leads her to question the common assumption that plazas with restricted access were generally used for exclusive elite rituals. During the Postclassic period the standardization in spatial plan decreased, and correlation between plazas and surrounding settlements became less clear.

The study of activities that took place in plazas is challenging because in those spaces artifactual remains were often swept away or significantly moved from the original locations of use. The analyses of chemical remains left in soils, however, open an important opportunity for the reconstruction of activities in plazas (Wells 2004; see also Fernández et al. 2002; Middleton and Price 1996; Terry et al. 2004). Rothenberg (chapter 7) applies this method to the study of plazas at Palmarejo, Honduras. Three plazas at this site exhibit different configurations of soil chemical concentrations, suggesting different patterns of use. In particular, the North Plaza and the South Plaza were both associated with ritual artifacts, but their chemical patterns were different, which possibly resulted from different types of ritual activities. Her study demonstrates that soil chemical data add important information for the understanding of plaza use, but it also shows that the interpretation of chemical data is not necessarily clear and straightforward.

The principle underlying these approaches is the explicit focus on human bodies that occupied and experienced plazas. In this regard, these studies of plazas and public events closely parallel the phenomenological study of space. Nonetheless, this is a controversial area. The phenomenological approach is criticized as lacking reliable evidential bases and methodological rigor (Fleming 2005), whereas the analysis of physical properties is viewed as "dehumanizing" accounts by phenomenologically oriented archaeologists (Tilley 2004:221). We probably should move beyond certain differences in styles of archaeological inquiry and pursue philosophical bases and analytical possibilities. The assumption of a unity in bodily experience existing prior to society and history, which is implied by some phenomenological archaeologists (e.g., Tilley 2004:221), is most certainly untenable (Barrett and Ko 2009; Blake 2006; Johnson 2012). If so, we need to evaluate critically the historical situatedness of researchers' own perceptions and to delineate potential experiences by past subjects through multiple external measures, including the formal analysis of physical properties of spaces and cross-cultural comparisons. The study of visibility, access, and capacity of plazas provides one of the starting points from which to examine how human bodies might have been positioned and how participants might have viewed and heard public events. But it never equates to the experience of past individuals. When recognized as such, these analyses still provide important bases from which to develop our interpretations. Technological developments offer us promising tools in this line of research, including GIS viewshed analysis, 3D reconstruction and visualization, and the analysis of acoustic characteristics of space (Zalaquett Rock 2011).

Meaning and History in Plazas

If human experiences are situated in specific historical and social contexts, the analysis of physical properties of space alone is never enough. Cultural values and senses of history associated with specific spaces, through their recursive relation with physical settings, shape people's perceptions (De Certeau 1984; Hirsch and O'Hanlon 1995; Knapp and Ashmore 1999; Low 2000; Low and Lawrence-Zúñiga 2003; Lynch 2000 [1960]; Munn 2003; Rabinow 2003). In the case of Classic and Postclassic Maya society, plazas may have been analogous to patios in common residential groups both in form and meaning. Various scholars have noted formal and functional replication at the levels of commoner residences, royal palaces, and polity centers, which has led them to suggest that polity administration was carried out in a sense as an extension of royal household management under the patriarchic authority of the ruler (Inomata and Houston 2001; Sanders and Webster 1988). Some scholars have observed that societies in highland Mexico developed political and economic organizations more detached from kinship or kinship-metaphor than the Maya (see Sanders and Webster 1988). Murakami in his chapter on Teotihuacan, however, sees certain characteristics in architectural style, building orientation, and construction technique shared by public spaces at the core and apartment compounds in individual neighborhood, which created some consistency in experience throughout these spaces. Ringle (chapter 10) develops a specific argument that there existed a metaphorical affinity between household patios and civic plazas at Teotihucan, Xochicalco, and later Nahua *altepetls*, particularly for nobility who were leaders of individual residential divisions and were main constituents of their polities. Although the house has often been emphasized as a principle and metaphor of social organization in Mesoamerica (e.g., Gillespie 2000; Inomata and Houston 2001), Ringle points out that the Nahuatl term, literally meaning "those of a single patio," refers to a family.

This point resonates with Matthew Restall's (2001) argument for the contact-period Yucatec Maya that plazas and adjacent open spaces in front of buildings served as the symbolic centers and anchors for the integration of royal courts and local communities. These observations imply that public plazas were not spaces detached from domestic spaces. Plazas may have elicited emotional attachments and senses of belonging, which possibly contributed to the development of communal identity and polity integration.

At the same time, plazas may have been liminal spaces that created experience distinct from the ordinary. On the one hand, the unique meaning and feeling attached to plazas may have been situational and fleeting. Their liminality may have been shaped in public ceremonies as extraordinary moments that allowed or even encouraged behaviors different from daily routines, whereas plazas may have become rather ordinary spaces when they were used as marketplaces or for other purposes (see Bakhtin 1984; Turner 1969). On the other hand, plazas may have been associated with more stable symbolism. For Classic Maya cases, for which texts and images provide rich information, scholars have proposed that plazas symbolically represented the watery world paired with pyramidal temples viewed as symbolic mountains (Schele and Mathews 1998) and that they are closely tied to the legitimizing ideology of the ruling dynasty (Looper 2009). The affinity of plazas to domestic spaces and their liminality should not be viewed as incompatible. The coexistence of these different qualities probably shaped the social significance of plazas. Thus, our study of plazas needs to situate them in a broader social world, including their relations to domestic life.

In the same vein, we should not assume the categorical distinction between the sacred and the secular. Scholars have noted that such categorization resulted from the imposition of Western concepts and that even in modern societies practices comparable to stereotypical rituals can be found in mundane daily life (Bell 1992; Bradley 2003; Brück 1999; Mills and Walker 2008b; Walker 2002). Such categorical distinction would be particularly problematic in the case of Mesoamerica. Archaeological, ethnohistorical, and ethnographic data show that various groups in Mesoamerica have viewed a wide range of activity, including agricultural work, craft production, and routine domestic work, to be interactions with what we might call supernaturals. These activities commonly involved abstinence, fasting, purification, prayers, and offerings, which often shared similar characteristics with public rituals held in plazas (Ciudad Ruiz et al. 2010; Hruby 2007; Monaghan 1998; Plunket 2002; Vogt 1969). As Mircea Eliade (1978) famously noted, this does not mean that time and space were perceived as all homogenous. The central issue continues to be how people constructed distinct meanings and perceptions in the web of diverse social fields.

It is misleading to conceptualize that such meanings are contained and transmitted by, or embedded in, plazas, architecture, or associated objects. Meanings are always deployed and perceived through people's engagements with places and objects, presenting the possibility of multivocality originating from different agents (Preucel 2006; Preucel and Bauer 2001; Robb 1998; Thomas 1996). We also need to recognize the presence of multiple layers of meaning. We may conceptualize two domains of meaning: the externalized or objectified forms of signification that can be shared and referred to by multiple agents on one hand and the meaning internalized by individuals that are tied to one's emotional and subjective states on the other (Shore 1996; Strauss and Quinn 1997). Narratives and representations associated with plazas seen in texts and images are squarely placed in the former type. They could have been recognized by many and probably emphasized by some groups, but they may not have necessarily been agreed on by others. The ways such narratives were internalized by agents with different social backgrounds were most likely diverse. Such multiplicity, ambiguity, and discrepancies associated with public spaces and events significantly shaped the process of political negotiation (Scott 1990).

As the negotiation of meaning and power relations takes place in specific historical contexts, the claim and interpretation of the past become its critical aspect. Social memory is a contested domain in which various parts of the past are reconstructed, reinterpreted, created, appropriated, and erased. Socially negotiated and constructed memory may naturalize power relations and create a sense of group identity (Connerton 1989; Mills and Walker 2008b; Van Dyke and Alcock 2003). Plazas at Mesoamerican centers probably served as primary stages for the two principal types of practice tied to social memory discussed by Paul Connerton (1989): inscription and commemorative ceremony. Plazas contained texts, images, and buildings on which memories of the past were inscribed, and there commemorative ceremonies that dramatized war victories and achievements of rulers were celebrated. As in the study of meaning, the interplay between individual agents and society at large is a critical issue. Most archaeologists are moving away from the Durkheimian notion of collective memory held by society (Mills and Walker 2008a:6), but Moore (2010) criticizes this theoretical shift arguing that archaeologists are in danger of reducing practice of remembering to individuals. We need to keep in mind that our focus should not be on memory as a cognitive state held by individuals but on practices concerning certain historical narratives and customs that may not be confined to individual life spans. Inscribed memory and incorporated memory that Connerton has highlighted as central processes are aspects of memory practice externalized beyond the domain of individual cognition into the forms of material media and embodied acts.

A relevant concept is that of citation. Plazas in prehispanic Mesoamerica are typically stages of repeated depositions of dedicatory caches and repeated performance of ritual acts. Various archaeologists have seen these acts as citations of past practices through which meanings are gained and referenced (Jones 2005:200; Mills and Walker 2008a:18–19). Although the notion of citation presents an attractive conceptual tool for archaeologists, we need to address its philosophical basis to avoid the superficial borrowing of a term. The concept draws on the discussion developed by Jack Derrida (1977). His conceptualization focused on the criticism of J. L. Austin's (1975) theory of speech act that emphasized the context of speech and the intentionality of the speaking subject. Derrida has argued that texts and signs must be repeatable (iterable in his term) and citable in different contexts. The texts and signs inserted in a new context produce a new meaning, which is partly similar to the previous meaning but is partly different. The iterability and citationality of texts and signs not confined by the intention of the subject and their contexts make successful communication possible. In examining social construction of gender and sex, Judith Butler (1993:1–2) has pushed this line of argument further and has contended that iterable and citational practices of discourses and acts create a regulatory ideal of sex and subjects with gender identities. In a broadly Foucaultian scheme, she has questioned the existence of a subject prior to discourse or citationality. Many archaeologists probably feel that Derrida and Butler have gone too much to the extreme of social constructivism, and that it is helpful to refocus our emphasis on the interplay between social processes and the role of human agency. Then, the main utility of the concept of citationality is to help us not to slip back into explanations that reduce social memory into individual minds. In our study of Mesoamerican plazas, a primary inquiry should be how plazas served as arenas for the construction and reproduction of authoritative versions of the past which may have been internalized in diverse manners or even been dissented by agents with different backgrounds.

In various Mesoamerican plazas, texts and images carved on durable materials played important roles in mediating the physicality of space and human practice, as well as the meanings and memories associated with them. They included stelae, murals, and stone sculptures, some of which have survived to the present, as well as wooden and clay sculptures, banners, fugitive paintings, and other perishable materials. These media significantly shaped people's experiences of the spaces and events and encouraged people to carry out certain types of practices. William Ringle and George Bey (2001), for example, have examined façade decorations and the placement of thrones associated with plazas at Chichén Itzá and other centers in northern Yucatan and have suggested that plazas were used for public ceremonies, particularly, investiture rituals. Importantly, they have noted that plazas were not secondary spaces defined after the placement of temple pyramids but social spaces of extreme importance in their own right (Ringle and Bey 2001:278). Matthew Looper (2001, 2009) has also examined stone monuments and has shown that plazas were central stages of public ceremonies focused on royal symbolism. However, as noted earlier, we should not assume that these spaces represented a coherent system of belief shared by community members. Our central inquiry should still be how dominant versions of meaning and memory represented by those texts and images shaped political processes as they were accepted, reinterpreted, and contested.

Urcid and Joyce (chapter 9) present striking new interpretations of visual programs at the plaza of Monte Albán, which will certainly invite spirited debate among Oaxacan archaeologists. They argue that carved human figures on Building L-sub represented the theme of a sodality organized around age-grades with images of young warriors, deity impersonators, a council of elders, ancestral spirits, and sacrificial victims. Carvings on Building J, according to them, represent revered individuals or fallen heroes from Monte Albán. Their interpretations highlight a tension between exclusionary and communal forms of authority, a certain level of polysemy of signs, and the commemorative nature of the visual narratives. The chapters by Ringle and by Solari explore intersections of material remains, images, and written texts. Ringle (chapter 10) continues to advance his discussion on plazas as stages for investiture ceremonies.

He sees certain continuity in practices of investiture of rulers and high nobles carried out in plazas of Teotihuacan, Xochicalco, Chichén Itzá, and contact-period Nahua groups. Sculptures and architectural arrangements found around those plazas were not purely mythical representations detached from people's bodily experiences but were tied to events carried out there and to their memories, which were also connected with more intimate experiences in households. In the time of drastic change imposed by the colonial regime discussed by Solari (chapter 11), the negotiation of meaning and memory in ritual took a distinct trajectory. She argues that Catholic ritual involving bodily movements framed in a quadrilateral space comparable to those of pre-Columbian rites were appropriated by the Yucatec Maya as an arena in which shared experience shaped communal memory and identity. The chapters by Urcid and Joyce, by Ringle, and by Solari draw our attention to the tension between the singularity of events set in their own contexts and persistent practices of citation that refer back to what went before.

New Directions

In compiling this volume, we decided not to follow the customary organization of chapters by time periods or geographic regions. Instead, we grouped them by important themes that emerged from those contributions: (1) plaza constructions and public events; (2) plazas in broader spatial contexts; and (3) plazas and images. All chapters obviously crosscut those themes to a certain degree, but this organization helps highlight the central focus of each chapter and illustrate directions for future studies.

The study of plazas is still challenging, and as Moore (chapter 12) notes, developing effective methods of study is of particular importance. In addition to theoretical discussion presented above, it is probably useful to recapitulate important methodological directions elucidated by the contributors. The main point is simple: we need more studies specifically focused on plazas. While earlier investigations focused largely on buildings surrounding plazas, chapters by Inomata and by Tsukamoto show that excavation programs specifically targeting plazas are highly illuminating. Detailed information on construction history of plazas, along with that of ritual deposits in some cases, is critical in understanding the social roles of these spaces. Large sizes of plazas and build-ups of later constructions may make their understanding difficult, but as Cyphers and Murtha show, systematic augering and other methods may present critical data. We expect that geophysical inspections will also be increasingly important.

For the reconstruction of activities in those empty spaces, the analysis of soil chemistry as applied by Rothenberg presents a promising approach. Similarly, the analysis of microdebitage and soil micromorphology should be effective. Another approach is to set plazas on multiple analytical scales, including the comparison of diverse types of plaza throughout the site as done by Tsukamoto and by Murakami, and the examination of plazas in broader regional contexts as developed by Stoll, by Liendo Stuardo, López Mejía, and Campiani, and by Ossa. The analysis of texts and images has a long tradition in Mesoamerican studies, but when we place them in the historical contexts of plazas, paying close attention to continuity and disjunction in the use of space and related practices, we may gain new insights as demonstrated by Urcid and Joyce, by Ringle, and by Solari.

As Moore points out, we need to frame the study of Mesoamerican plazas in a broader cross-cultural comparison. From the perspective of an Andean specialist, Moore comments that Mesoamerican plazas exhibit remarkable commonality across space and time. Following Moore's suggestion, we need to explore what kind of social processes underlie this continuity while paying attention to regional and temporal variations. The chapters in this volume indicate that in a general term Mesoamerican plazas were foci of substantially more intense engagements of people than, for example, the modern parks in the United States as described by Moore. People's engagements ranged from substantial investment of labor in their construction and repeated deposits of valued items seen in the archaeological record to periodical gatherings of numerous individuals recorded in historical documents and possibly applicable to prehispanic contexts. Despite the important variations and exceptions noted in various chapters, social interaction centered on plazas appears to have been a common mode of political negotiation adopted and perpetuated by various Mesoamerican groups. While we think that the study of plazas and other public spaces can be productively applied to various parts of the world, the remarkable intensity of people's engagements in such spaces commonly observed in Mesoamerica makes Mesoamerican plazas a particularly fertile ground for the development of new theoretical and analytical approaches.

PART I

Plaza Constructions and Public Events

CHAPTER ONE

Plaza Builders of the Preclassic Maya Lowlands

The Construction of a Public Space and a Community at Ceibal, Guatemala

TAKESHI INOMATA

The spacious plaza was the focus of communal life at virtually all Maya settlements during the Classic and Postclassic periods. The results of recent investigations at the Preclassic center of Ceibal (also spelled Seibal) have shown that a prototype of this form of social interaction and spatial practice emerged at the very beginning of a sedentary community during the Middle Preclassic period. The construction of a public space and the celebration of communal rituals there constituted a central process through which new forms of social relations were formed and negotiated. Although discussions and studies by archaeologists tend to focus on the role of pyramidal temples that are conspicuously visible in the landscape, at the early community of Ceibal the construction of a plaza was at least as important as those of pyramids; the construction volumes of the former likely surpassed those of the latter. When we initiated our research at Ceibal, our working assumptions were that the plaza was the focal point of communal activities and values, and that it deserved to be a central subject of archaeological investigations.

The early Middle Preclassic period was a time of major social change in the Maya lowlands when some groups began to adopt a fully sedentary way of life. We tend to assume that such transitions were gradual ones in which the first settlers began to live in small villages and then slowly formed larger settlements with formal ceremonial complexes. At Ceibal, however, there was a drastic transformation. A formal ceremonial center with a public plaza was founded at the very beginning of this settlement (Inomata et al. 2013). This transition probably involved the development of social inequality, new ritual practices, and reorganization of domestic activities. As the residents built a new form of community, public events held in the plaza probably provided a crucial field for fostering collective identities and negotiating social relations. Thus, the construction of a formal plaza meant not only the appearance of a new architectural form but also the emergence of new ways of social interactions and new senses of attachment to a place.

The lowland Maya were among the last Mesoamerican groups to adopt a fully sedentary way of life with the use of ceramics and substantial architecture (Clark and Cheetham 2002). Surrounded by sedentary agriculturalists, groups occupying the Maya lowlands during the Early Preclassic period appear to have maintained mobile life ways relying on a mixed economy of horticulture, hunting, and gathering (Lohse 2010). Their presence is indicated by evidence of maize pollen and forest disturbance dating to 2,000–1,000 BC, found in cores taken from Laguna Tamarindito, Lake Petenxil, Lake Quexil, and other lakes (Anselmetti et al. 2007; Brenner et al. 2003; Dunning et al. 1997; Islebe et al. 1996; Pohl et al. 1996; Rosenmeier et al. 2002; Tsukada 1966; Vaughan et al. 1985; Wahl et al. 2006). Archaeological remains of these groups, however, have not been confirmed in the Pasión region, indicating that their population density was low and that they did not use, or rarely used, ceramics and substantial architecture.

Ceibal is located atop an escarpment overlooking the Pasión River in the southwestern Maya lowlands. Researchers from Harvard University first explored this center extensively from 1964 through 1968. This research, led by Gordon Willey, included mapping, extensive excavations of monumental buildings, epigraphic studies, and survey and excavations in the peripheries, marking a milestone in the history of Maya archaeology (Graham 1990; Sabloff 1975; Smith 1982; Tourtellot 1988; Willey 1978, 1990). The results of their investigations showed that within the site of Ceibal the area named Group A was the focus of its earliest occupation dating to the Real-Xe phase of the early Middle Preclassic period (1,000–700 BC) (figure 1.1). A cruciform cache with greenstone axes (Cache 7) found in the Central Plaza indicated that this open space was an important stage of ritual activities (Smith 1982:118, 243). Except for deep plaza pits, however, the Harvard University investigations focused primarily on upper layers of buildings dating to the Classic period (AD 250–950), and much of the substantial Preclassic construction remained unexplored (Tourtellot and Hammond 2007; Willey 1990).

In 2006, nearly forty years after the Harvard University research, I initiated the Ceibal-Petexbatun Archaeological Project with Daniela Triadan, Kazuo Aoyama, and Erick Ponciano to re-examine this important site in light of recent developments in Maya archaeology. One of our main objectives was to examine the Preclassic origins of this center through deep stratigraphic excavations. Our excavations demonstrated that Ceibal was established around 1,000 BC as a formal ceremonial center with a spatial arrangement similar to contemporaneous centers in Chiapas and on the Gulf Coast, including La Libertad, Chiapa de Corzo, San Isidro, and La Venta (see Clark and Hansen 2001; Inomata et al. 2010, 2013). The residents of Ceibal deposited a series of greenstone axe caches (Inomata et al. 2010). These deposits closely resemble those found

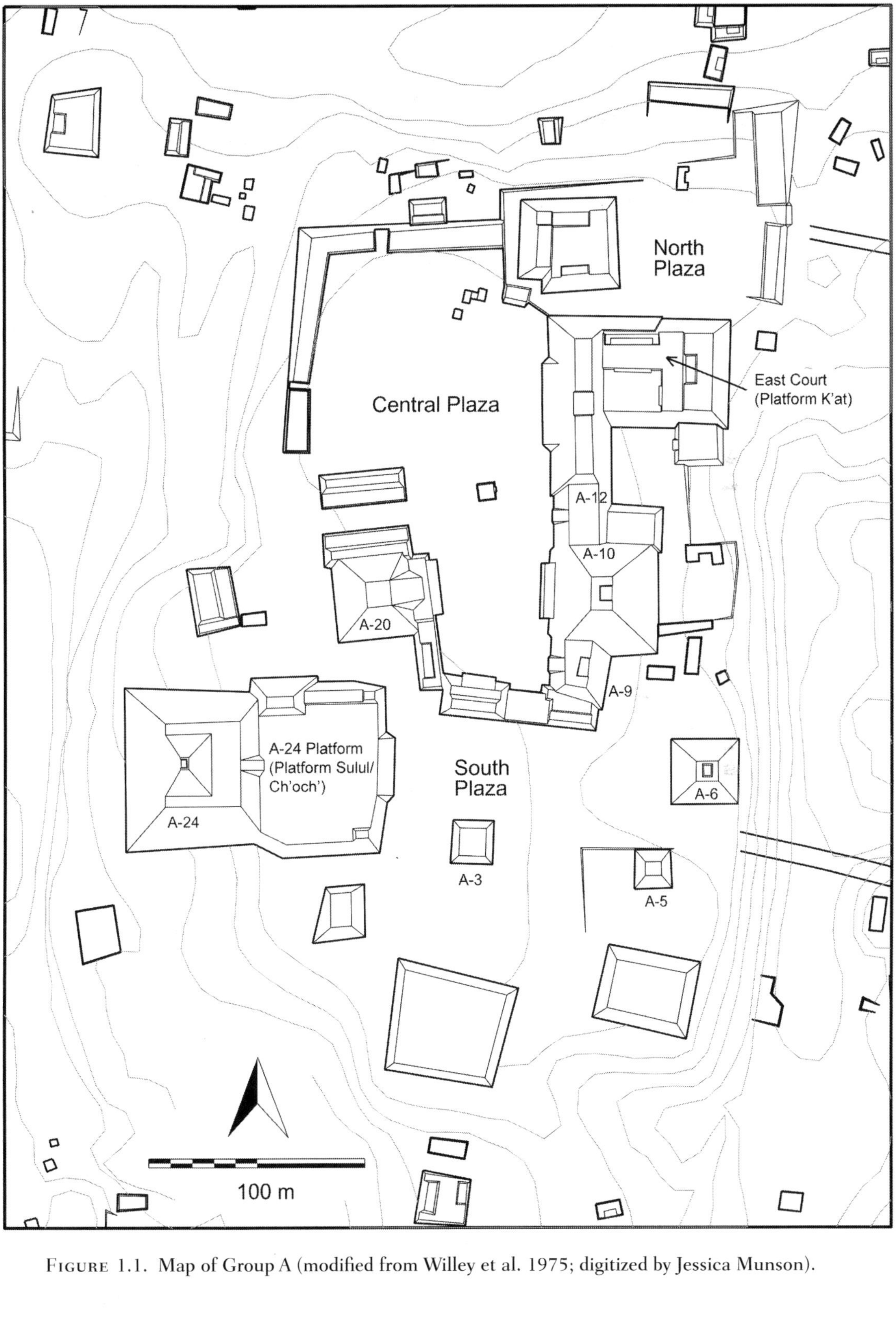

FIGURE 1.1. Map of Group A (modified from Willey et al. 1975; digitized by Jessica Munson).

at Chiapa de Corzo (Bachand et al. 2008), San Isidro (Lowe 1981), and La Venta (Drucker 1952; Drucker et al. 1959; Stirling 1943), suggesting that the residents of these centers closely shared ritual practices, and possibly religious ideas, through direct contacts.

The Construction and Use of the Plaza at Ceibal

In our investigations at Ceibal, we concentrated considerable effort in a series of excavations in the Central Plaza of Group A. The plaza is delimited by Structures 12, 10, and 9 on the east and Structure 20 on the west, which formed a so-called E Group assemblage. This complex was probably the focal point of the site plan that closely resembled the highly standardized spatial configuration of contemporaneous centers in the Grijalva drainage in Chiapas, which Clark called the Middle Formative Chiapas pattern (Clark and Hansen 2001). Through these excavations it became clear that at the beginning of the settlement at Ceibal the residents scraped the natural soil to create a leveled space and used the exposed whitish-yellow marl as the first plaza floor. Along the central axis of the probable E-Group assemblage, the early residents dug a 40 cm deep hole into the marl to place the first cache (or one of the first caches) with twelve greenstone axes (Cache 118) arranged in a form similar to Offerings No. 9 and No. 11 of La Venta (Drucker et al. 1959: Figures 47 and 48). Excavations by Otto Román demonstrated that, during the following twelve hundred years of the Preclassic period, the occupants of Ceibal constructed at least fourteen more plaza floors with fills measuring 2 m in total thickness at the location of Cache 118 (figure 1.2). Of these constructions, 1.5 m thick fills date to the Middle Preclassic period. Along with these plaza constructions, the Middle Preclassic residents of Ceibal deposited a series of caches. Excavations along the central axis of the E-Group assemblage by Román, Flory Pinzón, and Raúl Ortiz revealed twelve Middle Preclassic caches containing elaborately made objects with nine of them including greenstone axes. Other probable caches contained animal remains. The discovery of Cache 7 by the Harvard University team in the southern part of the Central Plaza indicates that there are more ritual deposits off the central axis. Toward the end of the Middle Preclassic period, common forms of ritual deposits in the plaza shifted from greenstone axe caches to those of ceramic vessels and sacrificial human remains (Inomata 2013). Excavations of the eastern part of the plaza by Pinzón showed that in the latter part of the Late Preclassic period a series of caches with numerous ceramic vessels were placed. Despite these changes in ritual deposits, the central axis of the E-Group assemblage continued to be the primary focus of public ritual throughout the Preclassic period.

The volume of Preclassic constructions is particularly impressive when we consider that plaza constructions during the Classic period measure merely 20 cm in thickness in the central part of the plaza. In the northern part of the Central Plaza, the Preclassic fills are even thicker because the residents tried to create roughly leveled surfaces over the sloping natural terrain. Excavations by Geraldine Fondevilla revealed 3.1 m thick Preclassic plaza fills with the Middle Preclassic layers measuring 2.2 m (figure 1.3). Patterns are similar in

Figure 1.2. Stratigraphy of the central part of the Central Plaza where Cache 118 was found.

Figure 1.3. Stratigraphy of the northern part of the Central Plaza.

TABLE 1.1. Estimates of Construction Volumes of Group A Plazas and Pyramids

Construction Period/Structure	Volume (m^3)	Years	Volume (m^3) per year
Plazas			
Real-Xe (early Middle Preclassic: 1,000–700 BC)	38,400	300	128
Escoba-Mamom (late Middle Preclassic: 700–400 BC)	52,800	300	176
Cantutse-Chicanel (Late Preclassic: 400 BC–AD 250)	86,100	650	132
Tepejilote/Bayal-Tepeu (Late-Terminal Classic: AD 600–950)	34,000	350	97
Pyramids (all periods combined)			
Structure A-3	1,400		
Structure A-5	900		
Structure A-6	3,900		
Structure A-10	19,600		
Structure A-20	9,900		
Structure A-24	38,200		
Pyramids total	73,900	1,600	46

The Early Classic period (AD 250–600) with weak occupation is excluded from the calculation.

the adjacent South Plaza. According to the excavations by the Harvard University team, the Preclassic fills in this area measured 2.4 to 3 m in thickness with nearly all layers dating to the Middle Preclassic (Smith 1982:108–114).

Table 1.1 shows estimates of plaza construction volumes of Group A for each period based on those excavation data from the Harvard University project and our investigations. These are compared to the total construction volumes of Group A pyramids. Since the process of plaza expansions, particularly that of the northern part of the Central Plaza and the eastern part of the Southern Plaza, is poorly understood, these figures may contain substantial errors. We have even less data for period-by-period estimates of pyramid constructions, and thus table 1.1 only lists the total volumes of each pyramid resulting from the building sequence through all periods. Despite these difficulties and uncertainties, table 1.1 demonstrates the most important point: Ceibal residents invested substantial labor in the construction of plazas. In particular, a comparison with the construction volumes of pyramids illustrates the importance of plaza constructions. The volume of plaza constructions during the Late Preclassic Cantutse-Chicanel phase alone surpasses the total volume of pyramids;

when we compare construction volumes for each period, the volume of plazas appears to be substantially larger than that of pyramids.

Another central point that table 1.1 shows is that plaza constructions were particularly important during the Preclassic period. The scale of Preclassic plaza constructions substantially surpasses those of the Late and Terminal Classic periods. In terms of the total volume, the Late Preclassic Cantutse-Chicanel phase may have witnessed the largest plaza construction, and as to per-year average, the late Middle Preclassic Escoba-Mamom phase may represent the most active period in plaza construction. However, to evaluate the social significance of plaza construction, we need to take the population levels of each period into account. Population estimates for the Preclassic period are extremely difficult, particularly for its early phases. Harvard University researchers assumed that Ceibal during the early Middle Preclassic Real-Xe phase was merely a small hamlet or village, although they did not dismiss the possibility that public buildings already existed (Willey 1990:193). Our investigations have demonstrated that Ceibal was already a formal ceremonial center from its inception, but its population level during the Real-Xe phase was certainly substantially lower than those of the subsequent Escoba-Mamom and Cantutse-Chicanel phases (Tourtellot 1988). Then, the per-capita plaza construction volume during the Real-Xe phase was most likely the highest in the history of Ceibal. The labor investment in plaza construction during the Real-Xe phase is even larger than what table 1.1 implies because the work of scraping off the humus for the creation of the first plaza floor is not reflected in the volume calculations. The first settlers of Ceibal were the most avid plaza-builders.

Plaza as a Monument and as a Stage

The precise process of the Middle Preclassic beginning of Ceibal is still under investigation. It remains to be determined whether there were migrations from the Gulf Coast and Chiapas or whether the local inhabitants adopted new cultural practices. Either way, the local lowland Maya probably constituted the majority of its population, and they maintained direct contacts with those regions to the west. As this society went through a major transformation from a mobile life way to full sedentism, the construction of a plaza provided opportunities on which people with different expectations and agendas gathered and worked toward common goals. Participants experienced collective work involving planning, coordination, and division of labor on a scale and in a manner unprecedented in the area. The resulting plaza was a monument of communal work, indexical of labor invested by many individuals. Plaza constructions were accompanied and followed by public ceremonies. Some precious and symbolic items buried during these rituals, including greenstone axes that came from distant places, give us glimpses of these events. The configuration of the E-Group plaza was highly open; it allowed, and probably was intended to encourage, the participation of all community members in events held there. Public gatherings likely involved music, dance, and feastings as well, in a manner similar to those from the Classic and Colonial periods and from ethnographically known cases (Ciudad Real 1976; Inomata 2006b; Miller 1986; Tozzer 1941). The plaza was a stage for public performance. Through these constructions and public events, the residents created and experienced social relations with other community members, shared common experiences and narratives, and negotiated individual and collective identities. The construction of plazas and public gatherings that took place there offered a central mechanism through which a new community was constituted. In other words, these activities were not simply outcomes of, or reflective of, an established sedentary community but an arena of the on-going process of creation, reproduction, and transformation of a community (see Inomata 2006a).

The plaza most likely served to tie the past, present, and future of the community in the mind and discourse of people. As a monument and a stage, the plaza constantly reminded people of their collective labor and communal gatherings that took place in the past, and it shaped people's imagination, planning, and narratives on future constructions and gatherings. This process was doubtless conditioned by the unique physical property of the plaza. Unlike the ever visible pyramids, the scale and significance of plaza constructions were not so evident once the building activities were completed. The same is true for caches of greenstone axes and other items; unlike stelae that continued to command people's attention through their perpetual visibility and tangibility, caches became sealed and invisible as soon as they were created. The continuous investments of substantial labor in plaza building and repeated depositions of precious items in these spaces indicate that, despite their invisibility, plaza constructions and caches were foci of community interests, most likely vested with significant symbolic and social values. Their importance primarily lived in people's shared memories, narratives, and understandings, as well as in the planning of replicated events in the future (see Connerton 1989). The physical acts of plaza constructions and public ceremonies, as well as their memories and narratives, probably served to tether the formerly mobile population to a fixed location.

We should not assume that the process of community-making at Ceibal was all harmonious. The invisibility of plaza fills and caches may have facilitated acts of forgetting meshed with those of remembering, leading to possibilities for reinterpretations of repeated acts and for the invention of new traditions, as hinted by changes in caching practices from those depositing greenstone axes, to dismembered human remains and to numerous ceramic vessels (see Gillespie 2008; Hobsbawm and Ranger 1983; Mills and Walker 2008a). These changes most likely involved negotiations and contestations among community members. A particularly important aspect of social setting in this regard was the relation between the Ceibal residents and the surrounding population. As the earliest sedentary center, Ceibal in its early history was most likely surrounded by mobile groups. According to our refined ceramic chronology, Ceibal is the only confirmed settlement in the Pasión region dating to the Real 1 and 2 phases (1000–800 BC), whereas other sedentary communities, including Altar de Sacrificios (Adams 1971), Itzan (Johnston 2006), El Caobal (Munson 2012), and Punta de Chimino (Bachand 2007) emerged during the Real 3 phase (800–700 BC) (Inomata 2013; Inomata et al. 2013). We suspect that this pattern reflects the coexistence of sedentary and mobile populations during the Real 1 and 2 phases and the transition of most mobile groups to sedentism during the Real 3 phases. Comparable coexistence of sedentary and mobile populations is suggested for other parts of the Maya lowlands and the southern Pacific Coast (Lohse 2010; Rosenswig 2011). The estimated two-hundred-year period required for the full transition to sedentism implies that many individuals in the region resisted the transition to the new way of sedentary life at the beginning of Ceibal. Even for the Ceibal residents who once had made this transition, return to mobile life ways continued to be an easy, viable option. It is conceivable that the boundary between the sedentary community and mobile groups was porous, which may have allowed some individuals from mobile groups to participate in public events held at Ceibal and some Ceibal residents to leave the sedentary community when internal animosity worsened. Still, the constant growth of the Ceibal population throughout the Preclassic period, as well as the increase in the number of sedentary settlements in the Pasión region and in other parts of the Maya lowlands, indicate that the sedentary, aggregated way of life was ultimately successful in attracting the lowland Maya. Incentives for the transition to sedentary communities may have derived in part from the functional or economic rationales of protection against enemy raids, the efficiency in agricultural work, and the better access to exchanged goods. Nonetheless, equally important was the attraction of communal activities tied to plaza construction and public ceremonies that cannot be fully explained through functional rationality. In addition, shared narratives and memories, mediated by these physical activities and by the material presence of objects and places, gave meanings and values to the new way of life.

Another important dimension of social context is the degree of social inequality. At Middle Preclassic Ceibal social inequality was present, but differences in prestige and power do not appear to have been strongly marked. To the southwest of the E-Group plaza under the A-24 Platform, our excavations revealed a substantial platform, which we named Sulul, dating to the onset of Ceibal settlement around 1,000 BC (Inomata et al. 2013). During the Real 2 phase (850–800 BC) a series of renovations transformed Platform Sulul into a monumental construction, which we call Ch'och', measuring 6 m in the maximum fill thickness and more than 34 m in width (Inomata et al. 2013). We are inclined to think that Platform Sulul/Ch'och' served as a residential complex although we still need to consider the possibility that it was a communal building. If our interpretation is correct, it would imply that its residents, who probably formed a corporate group at least partially based on kinship, lived in a building complex considerably larger than others. This was the most prominent group in this community and likely played leading roles in communal affairs, including the planning and organization of plaza constructions and public events. Our excavation of Platform Ch'och' revealed two caches containing greenstone axes and an axe preform, which point to the unique status of the group associated with this building. During the Real 2 or 3 phases another large platform, named K'at, was built to the northeast of the E-Group plaza. This platform supported multiple rectangular or L-shaped buildings that appear to have surrounded a patio. Its location and configuration are similar to contemporaneous platforms at central Chiapas, where excavations revealed possible evidence of their use as residential complexes (Agrinier 2000; Clark and Hansen 2001). It is not clear whether Platform K'at was built by the residents of Platform Sulul/Ch'och' or by a rival group, but this new platform was most likely used as a residential complex of the emerging elite. Besides the two greenstone axe caches, however, only a limited quantity of prestige goods has been found in those large platforms, and the ceramics recovered there are indistinguishable from those excavated from other parts of the site. If the leading groups of Ceibal lived on these platforms, their unique status was marked by the large size and the central location of their residences, but inequality in terms of other material possessions was suppressed. In this regard, we should note an important difference from Chiapas centers. At Chiapa de Corzo, the excavation of the western pyramid of the E-Group assemblage, Mound 11, by Bruce Bachand, Lynneth Lowe, and Emiliano Gallaga, revealed rich tombs containing numerous jade ornaments dating to around 700–500 BC (Lowe 2012). Our tunnel excavation of the western pyramid of the E-Group complex, Structure A-20, however, did not find any burials or caches along the central axis of its Real 1 and 2 constructions. At the Middle Preclassic community of Ceibal, its emerging elite could live in large residences, but they did not have power to claim pyramids or other buildings associated with the central plaza as their own monuments as their Classic-period descendants did.

In this social context, the residents of Ceibal invested substantial labor in the construction of the communal plaza although potential elite residential complexes located on large platforms were an additional foci of construction effort. Rituals held in the Middle Preclassic plaza of Ceibal probably had a strong character as communal events although the emergent elite possibly played a central role in those gatherings. The importance of the plaza is also reflected in the distribution of caches. Most Middle Preclassic caches were deposited in the plaza rather than in surrounding buildings. These patterns contrast to those of the Classic period in which pyramids tied to the royal family of each center commanded a substantial part of communal construction effort and were preferred locations for the placement of elite burials and caches (see Chase and Chase 1995).

In analyzing the process of community-making, we need to pay attention to the coexistence of different social implications presented by plazas and by practices associated with them. On one hand, plazas as formal spaces confined patterns of actions and interactions that contrasted to the less physically restricting spaces that mobile populations were accustomed to. The formalized spaces could have helped shape a certain type of political subject that conformed to norms of action expected in aggregated communities (Love 1999). They contributed to the emergence of a new kind of power relation (see Foucault 1977). On the other hand, Preclassic plazas afforded substantial flexibility in terms of its interpretation. Unlike the Classic-period settings where images and texts carved on temples and stelae narrowed down the range of associated narratives, the invisibility of previous constructions and cache deposits in Middle Preclassic plazas allowed individuals to create diverse meanings and values of the places and of events held there. As noted above, this flexibility could have caused tensions among the residents in relation to changes in practices and narratives, but it also meant that individuals with diverse backgrounds and expectations could internalize the values of the plaza and public events in various ways and could develop their own senses of attachment to the place. These complex implications of the plaza are comparable to the process of power relations shaped by ritual that Catherine Bell discusses (1992:221). She argues that ritual, or ritualization in her term, serves as a form of social control because it demands external conformance from the participants forcing them to act in expected manners. Ritual, however, allows a substantial degree of flexibility in terms of internal interpretations, making ritual effective in grounding a sense of community without overriding the autonomy of individuals. An analogous view applies not only to public events but also to the plaza in the Middle Preclassic community of Ceibal where an increasing number of individuals accepted and internalized new forms of power relations.

Comparison with Other Areas

Plazas appear to have been central elements from the beginning or in an early stage of many sedentary communities in Preclassic Mesoamerica. For example, Ann Cyphers and Timothy Murtha (chapter 4, this volume) and Javier Urcid and Arthur Joyce (chapter 9, this volume) show that public plazas were established at the inception of new communities at San Lorenzo and Monte Albán. In an even earlier period, excavations by John Clark and his colleagues demonstrate that a spacious plaza was already present in the Early Preclassic village of Paso de la Amada (Clark 2004). A few centuries after the foundation of Ceibal, the ceremonial center of Cival emerged in the eastern Peten, where the initial construction effort of public spaces was even more prominent than in the case of Ceibal. According to an estimate made by Francisco Estrada-Belli (2011), the initial leveling fills of the area including an E-Group plaza dwarfed any later construction efforts of monumental buildings.

In terms of labor investment in plaza construction, however, there exist diverse patterns. Significant investment in the early construction of plazas surpassing that of Ceibal may be found on the southern Gulf Coast as described for the Early Preclassic center of San Lorenzo by Cyphers and Murtha (chapter 4, this volume). A particularly impressive case is found at the Middle Preclassic center of La Venta (Drucker 1952; Drucker et al. 1959). In addition to the artificial fills measuring 1.5 to 2.5 m in thickness placed in the Ceremonial Court of Complex A, the invisibility of products resulting from substantial labor is epitomized by the five Massive Offerings excavated there, in which an enormous amount of serpentine blocks were placed only to be buried under thick construction fills. For the completely excavated Massive Offering 1, excavators estimated that serpentine blocks were arranged in twenty-eight layers in a 7 m deep pit weighed over 1,000 tons (Drucker et al. 1959:97). Similar emphasis on plaza construction and ritual deposits is found in Chiapas. At San Isidro, Early and Middle Preclassic fills of the E-Group plaza measured roughly 2 m thick, and excavations by Gareth Lowe along its central axis revealed numerous caches containing axes, pseudo-axes, and ceramic vessels (Lowe 1981). At Chiapa de Corzo, plaza construction in its E-Group assemblage was less impressive with Preclassic plaza fills measuring 1 m or less in thickness, but three large caches in front of the western mound contained roughly 340 axes and pseudo-axes in pits measuring up to 2.7 m in depth (Bachand 2011; Bachand et al. 2008).

The level of investment in plaza construction and ritual deposits in plazas is more varied in other parts of the Maya lowlands. At the centers of Tikal and Uaxactún, E-Group assemblages were foci of communal life in their early history, but extensive excavations of these groups revealed relatively thin accumulations of plaza constructions; much of the construction efforts were directed to pyramids and other above-ground buildings (Laporte and Fialko 1995; Laporte and Valdés 1993; Ricketson and Ricketson 1937). Extensive excavations of these groups failed to reveal axe caches comparable to those of Ceibal, Chiapas, and La Venta. The site of Cival mentioned above, however, reminds us that certain centers in the central and eastern lowlands emphasized the construction of plazas or plateaus over pyramidal structures. To build the ceremonial complex, the residents of Cival created a leveled surface by placing fills measuring up to 7 m in thickness on hill slopes (Estrada-Belli 2011:74). Excavations at Cival also unearthed the only known cruciform cache with greenstone axes in the Maya lowlands outside of Ceibal (Estrada-Belli 2006). It is not clear whether these similarities between Ceibal and Cival resulted from some contacts bypassing other settlements or whether our understanding is skewed because of limited excavations of Middle Preclassic remains. The process at Cahal Pech is somewhat similar to that of Cival (Cheetham 1995; Healy et al. 2004). The longest construction sequence was found in Plaza B, which was occupied by a small number of residential structures during the early Middle Preclassic Cunil phase contemporaneous with the Real phase. At the end of the Cunil phase, roughly contemporaneous with the beginning of Cival, this hilltop area appears to have been transformed into a ceremonial complex. At this time a level surface across Plaza B was created with construction fills over the slope in the southern part of the plaza measuring 0.9 to 1.9 m in total thickness. By the end of the Late Preclassic period, the total fill thickness reached 2.6 m in the southern part and 0.7 m in the northern portion where the bedrock was highest (Cheetham 1995). Unlike the one-time construction of Cival, the plaza buildup at Cahal Pech during the Cunil phase was achieved through a series of floor constructions. Still, the construction effort invested during the Cunil phase compared to those during the later phases is remarkable particularly when we consider the three hundred-year duration of the Cunil phase (within the 1200- to 1300-year total duration of the Preclassic period) and the lower population level in this early phase.

Different kinds of sequence have been identified at the Belizean sites of Cuello and K'axob. At Cuello, excavations focused on Platform 34. During the Middle Preclassic period when this part was a residential complex, the construction of its patio was modest, measuring 0.5 to 1 m in fill thickness. At the beginning of the Late Preclassic period, it was transformed into an open platform complex with a temple; the patio was filled with a 1 m thick layer of rubble in a single construction episode. By the end of the Late Preclassic period, the total fill thickness of the platform reached 2.6 m (Hammond et al. 1991). At K'axob, Plaza B was originally a residential complex, where the patio surface was gradually raised throughout the Middle and Late Preclassic periods. The fill thickness reached 1.2 m by the end of the Late Preclassic period when it was transformed to a temple-platform complex (McAnany 2004; McAnany and López Varela 1999). These sequences found at Cuello and K'axob are more comparable to that of the A-24 Platform than that of the E-Group plaza of Ceibal. The A-24 Platform also appears to have started as a residential complex (Platforms Sulul and Ch'och') and was transformed to an open platform at the end of the Middle Preclassic period. Structure A-24, the largest temple pyramid at Ceibal, may have been constructed after this transformation. Despite these similarities, the construction volume of A-24 Platform was substantially larger than those at Cuello and K'axob.

The results of excavations of E-Group assemblages and other public plazas in the El Mirador region have not been fully published. Regarding the construction sequence of Nakbé, a major center in this region during the Middle Preclassic period, Richard Hansen (1998) suggests that the late Middle Preclassic period witnessed major construction effort, in which substantial construction fills buried earlier residential remains and laid a basis for ceremonial complexes. Large platforms supporting residential structures have been found in the northern Maya lowlands as well. At Komchén, substantial platforms, 23F1 and 24G1, were built during the Ek' phase, possibly contemporaneous with the Real 2 or 3 phases (Andrews et al. 2008). Komchén continued to grow to become a densely occupied center during the Late Preclassic period with the addition of multiple platforms. Large platforms, 21F1 and 21J1, along with 23F1 and 24G1, defined a public plaza, but the buildup of plaza floors remained minimum throughout the Preclassic period (Ringle 1985; Ringle and Andrews 1988).

Different kinds of motivation and social circumstance appear to have affected these diverse ways in which plazas were built. In the case of Cival and Cahal Pech, substantial construction effort focused on the creation of a leveled surface for ceremonial cores in an early stage of occupation. At Cuello and K'axob, a major turning point was the burying of earlier residential remains for the creation of new temple complexes. At other settlements, including Tikal, Uaxactún, and Komchén, much of the construction effort was directed to visible structures above the ground level rather than to plazas. Even at these settlements, public plazas, particularly E-Group assemblages, were central foci of communal activities (Aimers and Rice 2006; Chase and Chase 1995). Like that of Ceibal, most E-Group assemblages, including those of Tikal and Uaxactún, exhibited open configurations that were probably geared toward communitywide participation. In terms of the labor investment in plaza construction and the emphasis on deposits of valuable objects there, the closest parallels to Ceibal are found on the southern Gulf Coast and in central Chiapas. Ceibal's sustained emphasis on plaza constructions and cache deposits as communal endeavors throughout the Middle Preclassic period was probably shaped significantly by the ideas and practices shared with these western groups.

Conclusions

Archaeologists have long directed their attention to pyramids and other prominent buildings, but the finds at Ceibal and related sites compel researchers to examine the importance of plazas more closely. Plazas were not simply empty spaces surrounded by more important buildings; they were vested with symbolic and historical values that shaped the constitution and identities of the community (Love 1999; Ringle and Bey 2001). At Ceibal, as well as at closely related settlements in central Chiapas and on the southern Gulf Coast, plazas were at once stages for communal gatherings, places where precious objects were deposited, and monuments that community members built in collaboration. Thus, plazas served as hubs and primary media of collective actions, of shared memories and narratives, and of negotiations of communal identities and values. The importance of plaza use and construction at Preclassic Ceibal may have been partly due to the relatively undeveloped social inequality, but similar emphases are also found in more hierarchically organized Chiapas and Gulf Coast groups. In other parts of the Maya lowlands, diverse patterns of plaza construction and cache deposit are found. While plazas are foci of communal life at many Preclassic Maya settlements, the ways people attached symbolic values to these plazas and invested physical work and material wealth in these spaces were shaped by different historical traditions and political situations. Although Classic and Postclassic descendants of the Maya lowlands and other Mesoamerican areas with institutionalized rulership tended to give greater emphasis to pyramids and other prominently visible buildings tied to the elite, plazas continued to be central elements of most settlements and stages for communal gatherings. In this sense, the early cultural practices seen at Preclassic Ceibal and other centers strongly shaped subsequent configurations of sociality in the Maya lowlands and other areas.

Acknowledgments

I thank the Instituto de Antropología e Historia de Guatemala for research permits. Investigations at Ceibal were supported by grants from the National Geographic Society, the National Science Foundation (BCS-0750808), the National Endowment for the Humanities (RZ-51209–10), and the Alphawood Foundation awarded to Inomata and Triadan, as well as the Ministry of Education, Culture, Sports, Science and Technology-Japan KAKENHI (21101003 and 21101002), and the Japan Society for the Promotion of Science KAKENHI (21402008), which were awarded to Aoyama.

CHAPTER TWO

Social Identities, Power Relations, and Urban Transformations

Politics of Plaza Construction at Teotihuacan

TATSUYA MURAKAMI

The built environment, including monumental buildings, public spaces, and urban forms, is an important locus where social identities and power relations are represented and enhanced, and is actively manipulated by central authorities and other sociopolitical and economic forces (e.g., DeMarrais et al. 1996; Low 2000; Rabinow 1989). However, the built environment is not a static representation of preexisting ideas (Hirsch 1995), but the meanings inscribed in it are continuously enacted and negotiated through both active and passive participation of people in public events, such as state rituals (Inomata 2006a). This is, in part, because these meanings are not necessarily shared by, or apparent to, all members of the society (Mack 2004) and may be contested (Bender 1992); but also because events are transitory by nature and enacted meanings and shared experience may fade through time after the events (DeMarrais et al. 1996:17). Thus, the durability of the built environment and the transitory nature of public events complement each other, perpetuating or transforming people's perceptions of social identities and power relations. Moreover, the physical settings are an integral part of activities taking place in the space (Giddens 1984), and thus the analysis of these settings, especially plazas and their associated features, provides a tangible means to make an inference about archaeologically intangible activities. This chapter explores how the creation and use of plazas and courtyards and their associated features served as an integral mechanism for the production and transformation of social relations at Teotihuacan, the capital of a regional state in Central Mexico (ca. AD 150–650).

Teotihuacan's history is highly dynamic (e.g., Cowgill 2000; Millon 1981; Murakami 2010) and there are several points at which the urban landscape underwent significant changes, including the initial urban growth during the Patlachique phase (ca. 150 BC–AD 1); the construction of monumental structures within the civic-ceremonial core along the Street of the Dead (the central precinct, hereafter) toward the end of the Tzacualli phase (ca. AD 1–150) to the Miccaotli phase (ca. AD 150–250); and the construction of apartment compounds around the central precinct (called an "urban renewal" by Millon 1981) from the Tlamimilolpa phase (ca. AD 250–350) onward (figure 2.1). Since the urban construction is often a cumulative process, the meanings inscribed in the final form of the city are not always apparent without referring to its historical antecedents (Duncan 1985). In this chapter, I examine diachronic changes in the use of plazas and courtyards from the initial period of state consolidation to the urban renewal project and discuss how bodily experience in plazas and courtyards was constructed to forge social identities and power relations at multiple scales of social interaction, ranging from domestic to neighborhoods to the city as a whole.

Technologies of Power and the Politics of Plaza Construction

Our understanding of the mutually constitutive nature of the built environment and social relations owes much to Foucault (1977, 2007), who demonstrated that the spatial control of bodily experience provides an important means to produce and reproduce power relations, which broadened our perspectives on the interface between experiential and spatial dimensions of political dynamics. Foucault (1977) identified two contrasting mechanisms of power in Europe: premodern, spectacle-based or sovereign power and modern, disciplinary power. Sovereign power is centered on the mortal body of the sovereign, be it an individual or collective sovereign, and is experienced in public spectacles, which, along with law and juridical systems, serve as an important means to define and enhance binary understanding of power relations, such as the sovereign and the subordinates, the permitted and the forbidden (Foucault 1977). The disciplinary technology of power is concerned with "the control and distribution of *bodies* and *individuals* in a spatial ordering" (Rabinow 2003:357, italics original). It is usually predicated on enclosure and its internal partitioning as seen in hospitals and prisons (Foucault 1977; see also Giddens 1984:145–147) and may also be devised in urban planning (Foucault 2007:15–17; Rabinow 2003). These technologies of power are an intrinsic part of social relations and are both effect and cause of social relations across the society (Foucault 2007:2). Such a conception of power allows us to explore "the notion of politics that includes everyday life" (Alonso 2005:28) and how technologies of power operate on the body of not only subject populations but also the dominant group (Foucault 2007; Giddens 1984:151–154; Rabinow 2003:358).

While the opposition of sovereign and disciplinary power has been critiqued by several researchers (e.g., Agamben 1998; Alonso 2005), who reevaluate

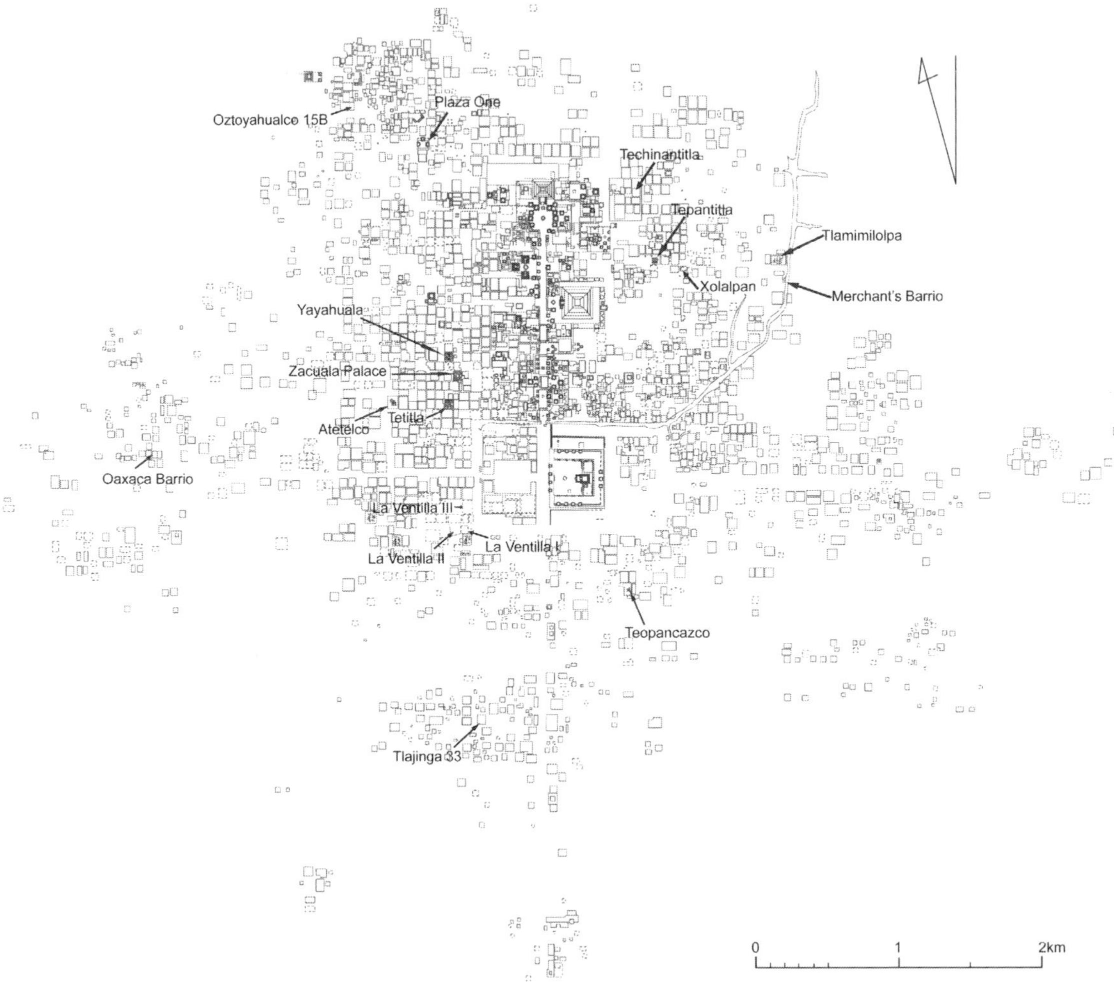

FIGURE 2.1. Location of architectural complexes mentioned in the text (redrawn from Millon 1973). Tlachinolpan is located outside the mapped area in the northwest periphery. See figure 2.2 for the location of architectural complexes in the central precinct.

the presence of sovereign power in modern contexts, Foucault (2007:7–8) acknowledges that disciplinary mechanisms are present within the regime of sovereign power and that some elements of premodern political technologies persist in the modern era. This leads to the question regarding what he calls "the system of correlation" between different technologies of power (Foucault 2007:8; see Tsukamoto 2009 for an archaeological case study). One of the major goals of this chapter is to explore how spectacle-based and disciplinary technologies of power were intertwined in activities that took place in plazas and courtyards to reinforce or transform social identities and power relations at Teotihuacan. As an integral part of public spectacles, physical settings such as plazas become an indispensable apparatus for the creation and maintenance of shared identity and power relations (e.g., Inomata 2006a, this volume; Tsukamoto, this volume). It is generally assumed that the size of open spaces has direct implications for the scale of social interaction and thus the nature of social identities and power relations negotiated during the events that took place in those plazas (Inomata 2006a). At the same time, standardized morphology of open spaces along with controlled access may indicate the control of bodily movement and experience in these events and the disciplinarization of apparatuses (e.g., Tsukamoto 2009). Building on Foucault's and other researchers' insight, I assess the size, morphology, and access patterns of plazas and courtyards at Teotihuacan. The size of plazas and courtyards will be used to make a rough estimate of their capacity and are not meant to represent the exact number of people these open spaces held.

Foucault's focus was on the operation of different mechanisms of power and not on their formation process. However, the development of different technologies of power is historically contingent and is both a cause and a consequence (both intended and unintended) of strategic actions of, and negotiations of power among, individuals and groups (e.g., Foucault 1982; Giddens 1984). Thus, technologies of power operating in open spaces can be conceptualized as both power strategies and elements of the spatial constitution of power relations. The second goal of this chapter is to examine how different technologies of power were implemented in plazas and courtyards as a consequence of strategic actions of individuals and groups. To this end, I present a summary of my study on the organization of urban construction, which examined the degree of state intervention in the urban renewal project (Murakami 2010).

State Formation, Public Plazas, and the Unified Architectural Style

The Teotihuacan state was comprised of multiple ethnic, linguistic, and/or regional groups (e.g., Rattray 1987; Spence 1992), and the creation of a shared identity along with a shared understanding of power relations was critical for the integration and operation of the state. Considering the explosive growth in construction activities in the central precinct during the Miccaotli phase, a strong central authority was likely established by this time. Conspicuous consumption of labor and material recourses for monumental construction represented the centralized power of the Teotihuacan state (Murakami 2010). The Sun Pyramid was built probably at the end of the Tzacualli phase or at the beginning of the Miccaotli phase (Millon et al. 1965; Murakami 2010; cf. Millon 1981). Shortly after the Sun Pyramid, Building 4 of the Moon Pyramid was built during the Miccaotli phase, which represents a substantial enlargement of previous structures (Sugiyama 2004; Sugiyama and Cabrera 2007). The canonical orientation of the city (15.5 degrees east of north) was likely established by this time as seen in the orientation of Building 4 (Sugiyama 2004). The Feathered Serpent Pyramid along with the Ciudadela was constructed in the Miccaotli-Tlamimilolpa transition (Sugiyama 2004). It is likely that these major pyramids were closely associated with the creation myth, the beginning of time, militarism, and/or rulership (Cowgill 2000; Headrick 2001; Millon 1993; Sugiyama 2004, 2005), and the construction process itself was an important means to legitimate the power of the state.

Along with these major pyramids, large plazas such as the Moon Plaza and the Great Plaza of the Ciudadela were constructed, which could have accommodated most city residents (table 2.1). The Street of the Dead, at least its northern half, was also in existence by the Miccaotli phase (Millon 1981). This suggests that the state ideology inscribed in monumental structures was actively and continuously disseminated through public events in these open spaces. Rituals, such as political rites (e.g., rulers' accession), state funerals, and temple dedications, would have been carried out in the plazas. The Moon Plaza in its final form could have accommodated up to approximately 35,000 people (table 2.1), but including the Street of the Dead, most city residents should have been able to attend public events in the plaza. The size of the Moon Plaza remained more or less the same throughout Teotihuacan's history because the Moon Pyramid was enlarged subsequently toward the north, never to the south (Sugiyama and Cabrera 2007). This may suggest that the size of the Moon Plaza was a major concern for planning spatial configuration of the central precinct. The Great Plaza of the Ciudadela is the second largest plaza within the central precinct,[1] and Cowgill (1983) estimates that the majority of city residents (i.e., ca. 100,000 people) could have been accommodated in the plaza (table 2.1). The Sun Plaza is considerably smaller than other major plazas, and it could have accommodated around 6,000 people (table 2.1). Possibly only high status people were allowed to enter the plaza or perhaps the audience was continuously circulated.

While both construction activities and public events in large plazas served to disseminate state authority, the control of subject population was further enhanced in these events through the control of individual bodies. The physical form of the Street of the Dead and its access pattern imply that the regulated and predefined movement of people and some degree of order was imposed on individual bodies. The lateral sides of the street were almost completely blocked by architectural complexes (at least in its final form), and there were likely three main entrances (figure 2.2). The absence of a formal entrance north of the Sun Pyramid implies the movement of people from the south to the north, suggesting that the Moon Plaza was the final destination. It is possible that ceremonies such as processions were carried out on the street. Access patterns of major plazas also indicate that the movement of people was highly regulated and/or predefined: the Sun Plaza and the Great Plaza of the Ciudadela have only one major entrance.

State buildings and large plazas also set a stage for the creation of a shared identity through bodily experience and sensory perception of the physical presence of other residents (Inomata 2006a). A shared identity was also enhanced by the creation of state symbols (Kertzer 1988). During the Miccaotli phase, *talud-tablero* style (a combination of a sloping wall and a vertical panel) was adopted from the Puebla-Tlaxcala region and was applied to almost all the platforms within the central precinct by the beginning of the Early Tlamimilolpa phase. This adoption of *talud-tablero* style might attest to the creation of a state

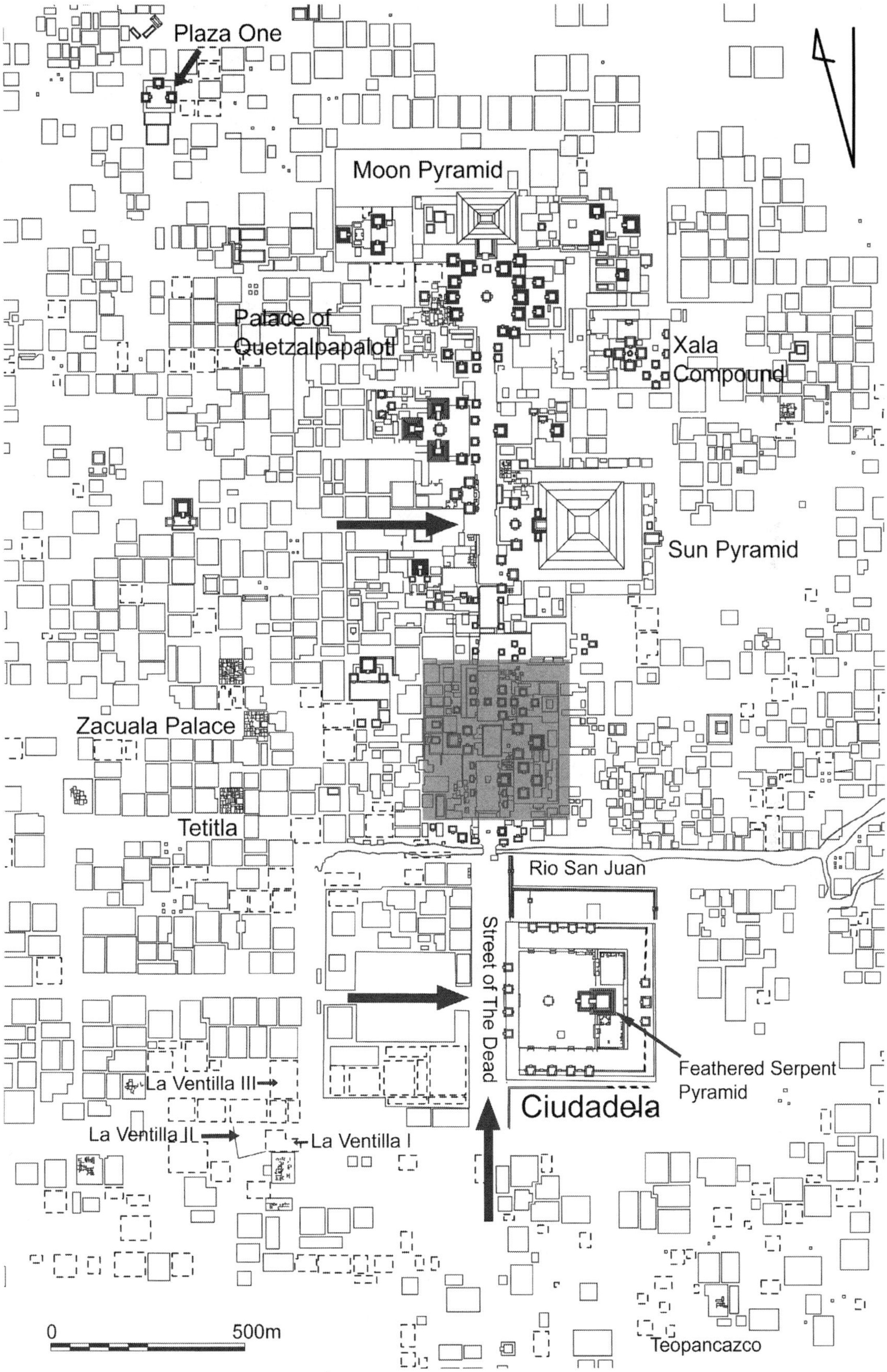

FIGURE 2.2. Architectural complexes in the central precinct (redrawn from Millon 1993). Arrows show the main entrances to the Street of the Dead. The shaded area is the Street of the Dead Complex.

identity, which was actively promoted through public events in major plazas. Current evidence suggests that there were multiple architectural traditions in the city before the Miccaotli phase, as seen in a public architectural complex in Tlachinolpan (Blucher 1971), a small circular pyramid in Plaza One (Cook de Leonard 1957), and small stepped pyramids (Buildings 1–3) at the Moon Pyramid (Sugiyama 2004; Sugiyama and Cabrera 2007). These different traditions might be associated with different ethnic and/or regional affiliations, suggesting that early Teotihuacan may have been an aggregate or a confederation of multiple communities, not necessarily under a single central authority (Angulo 2007; Murakami 2010). Thus, the use of *talud-tablero* style for nearly all the platforms can be interpreted as an intentional act to unify architectural styles. *Talud-tablero* style likely became a state symbol or a materialized identity (DeMarrais et al. 1996), which was re-created throughout the city (with some variants) as well as in other regions of Mesoamerica during the subsequent phases.

In sum, through the process of state formation, power relations (especially between state elites and subjects) and a shared identity were embodied in the size, form, and spatial organization of the central precinct and were continuously negotiated and reaffirmed or transformed in public events in large open spaces. Unfortunately, there is little evidence for residential architecture outside the central precinct in this period, and it is not clear how state rituals articulated with rituals in domestic contexts. The creation and maintenance of a shared identity and power relations are, however, continuous processes and the Teotihuacan state developed a new mechanism of forging a shared identity and power relations through the urban renewal project from the Tlamimilolpa phase (ca. AD 250–350) onward.

Urban Renewal and the Socio-Spatial Organization

The construction of apartment compounds marks the start of urban renewal (Millon 1981): over 100,000 people lived in approximately 2,300 apartment compounds (figures 2.1 and 2.2). Apartment compounds are walled enclosures and contain multiple residential units or apartments that consist of one or more courtyard units (figure 2.3). All the compounds were built following more or less the canonical orientation of the city. The concept of urban renewal can be applied not only to residential areas around the central precinct but also to the central precinct itself. A new spatial configuration of the central precinct was likely established in the Early Tlamimilolpa phase. Urban renewal throughout the city allows us to examine the use of open spaces at different scales of social interaction.[2]

It is generally assumed that there is a direct association between the size of open spaces and the type of activities (e.g., public vs. domestic), and the function and socioeconomic status of architectural complexes have been inferred based on the size of open spaces along with their location, associated buildings, access pattern, and other kinds of evidence (e.g., Manzanilla 2009; Millon 1976). Three broad socioeconomic urban strata have been defined at Teotihuacan: state elites, intermediate elites, and commoners (e.g., Millon 1976).

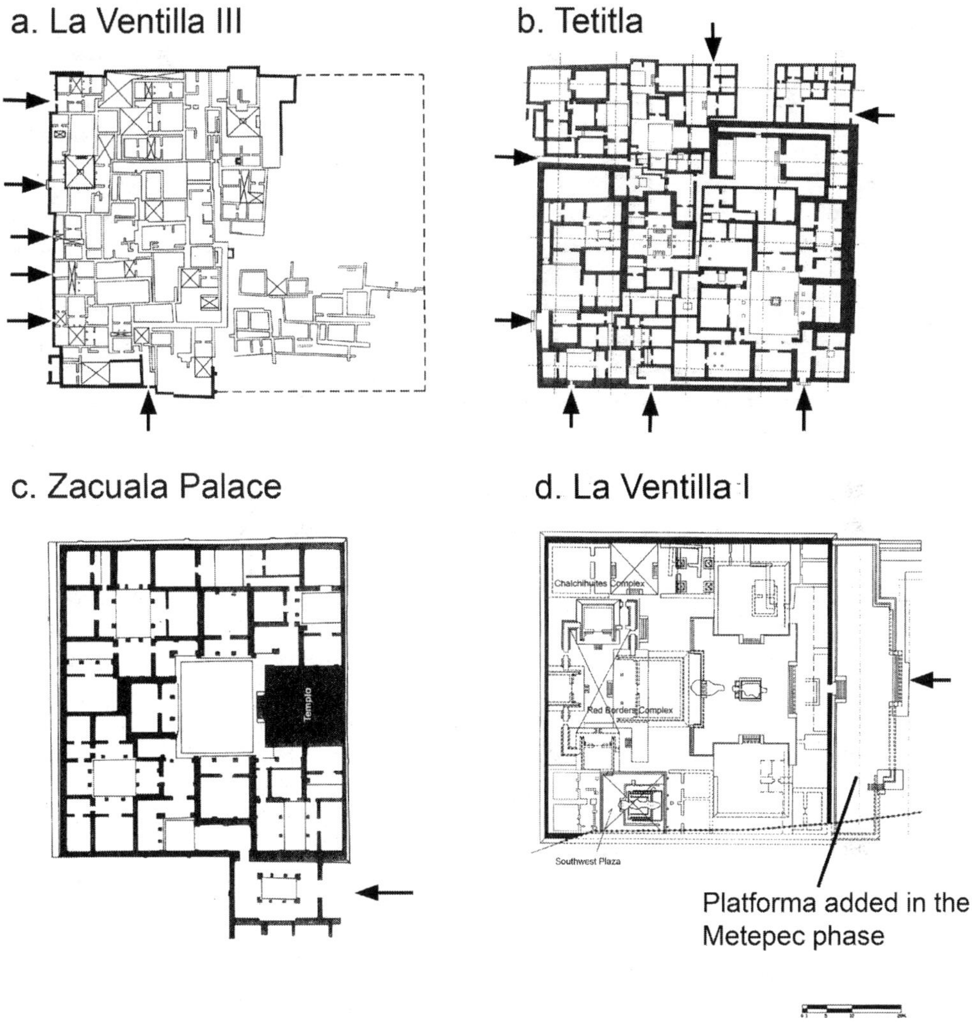

FIGURE 2.3. Layout and access pattern of some apartment compounds. (a) Modified after Gómez Chávez 2000; (b) modified after Manzanilla 2004:fig. 5.6; (c) modified after Manzanilla 2004:fig. 5.3; (d) modified after Gómez Chávez 2000. Arrows indicate entrances.

Below I describe plazas and courtyards associated with these socioeconomic strata and address the organization of the urban renewal project. Then I discuss how social identities and power relations were embodied in the reformed city.

The Central Precinct and State Elites

While state elites were probably responsible for the successful enactment of state rituals in large plazas, a number of different activities associated with state affairs were likely carried out within the central precinct. Besides major pyramids, other architectural complexes within the central precinct contain small plazas and/or large courtyards, and considering their size and restricted access pattern, it is likely that these plazas/courtyards served only a limited number of state elites, not the general public (table 2.1). Administrative duties were probably among the main activities carried out in these open spaces. Among a few excavated complexes, the Street of the Dead Complex (SDC) is thought to have been one of the central administrative facilities and/or royal palace (Cowgill 1983; Morelos 1993). The near absence of burials in the residential quarters suggests that the SDC housed institutionally affiliated groups, such as government officials, their retainers, and servants, not lineages. There were likely functional differentiations among plazas and courtyards at the SDC depending on their size (table 2.1). Probably during the Early Xolalpan phase (ca. AD 350–450) or earlier (Morelos 1993), the Street of the Dead between the Sun Pyramid and the Ciudadela was segmented by five transverse platforms, four of which are part of the SDC. It is not clear whether people could freely walk through the segmented street, but the presence of a stairway at each transverse platform implies the movement of people and it is possible that the general audience was allowed to walk through on special occasions (e.g., following the processions). In any case, the construction of transverse platforms implies a restricted access to the SDC, and the movement of people in this area was highly regulated.

Neighborhoods and Intermediate Elite Compounds

Apartment compounds defined as intermediate elite residences have a larger central courtyard and temple structures than those of other compounds and their internal rooms are profusely decorated with murals (Manzanilla 2006). The highly integrated spatial arrangement is also associated with some of these intermediate elite compounds. For example, at Zacuala Palace and La Ventilla I, there is only one entrance and all the courtyard units are connected through the central courtyard (figure 2.3). It is generally thought that higher ranked intermediate elite compounds were barrio centers (Manzanilla 2006, 2009:24–25; Millon 1976, 1981) or barrio temples (Cabrera and Gómez Chávez 2008:49; Gómez Chávez 2000:596–598), whose functions would include communal rituals and the administration of the production and distribution of various resources and political affairs.

The existence of neighborhoods (and, by extension, neighborhood leaders) is corroborated by data from the Teotihuacan Mapping Project (Cowgill 2008;

TABLE 2.1. Estimated Capacity of Plazas and Main Courtyards at Teotihuacan

	Area (m^2)	Estimated Capacity* (higher est.)	(lower est.)
Central Precinct (civic-ceremonial)			
The Great Plaza, the Ciudadela	45,590	99,109	12,664
The Moon Plaza	15,600	33,913	4,333
The Sun Plaza	6,474	14,074	1,798
N Sunken Plaza, SDC**	5,472	11,896	1,520
C Sunken Plaza, SDC	3,128	6,800	869
S Sunken Plaza, SDC	6,496	14,122	1,804
Central Precinct (administrative/residential)			
S Palace, the Ciudadela	896	1,948	249
N Palace, the Ciudadela	900	1,957	250
West Plaza Complex, SDC	630	1,370	175
Quetzalpapalotl Palace Complex	529	1,150	147
Quetzalpapalotl Palace	85	185	24
Intermediate Elite Apartment Compounds			
La Ventilla I	456	991	127
Zacuala Palace	285	620	79
Teopancazco***	275	598	76
Yayahuala	188	409	52
Tepantitla***	182	396	51
Atetelco	125	272	35
Tetitla	120	261	33
La Ventilla II	119	259	33
Xolalpan	108	235	30
Commoners' Apartment Compounds			
La Ventilla III	35	76	10
Tlamimilolpa	35	76	10
Oztoyahualco 15B***	25	54	7

* Higher estimated capacity is based on 0.46 m^2/person and lower estimate is based on 3.6 m^2/person (Inomata 2006a). A middle estimate would be based on 1 m^2/person and thus will be the same value as the area in m^2.

** SDC represents the Street of the Dead Complex.

*** The area was taken from Manzanilla 2009.

Millon 1981; Robertson 2001). Although the boundaries are not always clear, this does not imply that barrio-like spatial clustering did not exist. The presence of large main courtyards with temples at several apartment compounds attests that ritual practices and other kinds of social gatherings were carried out at a level larger than a single compound. These courtyards could have accommodated around a hundred to several hundreds of people (table 2.1), which suggests that members of multiple compounds participated in rituals and other activities. Moreover, Robertson's (2001) multivariate spatial statistical studies of surface-collected sherds suggest that social integration was enhanced by the reorganization of neighborhood composition during the Tlamimilolpa phase. Robertson has shown that the neighborhoods in the Miccaotli phase were relatively heterogeneous in socioeconomic terms and that this heterogeneity decreased with increased socioeconomic segregation in the subsequent Tlamimilolpa phase when apartment compounds were adopted. These observations imply that the intermediate-level spatial segments were probably important not only for social integration of a group of compounds but also for the internal administration of the city (Millon 1981:212; see also Gómez Chávez 2000).

Given the relatively large size of the main courtyard (table 2.1), La Ventilla I, Zacuala Palace, and Teopancazco might have served as barrio centers or temples. As for the other intermediate elite compounds, there were likely functional variations, ranging from public or institutional compounds to purely residential compounds with multiple entrances such as Tetitla (figure 2.3) (Cabrera and Gómez Chávez 2008; Gómez Chávez 2000:593–613).

Commoners' Apartment Compounds

Lower status compounds or commoners' compounds are characterized by their smaller size of rooms, temples, and courtyards along with inferior construction materials, such as adobe walls and earthen floors. Murals are present in those compounds, but are often limited to red paint and lack complex motifs that are common in intermediate elite compounds. A poorly integrated internal spatial arrangement also seems associated with commoners' compounds (figure 2.3). For example, at La Ventilla III, each residential unit or apartment has its own entrance and there is no internal connection among those units (Gómez Chávez 2000). Clayton's (2009) analysis of mortuary practice at commoners' compounds suggests that they were organized into *houses*, and members of each compound or *house* shared distinctive sets of artifacts and practices that can be distinguished from those of other compounds. It is likely that social and ideological integration of a house was enhanced through ritual and other activities carried out in courtyards (see also Manzanilla 2002, 2004). The main courtyards at commoners' compounds are very small (table 2.1) and could accommodate only a limited number of people at once (around several tens), which suggests that activities were carried out only by compound residents, probably with a limited number of participants from other compounds (e.g., some close kins). It is interesting to note that some objects that were symbols of militarism, such as portrait figurines and theater-type censers, have been recovered along with an altar in the form of a *talud-tablero* platform (possibly a representation of pyramids within the central precinct) at some compounds (Sugiyama 2004). This suggests that rituals in domestic contexts reinforced the participants' connection with state deities, rulers, or factions of ruling elites (see Ringle, this volume).

Standardized Architecture and the Organization of the Urban Renewal Project

It is clear that plazas and courtyards were used in diverse ways and often for multiple purposes at Teotihuacan, but I suggest that they served as integrative facilities at multiple scales, at a compound level, neighborhood level, institutional level, and city level. In view of the diversity in the nature of activities and scale, it is striking that the morphology of these plaza and courtyard units are highly homogeneous: a main temple (usually placed to the east) and an open space (usually plastered) with or without an altar at the center. The diverse architectural traditions at early Teotihuacan strongly suggest that the city's residents did not just happen to share architectural repertoire during the urban renewal project, especially if diverse architectural traditions during the Tzacualli phase served to perpetuate group identities of residents' place of origin. Rather, it is likely that standardized architecture was intentionally selected as a state strategy to create a new identity throughout the city. In this regard, considering the conformity of the orientation of the apartment compounds, Millon (1993) and Cowgill (2000) think that the decision to build such compounds derived from a strong and effective centralized authority. Furthermore, Millon (1993:29) postulates that the state must have sponsored the building of apartment compounds by organizing the supply of building materials. My study of construction labor and resources (Murakami 2010) partially supports Millon's interpretation and suggests that the state actively intervened in the actual construction processes of apartment compounds, and that the homogeneity of architectural traits was not derived from superficial imitation.

Analysis of labor investment suggests that a labor force necessary to build a single apartment compound (65,000 to 127,000 person-days) was beyond the ability of the compound's residents, who must have relied on external labor resources. I have suggested the possibility that barrio leaders and/or the state regulated labor mobilization for apartment compound construction. The distributional analysis of andesitic cut stone blocks has revealed that the majority of them were used for selected buildings within the central precinct, thus suggesting that the procurement was organized by the state. But some andesitic cut stone blocks were also used sporadically at apartment compounds, including commoner's compounds such as La Ventilla III. Geochemical analysis of these cut stone blocks ($n = 176$) indicates that their provenance was nearly identical between the central precinct and surrounding apartment compounds, which suggests that the same cut stone blocks procured by the state were distributed to apartment compounds. Compositional analysis of lime plaster ($n = 123$) demonstrates that its quality and recipe were homogeneous between the central precinct and apartment compounds. This suggests that the procurement of lime and the production of lime plaster were centrally organized by the state, although the possibility of open market exchange cannot be excluded. Lime and the majority of andesitic rocks are non-local resources, and the consumption of these resources on a substantially large scale implies a huge amount of state investment in securing their supply. In addition to these non-local resources, other construction materials and techniques were also highly homogeneous throughout the city (e.g., Morelos 1993; see Murakami 2010). Thus, the homogeneity of architectural traits was derived not from superficial imitation, but likely from an active control of construction processes (at least the procurement of some resources) by the state.[3]

All these observations strongly suggest that the repertoire of architectural traits, construction materials and techniques, and possibly construction labor along with the orientation of compounds were regulated to a great extent by the state. Such an active state intervention in urban construction suggests the exercise of a strong infrastructural power (see Mann 1984) and probably facilitated the administration of city residents. However, it is misleading to think that the reformed city was created only through the decisions of state elites. The size and internal layout of apartment compounds vary greatly, which likely reflected the decisions of each compound's residents (Millon 1976). Furthermore, Robertson's study (2001), as mentioned above, suggests that the decisions at the neighborhood level also played a role in reorganizing the urban communities. The size of apartment compounds may have been decided based on a mix of state regulation, negotiation among neighborhoods, and needs of individual compounds. Moreover, the presence of some variants of *talud-tablero* (Gómez Chávez 2000), Zapotec-style temples (Croissier 2007) and circular rooms (Rattray 1987) suggests that some architectural traits were more freely selected by some of the residents. Thus, not only the top-down and bottom-up processes, but decisions at multiple scales of social interaction were entangled in a complex way resulting in the reorganization of the city.

Bodily Experience, Group Identities, and Power Relations

As mentioned earlier, plazas and courtyards at Teotihuacan likely served as social integrative facilities at multiple scales. All these facilities consisted of the standardized architectural traits and standardized construction materials and techniques. The standardized architecture would have enhanced an understanding of the "sameness" not only in terms of visual form and sensory feeling of the material, but also through the experience of the identical spatial orientation, probably rooted in the religious meaning of cardinal directions (Millon 1993), as well as through predefined movements of the body implied by the standardized orientation. I suggest that the standardized architecture was an important medium for the creation of an imagined community (Anderson 2006) and its repeated experience may have fostered a shared identity. Architecture and urban planning are often an integral part of domination and social control (e.g., Foucault 2007; Rabinow 1989), and the active state intervention in the actual construction processes at Teotihuacan suggests that urban renewal was a state strategy to promote a shared identity and probably disseminate a corporate ideology (e.g., Blanton et al. 1996; Manzanilla 2006), which would have served to conceal from the daily practice of residents the contradictions inherent in the relationship among diverse groups of people in the city.

Nevertheless, while standardized architecture indicates a common setting for activities, these activities were diverse not only in scale, but also in nature as suggested by a wide range of activities and the functional diversity of apartment compounds. I argue that the standardized architecture can be conceptualized as a frame for diverse activities and experiences, a frame that moves between the foreground and the background depending on the nature of activities, but is always an integral part of these diverse activities (cf. Hirsch 1995). In a sense, the standardized architecture can be thought of as a structure in Giddensian terms (e.g., Giddens 1984) in that it both enables and constrains practices, which, in turn, reproduce or transform the structure. Within this frame or structure, multiple group identities, as a house member, a member of an ethnic group, a member of a neighborhood, a member of other institutions, and a member of the polity, were negotiated and were reaffirmed or transformed, thereby creating overlapping and often contradicting urban communities. Furthermore, there were people who did not follow or have access to the standardized architecture, especially those living in insubstantial structures (Robertson 2008), and they would have viewed and experienced the standardized architecture in different ways. In this sense, public rituals also provided moments in which social distinctions were pronounced to various degrees, providing a basis for forging conflicting identities within the city.

In the main courtyard of residential compounds, domestic rituals would serve to reaffirm or transform kinship relations. There were likely some occasions where the frame comes to the foreground and residents' connection with the polity was reinforced as seen in ritual objects associated with state ideology. At higher-ranked intermediate elite compounds, rituals of public nature likely took place (Manzanilla 2009). In addition, administrative activities and/or activities associated with specific institutions (e.g., military, priests) were likely carried out at some intermediate elite compounds. Those participants from commoners' compounds would have perceived both the shared identity through the bodily experience of standardized ritual settings and the reality of power relations through the differential scale and embellishment of ritual performances and settings. At both residential and higher-ranked intermediate elite compounds, rituals entailed face-to-face interactions among participants and served to reaffirm and transform group identities associated with houses, neighborhoods, and local institutions.

Within the central precinct, large-scale public events were continuously carried out in major plazas from the pre-urban renewal period and would have engendered an identity as a member of the polity. These public events would have had different implications after urban renewal. Participants would have realized the same architectural canons and spatial orientation used for the settings of these events. This is where the frame comes to the foreground and would have enhanced participants' identity as part of the polity. At the same time, public events and settings at an overwhelmingly larger scale and with accentuated sophistication would have fostered an understanding of the reality of power relations. Along with public events, smaller-scale activities carried out in a number of small plazas and courtyards would have entailed face-to-face interactions and provided arenas for the negotiation of power and identity among state officials.

Conclusion

As Inomata (2006a) emphasizes, public events would have been an indispensable means of social integration in preindustrial polities and would have provided critical moments in which central authorities and the unity of the polity could be perceived and experienced by subject populations. This seems to have been the case for Teotihuacan especially during the Miccaotli and Tlamimilolpa phases when monumental structures were actively built and rebuilt and a number of sacrificial burials were interred (e.g., Sugiyama 2004). Thus, spectacle-based power was likely the principal mode of power, which was reinforced by some aspects of disciplinary power as seen in the control of bodily movement within the central precinct. But the Teotihuacan state further enhanced social integration through the use of standardized architecture during the urban renewal project. A number of the same architectural traits, some of which were very likely associated with state ideology (e.g., *talud-tablero* style, canonical orientation), were re-created throughout the city, and plazas and courtyards became highly disciplinarized. Repeated bodily experience of standardized architectural canons with varying scales and embellishment would have engendered both a shared identity and the reality of power relations. At the same time, the presence of the polity deeply penetrated into the daily lives of city residents by enframing their diverse activities and experiences, which was likely a state strategy to integrate an array of people with different ethnic, linguistic, regional, and socioeconomic affiliations. Penetration of the state into the daily lives of the city residents represents a strong infrastructural power and a highly centralized and efficient state bureaucracy. However, this overarching pattern by no means implies that the standardized urban buildings were achieved solely through decisions of ruling elites. As Cowgill (2003) called for attention to differential costs and benefits of living in the city, residents might have voluntarily adopted or even emulated the standardized architecture.

An orderly laid-out city such as Teotihuacan seems to be exceptional and unique in the context of Mesoamerica, but some parallels can be drawn from cities in medieval Europe, specifically those described as "a disciplinary ordering of space" (Rabinow 2003:357–359), through which the spatial control of bodily experience operated on the middle and upper classes (Foucault 2007). Certainly, as I suggested above, the standardized architecture was a state strategy of social control, but at the same time the same disciplinary technology of power governed the activities of state elites, who would have been bound to a great extent to moral values and a social order reproduced continuously in rituals. Thus, it is likely that disciplinary power formed an important component of organizational principles at Teotihuacan. I suggest that the creation of the symbol of group solidarity, public spectacles associated with that symbol, and multiple levels of social integrative facilities with a disciplinary ordering of space provided an important basis for the successful operation and administration of highly nucleated and large urban settlements.

Acknowledgments

I would like to thank Kenichiro Tsukamoto and Takeshi Inomata for inviting me to contribute a chapter to this volume as well as for their invaluable comments on earlier drafts of this chapter. Part of the research presented here was funded by the National Science Foundation Dissertation Improvement Grant (BCS-0836716), Arizona State University (the Graduate and Professional Student Association and the School of Human Evolution and Social Change), and Sigma Xi (ASU Chapter).

Notes

1. A large open space at the Great Compounds, located to the west of the Ciudadela, is the largest plaza within the central precinct, but it is generally thought to be the central marketplace (Millon 1981) and is not considered here (but see Ringle, this volume).

2. Open spaces at Teotihuacan vary greatly in size (table 2.1) and are conventionally divided into four categories: plaza; courtyard (or patio); espejo de agua (water mirror or impluvium); and asoleadero or backyard floors (Angulo 1987:280–285; see also Morelos 1993:86, 88). Angulo (1987) and Gómez Chávez (2000) distinguish plazas from courtyards (or patios) based on the presence of an altar in plazas. Other terms are not always defined clearly and are sometimes used interchangeably. I limit the use of "plaza" to large open spaces within the central precinct. I group other open spaces directly associated with temples or rooms into the category of courtyard.

3. It should be noted that there are some apartment compounds in peripheral areas, which seem to have emulated apartment compounds in the dense urban zone, e.g., Tlajinga 33 (Widmer 1987). There were also insubstantial structures around the city (Robertson 2008). Thus, the state intervention in construction did not reach all the population in the city.

CHAPTER THREE

Multiple Identities on the Plazas

The Classic Maya Center of El Palmar, Mexico

KENICHIRO TSUKAMOTO

In Classic Maya society (AD 250–900), many centers had a wide variety of plazas in and around their civic core. A representative case in this regard is the Classic Maya center of El Palmar, where plazas of different sizes and means of access were constructed at both the civic-ceremonial core or the Main Group and at its outlying groups. How did these many plazas play roles in constituting social relations, more specifically, identities, in the wake of power negotiations among El Palmar's inhabitants? This chapter explores the relationship between the multiplicity of plazas and the formation of different identities in a community by examining both the scope of plaza construction and of ceremonial events on the plazas. In this regard, I will examine El Palmar's plazas from three perspectives: (1) how collective identities were formed and transformed by power negotiations in the process of constructing large-scale plazas and the spectacles conducted in these plazas; (2) how El Palmar's ruling elites accentuated social distinctions by means of physically and visually excluding the rest of the population from their ritual activities in a restricted plaza; and finally (3) how second-tier elites or intermediate elites claimed their group identity at an outlying plaza. A plaza can be an arena for producing and reproducing various identities, but in this chapter I will consciously focus on the most prominent identity perceived in the material remains of each plaza at El Palmar because this approach allows us to explicitly illuminate the different roles plazas played in Classic Maya society. While El Palmar consists of several discrete groups surrounding the Main Group, I will focus on the eight plazas at the Main Group and a small plaza located to the north in an outlying group, which we call the Guzmán Group (figure 3.1).

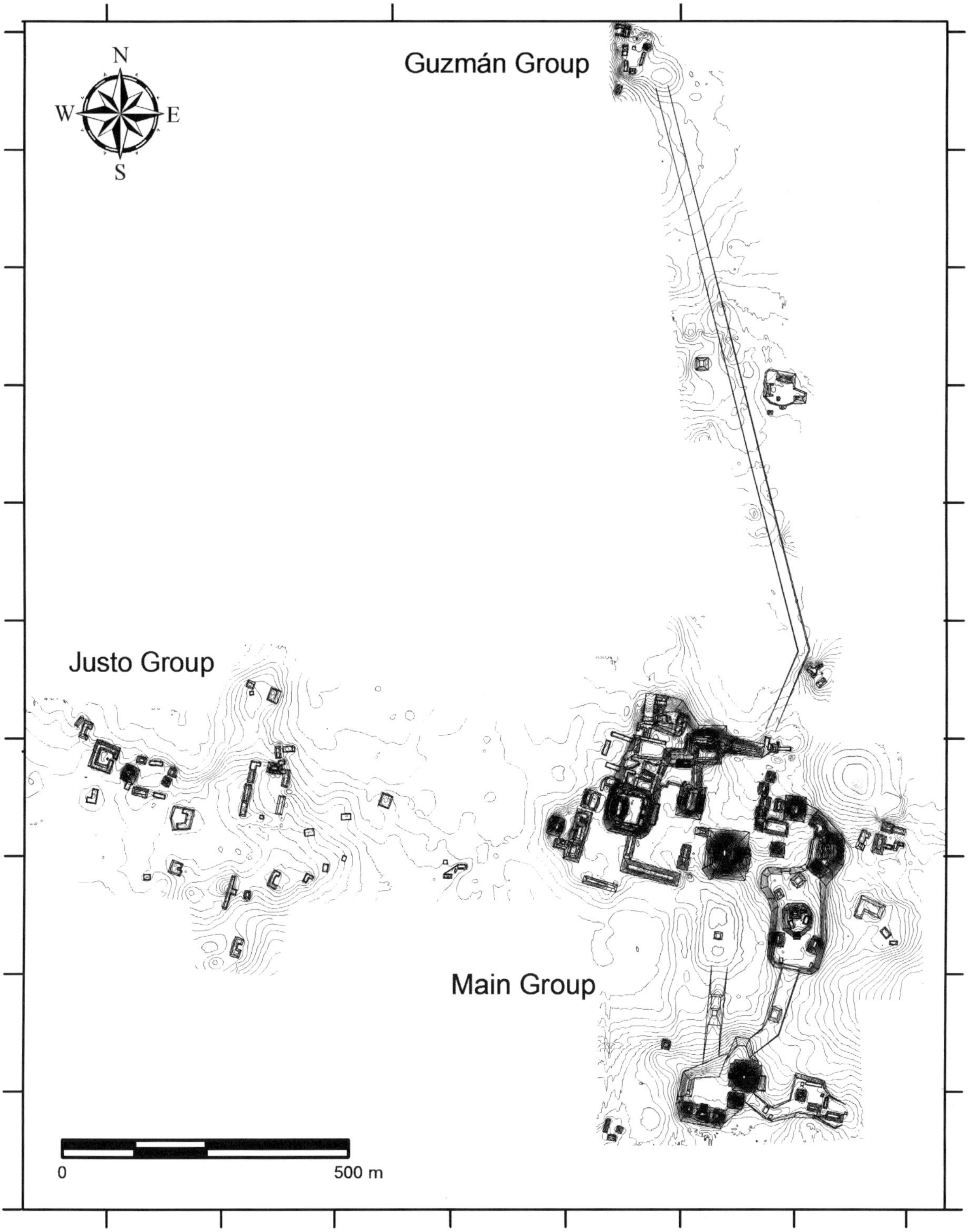

FIGURE 3.1. Topographic map showing the location of the Main Group, Justo Group, and Guzmán Group, created by Kenichiro Tsukamoto and Javier López Camacho.

Constituting Multiple Identities on the Plaza

Identity is the pivotal media through which social interdependence is cultivated. Holland et al. (2001 [1998]:57) argue that an identity is formed by practices of a social group in a figured world or field (see also Bourdieu 1977). An individual belongs to several fields in a society through being incorporated into the structural properties of rules or schema that regulate gender, family, race, ethnicity, occupation, ancestry, social status, and so on. As Giddens (1979), Bourdieu (1977), and other practice theorists argue, these structural properties are not determinative but reflexive mediations, which recursively guide and constrain human practices, perspectives, and emotions. Members in each field share similar bodily experiences and perceptions that evoke a group identity. Through being incorporated into various fields in one's life, an individual acquires multiple identities in daily practice, which often contradict one another. The multiple identities associated with an individual are never fixed, but are inherently a continuous flow of experiences and thoughts interwoven in several fields (Butler 1993). These identities perceived in daily life are emphasized or repressed in public life through social interactions.

The construction of public architecture and spectacles in a large plaza provide a critical opportunity for human interactions that create shared experiences among a large number of social members. In a small group, members constantly encounter face-to-face interactions in everyday life, sharing bodily experiences, structural properties, moral constraints, and emotions, all of which render a group identity. In contrast, once a population exceeds the capacity for its members to conduct regular face-to-face interactions in everyday life, public ceremonies endow participants with emotionally charged experiences that highlight their understanding of the community and themselves in the community (Geertz 1980; Inomata 2006a; Kertzer 1988). Similarly, a large construction program physically brings people together for a significant period of time beyond the daily circle of interactions (Inomata 2006a). The substantial labor investment in public buildings and the process of coordinating monumental practice create a new scale of social relations in a community (Pauketat 2001).

Nevertheless, physical gatherings in the plaza and in the building project are far from creating a coherent identity recognized among the entire community because such a sense of affiliation with a collectivity "embodies a distinct network of power relations" (Janusek 2004:17). Analyzing social space as a crucial module to reveal any exercise of power, Foucault (1977:80–88) stressed the transformable mechanism of power over time and space in the network of social relations. In premodern societies, he argued that spectacles were a vehicle of constituting power relations between sovereign and subject. Dramatic events in an open space were displayed for a large audience to see sovereign power in action. To institutionalize sovereign power, public events like public torture or human sacrificies were codified as a regulated practice, following well-defined procedures from instruments to duration of the execution. Meanwhile, Foucault argues that the rise of states in modern European society induced disciplinary power that produced docile bodies through controlling individual perceptions and physical movements in a given space.

However, even in premodern societies, disciplinary power emerges through a specific spatial setting that places participants in different roles or categories by which people learn how to treat one another and their own images (Inomata and Lawrence 2006; Inomata and Tsukamoto, this volume; Leve 2011; Love 1999; Murakami, this volume; Rabinow 2003; Tsukamoto 2009).

In early complex societies, rulers often enact theatrical performances in spectacles for publicly displaying the centralized authority to a large audience. During theatrical events, symbolic action and adornment are employed to make it easy for an audience to perceive ruling ideology as a community-wide identity. Kertzer (1988:52–53) argues that political reality cannot be established without public rituals and symbolic representations (see also Connerton 1989). Similarly, Turner (1969) and Geertz (1980) emphasize the dramatic nature of political rituals as entailed in symbolic representations and theatrical performances. In so doing, a substantial plaza in the Maya centers becomes a ritual field where the rulers legitimize and naturalize the hierarchical social distinctions embedded in ideology (Kertzer 1988:52–53; Moore 1996b, 2003; Yaeger 2003), though the audience was not simply a passive recipient of their political rituals, but they always evaluated and negotiated political realities (Inomata 2006a; Joyce 2010).

Moreover, as Foucault argues in the mechanism of disciplinary power, accessibility and exclusiveness of different plazas shape individual perceptions and bodily movements that lead individuals to perceive social hierarchy and different identities. While open plazas play a significant role in facilitating physical gatherings among a large number of community members who perceive and transform a shared identity, restricted plazas may promote elite identities among selected members of a community, distinguishing those groups from the rest of the population. For example, natural or artificial elevation and massive walls served not only to control visual and/or physical access to private plazas, but also to create exclusiveness in contrast to more public spaces. Ritual practices among rulers and nobles generated a different sense of self and different bodily experiences while the limiting of access to and participation in such rituals created a sense of social distinction visible to the rest of the society (Joyce 2004). Thus, the building programs of public architecture and spectacles create and re-create the political reality of a community, distributing values among its members (Inomata 2006a:808).

Shared practices and experiences in communal activities foster group interdependences, but emotions embedded in them may be only momentary and soon forgotten (Leach 1954:281; Lucero 2003:525). To perpetuate such emotional experiences as a hierarchically ordered identity, rulers commissioned the building of monumental architecture and commemorative monuments. Carved monuments on a plaza serve to exhibit social hierarchies in the community (Urcid and Joyce, this volume) and to publicly manifest the central authority of successive rulers over generations.

In Classic Maya society, many in the audience for the plaza rituals of the urban core probably were those who lived in surrounding areas. To integrate dispersed architectural groups into an overarching identity, Maya rulers could have commissioned the building of public architecture or commemorative monuments in the outlying areas as a political strategy (Yaeger 2003:137).

Nevertheless, outlying inhabitants must not have passively accepted a given social condition, but were actors who actively created and modified their political situations. One of the ways to accept or contest ruling ideological power is to conduct group rituals in their living spaces. In fact, many dispersed residences were grouped around small plazas in Classic Maya civic cores' outlying areas. I consider that these ceremonial plazas were not always sponsored by ruling elites, but local groups were capable of establishing their ceremonial spaces. Ritual practices conducted in this plaza would have been designed for fostering a group identity by consenting to and also contesting a politywide identity promoted by their rulers. For the member of a community, therefore, his or her multiple identities are continuously transformed and occasionally enhanced through various ritual practices and the modification of spaces situated in historically contingent ideological as well as power relations, present discourses, and symbolic materials (Holland et al. 2001 [1998]; Joyce 2010). Among different identities, people embrace mixed thoughts and feelings of subjective affiliation, often regardless of their potential incompatibility.

How can we articulate multiple identities and power relations embedded in ceremonial events with archaeological data? In Classic Maya society plazas were constructed in a variety of types and dimensions at both the urban core and in its outlying areas. Such various plazas were not constructed contemporaneously, but at certain historical moments as the outcome of social practices, historical contingencies, asymmetrical power relations, and negotiations of identities among social groups. I argue that the study of the different plazas at an archaeological site can lead to uncovering the different scale of negotiations. While identities are formed by a great array of social activities, this study focuses on the building program of plazas and associated ceremonial events including the erection of carved monuments at El Palmar.

The Classic Maya Center of El Palmar

El Palmar is located in southeastern Campeche, Mexico. Surface survey and topographic mapping conducted during fieldwork from 2007 to 2011 has shown that El Palmar extends over 10 km^2 and consists of at least eight outlying groups which are scattered at varying distances from the Main Group (Tsukamoto and López Camacho 2010). An *aguada* or reservoir (Central Aguada) lies at the center of the Main Group as a landmark of El Palmar's polity and around the Central Aguada there are substantial spaces (28,163 m^2) that were most likely used for some ceremonies such as procession rituals (figure 3.2). In fact, four commemorative monuments are erected in and around the aguada. To the north of the Central Aguada is Temple I, the largest pyramidal temple at the site, measuring 80 m by 70 m at its base and 30 m high. To the south of the plaza is Temple II, the second largest pyramidal temple with a height of 29 m. Other spatial features at the Main Group are eight ceremonial plazas: the Great Plaza, Central Plaza, K'awiil Plaza, López Plaza, and Plazas E, F, G, and H. Excavations show that El Palmar had a long construction sequence of plazas beginning from the Late Preclassic period (ca. 300 BC) until the Terminal Classic period (ca. AD 1000). We reported detailed construction sequences of these plazas elsewhere (Tsukamoto et al. 2012).

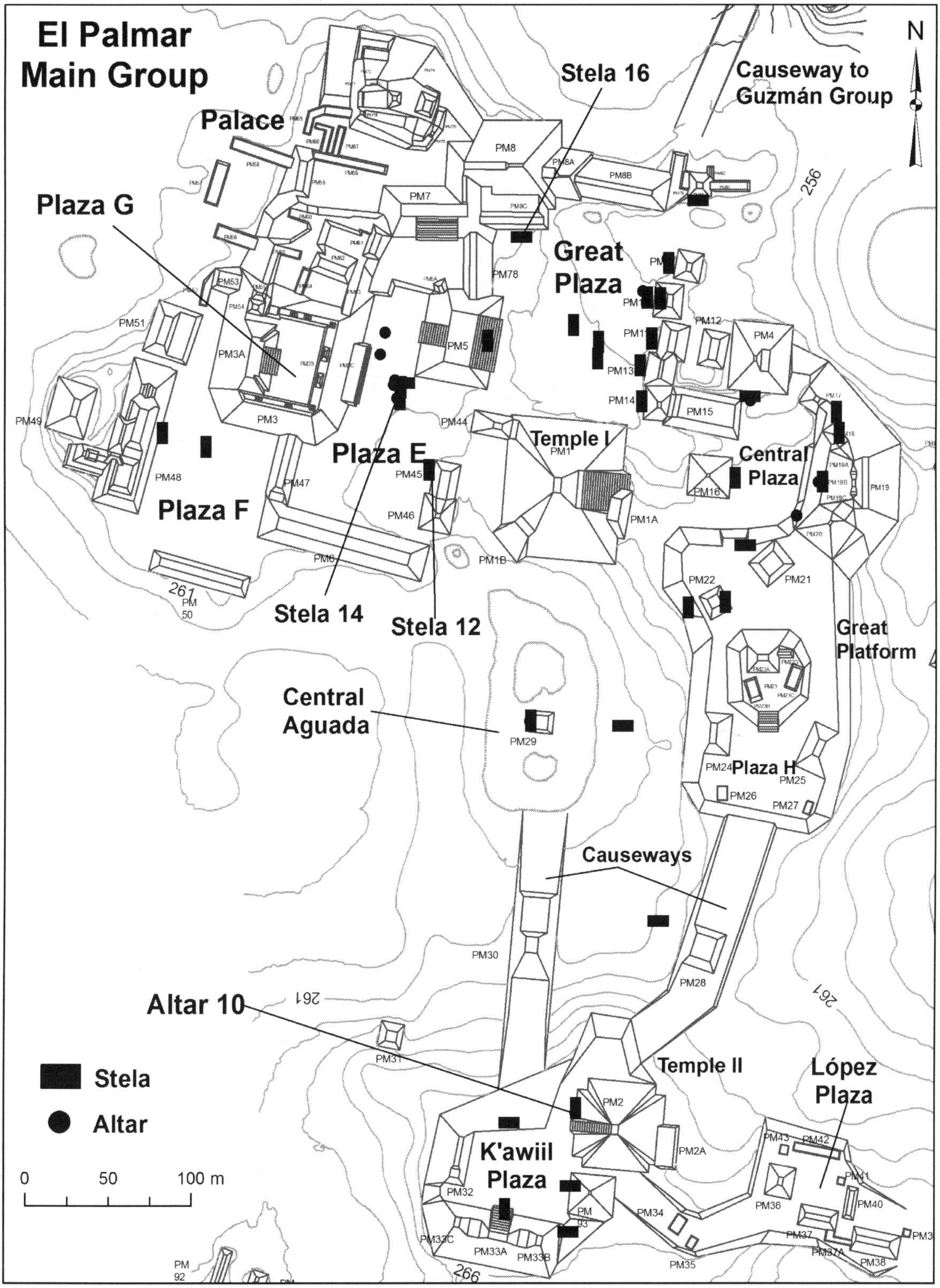

FIGURE 3.2. Map of the Main Group showing the location of eight plazas and carved monuments, created by Kenichiro Tsukamoto and Javier López Camacho.

The Rise of Ceremonial Spaces at the Main Group of El Palmar

During the Late Preclassic period, the Main Group was formed by only two of the eight plazas as ceremonial spaces: the Central Plaza and Plaza H (figure 3.2). The Central Plaza of 6,674 m^2 is located to the northeast of the Central Aguada. The Central Plaza possesses three entrances located at the northeast, northwest, and southwest corners, indicating that this was a public space. Particularly, the southwest corner was likely the main entrance because of its greater width. In addition to these entrances, the south end of the Central Plaza has a narrow staircase that ascends to the Great Platform. Temple I delimits the west side of the plaza, while the east side is defined by Architectural Complex PM19, consisting of six temples on a large platform. The excavation exposed a platform built with large rocks below the Central Plaza and one radiocarbon sample recovered from its fill dates to 361–93 cal BC, according well with Chicanel ceramic remains.

In contrast to the public space of the Central Plaza, a small square called Plaza H (2,455 m^2) might have been built as a private space, judging from the relatively confined access to the elevated Great Platform. Two radiocarbon samples recovered from the construction fill of the second earliest floor of Plaza H date to 206–41 cal BC, suggesting that the first floor of this plaza was paved at nearly the same time as the first construction of the Central Plaza. The main access to Plaza H is located at its south end where an internal causeway connects it to the south area of the Main Group. As I mentioned above, another access to Plaza H is at the north end of the Great Platform. Because these two entrances are narrow, I suggest that ceremonial organizers could control the flow of people entering Plaza H.

However, Plaza H may not have been designed as an exclusive space. The elevation of the Great Platform, about 5 m high without surrounding walls was unlikely to conceal ceremonial events from the areas surrounding the Great Platform. Furthermore, a stratigraphic excavation shows that the surface level of Plaza H during this period was 1.6 m lower than the latest floor level (Tsukamoto et al. 2012; Tsukamoto and López Camacho 2010:36–43). Thus, during the Late Preclassic period El Palmar's builders subtly set the visibility distinction between the Central Plaza and Plaza H.

The excavations of other plazas revealed unpaved areas, which originally exposed vertisol soils during the Late Preclassic to Early Classic (300 BC–AD 400). During rainy seasons such soils became muddy and unstable and, without a plaster floor, the areas would have been inadequate for conducting ceremonial events. Therefore, I suggest that the areas now occupying the Great Plaza and Plazas E and F were not ceremonial spaces before the Middle Classic period (AD 400–600).

During the Late Preclassic period (300 BC–AD 300) the size of public plazas presumably remained small. Analyzing the size of open plazas may not provide a straightforward answer about shared identities and power relations because these spaces probably were used in multiple ways and changed through time (Inomata 2006a; Moore 1996b). Yet calculating the size of the plazas provides a quantitative measure of capacity, which together with the location, visibility, and access of each plaza can elicit the magnitude of ceremonial spectacles in relation to participant members (Moore 1996b). Moore (1996b:151–153) estimated the capacity of open spaces for ceremonial participants in Andean archaeological sites. With some modifications in the percentage of space allotted per person, Inomata (2006a:811–812) estimated the capacity of plazas in lowland Maya societies. Since El Palmar is located in the central Maya lowlands, I use Inomata's formula, which allows me to compare my results to those of other Maya centers. Table 3.1 shows the estimated number of people that can be accommodated in plazas at El Palmar. Taking into consideration the possible variation of the area occupied by one person (0.46 to 3.6 m^2/person), the number of people that could have been accommodated in the Central Plaza ranges from 1,854 to 14,509 persons while Plaza H has a capacity of from 682 to 5,337 persons. The highest range of participant density could have occurred when important ceremonial spectacles were conducted.

The ratio between the open and private plazas sheds light on the proportion of selected participants. Through analyzing colonial documents, Restall

TABLE 3.1. Size and Estimated Capacities of Plazas at El Palmar

	Size	Estimated Capacity		
Plaza (Main Group)	**Area (m^2)**	**0.46 m^2/person**	**1 m^2/person**	**3.6 m^2/person**
Great Plaza	14,135	30,728	14,135	3,926
Central Plaza	6,674	14,509	6,674	1,854
K'awiil Plaza	3,161	6,872	3,161	878
Plaza E	9,096	19,774	9,096	2,527
Plaza F	6,134	13,335	6,134	1,704
Plaza G	1,050	2,283	1,050	292
Plaza H	2,455	5,337	2,455	682
López Plaza	890	1,935	890	247
Plaza A of the Guzmán Group	968	2,104	968	269

	Size	Total Estimated Capacity of Plazas per Period		
Period	**Area (m^2)**	**0.46 m^2/person**	**1 m^2/person**	**3.6 m^2/person**
Late Preclassic (ca. 300 BC–AD 250)	9,129	19,846	9,129	2,536
Early Classic (ca. AD 250–400)	9,129	19,846	9,129	2,536
Middle Classic (ca. AD 400–600)	36,571	79,502	36,571	10,159
Late Classic (ca. AD 600–800)	43,595	94,772	43,595	12,110
Terminal Classic (ca. AD 800–1000)	43,595	94,772	43,595	12,110

TABLE 3.2. Preliminary Results Showing Volumetric Estimates of Plazas at the Main Group over Time

Period	Volume of construction fill (m^3)
Late Preclassic (ca. 300 BC–AD 250)	6,777.65
Early Classic (ca. AD 250–400)	2,316.80
Middle Classic (ca. AD 400–600)	22,015.98
Late Classic (ca. AD 600–800)	16,133.50
Terminal Classic (ca. AD 800–1000)	2,685.05

(2001:353–358) argues that a dynastic elite comprised about 5 percent of the population. The maximum estimated capacity of Plaza H (5,337 persons) is 36.8 percent of the Central Plaza's maximum estimated capacity (14,509 persons). This result may indicate that the audience of Plaza H was not exclusively ruling elites.

Table 3.2 represents preliminary volumetric estimates for constructing plazas over time, based on the volume of construction fill between successive floors as derived from excavations. The calculation consists of the sum of the areas of the Central Plaza and Plaza H multiplied by the depth of each plaza's construction fill. Despite limited data and a lack of experimental analysis to estimate how many persons per square meter were required for building plazas, I believe that this preliminary result is suggestive of the amount of labor mobilization required for constructing ceremonial spaces. The results show that El Palmar's builders moved 6,777.65 m^3 of fill to construct these two plazas by the Late Preclassic period, although more excavation data are needed to generate more accurate estimates.

Building a Ritual Landscape at the Main Group of El Palmar

After the repavement of the Central Plaza and Plaza H in the Early Classic period (AD 250–400), the ritual landscape of El Palmar dramatically changed during the Middle Classic period (AD 400–600). The excavation at the Great Plaza revealed a brief occupation with a modest platform during the early phase of this period, and subsequently surrounding areas with vertisol soils were paved with plaster floors on which several commemorative monuments were erected. Table 3.1 shows how the estimated capacity of plazas changed throughout El Palmar's history. During the Late Preclassic and Early Classic periods, the sum of the maximum estimated capacity was 19,846 persons calculated at 0.46m^2 per person. In contrast, during the Middle Classic period this increased to 79,502 persons, about four times more than during the previous periods.

This spatial change may indicate that El Palmar became a regional center, with an increase in population and material flows, and alteration in the political organization, calling for ever larger ceremonial events. Above all, four large plazas had become essential elements in El Palmar's urban landscape by the end of the Middle Classic period: the Great Plaza, Plazas E and G, and K'awiil

Plaza. To the north of Temple I is the Great Plaza, the largest plaza at the site, measuring about 140 m by 100 m (14,135 m^2). This large open space has access from its northeastern corner where a causeway connects it to the northern outlying group, the Guzmán Group. The western and northern perimeter of the Great Plaza is defined by monumental architecture, which consists of several vaulted structures and a platform. Particularly, Structure PM5, a pyramidal temple with wide staircases at the west side of the plaza was presumably a main stage for ritual spectacles. The east side of the plaza is formed by five structures with eleven stelae and two altars, and beyond them farther to the east is a ballcourt. The stratigraphy of test excavations and ceramic analyses suggest that the Great Plaza was constructed during the Middle Classic period (AD 400–600) and used intensively with the erection of stone monuments during the Late Classic period (AD 600–800) (Tsukamoto et al. 2012). In fact, four of eleven stelae erected at the Great Plaza dated to AD 721, 731, 746, and 800, served to exhibit royal authority as well as to materialize the social memory of public rituals. The inscriptions of Stela 16, located at the northwest corner of the plaza, depict a period-ending ritual where a ruler of El Palmar conducted "a scattering incense ceremony" on August 16, AD 800 (9.18.10.0.0.0) (Esparza Olguín and Tsukamoto 2011). During this spectacle the number of people that could have been accommodated at the Great Plaza ranged from 3,926 to 30,728 persons, which is twice the capacity of the Central Plaza.

Other than the Great Plaza, Plaza E likely served for mass spectacles. It is located to the southwest of the Great Plaza and is irregular in shape, measuring about 140 m by 75 m (9,096 m^2). It is surrounded by monumental structures (PM3, PM5, PM6, and PM45–47) and similar to the Great Plaza, Plaza E could accommodate a large audience of nearly 20,000 persons if each person occupied 0.46 m^2 of the plaza. The main access opens to the east side while other areas are closed by monumental architecture. A test excavation suggests that Plaza E was constructed during the Middle Classic period and abandoned around AD 1000. There are four stelae and five altars erected on the plaza during the Late Classic period. A monument is Stela 12, which records a royal dance under the witness of Yuknoom Ch'e'n II, the most powerful ruler of the Kaan dynasty seated in Calakmul during this period (Esparza Olguín and Tsukamoto 2011). Despite the date's erosion, the iconographic style and the presence of Yuknoom Ch'e'n II, who reigned over the Kaan dynasty from AD 636 to 686 (Martin and Grube 2008), suggest that the stela was erected between AD 636 and 692 (see also Proskouriakoff 1950). Similar to Stela 16 on the Great Plaza, Stela 14 at Plaza E commemorates the half period ending with a scattering incense ceremony on May 3, AD 820 (9.19.10.0.0) (Esparza Olguín and Tsukamoto 2011). Moreover, the location of the stelae suggests that these royal rituals took place at Plaza E where a platform stage leads to the entrance of the immense structure PM3, whose upper part encompasses a flat space called Plaza G.

In contrast to the Great Plaza and Plaza E, visibility of and access to Plaza G would have been rigorously controlled by vaulted rectangular structures and Plaza G's elevation from the ground. Plaza G defines the west side of Plaza E and is elevated 10 m from the ground level of Plaza E. The inside area of Plaza G measures 20 m by 45 m (1050 m^2). The high elevation of the base along with the rectangular structures embracing the plaza make invisible any activities in Plaza G from the surrounding areas. When compared with Plaza H which was built during the Late Preclassic period, the access to and visibility of Plaza G of this period is much more restricted. The construction of this highly private space was contemporaneous with the construction of the largest public space at El Palmar, the Great Plaza. Two of three radiocarbon samples derived from the construction fill of the earliest floor of Plaza G date to 392–551 cal AD.

Besides the restricted access to and invisibility of Plaza G, the ratio of the maximum estimated capacity of Plaza G to that of the Great Plaza sheds light on social distinctions that emerged at the El Palmar dynasty during this period. The quantitative capacity analysis of Plaza G results in a much lower capacity range of 292 to 2,283 persons when compared to the Great Plaza. This maximum estimated capacity of Plaza G (2,283) is 7.4 percent of the estimated capacity of the Great Plaza (30,728 persons), which is close to Restall's data (2001:353–358) that 5 percent of the entire population comprised a dynastic elite in colonial Maya society. Thus, I suggest that the performers and audience for private ceremonies that took place at Plaza G were exclusively ruling elites, insomuch that asymmetrical interactions became more pronounced at El Palmar during this period.

In addition to the north part, a test excavation suggests that the south part of the Main Group was paved with a plaster floor at the end of the Middle Classic period. To the south of the Central Aguada is the K'awiil Plaza, which stands on a natural rise 7 m high, making the plaza broadly visible from the surrounding areas. The main access is by three internal causeways or sacbeob connecting to the Central Aguada, Plaza H, and López Plaza. K'awiil Plaza is a rectangular space embracing 3,161m^2 and Temple II stands at the east side of the plaza. While excavations in the plaza did not yield radiocarbon samples, the construction period of K'awiil Plaza can be dated from the inscription of a round altar (Altar 10) located in front of Temple II. Project epigrapher Esparza Olguín reads Altar 10 inscriptions as a record of the celebration of the sixth k'atun ending (9.6.0.0.0, March 20, AD 554) with deities and a ruler K'ahk' . . . laj Ch'an Yopaat who holds El Palmar's royal title of SAK-o-ka 6-PIIT AJAW [White valley?, the lord of Six litters]. This royal title was continuously used among successive rulers of El Palmar as a royal identity during the Late Classic period. We excavated a test pit in front of Altar 10 and recovered a cache beneath the plaza floor. The absence of intrusion into the cache suggests that the deposition of the cache and the construction of the plaza floor were contemporaneous, which means that the plaza was completed around AD 554, although the irregular surface marked by a large square pit cutting into bedrock suggests that this space was most likely inhabited in an earlier period. K'awiil Plaza was continuously used by maintaining the plaster floor until AD 884, a date carved into one of five stelae erected on the plaza.

The specific function of K'awiil Plaza remains unknown, but its limited capacity and three internal causeways may signal ritual processions, comparable to the use of a pair of causeways that connect to Temple IV at Tikal suggested by Reese-Taylor (2002:157–159) (see also Solari, this volume). The estimated capacity in the range of 878 to 3,161 persons for K'awiil Plaza is not enough to accommodate an entire population for full participation in large spectacles (table 3.1). Rather, with the causeways it was presumably designed for the continuous flow of people, such as in a procession ritual.

Labor mobilization that moved a fill volume totaling 22,015.98 m^3 during the Middle Classic period was about three times greater than that of the Late Preclassic (6,777.65 m^3). Despite the fact that I do not yet have population estimate data, this result shows that different social groups at El Palmar, including neighboring inhabitants, may have become more intensively involved in communal activities, such as large construction projects during the Middle Classic period.

During the Late Classic period (ca. AD 600–800), ritual spaces were further amplified at the Main Group. In addition to the remodeling of previous plazas, Plaza F (6,134 m^2) and López Plaza (890 m^2) were constructed. The new plazas and remodeling of previous plazas resulted in high labor mobilization (16,133.50 m^3). As mentioned above, theatrical performances were carved on stelae and altars at the Great Plaza, Plaza E, and K'awiil Plaza during this period. At this moment, most of the public plazas such as the Great Plaza, Central Plaza, and Plaza E became exhibition galleries for stelae and altars, which manifested the hierarchical nature of the El Palmar dynasty (see also Urcid and Joyce, this volume).

In the peripheral areas, excavation data show that some plazas were paved around AD 600 (Tsukamoto and López Camacho 2011). Two relatively large public plazas were constructed at a western group, which we denominate the Justo Group, while in a northern group known as the Guzmán Group one small plaza was built along with a hieroglyphic stairway. We extensively excavated this small plaza and surrounding structures to assess the negotiation of power relations between the royal elite and intermediate elites through ritual performances conducted on the plaza.

Extensive Excavations of Plaza A at the Guzmán Group

During fieldwork from 2010 to 2012, we conducted extensive excavations at the Guzmán Group, located 1.3 km to the north of the Main Group. The presence of a causeway or sacbe between the Main Group and the Guzmán Group suggests that people in these two groups had intimate political interactions. In the Maya area, ethnographic and ethnohistoric data show that the spatial organization of the core and its outlying groups is frequently associated with ritual circuits (Gossen 1974; Reese-Taylor 2002; Vogt 1976:42–44), and the placement of outlying settlements in cardinal directions reflects the legitimization of royal authority (Ashmore 1991; Ashmore and Sabloff 2002; Estrada-Belli and Tourtellot 2005). During the Colonial period, Bishop Diego de Landa documented that in the Yucatan Peninsula processional rituals were conducted from the outlying settlements at the cardinal directions toward the urban core (Tozzer 1941; Solari, this volume). The diachronic analysis of a plaza at the Guzmán Group helps us to assess whether the plaza formation of the Guzmán Group was intervened by El Palmar's central authority as a dynastic strategy of enhancing a politywide identity, as suggested for Teotihuacan (Murakami, this volume).

While monumental structures form the Main Group , the Guzmán Group consists of a small temple adorned by a hieroglyphic stairway (Structure GZ1) and six other structures (Structures GZ2–GZ7) surrounding a small plaza (Plaza A). The plaza is rectangular, measuring 40 m by 25 m (968 m^2). Structure GZ1 is located on the east side of the plaza and measures 15 m by 14 m at its base and is 3 m high. The stairway is attached to the west façade of GZ1 and leads to a large platform in front of a vaulted shrine.

Despite the presence of the hieroglyphic stairway, Plaza A was unlikely to have been established by El Palmar's central authority. Extensive excavations of three structures—GZ1, GZ5, GZ6—and Plaza A show that the Guzmán Group was founded in ca. AD 600. At the bottom of Structure GZ5-Sub 5, the excavation exposed linearly cut bedrock, which served as a platform. This modest building may indicate that minimal investment in labor was used to create this structure. Likewise, the north half of the plaza was occupied by a square platform (Platform A) built with uncut and roughly cut stones, which limited the already small plaza's ability to accommodate an audience for plaza rituals. Platform A measures 5.8 m by 5.8 m at its base and is 0.4 m high. Before building the hieroglyphic stairway attached to Structure GZ1, a modest stairway of roughly cut stones was first built with narrow steps measuring 23 cm in depth. All these data likely reflect the local foundation of the Guzmán Group rather than the intervention of El Palmar's royal authority.

Through the building of the hieroglyphic stairway in AD 726, the spatial configuration of the Guzmán plaza was transformed. The depth of the steps of the stairway at GZ1 was significantly enlarged to 77 cm with the adding of the hieroglyphic face blocks, suggesting that the stairway was designed not only for the stair function but also as a theatrical stage for ritual performances in front of an audience (figure 3.3). Apparently to better display the theatrical performances at GZ1 and to increase the plaza capacity, Platform A was buried contemporaneously to the building of the hieroglyphic stairway. Did the central authority transform this place as a political arena?

No epigraphic and archaeological data reflect the legitimization of the royal authority. Instead, the inscriptions record the identity claim and power negotiation of intermediate elites who would have occupied the Guzmán Group. Our epigraphic studies suggest that the main protagonist of the inscriptions is Ajpach' Waal who does not possess the El Palmar royal title, but is a descendant from second-tier elites called *lakam*. We will publish detailed epigraphic studies of the stairway soon (Tsukamoto and Esparza Olgúin 2014), and in the following I will describe its important parts associated with my arguments. The glyphic narrative begins with a journey to Copán on June 24, AD 726 (9.14.14.13.19), recording: T'AB[-yi] 3-wi-ti-ki CHAN-na CH'E'N ti-BAT-ku-pi? a-AJAW ti-18-u-BAAH-K'AWIL [An individual (most likely, Ajpach' Waal) went up to Copán (to see the thirteenth ruler of the Copán dynasty), Waxaklajuun Ubaah K'awiil]. Subsequently, Ajpach' Waal emphasizes his genealogical ties, listing the name of lakam ancestors beginning with his father and the serving rulers of El Palmar. The texts at R1-W1 of Step II and B1 of Step III record: yu-ne AJ-lu-#-chi-hi AJ-ti-xa-ha u-LAKAM u-pa-ka-la # ?? SAK-o-ka [the son of Ajlu . . . Chih, he of Tixah, he is a lakam of Upakal . . . White valley(?)]. In glyphic narratives, Ajpach' Waal repeatedly emphasizes that

FIGURE 3.3. Different depths of the stairways at the Structure GZ1 of Guzmán Group; the left side is the substructure and the right side the hieroglyphic stairway.

the stairway is carved by him on Step IV and it is his carving, BAT-lu-li AJ-pa-ch'a *wa-li, on Step V, representing his claims that the stairway is neither the possession of the El Palmar's ruler nor given by the ruler. After his possessive claim, the glyphic blocks record: *u-CH'AN-nu 18-u-BAH K'AWIL BAT-ku-pi? a-AJAW [he (Ajpach' Waal) is a guardian? of Waxaklajuun Ubaah K'awiil who is the lord of Copán]. Moreover, a Calakmul lord Yuknoom Took' K'awiil appears with the emblem glyph of the Kaan dynasty. Finally, the El Palmar ruler is recorded at the end of Step V, yi-ta-ji yu-ne . . . SAK-o-ka 6-PIIT? AJAW . . . BAT-ku-pi? AJAW [in the company of Yunen . . . , White Valley(?), the lord of Six litters . . . the lord of Copán]. This last statement indicates that El Palmar's ruler is referred to only once and almost at the end of the inscriptions. In addition, it is important to note that the glyphic text ends with the Copán's emblem glyph. Thus, the textual discourse makes an audience aware of an unusual relationship not only between the foreign ruler and Ajpach' Waal as a descendant of lakam elites, but also between El Palmar's ruler and a lakam group.

After the construction of the hieroglyphic stairway, there was a final resurfacing of the plaza's plaster floor. Then, about a hundred years later, ca. AD 850, lakam elites abandoned the Guzmán Group, conducting a termination ritual in and around Structures GZ1 and GZ6. As we recovered it from the earliest floor dating to ca. AD 660 at Structure GZ5-Sub 5, we found another top half of a broken jar on the latest floor of the inside room at GZ6. This continuity of ritual practices over time may indicate that the same lakam elites resided here for over two hundred years. Furthermore, such ritual practices reinforced the ideology of the social members, which, in turn, configured a group identity.

Plazas and Multiple Identities in the El Palmar Polity

The physical characteristics and construction sequences of different plazas at El Palmar open a window into illuminating the multiple identities and power negotiations embraced by Classic Maya society. From the Late Preclassic to Early Classic periods (300 BC–AD 400), the ambiguous spatial distinction between the Central Plaza and Plaza H suggests that group affiliations did not clearly distinguish ruling elites from the rest of the population even though the political symbolism of rulers would have played a crucial role in constituting a community identity. In contrast, during the Middle Classic period (AD 400–600), ritual knowledge exhibited on the plazas would have become a resource for royal elites to create ideological power for defining the relationship between people and deities, elites and nonelites, and among elites. The established power relations were likely reinforced by unequal access to ritual practices conducted in the elevated and restricted space of Plaza G, in which a privileged identity was fostered among ruling elites spatially differentiated from the rest of the population. The spatial restriction creates social distances between the rulling elites and other groups, and such control of social interactions is an important catalyst for the maintenance of dominance (Love 1999).

The project of building large plazas and associated mass spectacles may have served to articulate the affiliation of different social groups with collective identities during a period of political turbulence. Epigraphic studies suggest that the competitive political expansion of agents possibly from Teotihuacan, and subsequently the Tikal and Kaan dynasties provoked the redrawing of political landscapes in the central Maya lowlands during the Middle Classic period (Freidel et al. 2007; Martin and Grube 2008; Stuart 2000). Around AD 400 an enigmatic lord called Sihyaj K'ahk', who wears militaristic attire likely associated with Teotihuacan, arrived to establish a new political order at Tikal and other centers including Bejucal, El Perú-Waka', La Sufricaya, Río Azul, and Uaxactún (Martin and Grube 2008). Among these centers, Río Azul is located 34 km to the south of El Palmar. Under the tallest structure at Río Azul, Adams (1971) found three altars depicting five stripped captives. He suggests that these captives represent Río Azul's former rulers who were conquered and humiliated by Tikal. There is another influential agent known as Spearthrower Owl whose name is directly tied to Teotihuacan. His son is Yax Nuun Ahiin I, the first ruler of the Tikal dynasty after the establishment of the new political order (Martin and Grube 2008:30–31). The degree of Teotihuacan's sociopolitical involvement in the Maya polities is controversial, but archaeological and epigraphic data demonstrate that since Yax Nuun Ahiin I was seated, Tikal became a major player in the Maya lowlands. Likewise, the Kaan dynasty, an adversary of the Tikal kingdom, incorporated several centers into its political sphere. Grube (2008) identifies that Sky Witness, one of the most powerful kings of the Kaan dynasty, oversaw the enthronement of a Los Alacranes's ruler on April 30, AD 561. The archaeological site of Los Alacranes is located just 18 km to the southeast of El Palmar. Thus, two large Maya polities extended their hegemonic campaigns toward the El Palmar region during the Middle Classic period.

Changes in ritual performances in societies often occurred during periods of social and/or ecological disruption (Aldenderfer 1993, 2012; Schachner 2001). As mentioned before, the volume of material to construct plazas significantly increased from the Late Preclassic (6,778 m^3) and Early Classic periods (2,317 m^3) to the Middle Classic period (22,015 m^3). The consequent abrupt increase in plaza area may indicate that much of El Palmar's population was involved in experiencing construction projects and associated mass spectacles. These practices could have provided crucial opportunities for people who lived in dispersed settlements to experience moments of interactions and for rulers to create docile bodies of other social segments through dedicating long-term constructions. Likewise, the different accesses to and different forms of the plazas at the Main Group would have distributed both elite and nonelite bodies in an order, controlling their movements and perceptions as social norms that made them political subjects.

In addition to the ideological power of the rulers, I speculate that social anxieties, which resulted from the hegemonic extension of the Tikal and Kaan dynasties, motivated people to engage in cooperative activities, in turn providing critical opportunities for negotiating and claiming power relations and group identities in the process of creating a politywide identity. As Moore points out in this volume, we have not yet acquired robust data to support this interpretation. Nevertheless, the sacrifices of local elites depicted on the altars at Río Azul (Adams 1971) and the accession of Los Alacranes's ruler overseen by Kaan's ruler (Grube 2008) may signal that the El Palmar polity was not isolated from hegemonic pressures of the Tikal and Kaan dynasties. Simultaneously, mass spectacles at the Great Plaza and Plaza E might have served to release such social anxieties. Through ethnohistorical and ethnographic evidence, Taube (1989) pointed out that ritual humor and clowns played important roles in Classic Maya society during unstable moments of period-endings. There is no direct evidence of ritual humor at El Palmar, but ritual ceremonies recorded in many stelae and altars at the Main Group corresponded to period-endings. These ceremonies might have included humor and clowns, suggesting that spectacles served to release tensions among social groups. Such ritual relaxation of social status in festivals suggests the leading of participants in sharing a ritually figured identity. Thus, the Great Plaza, Plazas E and G, and K'awiil Plaza are the physical index of social interdependencies. Symbolic performances and the panoply of rulers' dress may have helped people visualize El Palmar's identity. Theatrical spectacles at the Great Plaza and Plaza E were witnessed by a large audience that collectively experienced emotional practices as a medium of understanding the community and themselves in the community. The visual impression of the king's costumes and theatrical performances were perpetuated by stelae of the plazas at the Main Group, which shaped and reshaped social memories of belonging to the community, though such dominant versions of memories were reinterpreted, modified, and erased by the same and next generations.

People rarely possess a coherent identity. We always live with multiple identities, some of which are occasionally emphasized, shared, contested, or even contradicted through human interactions (Janusek 2004; Joyce 2010:24). In the case of Ajpach' Waal, he consciously or unconsciously expressed multiple identities in the glyphic discourse of the hieroglyphic stairway and ritual practices conducted at the Guzmán Group. In the glyphic narrative, Ajpach' Waal emphasizes his intimate relationship with a Copán's ruler, Waxaklajuun Ubaah K'awiil. This Copán's ruler appears twice in the inscriptions from the beginning of the text while the name of the current ruler of El Palmar was carved almost at the end of the inscriptions. This text clearly represents that Ajpach' Waal bound his identity to Waxaklajuun Ubaah K'awiil rather than to El Palmar's ruler. By claiming the intimate relationship with the foreign king as well as the placement of the hieroglyphic stairway at his residence, Ajpach' Waal may have differentiated lakam elites from other El Palmar elites. On the other hand, El Palmar's ruler, who should have had governing status over the lakam elites, appears with a relational glyph block S1, yi-ta-ji, [in the company of], without any expression of specific esteem. This phrase could indicate that although El Palmar's ruler was perhaps physically present at the unveiling ceremony of the hieroglyphic stairway, he exerted less authority over second-tier elites at their outlying plaza. Nevertheless, to claim his genealogical ties to lakam ancestors, Ajpach' Waal needed to list the successive rulers of El Palmar, implying that his identity was derived from the El Palmar dynasty that was established and inherited by rulers. His identity as a lakam elite in part was derived from his ancestors' practices at Plaza A of the Guzmán Group over generations. Finally, as a member of the El Palmar dynasty Ajpach' Waal likely participated in and organized mass spectacles in the Great Plaza and Plaza E of the Main Group, where he must have perceived and reinterpreted the community-wide identity manipulated by rulers through interactions with other community members.

Conclusion

In this chapter, I examined multiple identities generated by the physical characteristics of plazas and ritual activities conducted at the different plazas of El Palmar. While a politywide identity emerged as a result of power negotiations among different social groups in the spacious Great Plaza, Central Plaza, and Plazas E and F, a privileged identity was fostered under the limited space and restricted access of Plaza G. These various plazas with formalized ritual activities at the Main Group could have normalized individual movements and perceptions in a particular order of materiality. Simultaneously, spectacles at the Great Plaza and other public plazas might have served to release social tensions among social groups through repudiation or jesting of current authority (Bakhtin 1984; Turner 1969). We should note that the politywide identity never became uniform, but was perceived and re-created differently by members of the El Palmar dynasty. In the outlying areas, where many of the participants who shared in the mass spectacles conducted at the plazas of the Main Group lived, second-tier elites could establish a plaza where they claimed their local identity. These three identities were not mutually exclusive but coexisted and overlapped in human bodies through social practices. To highlight different roles of plazas, I have stressed the creation of a specific identity in each plaza. However, multiple identities are always interwoven and three identities shown could easily emerge in any kind of these plazas.

The relative dimensions and volume data over time for the plazas of the Main Group at El Palmar are preliminary and more excavations are needed. Furthermore, I did not scrutinize the role of ritual processions utilizing causeways in this chapter, but they are arguably critical elements in understanding the formation of identities. I believe that future archaeological research could reveal further complex identities among the inhabitants of El Palmar who negotiated power and ideological relations on the plazas.

Acknowledgments

I would like to thank Takeshi Inomata and two anonymous reviewers for their thoughtful comments on my earlier manuscript. I also thank Stephen Houston, Simon Martin, David Stuart, Guillermo Bernal Romero, Dmitri Beliaev, Erik Velásquez García, and Marc Zender for their invaluable comments and suggestions on our epigraphic studies. I am indebted to Javier López Camacho, the codirector of the El Palmar Archaeological Project, for his untiring support and patience. The data presented here are results of team efforts, particularly by Luz Evelia Campaña, Hirokazu Kotegawa, Octavio Esparza Olguín, and Yareli Jáidar Benavides. I am deeply grateful for their dedication and efforts on making it possible to conduct archaeological research at El Palmar. The El Palmar Archaeological Project has been supported by the National Science Foundation (BCS-111640), National Geographic Society (W93–10), American Philosophical Society, the University of Arizona, Escuela Nacional de Antropología e Historia (ENAH), and the Centro INAH Campeche. I thank Dumbarton Oaks for its generous fellowship which enabled me to finish this chapter. Permission to excavate was generously granted by the Consejo de Arqueología of the Instituto Nacional de Antropología e Historia (INAH), Mexico.

PART II

Plazas in Broader Spatial Contexts

CHAPTER FOUR

Early Olmec Open Spaces at San Lorenzo, Veracruz

ANN CYPHERS AND TIMOTHY MURTHA

Plazas are important elements of the prehispanic built environment in Mesoamerica. The human interaction that takes place in plazas varies from informal public gatherings to specialized activities carried out in carefully designed spaces (Low 2000). They are considered "*recognizable* elements in the built environment" (Moore 1996a:789, emphasis added). Understanding the myriad of interpersonal relations that may be played out within plazas is contingent upon the accurate identification of these spaces, their shapes, built form, and compositional elements. In many archaeological sites, their recognition is a straightforward process because they are observable components of the architectural layout.

The purpose of this exploratory essay is to investigate whether plazas can be identified for the Olmec capital of San Lorenzo using a creative approach for identifying buried open spaces. Identifying plazas at the Early Preclassic capital provides unusual challenges since these features cannot be identified using visible architectural cues, as is the case of the later capital of La Venta, Tabasco, often considered a model for the Olmec. At La Venta, a central zone of monumental architecture surrounds a great plaza covering 42,000 m^2, which is described as a public space where messages about the gods, the power of the rulers, and divine legitimacy were communicated to large congregations of people attending special events and ceremonies (González Lauck 1996).

Those familiar with San Lorenzo may point to the standing architecture (figure 4.1, inset), which, at quick inspection, appears similar to the design of La Venta. This similarity motivated Matthew Stirling to cut into the center line, across the conical mound and plazas, in a search for spectacular offerings comparable to those he had located at the aforementioned Middle Preclassic capital (1947; see also Coe and Diehl 1980:I:33–37). Decades later, Michael Coe and Richard Diehl (1980) similarly explored this Classic period earthen

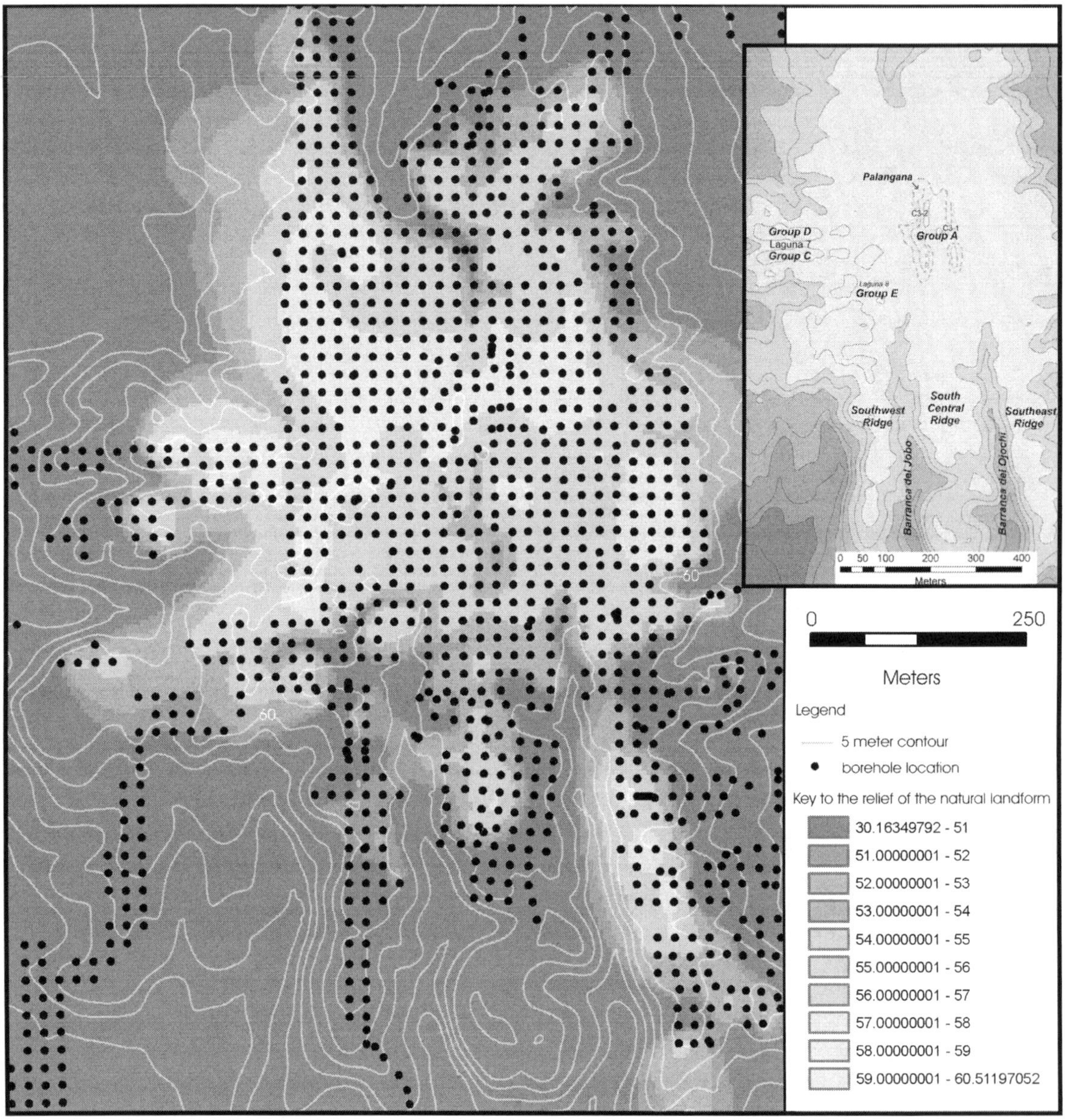

FIGURE 4.1. Topographic map of the San Lorenzo plateau superimposed on the preliminary relief map of the underlying natural landform with an inset map showing features mentioned in the text.

architecture in another equally unrewarding search for the early Olmec architectural template expected to precede the layout of the great Tabascan site (I:50–70).

This search continues to the present day. We attempt to assess a basic fact: whether open spaces for collective activities were present during the Early Preclassic period in the San Lorenzo plateau. The "invisibility" of these features as buried elements necessitates an evaluation of the archaeological evidence obtained in excavations and borehole samples. Consequently, in this chapter, we peel away the layers of overburden and successive occupations of the plateau summit of the early capital, as an essential step to ascertain if centrally located Olmec open spaces once existed in the heart of San Lorenzo.

The Changing Shape of San Lorenzo

San Lorenzo's great plateau has been shaped by human action and agency over the past four millennia. The form and shape of the present plateau, while influenced by the past, do not reflect the Olmec-period configuration of the site. In order to interpret this period, it is first necessary to identify and strip back the layers of post-Olmec modifications. The identification of these alterations is essential to understanding the Olmec layout of the site from its earliest occupation in the Ojochi phase, 1800–1600 cal BC, to the apogee San Lorenzo B phase, 1200–1000 cal BC. What follows is a brief description of the changes that have occurred on the plateau beginning with the most recent and working back to the Olmec period.

The most recent events that have caused alterations likely date to times prior to the Mexican Revolution, when oil exploration began in southern Veracruz, spearheaded by the famous English oilman Weetman Pearson. Once part of the communal lands of Potrero Nuevo (also called "San Lorenzo"), the archaeological site of San Lorenzo then was acquired by the Compañía Mexicana de Bienes Inmuebles (CMBI), as shown on a map dated to 1917 from the Archivo de la Nación. It is during the period of CMBI ownership that it is likely that the company rented the land to third parties, a custom we have seen in rental contracts in the historical archives of Petróleos Mexicanos PEMEX. Since the site has no evidence of modern constructions, the third parties using the San Lorenzo site likely were ranchers who constructed numerous ponds as seasonal water sources for their livestock. One such pond (laguna 8) was dug into Group E to take advantage of a sunken spot, now known to be the patio of an ancient Olmec architectural precinct (Cyphers et al. 2006). Not only did they create ponds but they also dug drainages to siphon off excess water due to pond overflow, such as the one draining laguna 8 to the northwest. Laguna 7, separating Groups C and D, may be another such drainage feature. Fill removed during these earth-moving operations was deposited next to the ponds and drains so that ponds are ringed by piles of earth and the drains are lined by what look like linear mounds. Stratigraphic and artifactual evidence from excavations by the San Lorenzo Tenochtitlán Archaeological Project (PASLT) uphold the late date for these rings and piles of earth, the latter sometimes interpreted as Olmec habitation mounds by Coe and Diehl (1980).

The Terminal Classic period, the Villa Alta phase, contributed to perhaps the most misunderstood and misinterpreted constructions at the site. Terminal Classic residents erected standard monumental architecture in the center of what was once the great Olmec artificial plateau. They built two plazas in Group A, each delimited on the east and west by elongated earthen mounds and separated by a central conical mound (figure 4.1, inset). The formal similarity of San Lorenzo's Group A architecture with La Venta's Complex A, further highlighted by the alphabetical designations, stimulated fruitless quests for comparable center-line offerings in the plazas (Coe and Diehl 1980:I:50–70; Stirling 1947).

Testing in the mounds and plazas by the Río Chiquito Project was the basis for Coe and Diehl's (1980:I:29) suggestion that certain components of Group A, specifically the Central Court and Palangana, dated to the Middle Preclassic despite the presence of Villa Alta material in mound fill.[1] Following from the assumption that pre–La Venta mound and plaza groups at San Lorenzo should bear a formal similarity to those at the Middle Preclassic Olmec capital (1980:I:24), they tendered the proposition that the site's early layout was similar to the architectural arrangement visible today.

Importantly, these researchers provide evidence that Villa Alta phase construction activities predominated in Group A. First, they certify that ceramics from Early and Middle Preclassic phases were found in the mound fill, thus indicating the removal of fill from preexisting strata for these constructions. Second, a clear stratigraphic unconformity documented in their report is represented by the direct superposition of Villa Alta strata upon San Lorenzo B phase strata (see Coe and Diehl 1980:I:55) with the absence of temporally intermediate Nacaste and Palangana phase deposits.

Recently, we completed a program of manual coring of the site of San Lorenzo conducted at 20 m intervals. These data, while complex and resulting in over 2600 soil cores, also referred to as boreholes,[2] can provide an interpretive window into the built environment of the past constructions at San Lorenzo (Cyphers et a1. 2007–2008; Cyphers et al. n.d.). The stratigraphic sequence obtained in 279 soil cores from the plateau confirms the aforesaid stratigraphic unconformity, indicating that, in the process of constructing the small ceremonial layout, Villa Alta people razed part of the plateau heights in order to obtain clay fill for these buildings. This process eliminated evidence of the final moments of the apogee occupation in the plateau center, but left intact the deeper floors dating to the early part of the San Lorenzo B phase, 1200–1100 cal BC.

Even during the Early Preclassic period the site underwent transformation as a result of the massive modifications of the terrain involved in the continual shaping of the plateau. Coe and Diehl (1980) accurately assessed that the plateau was an artificial construction and, in addition, proposed that it was an unfinished cosmogram, an effigy of a giant headless bird flying eastward. Their proposition that Group A was an early Olmec ceremonial center set atop an artificial effigy plateau is best summarized in their own words: "Group A . . . can be thought of as borne on the back of a great bird flying east" (I:388).

Recent evidence suggests that the hypothesized bird cosmogram is unlikely. The results of the systematic coring program indicate that the underlying natural landform was irregularly shaped until the Olmec modified it over the centuries by adding clay fill to produce a relatively flat plateau ringed by stacked residential terraces. Planes of weakness occur where the earthen terraces abut the natural landform. Along these planes, the great ravines formed due to the related natural processes of erosion and uplift of the deep underlying salt structure, an effect exacerbated in some places by the presence of weighty stone monuments.

The coring program combined with what we know about recent history clearly demonstrates that the present-day topography of the plateau heights is the consequence of multiple factors unrelated to Olmec use. These observations, including information from the stratigraphic deposition also indicate that the proposed "bilateral symmetry" of the plateau and the related identification of the wings and tail feathers of the alleged bird cosmogram (Coe and Diehl 1980:I:27–28, II:387) are, in fact, mostly the result of erosion and post-Olmec activities. Group A is built on top of Olmec strata but the buildings themselves date to the Villa Alta phase. The fact that the Classic period people placed their small ceremonial center in the geographic center of the plateau, which coincides with the center and highest portion of the underlying natural landform, simply could be the result of accurate calculations even as it might be possible that, upon their arrival at the site, they may have observed a noteworthy Olmec landmark at this location.

Open Spaces at San Lorenzo

The coring program provides an opportunity to reconstruct the general shape of the natural landform and investigate, through the samples, the continuous design and construction changes that occurred at the site. While the 20 m sample doesn't necessarily provide architectural details, it is perfectly adequate to define use areas through time. It also allows us to reconstruct in a preliminary fashion the early leveling operations, the construction and continual modification of the stacked terraces, and the final massive clay cap applied to the plateau during the site's apogee (Cyphers et al. 2007–2008). These data also are the basis for evaluating the presence of early Olmec open spaces through time. We can trace open spaces by the process of elimination, in other words, by plotting the distribution of floors that are typical of building interiors. Figure 4.1 shows the location of the borehole sample in relation to the present-day topography and to that of our reconstruction of the underlying natural landform.

The study universe consists of the top of the San Lorenzo plateau, specifically the relatively flat 43-hectare area above the 60 m contour interval, which is the area with the highest concentration of stone monuments and prestigious constructions. Within this area, we define the "core" as that space centered on the Group A architecture, which is found at the geographic hub of the plateau and is coincident with the highest part of the underlying natural landform.

We selected the following three periods for the present study: (1) ca. 1600 cal BC, the date corresponding to the end of the Ojochi phase and beginning of the Bajío phase; (2) ca. 1400 cal BC, which falls at the transition from Chicharras to the San Lorenzo A phase; and (3) ca. 1200–1100 cal BC, corresponding to the early San Lorenzo B phase, which appears to be unaffected by Villa Alta phase razing. These general time frames provide initial parameters for tracing changes in open spaces on the San Lorenzo plateau heights.

Based on the ongoing comprehensive study of excavation and the stratigraphy of 279 cores from the plateau heights, we offer a preliminary assessment of diachronic floor distributions enabling us to define open spaces. Previous work at the site indicates that the surfaces of external spaces are compacted earth and lack the formal preparation of structure interiors. Unfortunately, tamped surfaces are virtually impossible to define in borehole samples, meaning that the recognition of open spaces in the data set is contingent on the absence of well-defined structure floors. Therefore, we examine the diachronic distribution of all structure floors, defined as those composed of sand and gravel, compacted colored clays, as well as red (hematite stained) sand and floors paved with bentonite stone. Red and bentonite floors may be considered "prestigious" because their peak frequency is found in structure interiors on the plateau rather than the periphery, and their creation with uncommon materials required a higher labor investment in procurement than the floors made of sand, gravel, and packed colored clays.

It is important to note that the boreholes that are plotted in figures 4.2, 4.3, and 4.4 merely mark the location of structure floors, and each floor is not necessarily indicative of a separate construction. Their simple distribution does not reflect structure density, above all, during the apogee period, when the length of domestic structures are known to surpass the 20 m borehole spacing interval, at times covering 800 m^2 or more. Clusters of boreholes with floors, on the other hand, may reflect multiple structures pertaining to residential groups and other kinds of architecture.

The 1600 cal BC floors are found in fifty-two boreholes in the 43-hectare space above the 60 m contour interval (figure 4.2). The highest frequency of floors is concentrated in the southern and eastern sectors of the plateau heights. Of these, twenty-six boreholes contain prestige flooring consisting of red or bentonite surfaces, the majority positioned near the plateau center. Six red floors are present in the southern and eastern sectors of the plateau heights. The trail of floors extending along the Southeast Ridge may mark one of the time-honored natural accesses to the site center insofar as it is superimposed on a prolonged crest of the geologic landform.

The absence of floors on the Southwest Ridge and in the southern part of the South-Central Ridge is due to the fact that this area was not completely built at this time. These two peninsulas of terrain, called "ridges" by Coe and Diehl (1980), once were stacked terraces abutting the natural landform that were leveled to their maximum height during the San Lorenzo B phase. Their present-day form is largely the outcome of the great ravines cutting through the original Olmec built landscape.

There is a considerable amount of open space on the plateau heights at this time since structure density is low. The key area is the centrally focused open space, which is amorphous in shape and measures more or less 275 by 250 m (roughly 68,750 m^2), and may have been used for community activities. It contains two boreholes with floors that are separated from each other by 85 m but lacks clear boundaries defined by the remaining floors. Its core

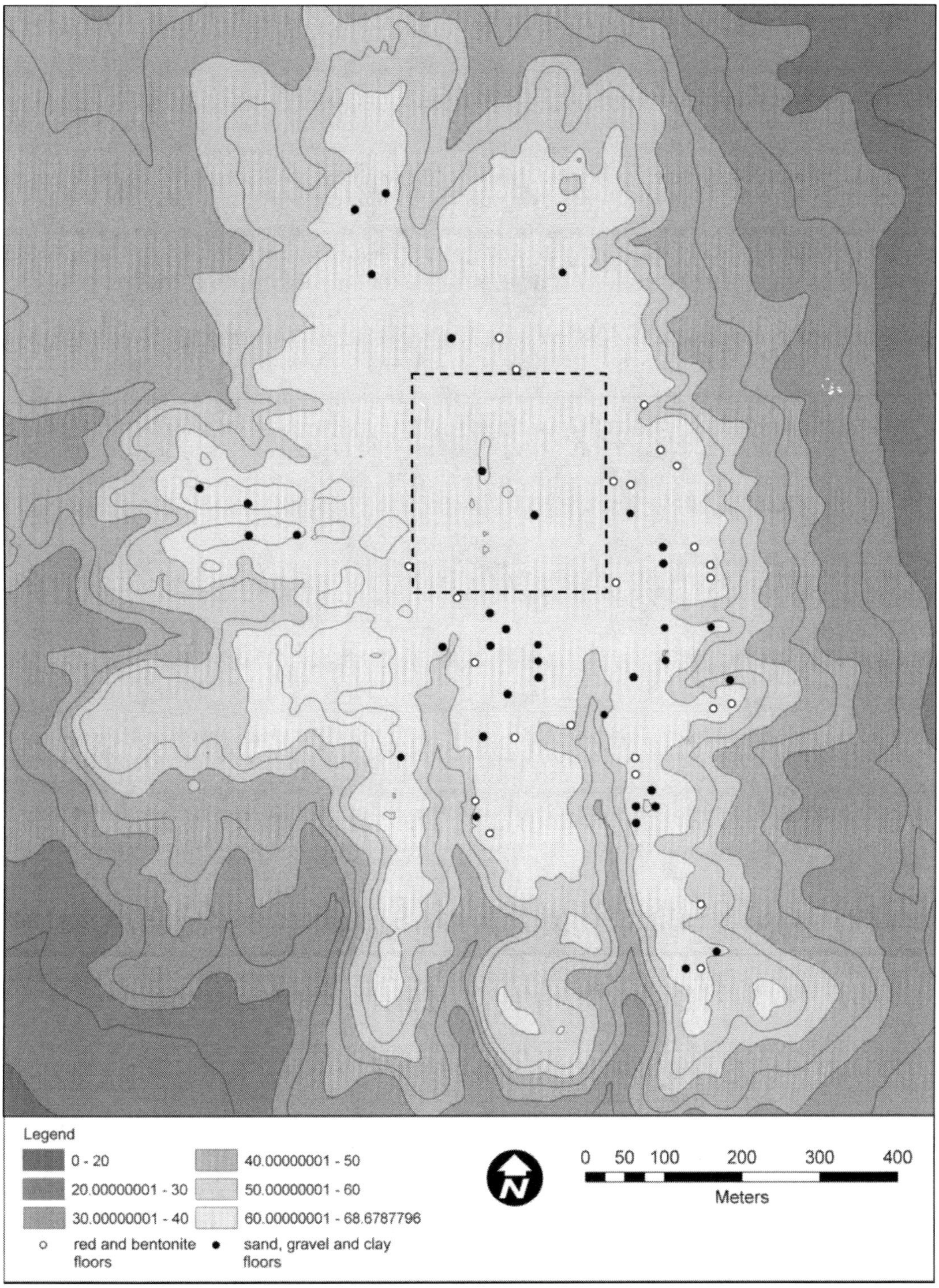

FIGURE 4.2. Map showing the distribution of boreholes containing floors dating to 1600 cal BC. The dotted line marks the open area.

position is coincident with the highest section of the underlying natural landform. The floor found below mound C3–2 of Group A may mark the site center at this time.

Following the initial colonization of the site ca. 1800 cal BC, construction on the plateau was focused on filling in low areas in the irregularly shaped natural landform to create unbroken horizontal space for domestic and ceremonial activities. During this period, settlement was dispersed, and the lack of construction in the central area of the plateau suggests that it was used as open space for collective activities. Due to its great size, this space could easily accommodate the whole population of the site and that of the near hinterland. The prestigious red and bentonite floors are positioned so their occupants could have ready access to this area.

At 1400 cal BC, floors are registered in seventy-four boreholes. Their distribution illustrates a more tightly clustered set of constructions and a filling in of earlier open spaces in the central, northern, and western sectors of the plateau heights (figure 4.3). Of these boreholes, thirty-nine with red and bentonite floors are centrally located. Red floors continue to be present in the eastern and southern sectors, and there is intensified occupation of the western sector, later to become the locus of ostentatious residences in Groups C and D. The previously existing amorphous open space now measures only 200 by 90 m (18,000 m^2), 25 percent of its previous size. It lacks internal floors but is quite clearly surrounded by red and bentonite ones. The simultaneous occurrence of size reduction and circumscription by high status floors suggests possible elite appropriation of this key space, which would have been an essential element underwriting their sponsorship of public events.

A total of 212 boreholes show floors for the 1200–1100 cal BC time frame (figure 4.4). Of these, 138, or 65 percent, have red or bentonite floors. Most red floors occur in the western sector, and, notably, there is a red floor under the long west mound, C3–2, of Group A. During this period, there clearly was a greater variety of open spaces, some very clearly defined as traditional plazas, whose diversity probably reflects broader societal patterns. A central but sparsely occupied zone measures 250 by 250 m (62,500 m^2). For the first time, the central open space may merit the term "plaza" based on the criterion of well-defined boundaries. Nested within this zone, there is a smaller empty space measuring 200 by 50 m (10,000 m^2) that is found directly below Group A; again, its boundaries are fairly clear as it is delimited by thirteen floors, ten on the west and three on the east, all under Group A architecture. Of these floors, the only red one is located under the Palangana. Although the eastern sector shows a lighter density of floors than the rest of the plateau heights, there is a nearly continuous pattern of floors around the perimeter of the large plaza. Overall, the circumscription of the nested plazas by high status floors may indicate reduced access to this district. In similar fashion, it may be observed that the habitation on the stacked terraces surrounding the heights also may have served to regulate access to the center.

In addition, another floorless space measuring 100 by 100 m is found on the midsection of the South-Central Ridge and sits at an elevation at least 1 m below the core. As we will discuss below, this space may be the best candidate for a civic-ceremonial plaza due to its capacity to accommodate many

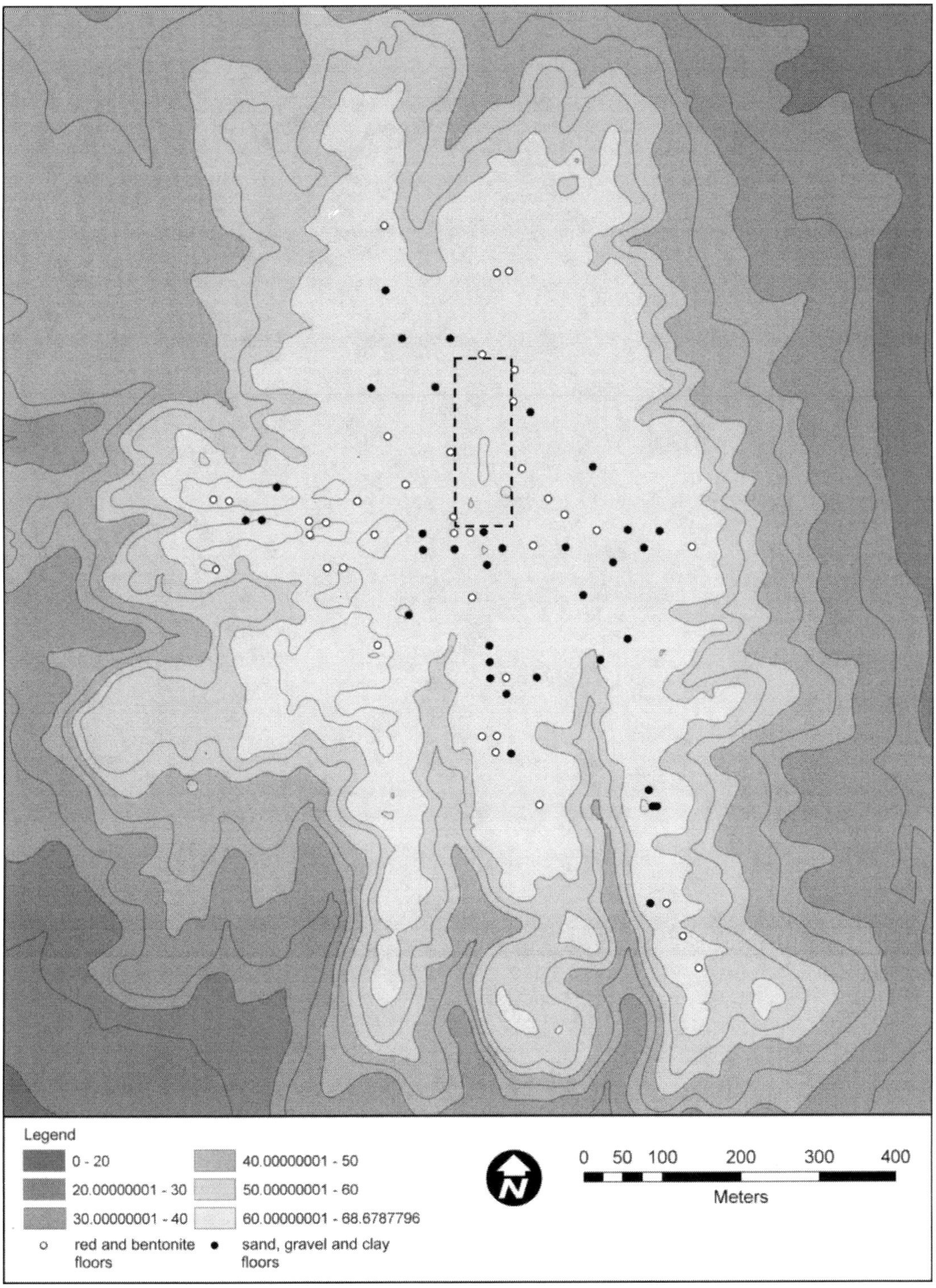

FIGURE 4.3. Map showing the distribution of boreholes containing floors dating to 1400 cal BC. The dotted line marks the open area.

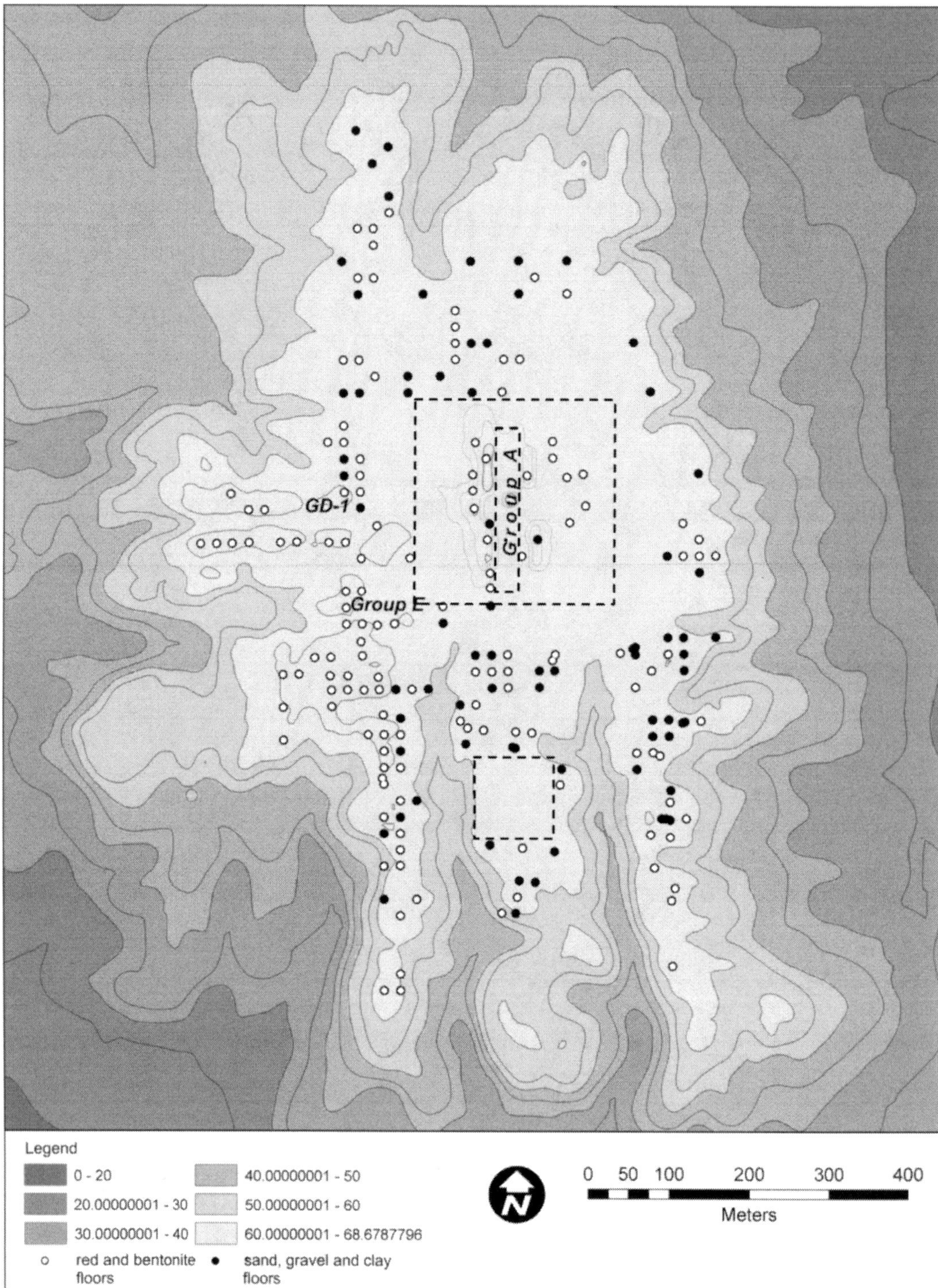

FIGURE 4.4. Map showing the location of boreholes containing floors dating to the 1200–1100 cal BC period. The dotted lines mark the open areas.

individuals, its outline defined by a stone monument display centered on the theme of rulers, and its accessibility and relative visibility from the south.

The data presented above indicate several possible temporal tendencies in the diachronic organization and reorganization of open space in the central plateau (see figure 4.5). The first trend is formal in nature, starting with a large central open space without defined architectural boundaries. It is followed by a clearer delimitation of boundaries by 1200–1100 cal BC and the nesting of a rectangular plaza within it. The second trend is the reestablishment of a large open space, now with an adjacent delimited space. Beginning with an irregularly shaped 68,750 m^2 open area that was present at 1600 cal BC, subsequent encroachment by prestigious structures reduced it to 18,000 m^2 by 1400 cal BC, possibly indicating the elite appropriation of the open space and the addition of some formality to the design and the behaviors carried out there. By 1200–1100 cal BC, it increased in size to 62,500 m^2, a formal area, which includes the smaller nested, and perhaps exclusive, plaza covering 10,000 m^2. At this time, the southern open space on the South-Central Ridge functioned as another, perhaps public, plaza. The low density of floors in specific portions of the terrain, such as in the northeastern sector and along the South-Central Ridge, may signal the points of entry into the heart of the plateau and a focus away from the centralized area for specialized public gatherings.

The shift in the location of high status floors, from the eastern sector of the plateau heights to the western one in the San Lorenzo B phase correlates well with information from excavations. The Group E precinct, built since 1400–1200 cal BC, dominated the southwest sector of the plateau heights, and the ostentatious structure, GD-1, also known as the Red Palace, also built since the 1400–1200 cal BC period, stands out in the western sector where the greatest number of red floors occur.

On the whole, the start of the San Lorenzo B phase is characterized by a period of intensified construction in the plateau, a process that defined the boundaries of a central plaza. Preexisting open space was reshaped and resized as central nested plazas with reduced access for outsiders. The nesting, which restricts access to space, bespeaks ritual exclusivity in the inner plaza. For the first time, a plaza with stone monuments is created just outside the plateau core, perhaps to provide space for civic-ceremonial spectacles while reserving the core, notably lacking in stone monuments, for restricted and specialized pursuits.

Stone Monuments, Structures, and the Central Plaza

In Mesoamerica, large plazas tend to be areas for congregation and interaction and often contain displays of stone monuments carrying cosmological messages. As open spaces forming part of a complex layout of special buildings and monuments, they are necessarily defined in terms of the surrounding architecture and stone monuments, which are related to the kinds of activities conducted in them. In the case of the plazas at San Lorenzo, we lack specific information on the behavior and actions of the people that congregated in these spaces due to the absence of extensive excavations and the nature of the

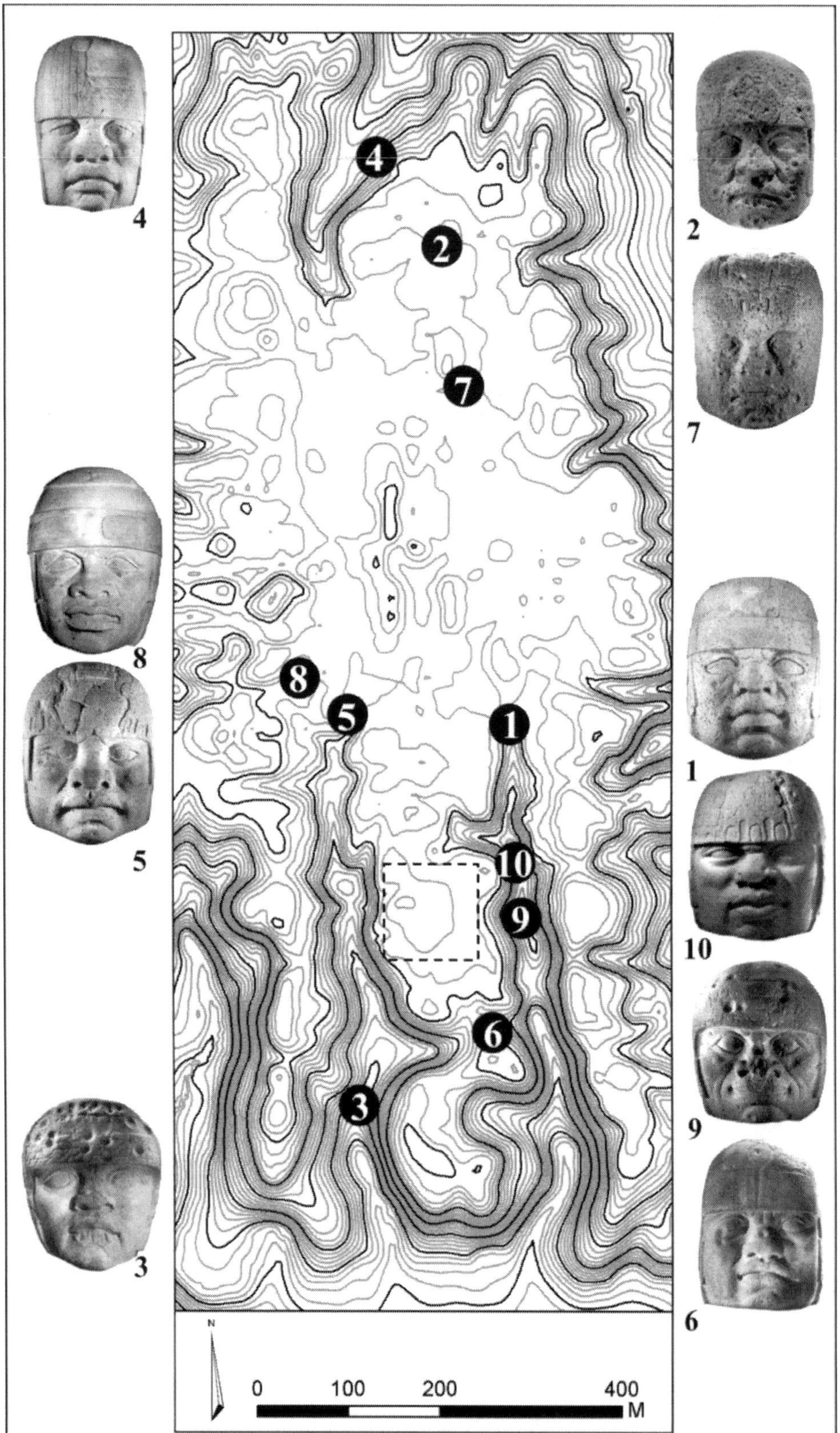

FIGURE 4.5. Location of colossal heads on the San Lorenzo plateau. The dotted line marks the open area on the South Central Ridge.

borehole data. Nevertheless, we can glean some understanding from the distribution of stone monuments and the known structures around them.

With regard to stone monuments, there is a virtual absence of in situ sculptures of all sizes in the core. The sector located east of the core curiously lacks any, while their distribution in the north, south, southwest, and western sectors appears to surround, but not closely border, the nested central plazas on three sides.

However, we should ask if Olmec monuments were moved out of the core by the Villa Alta people since these later occupants actively modified the central plateau surface in preparation for the construction of their architectural group. It is possible, even likely, that relatively small pieces, such as monuments 12, 13, and 54, which were found on the surface of Group A (see Coe and Diehl 1980), were relocated in the Villa Alta phase or later. On the other hand, the large stone monuments are a different case. If large sculpture once had been set in and around an early Olmec central plaza, it is highly improbable that the Classic period inhabitants could have mustered the labor force to move them out of their way since their total population was, at most, 1,000 strong (see Symonds et al. 2002). Consequently, it is to be expected that such monuments should rest in their original locations unless none were erected there or they were moved out by the Olmec themselves. Thus far, the most parsimonious explanation for the absence of voluminous weighty pieces in and around the central plaza is that the Olmec never placed them in this context.

Thus, the spatial distribution of stone sculpture seems to indicate that the central core was not the key space used for the display of large monuments (see also Grove 1997) whose mobilization even over short distances required considerable labor.[3] This leads us to propose that the central plaza was a space largely reserved for the occupants of the plateau heights but also could have been used for public congregation on specific occasions.

At the same time, in situ sculpture of lesser size also is absent in the core, but this is not surprising since relatively portable pieces may be moved and reset with greater ease. It is conceivable that small- and medium-sized sculptures may have been temporarily displayed in the core area since the majority of known sculptures in these size categories are located relatively nearby, at a short distance of about 100 m on the west rise. These monuments are concentrated in and around the monument recycling workshop and storage area pertaining to the palatial structure GD-1. The ritualistic decapitation and mutilation of many of these sculptures clearly occurred prior to their deposition in GD-1. One possibility is that such rituals could have been conducted in the core, and afterward the damaged monuments were channeled to the recycling workshop under the direct control of the palace residents. Even as such expediency may have been exercised, other possibilities also exist, including their use and destruction in other site areas and off-site.

As at La Venta, where numerous monument fragments were found associated with central structures (González Lauck 1996), there is evidence for other recycling spots on the plateau summit. In the northern plateau sector, three colossal heads (monuments 2, 4, and 53) and one large monolithic throne (monument 20) were in the process of recycling, each at a different crafting locus (see Coe and Diehl 1980; Cyphers n.d.; Grove 1997; Porter 1989). Monument

SL-109, the largest, but highly mutilated, stone monument from San Lorenzo, was tumbled into a large pit located about 40 m west of the Palangana. The presence of these large pieces in the central plateau strongly suggests that their recycling was conducted under the aegis of the ruling establishment and may have involved ritual activities.

With regard to structures located around the central nested plaza, there is far more information available about ones on the western rise than those on the eastern rise. One important special function structure is located just 150 m west of the Group A core and 60 m north of GD-1. Monument SL-112 was deliberately deposited in its interior in such a way that most of the monument is hidden under the floor, leaving visible only a small section with hundreds of "cut marks,"possibly sharpening scars made by tools or weapons. The buried or hidden side of the five-ton monument bears the relief image of a possible fallen warrior (Cyphers 2012; Zurita and Cyphers 2008).

Further south, the area known as Group E is found some 80 m southeast of GD-1 and 80 m west of the southern tip of the Group A core. This administrative and ceremonial precinct, containing rulership symbols and lacking evidence of domestic occupation, covers an estimated 10,000 m^2 and is composed of four low earthen platforms oriented to the cardinal directions, which delimit a 2,500 m^2 interior patio (Cyphers et al. 2006). The theme of rulership predominates in the precinct, as illustrated by the interment of a colossal head ruler portrait (monument SL-61) in the eastern platform and the placement of the great monolithic throne (monument SL-14) in the patio at the foot of the northern platform. Entrance to the patio from the south was controlled by at least one narrow access. The size of the patio suggests that extremely large congregations of people did not enter this space, which was likely reserved for the ruler and his attendants. Group E's patio could hold a relatively limited number of people for a given event, so that its exclusive nature and the close interactions held within it were important in shaping elite behaviors. Although the experience of commoners in this space would have been limited, their restricted access was counterbalanced by their knowledge of its existence—and that the structure of the cosmos was replicated, reinforced, and maintained in the sacred precinct on the artificially tiered hill.

Interestingly, another throne, monument SL-60 (Brüggeman and Hers 1970), was found 80 m southeast of Group A, but its overall context and its relationship to a nearby colossal head (monument SL-1) and a massive stone column (SL-55) remains unknown. Consequently, it may be premature to speculate on the possible presence of paired opposites, that is, another precinct located 200 m east of Group E.

In sum, during the apogee period, the plateau core contained a formal plaza delimited by prestigious structures, which was nested within a broader central plaza surrounded on three sides by exclusive buildings with stone monuments. Even though much information still is lacking about intra-site patterning, we know that the central plaza is bounded on the west by the major residence, GD-1, and associated structures in the same residential cluster, as well as the nearby special structure housing monument SL-112. The administrative-ceremonial area of Group E with its restricted-access patio is located on the southwest fringe of the core while the northern plateau heights were reserved for special craft activities consisting of the recycling of large monuments into new forms, such as thrones or colossal heads. The structures on the top of the plateau and terraces would have created an effective impediment to casual intrusion into this space, which was not visible to observers positioned below the heights.

Overall, the apogee phase witnessed a reduction in generalized access to the plateau heights. The construction of terraces for elite dwellings was involved in the spatial segregation of the population into summit, terrace, and periphery dwellers. In this roughly concentric pattern, altitude and distance from the center tend to roughly correlate with social status, such that the hilltop became the locus of the most prestigious residents and activities. If these trends had been related to the creation of public space in the central plateau, then it is expected that carved monuments, which are generally displayed in such contexts, should be found there. Since this is not the case, it may follow that plateau remodeling was intended to reserve the highest portion of the site for the most important people and their activities, which may have included specially sponsored sizeable events. Taken in conjunction with the appearance of the nested and split-level plazas, this likely is a reflection of increasing sociopolitical differentiation within San Lorenzo.

Stone Monuments and the Southern Public Plaza

The 10,000 m^2 plaza located on the midsection of the South-Central Ridge likely was a public space that was framed by imposing stone monuments (table 4.1). The existence of two parallel lines of colossal heads in this sector of the plateau was first noted by Francisco Beverido Pereau (1970), who included all the then-known heads in these rows. His proposal illustrates the problem of using simple monument distributions without taking into consideration their context. Today we know that head #8 (monument SL-61) forms part of Group E and that heads #2, 4, and 7 (monuments SL-2, 4, and 53) were in the process of recycling in the northern plateau sector (see Cyphers 2004a, n.d.; Grove 1997; Porter 1989).

The distribution of the remaining colossal heads is as follows: four heads, aligned north to south along the eastern Barranca del Ojochi; and two heads, one at each end of the western Barranca del Jobo (figure 4.6). The asymmetry in the number of heads on the eastern and western sides of the South-Central Ridge, taken in conjunction with the evidence of others in process, is the basis for proposal that they constituted an unfinished commemorative macro-scene of ancestral ruler portraits (Cyphers 2004a), which is akin to Grove's (1997) concept of a "processional" arrangement designed to be viewed sequentially in public rituals.

The southern plaza rests between the lines of colossal heads and at a slightly lower elevation than the core. The multiple functions of this plaza likely included its role as the principal plaza for public congregation, a place where spectators could observe the grandeur of the stone portraits of powerful ancestral rulers. Additionally, on certain occasions when access to the central plaza was permitted, it may have been a kind of esplanade, an entrance or reception

TABLE 4.1. Summary of the Characteristics of Open Spaces at San Lorenzo through Time

Timeframe	Location	Shape	Size (m^2)
1600 cal BC	central plateau	amorphous	68,750
1400 cal BC	central plateau	amorphous	18,000
1100 cal BC	central plateau	quadrangular	62,500
1100 cal BC	central plateau	rectangular (nested)	10,000
1100 cal BC	southern plateau	quadrangular	10,000

area for spectators en route to the core. Not only did the visual impact of the combined tonnage of these monuments signal a huge concentration of wealth, but also their placement on the plateau heights was a cosmological message relating the rulers to the artificial sacred mountain.

Since the southern tip of the South-Central Ridge was not covered in the systematic coring program due to dense plant cover, we cannot evaluate if there is another plaza there; however, its configuration as another step 2 m below the aforementioned one, as well as its position within the colossal head scenic display, suggests that the possibility should be investigated.

Observations on Exclusion and Inclusion

Throughout the development of the San Lorenzo Olmec, there clearly were social mechanisms of exclusion and inclusion at work. The former acted to increase social distances and the latter for sociopolitical integration. Plazas were key instruments of both forces; for example, Takeshi Inomata (2006a) has shown that Classic period Maya theatrical spectacles held in plazas served to counteract inherent centrifugal tendencies caused by high population dispersion and mobility. On the other hand, the trend discussed by Arthur Joyce (2004) for Monte Albán during the Late Classic period included the elite appropriation of the great Oaxacan capital's Main Plaza, which shifted ritual activity from public spectacles to privileged audiences, perhaps as a result of competition among the nobility.

Below, we consider facets of early Olmec life that contributed to social inclusion and exclusion. The public plaza, the "layers of reciprocal metaphors" and the "traveling theaters" appear to have acted as mechanisms of social inclusion that worked simultaneously with those promoting increased social exclusion, such as the privileged central plazas at San Lorenzo.

Since privileged pre-apogee spaces are known to have existed at San Lorenzo (through excavations), the initial conformation of a public space must have been important for cohesion and unification rather than as a social exclusionary strategy. However, with time, social exclusion became associated with the core. The edification of the largest sacred artificial hill in the Olmec region had profound impacts on intra-site organization.[4] Population was relocated on newly created residential terraces while prior open space on the summit eventually became reserved for elite activities, and a new public plaza bordered by colossal heads was created at a slightly lower level south of the core. The reshaping and relocation of open spaces reduced the frequency of large public events in the heart of the site and displaced them to the southern plaza locus bordered by colossal heads, a trend that propitiated greater internal social distances at the capital. The exclusive central plazas and the lower elevation of the southern public plaza bespeak the use of horizontal and vertical scale to illustrate and accentuate sociopolitical distinctions.

On the whole, metaphors embedded in the constantly changing built landscape gave sensory and spiritual qualities to early Olmec life, and the thorough saturation of quotidian life with all-embracing theatrical meanings suffused with grandiose significance widened perceptual thresholds. The sacred mountain paradigm stands out in this regard insofar as it was solidly imbedded in the Olmec built landscape in the form of material replicas. The interplay of the built landscape with the cosmological concept was essential to reinforcing beliefs, behaviors, and values. The design and symbolism of ostentatious constructions and plazas on the plateau summit participated in the paradigm, whose replication contributed to the reinforcement of identity and social cohesion.

These constitute "layers of reciprocal metaphors," as defined by Stephen Houston (1998:348–349), and may be identified on multiple scales. On the grand scale, the island location of San Lorenzo constitutes a sacred artificial hill surrounded by water that contains monumental evidence supporting the associations of hills, power, legitimacy, founding ancestors, and the monster deity. The scale of this built metaphor made it visible from afar. At the next level, the plateau, the artificial version of the sacred mountain, was constantly remodeled to accommodate a roughly concentric pattern of population distribution in the San Lorenzo plateau and its periphery. As well, ceremonial and residential architecture replicates the cosmological messages in several ways, such as in the placement of the plazas in the center summit and the cosmic symbolism of the Group E architectural precinct and the Red Palace (Structure GD-1).

Also at the regional level, population integration was an important political issue for the early Olmec of San Lorenzo due to the dispersed settlement pattern conditioned by the isolated locations of appropriate terrain for permanent human habitation, in other words, the "islands" of high ground set within the soggy coastal plains (Symonds et a1. 2002). The dynamic way of life in the wetlands posed significant problems for early Olmec sociopolitical integration, which were approached with equally dynamic strategies.

One regional strategy is reflected in the distribution of stone monuments in key hinterland communities (Cyphers and Zurita 2006). These monuments were in a sense "milestones" that symbolized the relationship of lesser sites and the position and identity of the local rulers to the centers. They were intended to encourage regional interdependence and resource flows and, in turn, the development of economic interaction spheres, regional specialization, administration, and disaster relief.

Another strategy was the creation of multicomponent sculptural scenes that involved the setting and resetting of pieces in a variety of contexts with potentially variable meanings (Cyphers 1993, 1994, 1997a, 1999). Because this activity afforded the opportunity for associated public events to be held in different places at different times, it was instrumental in efforts toward the formation and maintenance of certain identities. It ideally would have favored the creation and maintenance of social identities as well as political and religious integration by promoting the lateral unification of a poorly developed distant hinterland in the belief system.In the case of the vast coastal plains inhabited by the San Lorenzo Olmec where centrifugal tendencies prevail, the public spectacles involving scenic sculptural displays perhaps could be likened to traveling theaters that entailed conspicuous displays of prestige and manpower. They would have reinforced regional integration by broadening the spatial occurrence of icons and rituals related to the prevailing ideology. Notwithstanding, this broad information exchange may have had both positive and negative consequences for the constant early Olmec struggle with economic and political integration since the concepts and associated icons of the ideology of power became widely accessible in the landscape.

Final Comments

The analysis of open spaces at San Lorenzo is challenged by the lack of visibility of both architecture and plazas. Borehole stratigraphy obtained in a systematic manual coring program provides a creative data set for identifying areas of construction and open spaces and tracing their physical transformation over time. Observations of their shape, size, and location, along with the consideration of structure and monument distributions, allow insights into the changing central layout of the site in terms of function, status, and accessibility. Even though we cannot yet provide specific information on the quotidian and ritual human behaviors conducted within these spaces, nonetheless, their recognition lays the initial groundwork for further investigation. At San Lorenzo, there appears to be not only an increase in the formal design of open spaces, but also an enhanced complexity in their forms and distributions. This likely reflects the complex interplay between ideas and/or agency and the political theaters in which they were performed.

Acknowledgments

It is a pleasure to recognize the support and generosity of the following institutions that have made possible the research conducted by the San Lorenzo Tenochtitlán Archaeological Project: El Instituto de Investigaciones Antropológicas y La Dirección General de Asuntos del Personal Académico de la Universidad Nacional Autónoma de México; El Consejo de Arqueología del Instituto Nacional de Antropología e Historia; The American Philosophical Society; El Consejo Nacional de Ciencia y Tecnología; The National Endowment for the Humanities; The National Geographic Society; The National Science Foundation; and The Foundation for the Advancement of Mesoamerican Studies, Inc. Fieldwork was authorized by the Consejo de Arqueología del Instituto

Nacional de Antropología e Historia. We also wish to gratefully acknowledge the noteworthy efforts of all the project participants over the years.

Notes

1. Coe and Diehl (1980:I:62) argue that, despite the presence of Villa Alta material in Strata B, B1, and B2 of the Palangana excavations, it dates to the Middle Preclassic Palangana phase. As well, their dating of Stratum F in the Central Court excavations does not jibe with the stratigraphic correlation between these excavations and the C3–1 trench (see 1980:I:52–62). In this latter case, Stratum H of C3–1 clearly coincides with Stratum F in the Central Court in color, consistency, and stratigraphic depth, and both are overlain by a gravel lens or floor (e.g., stratum E in the Central Court and an unnamed lens atop Stratum N in C3–1). Insofar as these authors cite the presence of Villa Alta material in Stratum N of C3–1, it holds that its counterpart, Stratum F in the Central Court, dates to the same phase. Consequently, it appears that both the Palangana and mound C3–1 were built atop a gravel lens and/or floor dating to the Villa Alta phase.

2. The borehole study of San Lorenzo is facilitated by the earthen construction and absence of hard-stone masonry.

3. The study of monument distributions at San Lorenzo is a challenging endeavor, and spatial location cannot always be taken at face value due to the possibility that post-Olmec forces have intervened in their positioning. Small- and medium-sized monuments are more likely affected by later human activities than the large monuments, and monuments of all sizes have fallen into ravines due to the forces of erosion and gravity. At the same time, the bottom line is that the most reliable data regarding monument distributions derives from the contexts of in situ pieces, which have a greater potential for accurate interpretation. However, the locations of large redeposited pieces, such as the colossal heads found in ravines, also may be used as general parameters for interpretation since they are unlikely to have been moved great distances by non-Olmec forces.

4. The plateau contains seven million cubic meters of artificial fill (Cyphers et al. 2007–2008).

CHAPTER FIVE

Empty Space, Active Place

The Sociopolitical Role of Plazas in the Mixteca Alta

MARIJKE STOLL

There is no question that plazas were important for many prehispanic Mesoamerican communities. Serving multiple purposes, plazas were made most meaningful through human interaction and social bonding where community members could gather to participate in and witness ceremonial events. Public architecture such as plazas surely affected the spatial arena in which social agents interacted and related to each other.

The Mixteca Alta is a ruggedly mountainous area in the northwest part of Oaxaca State with a long history of occupation and complex settlement. In comparison to many Zapotec Valley of Oaxaca sites, monumental architecture in the Mixteca Alta arguably emphasized terraces, platforms, and plazas over pyramidal mounds. Because prehispanic occupation focused on the hills and piedmont areas, plaza construction by necessity involved the transformation of rugged ridgetops into artificial flat, open spaces. The naturally restrictive topography meant that, with a few exceptions, most plazas in the Mixteca Alta were small. Building on the ridgetops would also have influenced how accessible plazas were. How did size and access affect the use of plazas in the Mixteca Alta as public, communal spaces?

In the preliminary analysis presented here, I take a quantitative and qualitative look at plazas in the region, drawing on data from the 1999 Central Mixteca Alta Survey project (Kowalewski et al. 2009) as well as Pluckhahn's (2009) analysis of Mixtec plazas as marketplaces.[1] I approach this analysis following Setha Low's (2000) argument that analyzing the social production and significance of plazas require that we also understand their historical context, that is, those economic, ideological, social, and technological factors that resulted in the physical creation of a material setting (Low 2000:127–128).

In the first section, I consider the overall historical and cultural context of the Mixteca Alta, looking at the evidence on settlement patterns, political organization, and the religious and ritual system. How was the architecture of civic-ceremonial spaces influenced by, and how did it influence, the particular political systems of Mixtec communities? The second section presents the statistical analysis on plazas, including plaza measurements and the number of plazas per phase. Following Inomata's (2006a) study of Maya plazas, I calculate the capacities of Mixtec plazas. These plaza capacity figures serve as heuristic tools only. While useful for understanding the possible patterns of interaction in plaza spaces, how we determine actual use still requires multiple lines of evidence. To do this, I examine the data according to chronological period, linking changes and continuities in plaza characteristics to transformations in the social and political organization of settlements during the Preclassic, Classic, and Postclassic periods.

Finally, given the plaza statistics and our knowledge of Mixtec politics and religion, I attempt to define who the intended users of these plazas were and how they may have used them. I use Hall's (1972) theory on communication and social distance known as "proxemics" to consider what kinds of ritual activity would have been possible in the spatial dimensions of Mixtec plazas, given specific types of practices and the size of the audience witnessing the performance. By breaking down the statistics of plazas in the Mixteca Alta and looking at the data by chronological periods, I aim to place Mixteca plazas in their sociopolitical and historical context.

Plazas as Social and Ritual Spaces

Plazas are more than simply empty spaces. They are also physical and social spaces where both the everyday and the extraordinary occur (Inomata and Tsukamoto, this volume). In their everyday use, plazas would have served as locations for marketplaces, for informal socializing, or for moving pedestrian traffic through a site (Inomata 2006a:811). One of their most socially significant functions lies in their use as stages or gathering areas for large ceremonial events. Through shared experiences, communal bonds and a common identity are forged, turning individuals into community members (Inomata 2006a:805; Inomata and Coben 2006:11; Swenson 2008). We perceive and experience our cultural worlds through our bodies most often within the context of ritual and religious practice. Rituals are believed to open or allow communication with the sacred, and power is often predicated on controlling access to ritual practice (Dornan 2004:29).

The purported purpose of public performances is to communicate culturally salient ideas or meanings (Bloch 1989; Bradley 1991) to a receptive audience in promotion or reinforcement of an ideology. A performance is only considered to be effective if these ideas or meanings are communicated successfully, and the aims of the rituals (whatever they may be) are achieved or the expectations of the audience and participants have been met. This is the ideal of course—a performance may successfully communicate the intended message according to the performers, but the audience may be unaffected. Nor are ideas or meanings ever unambiguous. The audience may understand the communicated message in a different way than intended.

Research shows that the spatial properties of the built environment and the thresholds of human perception affect the modes of communication possible within those spaces (Hall 1972; Moore 1996a:798–790; 2004:791; Robin 2002:54). Different types of ritual will therefore be conducted in different kinds of spaces (Moore 1996b:164). The design of a performance space could thus be considered critical to successful performances, although it would be difficult to argue that the designers and sponsors of performance spaces were always concerned with or conscious of maximizing the successful communication of their (intended) meanings.

In developing proxemics theory, Hall (1972) recognized four distance sets at which particular social behaviors are carried out: the *intimate*, *casual-personal*, *social-consultative*, and *public*. Each has a close and a far phase. The first two, *casual-personal* distance and *intimate* distance, involve both parties being within arm's length of each other and touching is possible (Hall 1972:144–146).

At the *social-consultative* distance, the intimate visual details in the face are not perceived, voice level is normal, and special effort must be made if one is to touch another individual. The entire body can be seen at a distance of 2.13 m (seven feet). At the close phase of *public distance*, between 3.66 to 7.62 m (12 and 25 feet), a speaker's voice is loud but not at full volume. Importantly, there are notable grammatical or syntactic shifts in speech as the choice of words and phrasing of sentences are more carefully and distinctly pronounced (Hall 1972:147). The far range of the public distance phase begins around 9.14 m (30 feet) or so, and it is notable that this is the preferred distance to set between important public figures and their audiences. Body stance and gestures as well as facial expression are much more exaggerated, and the voice is louder though tempo drops (Hall 1972:148–149).

A Note of Caution regarding Proxemics

While certainly useful for inferring the level of interactions possible within a given space, it is not clear how archaeologists can actually investigate meaning, intention, experience, or even a combination of these three using the social distances outlined by Hall. As a theory, proxemics cannot answer exactly how a physical setting shapes human interaction, only what is possible. It is unlikely, for example, that public Mixtec ceremonialism involved *casual* and *intimate* distances between a larger audience and the participants. Rather, it was more probable that only elites, priests, other ruling officials, and visiting elite guests directly participating in a ceremony would have been interacting at these levels of personal distances.

The chapters in this volume certainly show that the different sizes of Mesoamerican plazas relate in some way to how they were used in ceremonial contexts. Many Maya plazas, for example, were fairly large and accessible, with substantial capacity for holding large audiences (Inomata, this volume; Stuardo, Mejia, and Campiani, this volume; Tsukamoto, this volume). Smaller plazas, on the other hand, would probably have been used for performances intended for elites or restricted audiences only (Inomata 2006a:814). Murakami (this volume) argues that the plazas and patios at Teotihuacan in fact served different types of audiences where different rituals were performed, based on size and location. Small-scale public rituals and ceremonies, for example, would likely have taken place in the higher-ranked intermediate-elite compounds, whereas more intimate rituals related to ancestor worship and familial concerns would have occurred within the main courtyard of residential compounds. The Street of the Dead and the plazas in front of major architectural features were stages for much larger-scale public rituals.

Even though a plaza may have the potential to hold a sizable number of people, we cannot assume that it necessarily did at all times. The nature of the ceremony, whether it was intended for the community at large or for a restricted audience, and the rituals involved would have influenced the size and composition of the audience, and vice versa. Significant crowding in a plaza, for example, would have reduced the effectiveness of large-scale performances and ceremonial events (Inomata 2006a:814) as ample room would have been required for staging. This is particularly true for smaller plazas, where the limited space would have constrained the movement of relatively large numbers of people. A small plaza would thus imply different types of ritual performances than those that would occur in much larger spaces. Additionally, the location of the plaza within the site and the arrangement of buildings associated with or near the plaza would also have influenced the audience and performances staged there. While other buildings surrounding the plaza could have acted as theatrical stages for setting performers apart from the audience, they could have also effectively obstructed sight lines, rendering some plazas ineffective for large audiences.

Finally, though it may not have always been desirable to fill a plaza to capacity, it is also possible that at certain particular times large numbers may have gathered in plazas for other, nonceremonial purposes. Plazas that also served as market spaces would certainly have seen large volumes of people moving through on market days. Other economic factors may have influenced plaza dimensions and size as well. It is therefore important to keep in mind that plaza spaces are inherently flexible, and that they may have been used in ways distinct from the designers' original intentions, adapted to the needs of the community that used them.

The analysis of the data will show that Mixtec plazas contrast in many ways with plazas from other regions of Mesoamerica as demonstrated by several authors in this volume. The surprisingly small sizes of the majority of the plazas and the small number of sites that actually feature plazas, suggests that in the Mixteca case there may be something different going on here than what is occurring in, for example, the Maya region. I will explore the social implications of the Mixtec plaza data later in this chapter.

The Geography and History of the Mixteca Alta

The Mixteca Alta region is located in the northern and central part of the state of Oaxaca. It is a highly fragmented zone both geographically and socially. The rugged topography greatly restricted the size of population clusters and the availability of arable land, creating the need for a high level of economic exchange and intercultural communication between communities for even basic subsistence needs (Kowalewski et al. 2009:5; Spores 1974:300)

Beginning early in the Late Formative and continuing throughout much of the prehispanic era, the dominant settlement pattern was based on a city-town-ranchería scheme (Balkansky 1998b:38)—that is, a subregional capital and its allied small towns and isolated households. By the Postclassic, most subregions had a large urban center or *cacicazgo* that heavily influenced intraregional politics (Kowalewski et al. 2009:315–317). Boundary maintenance between cacicazgo territories appears to have always been a great concern (Kowalewski et al. 2009:310, 324; Pohl et al. 1997:207, 218–225).

Most of our knowledge about ancient Mixteca society pertains primarily to the Postclassic or Natividad phase (AD 1000–1500). During this time, Mixtec political relationships were characterized by a deep factionalism and constant competition (Pohl et al. 1997:224). The political system was dominated by multiple ruling families where the legitimacy to rule was determined by a descendant's proximity to the deified ancestors of royal lineages (Bellas 1997:42; Joyce and Winter 1996:45; Monaghan 1990:133; Pohl 1984:20, 1994:69–70). The competition and cooperation of multiple small kingdoms via the means of kinship networks, martial alliances, and warfare meant that there was a constant flux in the political structure (Balkansky et al. 2000:379–380; Kowalewski et al. 2009:315; Pohl 1984:137).

Of course, how far back we can project these characterizations is a question that all archaeologists must wrestle with, especially for a political system that went through several periods of reorganization and collapse. However, similarities in settlement organization, ritual paraphernalia, and formal architectural style (Balkansky 1998a) reveal strong continuities between periods, despite drastic changes in social complexity and settlement patterns.

Ritual and religion were significantly important means of accessing power in Mesoamerica (Clark 2004; Elson 2006; Finsten et al. 1996; Flannery and Marcus 1976; Hamann 2002; Joyce and Weller 2007; Marcus and Flannery 1994; Masson and Orr 1999). Affairs of the supernatural were also highly political in the Mixteca Alta and, arguably, part of the power and authority of Mixtec elites was rooted in their roles as ritual specialists (Joyce 2010; Joyce and Winter 1996). Nonroyal religious authorities, however, also wielded a great deal of influence over Mixtec political affairs and were often consulted by Mixtec rulers, particularly during power conflicts (Pohl 1984:76).

Our primary sources for much of what we know about prehispanic Mixtec religious worldview and ceremonial practices are the prehispanic codices. Aside from genealogical and historical information, they also depict deities and elites engaged in various ceremonies and rituals as well as the interactions between and among historical elite personages and deities (Jansen 1990:104; Pohl 1984:25). According to the literature, Mixtec religion placed emphasis on maintaining balance in the universe through "deliberate acts of ritual and through maintaining respect for nature and the spirit world" (Bellas 1997:30), rather than on the creation of the world as was emphasized in Aztec beliefs. Aside from this, ancient Mixtec beliefs had much in common with other contemporaneous groups throughout Mesoamerica (Bellas 1997:57–58; Lejarazu

2007:93; Marcus et al. 1983:38). Spores (1967:82) characterized Mixtec religion as being based around agriculture, fertility, and curing, but certainly other underlying themes were sacrifice and rain (Bellas 1997:3; Forde 2002:103; King 1990:141; Monaghan 1995).

Mixtecs of all social levels, like other Mesoamerican groups such as the Zapotecs, Teotihuacanos, and the Maya, practiced ancestor veneration. Deceased royal elites were wrapped in bundles and placed in caves, and their descendants' right to rule centered on their preservation and care (Pohl 1984:48–49). The bundles were "consulted," with oracular priests acting as mediums, by their descendants for guidance on political questions and everyday matters (Bellas 1997:7; Pohl 1984:48). This way of directly interacting with the deceased ancestral bundles (Bellas 1997:24; Williams 2009:91), however, is particularly similar to Inkan practices where ancestral mummies were treated as animate beings (Gose 1996; Moore 2004; Wernke 2006).

Many ceremonies were performed in front of temples, on top of platforms, and inside plazas. What was civic-ceremonial architecture like in the Mixteca Alta? Some scholars argue that the degree of diversity in the form and function of civic-ceremonial architecture may reflect diversity in ceremonies and ritual practices at the regional level. However, there is not much description of how exactly ceremonial architecture in the Mixteca varied. On the other hand, the dispersed distribution of small mounds and plazas across the Mixteca Alta would seem to indicate that neither the political nor the religious systems were particularly centralized. Certain ceremonial and political activities may have been primarily concentrated in the subregional capitals, given the limited monumentality of the second-tier centers (Kowalewski et al. 2009:310, 321). With a few exceptions, most Mixtec mounds were rather small. Instead, sites were dominated by monumental terraces, some stretching around the entire length of a hillside slope. These terraces were primarily dwelling space and therefore were probably not public space (Pérez Rodríguez 2006).

Plazas in the Mixteca Alta by the Numbers

Some 999 sites were registered by the Central Mixteca Alta Survey project in the Central Mixteca Alta, dating from the Late Archaic to the Spanish Conquest period. The majority of these sites are low-level rural settlements lacking ceremonial architecture (Pérez Rodríguez 2003:41). Out of the sites registered, only 166, or 16.6 percent of the total, featured plazas across all phases (table 5.1). Because some sites were occupied over the course of several different phases, the true count is only 98 unique sites with plazas, or about 10 percent of total sites registered. The relatively low presence of plazas—in comparison to the settlements of other Mesoamerican groups such as the Maya and even the neighboring Zapotecs—may of course be partly due to the destruction of plaza surfaces in later times from natural and cultural factors, making their identification in the field incredibly difficult. However, other factors both social and geographical may explain this phenomenon as well, and will be explored later in this chapter. Overall, 232 plazas were recorded by survey crews. Because some of the plazas were reused from one period to the next, and thus

TABLE 5.1. Plazas in the Mixteca Alta, Formative to Postclassic Periods

Phases	Total sites	Sites with plazas	Sites without plazas	Sites with plazas %	Sites without plazas %	Number of plazas per phase	% of total plazas	% of total sites
Early/Middle Cruz	51	1	50	1.96	98.04	1	0.43	0.10
Late Cruz	237	7	230	2.95	97.05	7	3.02	0.70
Ramos	169	38	131	22.49	77.51	61	26.29	3.80
Las Flores	341	62	279	18.18	81.82	85.5	36.85	6.21
Natividad	843	51	792	6.05	93.95	77	33.19	5.11

were more than likely counted several times, the true plaza count is probably much lower (given some inconsistences between the data sets used in this chapter). The majority of the identified plazas were dated by survey crews to the Classic and Postclassic eras, based on associated surface collections. Most sites only have one plaza ($n = 64$).

Plazas in the Mixteca Alta are more or less standardized in their length and width measurements, ranging between 15 and 30 m (figure 5.1). Though there are some relatively large plazas ($n = 5$), such as those at the Cerro Volado in Huamelulpan Valley, Yucundaa in Teposcolula Valley, and Ñunducha in the Lagunas subregion, when we look at the plaza area measurements we see that, with the exception of these few, most plazas are small-to-medium sized. In fact, 75 percent of Mixtec plazas fall within the range of 300–1500 m^2. As figure 5.2 demonstrates, these proportions do not change much over time—that is, plazas do not increase or decrease considerably in dimension from the Preclassic to the Postclassic (i.e. Postclassic plazas are not much larger than Classic-era plazas). It is entirely possible that plazas built in earlier phases could have been expanded later on; due to a lack of excavation data we do not have information on plaza construction phases. The restrictive topography would suggest that if plazas did expand it would not have been by very much, as would be possible on flatter terrain.

In comparison, plazas in the Maya region were on a whole much larger and seem to expand in size from the Preclassic to the Classic period. The West Plaza of Tikal alone measures over 22,000 m^2 in area, while the smallest plaza at the lower-tier site of Aguateca measures over 7,000 m^2 in area (Inomata 2006a:816). Many other plazas discussed by the authors in this volume are also fairly large. Plaza H at El Palmar, described by Tsukamoto (this volume) as the smallest plaza at the site, measures 2455 m^2, while the sunken patio of Group E at San Lorenzo is only a few meters larger (Cyphers and Murtha, this volume). Both are much bigger than most plazas in the Mixteca Alta.

In contrast to claims that public buildings and spaces were relatively open in the Mixteca Alta, the analysis reveals that plaza access appears to have been fairly restricted—around 59 percent ($n = 137$) of plazas could be considered closed access (table 5.2). Open and closed access refers to how accessible

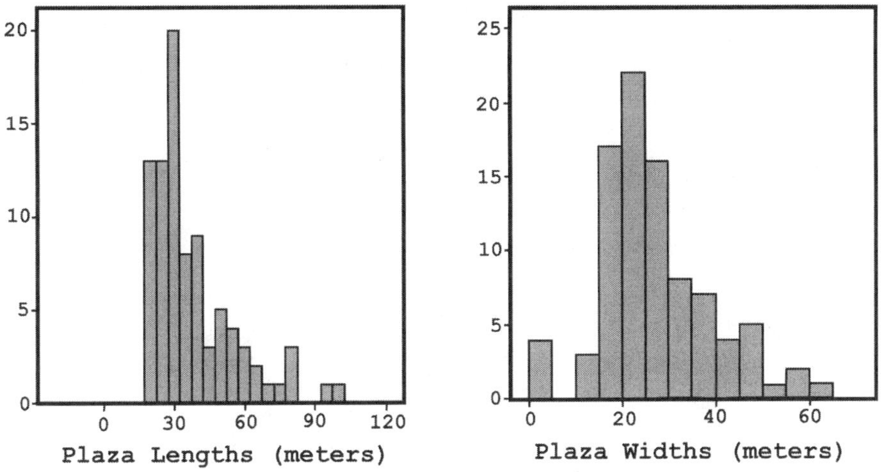

FIGURE 5.1. Length and width measurements of plazas in the Mixteca Alta.

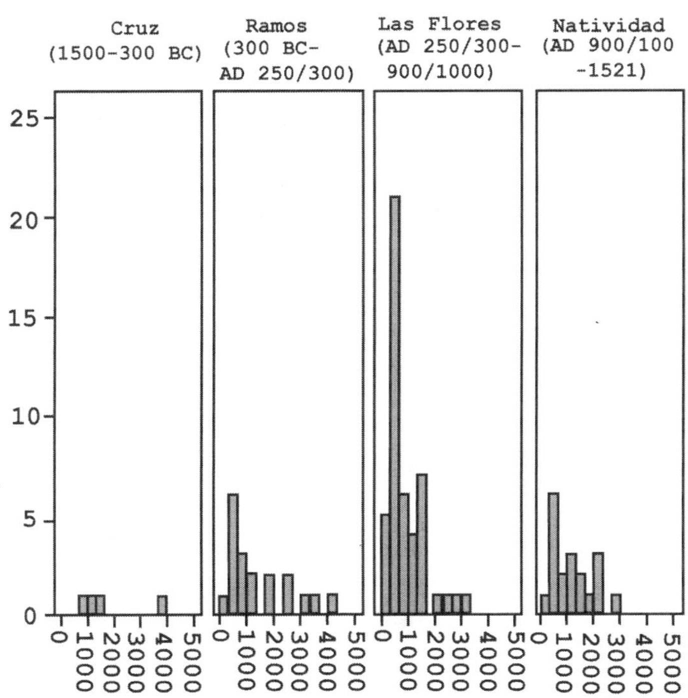

FIGURE 5.2. Plaza areas by phase.

TABLE 5.2 Plaza Accessibility by Phase

Phase	Sites with plazas	Number of plazas per period	Open: Number of plazas	Open: % of total plazas	Closed: Number of plazas	Closed: % of total plazas
Late Cruz	7	7	2	28.57	5	71.43
Ramos	38	61	12	19.67	49	80.33
Las Flores	62	85.5	42	49.12	43.5	50.88
Natividad	51	77	37	48.05	40	51.95

a plaza is to people of different social statuses. A plaza with multiple entry points where pedestrians could easily move through the space can be considered open, while a plaza with tightly controlled access points where the movement of people was greatly restricted would be described as closed. Restriction in access was achieved either by the design of the plaza itself, the construction of other architectural elements (other mounds or platforms), or its location within the site. The common linear arrangement (figure 5.3) of monumental architecture found at many sites in the Mixteca Alta, where the plaza was often located behind a mound on a narrow ridgetop, could have made access difficult.

Breaking these figures down by chronological phase, we see an interesting pattern emerge. Referring to table 5.2, it appears that access to plazas was more restricted in the Late Cruz (700 BC–AD 300) and Ramos phases (300 BC–AD 250)—nearly two-thirds of sites with plazas can be classified as closed access. We see the opposite pattern for the Las Flores (AD 250–900/1100) and Natividad (AD 900/1100–1521) phases—the Classic and Postclassic respectively—when nearly half of the plazas were more accessible. While the increasing access to plazas in later periods could suggest changes in ritual and performance acts, it may also reflect political and economic motives on behalf of the ruling nobility.

Previous research has shown that there is no consistent correlation between plaza sizes and the estimated populations of settlements, probably due to the various ways plazas were used for performances (Inomata 2006a:812). The Mixteca plaza data bears out this observation. Although most Mixtec settlements tended to be smaller and more dispersed, there is only a weak, though significant, correlation (Pearson's $r = 0.537$, $p = 0.0005$) between the total area of a site and the presence and number of plazas. Thus, even sites that would not be classified as headtowns or regional centers have plazas. Some sites, such as TLA-TLA-TLA-1, even have multiple plazas though their populations were quite low.

As stated previously, ritual practices will vary not only according to the number of performers but also the composition and size of the audience. The capacity of a plaza can affect not only how large or small an audience will be, but also the types of interactions that will occur there. Taking the average

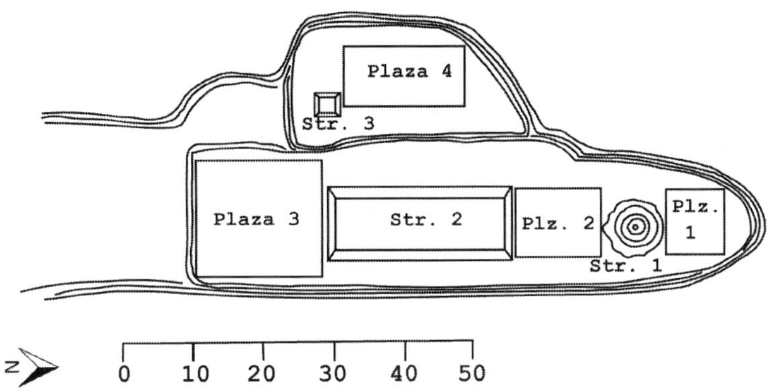

Typical Mixtec Plaza Layout with Civic-Ceremonial Architecture in Linear Arrangement.

FIGURE 5.3. A typical linear arrangement of civic-ceremonial architecture found in the Mixteca Alta.

population of Mixtec sites as determined by the 1999 survey team in combination with the areas of individual plazas and the total areas of all plazas provided by Pluckhahn, I calculated the occupancy capacity of plazas (data was available for 86 out of 232 plazas or 38 percent). I used the figures of 0.46 m^2/person, 1 m^2/person, and 3.6 m^2/person, following Inomata (2006a).[2] As explained previously, these figures are heuristic tools only and simply represent possibilities of plaza space based on their dimensions.

If the average population is accurate, at a tight squeeze of only 0.46 m^2 per person, about 79 percent of the plazas had enough capacity to fit the entire estimated population of the settlement. In fact, nearly three-quarters of those plazas may have even been large enough to accommodate neighboring settlements, as Moore correctly observes (this volume). On the other hand, at a generous 3.6 m^2 per person, only 29 percent of plazas could have held the entire population of the settlement. However, if Mixtec plazas were packed to capacity, would large-scale staged events like that of the Maya have been possible in the available plaza space? Furthermore, would these plazas have necessarily been packed to capacity with people standing shoulder to shoulder?

Another possibility that should be considered here is that the majority of Mixteca Alta plazas were not actually constructed for holding the entire community, but instead were designed for specific events to which only certain community members would have been invited to participate. Unfortunately, the plaza capacity figures cannot tell us directly how Mixtec plaza space was actually used. One could imagine that more people would have occupied the space if the plaza was also used as a marketplace; however, the analysis of plaza access demonstrates that most plazas were probably not used for economic activities. We therefore cannot assume a simple correlation between plaza size, its total calculated capacity, and the actual audience size. As flexible spaces, the plaza would have accommodated audiences of different sizes depending on how it was to be used on a given day.

Plazas in the Mixteca Alta through Time

Formative period—Cruz (1500–300 BC) and Ramos (300 BC–AD 300) Phases

Throughout the Early and Middle Formative period (the Cruz phase in the Mixteca Alta, 1500–300 BC), the dominant settlement pattern consisted of small sites clustered around a centrally located headtown (Kowalewski et al. 2009:290), indicating a high level of interaction and integration. Beyond the regional level, evidence also suggests links with foreign ideational and symbolic systems, pointing to an emergent social complexity.

In the Early Cruz to Middle Cruz phases (1500–700 BC), a suite of shared symbols and new artifact types begin to appear at different archaeological sites throughout Mesoamerica (Blomster 1998:309; Joyce 2010:88), including Oaxaca and the Mixteca Alta. Some of the new ritual paraphernalia included items such as prismatic blades, sting-ray spines, spouted trays, magnetite and illmenite mirrors, shell and mica objects, and other ceramic objects (Blomster 1998:323; Flannery 1976:341–344; Joyce 2010:88–89). We also see more evidence of feasting and ceremonial gatherings during the Middle Formative phase (Blomster 1998:309, 319–320). Other major changes included the ennobling or deification of ancestors by groups vying for leadership positions, and the increasing restriction in access to powerful symbols of authority (Blomster 1998:323–324; Joyce 2010:111–114).

Only one plaza, located at the site designated SPP-SPP-TEC-4 in the subregional valley of Teposcolula, was securely identified for the Early and Middle Cruz phases. By the Late Cruz (700–300 BC) or the Middle Formative phase, plaza construction had increased. Survey crews registered seven sites with plazas, representing about 3 percent of the total sites recorded for that phase (n = 237), or 0.70 percent of total sites. Only two Cruz plazas, or 28 percent of the total recorded for that time period, could be described as open-access. This suggests that formal architecture was more restrictive in comparison to later periods; however, the population size is so small that it is difficult to draw any real conclusions. Instead, given that Pluckhahn's criteria is more market-focused, fewer open-access plazas could be due to there being less market-oriented activity this early on.

By the Ramos (300 BC–AD 300) phase or Late to Terminal Formative, society had become even more complex with the transition to urbanism and the establishment of early cities in the Mixteca Alta. Many of the villages of previous phases were abandoned and populations coalesced into fortified hilltop towns (Balkansky et al. 2004:36–37; Joyce 2010:160–164; Kowalewski et al. 2009:297). These early urban centers had much larger populations and featured shared architectural styles, clearer class and social divisions with more elaborate elite housing and segregated residential zones, and hieroglyphic writing (Balkansky 1998b:38; Balkansky et al. 2004:37).

There is a clear increase in plaza construction compared to the previous phases. The architecturally unique city of Monte Negro had two plazas, while Huamelulpan—one of the earliest urban centers in the Mixteca Alta—had seven! Still, sites with plazas represent only 22.5 percent of the total sites for this phase (n = 169), or 3.80 percent of all sites registered. Interestingly, the accessibility of plazas slightly decreases from the previous phase, with 80 percent of plazas considered to be fairly restrictive in access. The decrease could be explained in part by the larger sample size of plazas, but the shift to a new form of sociopolitical organization, urbanism, with its attendant increases in social stratification may also explain why plazas are less accessible in the Ramos phase.

Only a few centuries after they first appeared, the urban centers of the Ramos phase were abandoned (Joyce 2010:195; Kowalewski et al. 2009:303). Though they existed only briefly—Monte Negro lasted only a century (Balkansky et al. 2000:374)—the social patterns that emerged in this time period would characterize Mixtec social systems and political hierarchies for millennia.

Classic Period–Las Flores (AD 300–900/1100) Phase

The political upheaval during the Terminal Formative was followed by the settlement reorganization and population expansion of the Classic or Las Flores (AD 250–900) phase. The dozens of small polities that existed at this time were organized in a manner resembling later Postclassic sites (Joyce 2010:226–227). Subregions within the Mixteca Alta all had substantial but fairly dispersed occupation during the Early Classic (Kowalewski et al. 2009:306–307).

Settlement and civic-ceremonial hierarchies were more complex and differentiated in the Las Flores period (Kowalewski et al. 2009:308). Status distinctions between rulers and commoners were more formalized (Joyce 2010:197). The scale of mounded architecture was also greater: mounds were taller, platforms were much more massive, and even the areal extent of civic-ceremonial complexes was larger during this time period (Kowalewski et al. 2009:308–309). However, there is much continuity from previous periods as well, particularly in the political and religious systems (Joyce 2010:197). Formal architectural style, for example, remains much the same from the Ramos to Las Flores phase.

Evidence confirms that there were indeed more plazas—a 61 percent increase over the Ramos phase. This represents both the reuse of Ramos-era plazas and new construction as well. However, the relative number of sites with plazas (n = 62) in comparison to the total number of sites for this phase (n = 341) is still very low. Only 18 percent of Las Flores sites had plazas. Some of these sites included Cerro Jázmin in the Nochixtlan Valley, which alone featured five different plazas, several sites within the Greater Teposcolula area, such as Ñunducha and Yucunee, and Cerro Encantado in the Greater Tlaxiaco region.

Again, it has been argued that access to public space was increasingly restricted in the Las Flores period (Joyce 2010:234; Kowalewski et al. 2009:310). Data, on the other hand, suggest that in actuality there are more open-access plazas (49 percent of the total, n = 42) during this time than in previous phases. How might we interpret this increase in accessible plazas? While it is entirely possible that this increase is linked to ritual practice, we must also consider economic factors as well. The need for marketplaces would have become increasingly critical as Mixtec Classic societies began extending their social and economic influence.

Occupation and population contract during the Late Las Flores (Kowalewski et al. 2009:313). Where Late Las Flores occupation is found, archaeologists also find evidence of a violent reorganization of settlement patterns that results in the abandonment of Classic-era urban centers and the establishment of the new Postclassic cacicazgos.

Postclassic Period–Natividad (AD 900/1100–1521)

The end of the Late Classic (AD 500–900) through the Early Postclassic period (AD 900–1200) was a time of severe conflict in the Mixteca Alta (Byland and Pohl 1994:13; Hamann 2002:358–363; Joyce 2010:259–260; Pohl 1984:70) that lead to great changes in the political landscape. A major Terminal Classic to Early Postclassic conflict described in the prehispanic codices (Bellas 1997:82; Pohl 1984:71; Williams 2009:99) has been documented archaeologically by Byland and Pohl (1994). They believe that the conflict, known as the War of Heaven, is related to a shift in power between two different groups of elites during the Classic to Postclassic transition.

While the collapse of urban centers occurred throughout Mesoamerica (albeit at different rates), how much of this conflict was localized only to the Nochixtlan Valley (Williams 2009:44, 99), or had spread throughout the Mixteca Alta, remains to be seen. Settlement shifts from the piedmont region in the Early Postclassic to the valley floors during the Late Postclassic may indicate that the political environment was more militaristic during the former (Pohl 1984:70–71).

Throughout much of the Natividad phase then, the Mixteca Alta was populated by numerous autonomous states (Balkansky et al. 2000:368; Furst 1990:123; Pohl and Byland 1990:126; Pohl et al. 1997:224; Terraciano 2001:1) that considered themselves distinct from one another yet recognized their shared histories and culture (Byland and Pohl 1994:123; Pohl et al. 1997; Terraciano 2001:1). These small states had attained high levels of artistic expression, as seen in the widespread iconographic tradition known as the "Mixteca-Puebla" style (Forde 2002:9) and the expansion of cacicazgo political influence into other territories. Mixtec rulers maintained influence and political control by forging strong marital alliances with the Zapotecs as well as the various kingdoms of Puebla and Tlaxcala (Joyce 2010; Kowalewski et al. 2009; Pohl 2003a, 2003b, 2003c; Pohl and Byland 1990; Spores 1974; Terraciano 2004).

There appears to have been less investment in infrastructure for public religious events and communal gatherings during the Postclassic than in previous periods. Forde claims that there is a clear decrease in the scale and frequency of civic-ceremonial architecture and monuments (2002:148); Kowalewski et al., however, argue that there was plenty of new construction of civic-ceremonial mounds (2009:321). The evidence from the plaza data reveals that the number of sites with plazas does decrease in comparison to the Classic era, although Natividad plazas do represent 33 percent of total plazas recorded. Out of 843 sites dating to this time period, only 51, or 6.05 percent of the total, featured plazas (5.11 percent of all sites recorded). Most of these are located in the Greater Teposcolula and Inner Basin regions. Indeed, the site with the most plazas (n = 7) is Yucundaa in the Teposcolula Valley subregion, which was a powerful cacicazgo in the Late Postclassic with a highly elaborate civic-ceremonial complex.

Access to plazas is still less restrictive in the Postclassic, with 48 percent classified as open. While this represents a small decrease from the Classic, the difference is not great enough to conclude that this change is socially significant. However, given the fluorescence of Mixteca Alta states and their increasing role in the supraregional politics of Mesoamerica during this time, the opening up of plazas again could be related more to economic activity, as it may have been in the Classic. While the increasing access to plazas in later periods may suggest changes in ceremonial types and ritual practices, it could also reflect political and economic motives on behalf of the ruling nobility.

Discussion

Given these statistics and historical background, how do we interpret the role of plazas in the social lives of Mixtec communities? We know that plazas probably acted as important boundary markers (Pohl et al. 1997), and that some were more than likely used as marketplaces (Joyce 2010; Kowalewski et al. 2009; Pluckhahn 2009). Most were certainly used for ceremonial and ritual activity. But what kind of ceremonies took place there? Were the plazas host to mass spectacles on the scale of ceremonies in the Maya region, or were the performances restricted to more specialized audiences? An exploration of Mixtec ceremonialism is in order if we are to investigate the social roles of plazas further.

From the codices, we know that a range of ceremonies were performed by Mixtec royals, priests, and other elites. Major ceremonies included the ritual sacrifice of captives (Bellas 1997:153; Dahlgren 1966:154–155; Pohl 1984:25); marriage rites; rites related to the birth and death of royal elites; peregrinations to sacred sites (Pohl 1984:25); and the ascension of lords to rulership, and the confirmation of their associated rights and prerogatives (Furst 1990:123; Lejarazu 2007:95, 102; 2008:126; Pohl 1984:25). Some of these ceremonies may have been performed, particularly those rituals related to birth, death, and marriage, and more likely on a much smaller scale, by commoners and lower-status individuals.

Elite (and maybe even commoner) ceremonies included various ritual practices and elements. Ritual practitioners burned copal; used powdered tobacco (piciete); performed auto-sacrifice using maguey spines or obsidian blades (Forde 2002:100; Lejarazu 2008:125, 127); and made offerings of quail blood, bound stick bundles, and grass mats (Bellas 1997:124, 125). Batons and scepters were also used in many rituals. As objects of power linked to rulership, they were often placed inside or at the foot of temples (Lejarazu 2007:88, 91–92).

Some ritual practices were linked to specific ceremonies. The fire-drilling ritual is often associated in the codices with the establishment of new dynasties (Bellas 1997:76; Byland and Pohl 1994:155; Jansen 1982:206–217; Lejarazu

2007:102). Bloodletting was supposedly performed before the sacred bundles (Pohl 1984:68–69), though this practice may have also been included in other ceremonies, as bloodletting was a common practice throughout Mesoamerica. The offering of pulque to drink was viewed as a demonstration of power (Lejarazu 2008:126, 133), while the scattering of piciete usually occurred at ceremonies related to change and metamorphosis, such as marriage and death (Bellas 1997:102). It is believed that the myths and histories portrayed in the codices themselves were also performed, most likely sung or chanted by trained priests and storytellers (Monaghan 1990:133).

Both oracular priests and the Mixtec elite spoke in a ritualized language (Bellas 1997:151) that would have probably worked very well in performances, given that speech becomes highly performative starting at a distance of 3.66 m (12 feet). Performances of the codices, for example, would have been conducted in this ritualized language and would probably have been most audible and visible to those positioned between 3 and 15 m from the staging area (depending also on the acoustic characteristics of the performance space). Depending on how tightly packed audience members were, it is possible that a sizable percentage of the community witnessed these performances. How much these narratives resonated with nonelite members of the community who did not speak this ritualized language, on the other hand, is still a subject of debate (Ford 2002:155; see Monaghan 1990 and Pohl 1984 for contrasting opinion).

Based on the evidence from the codices, it appears that most ceremonies involved a series of ritual practices that were rather personal and intimate in nature. Such activities would have been difficult to see at distances greater than 9 m (30 feet) (Hall 1972:148), wherein the human figure begins to diminish in view. In a crowded plaza, those audience members standing at 10 m or more away from the performance stage would have had difficulty discerning the performers' movements, although in the case of the fire-drilling ritual they would have been able to see and smell the smoke. Of course, as is the case with the Maya, surrounding temples and platforms may have been used as staging areas, which would have elevated performers and allowed more audience members to view the ritual performances. The codices do show many ceremonies being staged on and around temples; however, the small sizes of many Mixtec mounds could indicate that ritual activities would have been somewhat obscured as well.

If Mixtec ceremonialism was indeed so intimate and restricted in nature—and again, our knowledge of these ceremonies is limited to the activities of Terminal Classic and Postclassic elites as depicted in the codices—then what role did plazas play as performance and ritual spaces? The evidence seems to argue against plazas as community integrating spaces in the Mixteca region, a contrast with other areas of Mesoamerica as described by the authors in this volume. The low numbers of plazas suggest that they were not highly critical architectural elements for the entire community in comparison to platforms and terraces, which in the Mixteca Alta are quite numerous and fairly monumental (Kowalewski et al. 2009:303).

Referring back to table 5.1, only 16.6 percent of sites registered by the Central Mixteca Alta survey project had plazas. Additionally, as figures 5.1 and 5.2

demonstrate, most of these were small-to-medium sized—measurements that remain surprisingly stable throughout the prehispanic era. Those sites that did feature plazas typically only had one; rarely did a site have more than two. Furthermore, excepting those few that have been identified as potential marketplaces, most plazas were highly restricted in access. The linear arrangement of civic-ceremonial architecture, as seen in figure 5.3, at many sites in the Mixteca Alta, and the location of these architectural groups on the ridgetops near elite residential space, would have precluded a large majority of the community from using the plaza space. The nature of Mixtec (primarily elite) ceremonies and ritual practices meant that, with a possible few exceptions, most audience members would have been unable to clearly see or hear the activities taking place if the plaza were packed to capacity. Thus, while Moore (this volume) is correct in arguing that the low population estimates meant that a large portion of the community could have fit in a plaza, we cannot assume that they necessarily did at all times for all occasions.

I would argue that most plazas, depending on location and accessibility, would have been used for those ceremonies directly related to elite concerns and involving select members of the community whose presence would have been considered critical for validation of the rituals' results. These select members would have included the ruling lineage, other members of the nobility, noble and nonnoble ritual specialists, and most likely important leaders and community representatives from the allied towns and smaller villages. Excepting perhaps special occasions, commoners would have been excluded from these ceremonies and from the use of the plazas, particularly those plazas located within the civic-ceremonial sectors of the sites, as most were. Nonelite ritual practices would have most likely occurred within the household or the barrio, rather than in the headtowns. Previous research has shown that commoner households often acted and organized themselves independently of nearby elites, such as in the case of *lama-bordo* terrace (agricultural terraces built in mountain drainages) construction (Pérez Rodríguez 2003).

As always, however, there are exceptions to this rule. As Moore (this volume) points out, there are specific sites in the Mixteca Alta that feature disproportionately large plazas for the given population estimates. TLA-TLA-TLA-1 was specifically cited as one site that could have easily fit its estimated population in any one of the three plazas registered there by the 1999 survey crews. The seven plazas of Huamelulpan surely could have hosted quite a number of people and were probably the location for some spectacular ceremonies. However, the lack of excavation data means that we can only speculate on the significance of these exceptional sites, and I agree with Moore that more investigation into the unusual cases is certainly warranted.

One final observation worth mentioning here is the seeming stability in the plaza measurements over time. What does this stability imply given the evident changes in political and social organization? Could we connect this stability to continuity in ritual practice, or perhaps to continuity in the size of the social unit? The explosive increase in population growth during the Las Flores and Natividad phases would argue against continuity in the size of the social unit. On the other hand, the organization of sites into the headtown-village-ranchería scheme was established early, and remained the predominant way of organizing socially on the landscape despite several systemic political collapses and reorganizations, which may have affected elites more than commoners. The stability in plaza measurements could be related to continuity in ritual practice, though once again it should be repeated that our time-depth for knowledge on Mixtec rituals and ceremonies only extends so far into the past.

Our inability to answer these questions is due entirely to the lack of excavation at many of the sites registered by the Central Mixteca Alta project. Without this data, we can never know if individual plazas did indeed expand from one phase to another—the stability therefore may be an artifact of the data being primarily derived from survey. Finally, the simplest explanation may be found in topography. Ridgetops in the Mixteca Alta, where civic-ceremonial architecture is typically found, are often narrow and highly restrictive in spatial terms. Even if an individual plaza was built up over time, it would not have much room for expansion given the nature of the topography where these structures were built.

Conclusion

If plaza design constrains the communicative potential of rituals, then the small sizes of many Mixtec plazas may indicate that most of the ceremonies and other ritual practices were perhaps intimate affairs involving only select groups or members of the community. The low numbers of plazas and their location near elite residential sectors possibly indicate that the majority of nonelite religious ceremonies occurred on the local level within barrios by kin groups, and that elite ceremonies were exclusively held in the civic-ceremonial districts of headtowns. The decentralized distribution of civic-ceremonial architecture and the location of some small mound groups on the barrio level support this conclusion.

Unlike many of the plazas spaces discussed in this volume, plazas in Mixtec communities may not have been used to integrate the entire community together across social hierarchies. Rather, those plazas that did not also serve as marketplaces were used to promulgate the dominant political ideology to the nobility and other community leaders alone. Elites and commoner households may have been loosely linked together more through their participation in a pan-regional ideology and use of similar ritual practices (bloodletting and feasting, for example), than through participation in performances together within the same space.

The data presented in this chapter challenge our assumptions about how public architecture such as plazas was utilized and viewed by different Mesoamerican communities with distinct traditions. The analysis suggests that social integration may have taken a different form in the Mixteca Alta, distinct from those traditions and practices we find in other areas. Further investigation is necessary to explore fully the range of material expression that community integration took not only in the Mixteca Alta, but elsewhere in Mesoamerica as well.

Notes

1. Unfortunately, there are some inconsistencies between the two data sets. I have tried to accommodate and account for these inconsistencies as much as possible.

2. Although Moore cites a much larger range of space of 0.46 m^2 to 21.6 m^2 available to participants and audience members (1996b:147), I agree with Inomata that this higher figure would not have been possible given the geography and site layout of most Mixtec sites (2006a:812).

CHAPTER SIX

The Social Construction of Public Spaces at Palenque and Chinikihá, Mexico

Rodrigo Liendo Stuardo,
Javier López Mejía, and
Arianna Campiani

In this chapter, we reflect on the mechanisms through which political activity becomes incorporated into communal social and cultural life by the creation of spaces for permanent collective action. Our impression is that routine aspects of communitarian life are usually framed by cyclical events capable of attracting a sizable number of individuals leading to a collective experience with political connotations. Hence, our goal is to highlight the potential of the study of public spaces for the understanding of the political phenomena from an archaeological point of view.

We start from the position that there is no clear boundary between the "political" and the "social"; we firmly believe that the political component should be looked for in those acts or events that constitute a fundamental part in the daily life of ancient communities like the Maya: for example, festivities, carnivals, public ceremonies, markets, games, and processions. In such societies, daily community life was commonly shaped by cyclical events with clear symbolic meaning, renewing and reinforcing the sense of community through important representations of social order repeated each year in certain moments and places. Our premise, following Takeshi Inomata (2006a), is that within Classic Maya political regime, the feeling of belonging to a particular community and the obedience to a particular political leader was manifested and intensified only in certain spatial and temporal contexts (cyclic communal events or within specially built environments) and hence generally absent from the everyday experience of ordinary citizens. We will use information recovered by our settlement pattern project in the Palenque region, Chiapas, Mexico, to underscore that the study of public architectural space provides significant insights into understanding ancient Maya political organization.

The Palenque Settlement Project

During the last fifteen years, our research in the Northwestern Lowlands has tried to elicit the nature of political integration in the area with the special aim of identifying significant material signatures in the archaeological record (Sabloff and Henderson 1993:455). These might lead to a better appraisal of the political regime characterizing the region in prehispanic times. According to our site typology, the single most important element distinguishing the relevance of any of them is the existence of civic-ceremonial architecture. All sites show, at least for Late Classic times, a clear architectonic pattern composed of plazas surrounded by buildings with a limited range of functions (temples, ballcourts, and palaces). This architectural program bespeaks the political importance of creating a significant built environment capable of bringing together a dispersed population on certain important occasions.

In this regard, some authors have suggested that regal-ritual Maya centers were practically "grandiose palace complexes," "great concentrations of tombs, temples, ballcourts, plazas, causeways and monuments" (Webster 2001:132). In sum, the built environment is the setting where paramount leaders, surrounded by stunning and ever-growing architecture, administered the affairs of the state in a personal and nonspecialized manner. We believe that two aspects of this proposal have particular relevance in our discussion of the archaeological data recovered from our research area. The first deals with the nature of ancient Maya urbanism under the premise that ancient Maya politics basically meant the administration of a royal household compound writ large. The second proposal is that the ancient Maya royal court was an institution centered on individuals and not clearly defined institutions, with an observable hierarchy. Both premises will be further discussed in detail.

Palenque and Its Built Environment

Palenque's palace complex sits at the center of its urban landscape (figure 6.1). It is composed of temples, a ballcourt, buildings, and plazas with civic-ceremonial functions. The built space within the complex is divided into three sectors encompassing a vast area of approximately 8.5 hectare without major architectonic barriers, with the exception of plazas at different levels and stairs encouraging circulation. It is also highly significant that the overall architectural complex scheme corresponds very clearly to what several authors (Ashmore 1981; Coggins 1967; Hammond 1991) have identified as a repetitive pattern of architectural associations with a highly symbolic content that "materialized" a worldview in which the ruler is located at the center of their community and the cosmos.

The archaeological evidence indicating the multifunctional character of the Palace Complex at Palenque is another interesting aspect of its spatial

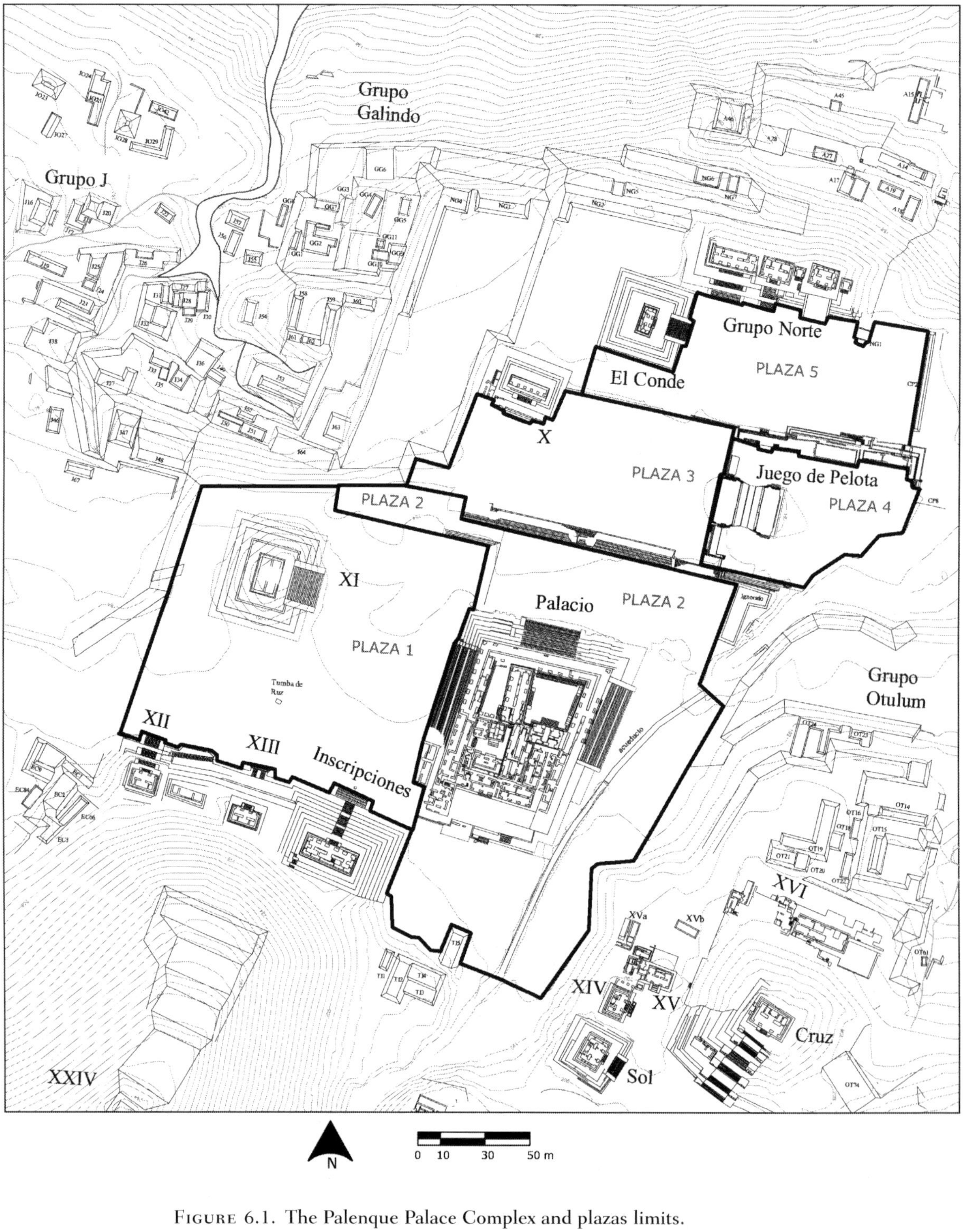

Figure 6.1. The Palenque Palace Complex and plazas limits.

configuration. In a previous analysis of the Palenque Palace compound (Liendo Stuardo 2003:196–198) using graphical methods available for architectural analysis we were able to detect several areas within the compound showing differences in patterns of accessibility and privacy. In this analysis, the southeastern section of the palace represents an unusually segregated space within the compound. This evidence added to other archaeological indicators (the existence of a complex sewer system framing the area, the abundant utilitarian wares found in the corridors and floors of several structures forming the compound, and the existence of a sizable midden containing several thousand sherds of serving vessels, jars, figurines, needles, bone awls, obsidian blades, jade beads, and faunal and macrobotanical remains) (Liendo Stuardo 2003:198–199) attests, we believe, to the residential function of this sector of the palace. Nevertheless, we suggest that the group composed by the Otulúm, the Cruz, and the South Acropolis complexes is the most likely candidate for the residential area of the ruling lineage of Palenque, judging from the volume, size, area of plazas, quality of its monuments, and the importance of texts and images represented in its buildings, which surpass the magnitude and relevance of all the evidence found in any other city groups. In the case of Palenque it is interesting to note that, contrary to what happens in other Maya centers, the residence of the ruling family was not confined to the palace.

Palenque's Main Plaza (Plaza 1 in figure 6.1) is connected to the rest of the city by a circulation axis from west to east, directing the flow of people from the margins of the city where the Main Plaza is located. Although the actual architectonic scheme observable today belongs to Palenque's latest occupation phase (Balunté AD 730–830), it is certain that the first buildings of the Main Plaza belong to the Early Classic Motiepa ceramic phase, a date corresponding to the founding of the Palenque dynasty (AD 431). The results of a recent test-pitting program carried out in the city (López Bravo et al. 2003, 2004) suggest that the construction of the Main Plaza at Palenque was done as a major architectonic effort aiming to join in a single urban plan two independent sectors of an earlier settlement configuration. The building program surrounding the Main Plaza has an evident public orientation. Contrary to other cases, it has no architectonic elements segregating it from the rest of the city indicating perhaps, the communal nature of this urban space.

The Palace Complex at Chinikihá

The magnitude of the civic-ceremonial core of Chinikihá, the density of its total population, and the characteristics of the regional settlement pattern indicate the possibility that this center was the head of an autonomous political entity, like Palenque, PiedrasNegras, or Pomoná. Chinikihá has an extension of 1.08 km^2, a total of 362 structures with a maximum population figure of 1,014 to 1,520 inhabitants and a density of 335 structures per km^2. When comparing Chinikihá to Palenque we notice that the latter has an extension and density of structures that is slightly more than double that of Chinikihá, and a population index four times greater (Campiani et al. 2011).

Furthermore, the Chinikihá palace complex is located at the center of the urban settlement, side by side the city´s main circulation axis. This complex, where most of the major civic-ceremonial buildings are located, has an area of 7.5 hectare (figure 6.2). In order to build it, ancient masons and designers took advantage of a wide plain area framed by hills on three of its four sides, a condition that provides privacy to the Main Plaza (Plaza Norte rather than Plaza Sur in figure 6.2): it has only one access, which is located to the west, marked only by a moderate slope in the terrain. All the buildings framing the main square correspond to an array of emblematic constructions for the whole community: to the north, a pair of temples located 8.5 m above the Main Plaza level and to the south a four-tiered building (named “La Gran Pirámide” in 1901 by Teobert Maler). This building rises on top of a series of terraces having principal importance over the site. The palace uproots from the plaza level and occupies its northeast corner; it is built around two squared patios bounded by vaulted corridors two levels high on its eastern side, both leaning toward the hill slope. Simultaneously, the palace and the ballcourt create a private courtyard on the east. The Main Plaza is divided into two sectors (North Plaza and South Plaza) of approximately the same size (about 6,000 m^2) by a central building, the A-1 Structure. The placement of A-1 divided a spatially continuous space creating two plazas characterized by a different frame of buildings: the northern sector surrounded by the paired temples and the palace, whereas the southern sector is delimited on the east by the ballcourt and to the south by the monumental access to the Gran Pirámide.

The palace complex with its central position and restricted access contributes to the spatial separation and identification of residential groups: the east group stands clearly for its size, for the privileged entrance that links it to the Main Plaza, and for the characteristics of its households. Here we find the biggest and most formally elaborated architectonic compound of the site. As it happens with the palace of Palenque, we cannot confidently infer a residential function for Chinikihá’s palace, but it is plausible that this compound functioned as the residence of the ruling family at least in its first moment of occupation. These two occupational stages have been detected in ceramic assemblage variation found in several of the palace’s deposits as well as in the evident changes in building technique present over the site during Chinikihá’s last occupation phase. These changes coincide with a strong presence of Palencano material markers (both stylistic, in ceramics; and technological, in construction materials), which signals the clear Palenque influence in the eighth century. This moment corresponds to a period of major construction effort at Chinikihá, despite the fact that the architectonic constructions and enlargement of several buildings might suggest a less elaborate quality in the carving of the stone façades and in the structural composition of the buildings, leading to diffused collapse of the constructions. These elements show the short-lived nature of Palenque presence at Chinikihá and emphasize the haste of those works. Looking at the architectonic composition of Chinikihá, it is easy to appreciate the emblematic position of its urban core, which stands literally at the center of the site, reaffirming its political and social significance. This area functioned as a physical node but also as the heart of the communitarian dynamics. Its monumental buildings are markers inside the settlement,

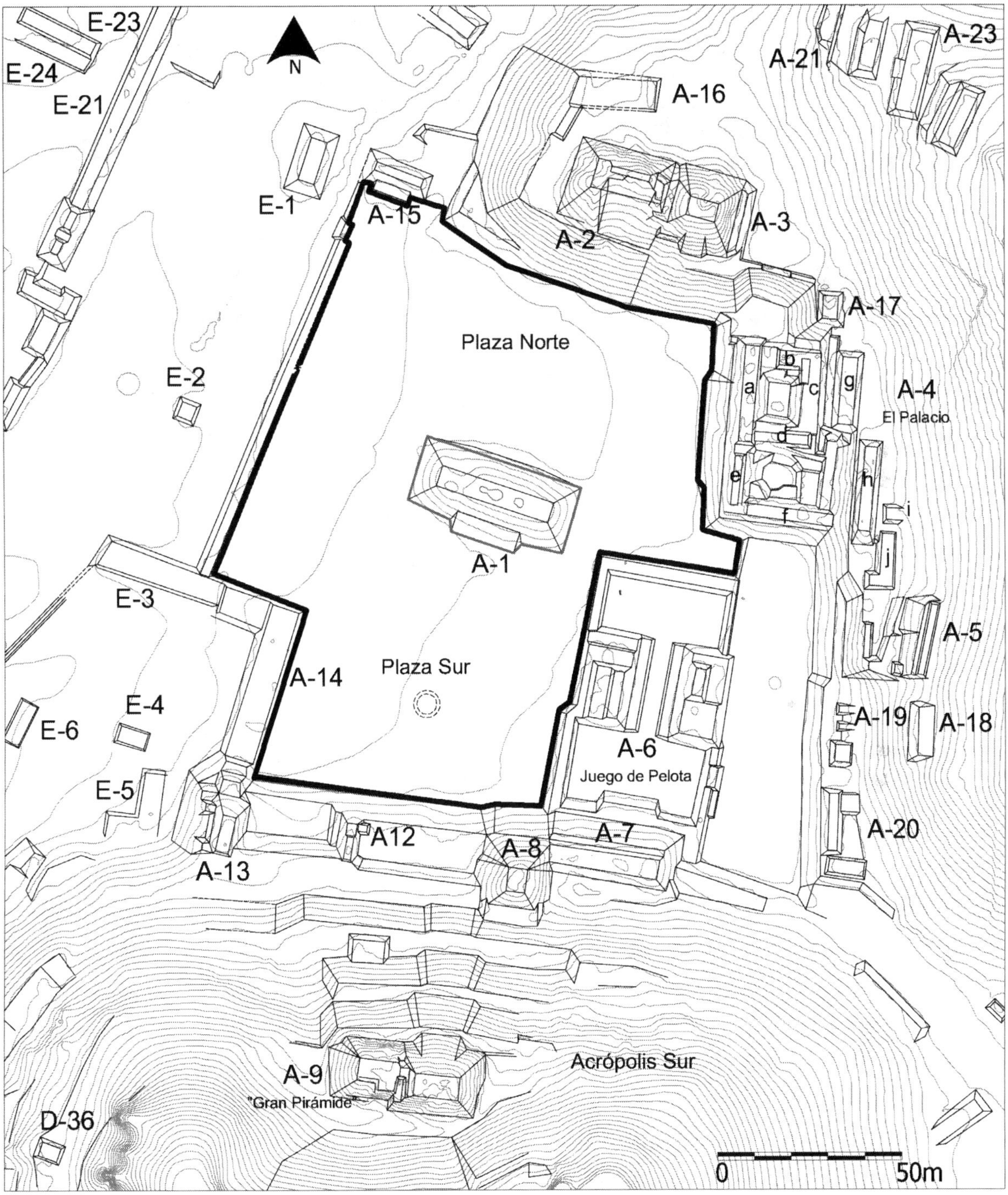

FIGURE 6.2. The Chinikihá's Palace Complex and plaza limit.

constantly indicating where the center of political power is located and where public events were going to be carried out.

The Expansion of Palenque Influence in Its Hinterland

Recently, our research in the region has allowed a clearer understanding of Palenque settlement patterns. Needless to say, our current knowledge is heavily skewed toward the last moments of regional occupation (Murciélagos-Balunté ceramic phases: AD 730–830). Nevertheless, we consider that these one hundred years of regional occupation constitute a moment of great innovation and development from several points of view, especially as indicated by the filling-in of unoccupied territory by new settlements. On the other hand, textual evidence indicates the existence of important individuals who lived in centers that were capable of amassing a sizable population surrounding its civic-ceremonial complexes. Approximately 28,000 individuals inhabited the study region during Balunté times (AD 730–830) and were distributed over 609 discrete settlement units ranging from isolated platforms to complex civic-ceremonial centers. Nine civic-ceremonial centers are regularly spaced in this region (see figure 6.3). They are surrounded by minor settlements forming discrete areas of settlement nucleation, each one of them reproducing the format of a palace compound.

As we will try to argue, the settlement data show a similar phenomenon of population concentration (as shown by the Palenque and Chinikihá cases) within the political microcosm formed by rural palace complexes and the communities in their respective regions of influence. It is very clear from a glance at distributional maps that settlements in the region tend to congregate around minor centers showing civic-ceremonial architectural features.

To further analyze this capacity of attraction we use a digital elevation model (DEM) and digital image shading (DIS). With a resolution of 20 m by 20 m, we were able to carry out a geographic information system (GIS) analysis aimed to characterize the ground in terms of numerical values, depending on the different angles of slope, expressed in degrees (0°–90°) or percentage (where 0° = 0 percent and 90° = 100 percent) (Wheatley and Gillings 2002:120). The slope map generated in this manner shows graphically the places where the slope is more pronounced and therefore, more difficult to move. From the slope calculation, several maps were created (Wheatley and Gillings 2002) with a main focus on accessibility and degree of resistance of the ground (friction).

Armando Anaya, in his work on the upper Usumacinta, carried out empirical observations over time and distance in which a person could walk with or without a load on a given slope. He expressed this relation in the following formula: $Y = [0.031\ X^2] + [-0.025\ X + 1]$ where Y = Friction, X = slope, and 0.031 and –0.025 (Anaya 2001; Anaya et al. 2011). Closely related to this formula is the effort involved in navigating through the environment or anisotropic cost calculation (Conolly and Lake 2006; DeMers 2009; Wheatley and Gillings 2002). This calculation involves not only the proximity between points but also the roads and restrictions provided in the field, from a source to different destinations. For the area of Palenque, the first- and second-order sites were used as

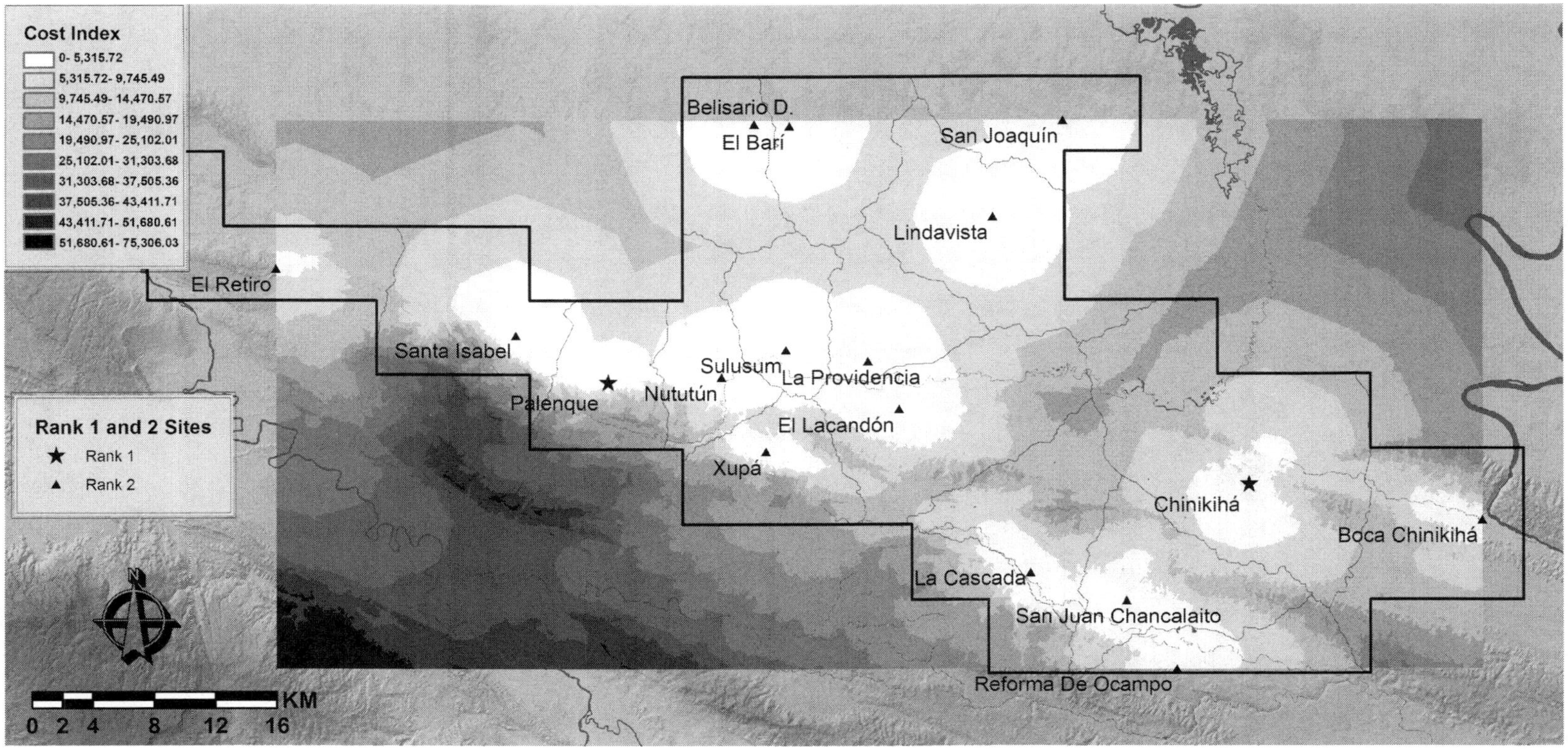

FIGURE 6.3. GIS cost map and area of influence around first and second rank sites.

points of origin and destination for spatial analysis in GIS (Flores 2011; Liendo Stuardo 2011).[1]

The result creates a map with hues of black, from dark to white emanating from each of the sites of rank 1 and 2 (figure 6.3). This variation is determined by the combination of two parameters: the distance and the effort needed to arrive from one place to another. Thinking in archaeological terms, the area showing the same tone of black could be seen as the primary area of access from secondary centers. All the sites located within each one of these sectors have the same potential to be influenced or directly controlled by the nearest secondary center (in terms of distance and easy access). The GIS analysis carried out in this way helps a logical interpretation that goes beyond the traditional maps and spatial analysis, adding an element of reality.

We think that the areas formed this way show a clear pattern of frequent and regular relationships among populations living close together. There are several reasons for the conformation of a pattern like this: coordination of productive activities or the regular participation in public ceremonies. Hypothetically, we could define these territories as places where a broad array of social relation was concentrated through the daily interaction among individuals (figure 6.3). We propose that main plazas spread across minor ceremonial centers played a central role in the integration and reproduction of the settlement system at large. Within each minor ceremonial center, the civic-ceremonial architectonic elements associated with the Main Plaza replicate the format of a palace complex. In a similar manner each one of these minor ceremonial centers reproduces the same process of population congregation around Palenque or Chinikihá's palace complexes in their own areas of influence.

To advance the idea that main plazas at major sites in our study region might have served as places for communal periodic events, we followed Inomata's suggestion that those places served as potential theatrical spaces, and we investigated the capacity of those areas to accommodate a number of spectators (Inomata 2006a). Based on a study of the Andean world by Jerry Moore (1996b:146–152), Inomata approached the capacity of Tikal, Copán, and Aguateca plazas according to three different values of square meters per person: 0.46, 1, and 3.6 (Moore 1996b:811–816). We decided to apply those same values to first- and second-rank sites surveyed by the Proyecto Integración-Política en el Señorío de Palenque and Proyecto Arqueológico Chinikihá (table 6.1) as a heuristic tool in order to search for meaningful patterns of possible plaza uses. We then proceeded to extend this analysis to their own sectors of influence, considering the probable population size of each settlement (table 6.2). The 3.6 m^2/person result turned out to be the best representative value of our analysis, because it provides the most useful correlation between the area of public space at secondary sites and their local population (areas of influence). As we see in table 6.1, in the majority of cases the plaza's capacities exceeded the resident population. Nevertheless, the result of the regression analysis presented in figure 6.4 shows a very strong and significant correlation between the capacity of the plaza and its local and surrounding population ($R = 0.914$, $Rsqr = 0.835$, $t = -2.864$, $p > 0.005$).

This result strengthens our hypothesis that residents living in discrete settlements in their respective regional sectors might have attended regularly their

TABLE 6.1. Estimated Capacity of Plazas at the First and Second Rank Sites

Site	Estimate Population (5.6 person/plat)	Plaza Area (m^2)	0.46 m^2/person		1 m^2/person		3.6 m^2/person	
			Capacity	% Population	Capacity	% Population	Capacity	% Population
Palenque*	8,388.8	40,840	88,783	1,058.3	40,840	486.8	11,344.4	135.2
Chinikihá	1,960.0	12,965	28,184	1,437.9	12,965	661.5	3,601.0	183.7
Xupá	78.4	5,577	12,123	1,5463.0	5,577	7,113.5	1,549.0	1,975.8
El Lacandón	403.2	3,004	6,350	1,574.9	3,004	745.0	834.0	286.4
La Cascada	190.4	10,188	22,147	11,631.0	10,188	5,350.0	2,830.0	1,486.3
La Providencia	84.0	3,639	7,910	9,416.7	3,639	4,332.1	1,011.0	1,203.6
Nututún	145.6	4,208	9,147	6,282.3	4,208	2,890.0	1,169.0	802.9
Santa Isabel	229.6	5,375	11,684	5,088.9	5,375	2,341.0	1,493.0	620.3
Sulusum	106.4	1,773	3,854	3,622.2	1,773	1,666.3	492.0	462.4
Boca Chinikihá	106.4	17,499	38,041	35,752.0	17,499	16,446.0	4,860.0	4,567.0
El Retiro	173.6	3,682	8,004	4,610.6	3,682	2,121	1,023	589.3

*Note that the area of the plaza presented here is the result of the sum of five areas (see figure 6.3).

TABLE 6.2. Estimated Capacity of Plazas at the First and Second Rank Sites in Relation to the Population of Each Area of Influence

				3.6 m^2/person	
Site	Plaza Area (m^2)	Sites/ Region	Population/ Region	Plaza Capacity	% Population
Palenque	40,840	71	9,402.4	11,344.4	121
Chinikihá	12,965	97	2,419.2	3,601.0	149
Xupá	5,577	25	470.4	1,549.0	329
El Lacandón	3,004	94	1,702.4	834.0	49
La Cascada	10,188	29	548.8	2,830.0	516
La Providencia	3,639	13	246.4	1,011.0	410
Nututún	4,208	33	560.0	1,169.0	209
Santa Isabel	5,375	18	347.2	1,493.0	430
Sulusum	1,773	21	744.8	492.0	66
Boca Chinikihá	17,499	109	868.0	4,860.0	560
El Retiro	3,682	23	543.2	1,023.0	188

*Note that after receiving Jerry Moore's commentary chapter, we realize that some of the centers listed above lack exhaustive maps that express their real extension, for example, Xupá and La Providencia, both show huge plaza capacity in comparison to their actual population.

immediate major sites during significant gatherings. Main centers are not the only focal points of political, economic, or religious superstructure (materialized in the public buildings of their core) but places where their public plazas and the cyclical events that took place in them brought together the majority of the population and offered people the occasion to meet, exchange, negotiate, and strengthen their sense of community.

Final Thoughts

We can argue that the political importance of plazas in our study region might stem from the fact of their being culturally defined and of having, at least, three common features:

Plazas functioned as social markers that allowed the sharing of a common social identity.

Plazas were relational spaces where more extended social contact was possible, and where the differences between class, gender, or age could be suspended by the participation in collective activities that created a common identity.

Plazas served as historic mediators connecting generations and moments within a shared history.

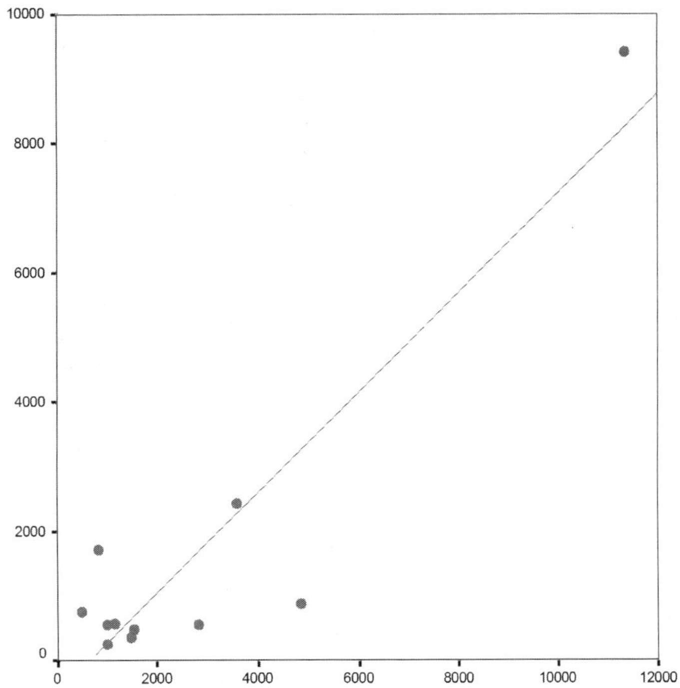

Plaza Capacity (3.6 msqr / pers)

Model	R	R Square	Adjusted R Square	Std. Error of the Estimate	Change Statistics				
					R Square Change	F Change	df1	df2	Sig. F Change
1	,914	,835	,816	1140,8671	,835	45,397	1	9	,000

Model Summary
a Predictors: (Constant), Capacidad 3,6

FIGURE 6.4. The correlation can be considered very high with a correlation coefficient of 0.914 Pearson's *r* close to 1. The correlation is directly proportional, in which a larger plaza capacity corresponds to more population. Furthermore, the correlation coefficient *Rsqr* suggests that 83.5 percent of the variation in population size is explained or represented by the capacity of the plaza. In other words, the independent variable (capacity of people in plazas) explains up to 83.45 percent of the observed variability in the dependent variable (population number). The model has a confidence between 99 percent and 99.5 percent (99–995) and a significance between 1 percent and 0.5 percent (.01 > p > .005), with 22 degrees of freedom.

As mentioned above, 609 discrete units ranging from isolated platforms to complex civic-ceremonial centers forming a continuous string of settlements stretching in an east-west direction along the first hills of the Sierra de Chiapas held a population figure of about 28,000 individuals. The archaeological evidence gathered so far (chronological, settlement structure, and architectural patterns) attests to the existence of a fractured political landscape. Populations within the Palenque area might not have constituted a homogeneous sociopolitical unit responding in similar ways to strictly top-down mechanisms impinging upon them. The evidence also indicates a high level of redundancy among the components of Palenque's and Chinikihá's urban and rural landscapes, although the size, density, and architectural complexity present at paramount centers (Palenque and Chinikihá) exceed in several orders of magnitude all other archaeological remains in the region. This alone reveals the disproportionate importance that major centers might have held in practically every single aspect of daily life for the rural population in the region, regardless of social status or settlement residence type. Nevertheless, it would be a mistake to deny the existence of strong local networks of social obligations that integrated rural populations into socially discrete units. In this last regard, the importance of plazas as social mediators allowing the creation of a shared social identity through the participation of people in collective gatherings of a sacred character (processions, rituals, sacrifices, offerings, etc.) or of a more mundane nature (commercial enterprises, feastings, sports, scenic representations, etc.) holds important clues for future research.

Acknowledgments

We would like to thank Takeshi Inomata and Kenichiro Tsukamoto for their kind invitation to participate in the 2011 SAA Symposium, "Mesoamerican Plazas: Practices, Meanings, and Memories." We are sincerely thankful to Gerardo Jiménez for his support in the design and interpretation of several of the analyses presented here.

Finally we would like to thank all the members of our research project at Palenque and Chinikihá.

Note

1. It is interesting to observe another use of the GIS analysis that Alanna Ossa (this volume) proposes with a Monte Carlo simulation to test the existence of and the scale (if it existed) of settlement associations with monumental architectural groups.

CHAPTER SEVEN

Interpreting Plaza Spaces Using Soil Chemistry

The View from Honduras

Kara A. Rothenberg

Archaeological research is often based on material remains, such as architecture, lithics, and pottery. However, much of ancient material culture was made from biodegradable material and has thus not survived in the archaeological record (Cavanagh et al. 1988). This is especially true in humid tropic and subtropic areas of Mesoamerica. Additionally, analysis of the use of space can be difficult at archaeological sites that were abandoned gradually. In gradual abandonment, important objects for interpretation are often carried away, and their context, distribution, and presence are significantly affected and modified (Fernández et al. 2002). To further complicate archaeological interpretation, many spaces, particularly plazas, were often kept clean of material debris thus leaving even less material remains for archaeologists to examine. Nevertheless, chemical signatures of human activities remain, even in tropical areas. Such soils modified by human activity, called *anthrosols*, provide important clues to past activities and space use. The integration of soil chemical residue analysis with excavation data in archaeological research can be used as a powerful method to help researchers understand spatial usage patterns and activity loci. Previous geoarchaeological studies of anthropogenic soils and sediments have shown that specific activities leave characteristic chemical signatures on prepared earthen surfaces (e.g., Fernández et al. 2002; Middleton and Price 1996; Wells 2003, 2004). By analyzing the spatial distributions of a variety of elements within soils, coupled with excavation data, researchers can infer spatial use. Through spatial use, we can further attempt to understand societal relationships. The purpose of this chapter is to show how soil chemical residue analysis can enhance the interpretation of activities within plazas. I will focus on three Late Classic plaza spaces at the prehispanic settlement of Palmarejo, Honduras.

Soil Chemical Residue Analysis and Interpreting Plaza Spaces

The underlying premise of soil chemical residue analysis is that specific chemical compounds are generated as a result of particular repeated human activities (e.g., cooking or tool making). The elements are deposited into the soil, then adsorbed and rapidly fixed to soil particles (Wells and Terry 2007b). This occurs because soil particles hold anions that act like magnets to attract ions of an opposite charge, cations, which create a very strong bond (Wells 2006). Due to this bond, the deposited elements tend to be very stable and resistant to horizontal and vertical movement over time (Wells 2006; Wells and Terry 2007b). By comparing relative concentrations and combinations of elements in the soils, researchers can examine patterns of repeated activities. Relative concentrations rather than absolute concentrations are recorded as many variables affect elemental levels in soils (Wells et al. 2000; Wells et al. 2007). Much of what we know about the relationship between elements and human activities comes from various ethnographic studies on contemporary floors. Most notably, Luis Barba and his colleagues at the Laboratory of Archaeological Prospection, part of the Institute of Anthropological Investigations at the National Autonomous University of Mexico, have worked with indigenous people in their households in rural villages throughout Mexico (see Barba 1986, 1990; Barba and Bello 1978; Barba and Denis 1984; Barba and Ortiz Butrón 1992; Barba et al. 1995). Other ethnoarchaeological studies have focused in different parts of Mesoamerica including Oaxaca, Mexico (Middleton and Price 1996), Guatemala (Ferdández et al. 2002; Terry et al. 2004), and Honduras (Wells and Urban 2002). Studies such as these have found connections between specific domestic activities, such as cooking and craft manufacture, and certain chemical elements, compounds, and soil properties (Wells et al. 2007). Specifically, areas near ovens, fireplaces, and hearths tend to have high pH values and low phosphorus (P) concentrations while also maintaining high levels of calcium (Ca) and carbonates (Wells et al. 2007:213–214). The presence of wood ash, possibly from a hearth or kiln, is associated with high levels of potassium (K), sodium (Na), and magnesium (Mg) (Holliday 2004:302; Wells 2004:71; Wells et al. 2007:217). The deposition of extremely high levels of P can be associated with food and beverage consumption and preparation, with low pH indicating food consumption (Wells and Terry 2007b:385; Wells et al. 2007:213–214). Additionally, Ca and strontium (Sr) have been shown to be associated with the preparation of corn-based food and beverages whereas the presence of iron (Fe) with P has been shown to be associated with areas used for processing agave; these same elements are low in areas where the food was consumed (Wells et al. 2007:214). The elements barium (Ba), manganese (Mn), and phosphorous (P) have been shown to indicate organic refuse disposal, and mercury (Hg) and lead (Pb) have been demonstrated to be associated with craft production (Holliday 2004:303). Finally, the deposition of iron oxide and mercuric sulfide suggest the use of certain pigments, such as hematite and cinnabar, which were often used in ceremonial settings including burials and caches (Wells and Terry 2007b:387). The interpretations of activity loci based on chemical concentrations can aid in further evaluating hypotheses surrounding structures and functions of archaeological sites. Further, soil chemistry has recently been introduced in the investigation of proposed marketplaces. For example, Dahlin et al. (2007) used soil chemistry to support their contention that a plaza space at Chunchucmil, Mexico, housed activities associated with a utilitarian market. This interpretation presents larger organizational implications including the possibility that Chunchucmil operated under a market economy.

Case Study: Palmarejo, Honduras

Turning to the prehispanic settlement of Palmarejo, this section will discuss the use of soil chemistry in the interpretation of human activity patterns at three Late Classic (ca. AD 600–900) spaces. Palmarejo, located in northwestern Honduras, is located in a region referred to as the Palmarejo Valley, which is a part of the larger Naco Valley.

The Palmarejo Valley and Palmarejo

The Palmarejo Valley is a geographically isolated side pocket of the Naco Valley in northwestern Honduras located approximately 20 km southwest of modern-day San Pedro Sula. The Palmarejo Valley is characterized by mountains to the east and west with at least three passageways that lead to the rest of the Naco Valley (Urban 1986). The 15 km^2 valley lies at approximately 100–200 m above sea level and experiences about 1,300 mm of precipitation per year (Schortman and Urban 1994; Schortman et al. 2001; Urban 1986). Alluvial and colluvial fans and fluvial valley fills represent the predominant geomorphic landforms in the valley and the area lies on top of carbonate rock, most of which is schist and limestone (Wells et al. 2013). In prehispanic times, maize and cacao were intensely cultivated in the fertile soils characteristic of these landforms (Urban 1986). The region is home to a large variety of plant and animal species, including deer, peccary, birds, and rabbits, another factor that likely drew people to settle in the region (Urban 1986). The soil record at Palmarejo includes a dark brown to black over-thickened Mollisol epipedon with an argillic subsurface illuvial horizon overlying a limestone substrate. Soils are moderately acidic to neutral, where pH ranges from 6.5 to 7.5, and include clays—varying from 5 to 25 percent—and organics—varying from 5 to 15 percent (Wells et al. 2013).

A total of ninety-six prehispanic sites of various sizes with 665 visible surface structures have been recorded within the Palmarejo Valley (Davis-Salazar et al. 2007). Though Palmarejo Valley occupation stretches back to the Early Classic period, ceramic data suggest that occupation within the valley primarily dates to the Late Classic period (AD 600–900). During this time, Palmarejo emerged as a major political and economic center within the Palmarejo Valley (Davis-Salazar et al. 2007).

With ninety-three structures visible on the surface, Palmarejo is the largest site in the Palmarejo Valley (Davis-Salazar et al. 2007). The settlement dates to the Classic Period (ca. AD 400–1000) and appears to have been the politically dominant center in the valley, due to its large size and location as well as its site layout and architecture (Wells et al. 2007). Excavations have shown a two-stage construction history representing the Early and Late Classic periods. Twenty-eight of the buildings represent monumental platforms with dressed-stone architecture that may have had administrative or religious functions. The placement of Palmarejo seems to be strategic, as it rests near water sources as well as sources for building materials, perlite, and clay (Hawken 2007). Further, it is located near alluvial fans and floodplains containing the most productive and fertile soil in the valley, which would have been ideal for intensive maize agriculture (Wells et al. 2013).

The discussion in the remainder of this chapter surrounds a 1,600 m^2 open space within the heart of Palmarejo that has been designated the North Plaza in addition to two nearby plaza spaces: the South Plaza and East Plaza. The South Plaza measures approximately 1,000 m^2 while the East Plaza covers an area of approximately 2,500 m^2 (Wells et al. 2007). These two spaces were investigated and compared chemically by Wells et al. (2007). This chapter presents additional data collected from the North Plaza.

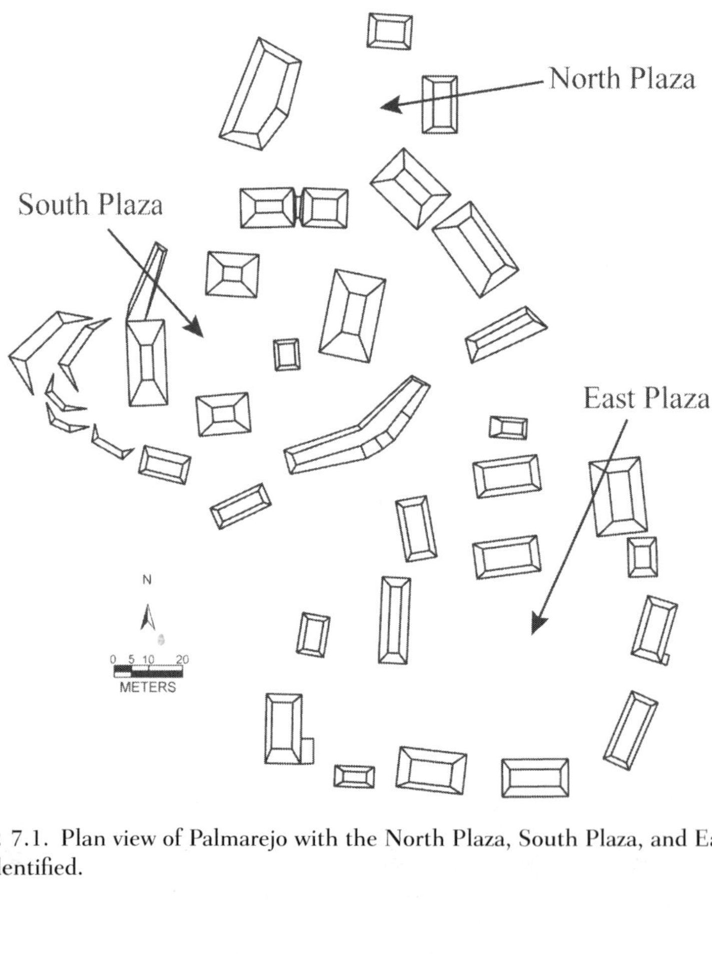

FIGURE 7.1. Plan view of Palmarejo with the North Plaza, South Plaza, and East Plaza identified.

ARTIFACT ASSEMBLAGES

Excavations at all three plazas provided few artifacts on their central surfaces, but a wide variety of materials were in abundance on the edges, indicating that objects were swept to keep the plaza spaces clean. Materials uncovered from the edges of the South Plaza included "large grinding stones, presumably used to prepare foods and beverages, large polychrome serving plates, and large effigy censers (for burning incense) in anthropomorphic and zoomorphic forms" whereas the East Plaza produced "smaller examples of groundstone, small dishes including bowls and cups, and small figurines depicting humans" (Wells et al. 2007:218–219). These patterns suggested to the investigators that those utilizing these two spaces used similar materials, but in different ways. For example, the considerable size of certain ceramic vessels in the South Plaza (such as large cooking and serving implements) indicate that this space was used by larger groups of people than the East Plaza for feasting and other collective activities. Wells and colleagues suggest that the South Plaza may have been primarily a ceremonial space, whereas the East Plaza may have functioned largely as a residential space. Turning to the North Plaza, a large proportion of the material uncovered from excavations were objects primarily associated with ritual use, including *candelero* and censer fragments along with *Spondylus* shells. Though ceramics were uncovered, the small sizes of sherds and the low quantity of recovered materials did not allow a reconstruction of vessel sizes.

CHEMICAL PATTERNING

Though the soil chemistry studies of the East Plaza and South Plaza (Wells et al. 2007) and that of the North Plaza (Rothenberg 2010) were conducted at different times, they were performed in similar manners and therefore can be compared and discussed. We collected soil samples from the ancient prepared surfaces using a lattice grid matrix, at regular 2 m intervals in the South Plaza and the North Plaza and at 5 m intervals in the East Plaza. A mild acid extraction procedure was used in the extraction of anthropogenic inputs from the soils, then the solutions were chemically characterized with inductively coupled plasma-optical emission spectroscopy (ICP-OES) for the samples from the South Plaza and East Plaza and with inductively coupled plasma-mass spectrometry (ICP-MS) for the samples from the North Plaza. Statistical analyses, including principal components analysis (PCA) and discriminant function analysis, were conducted on the data sets to investigate which elements most contributed to the variation within each space. Spatial patterning throughout each space was examined through Kriging, an empirical model used for interpolating unknown values based on known values, in the computer program Surfer, which visualizes the spatial distributions of the elements. Grid intervals were set to equal sample intervals.

Several patterns emerged from the chemical comparison of the South Plaza and East Plaza by Wells et al. (2007). In the South Plaza, activities appear to be differentiated by the north versus south portions of the space. In other words, the northern part of the South Plaza was used for different activities, or combinations of activities, than the southern part. This north-south separation was also present at the North Plaza. In contrast, in the East Plaza, use

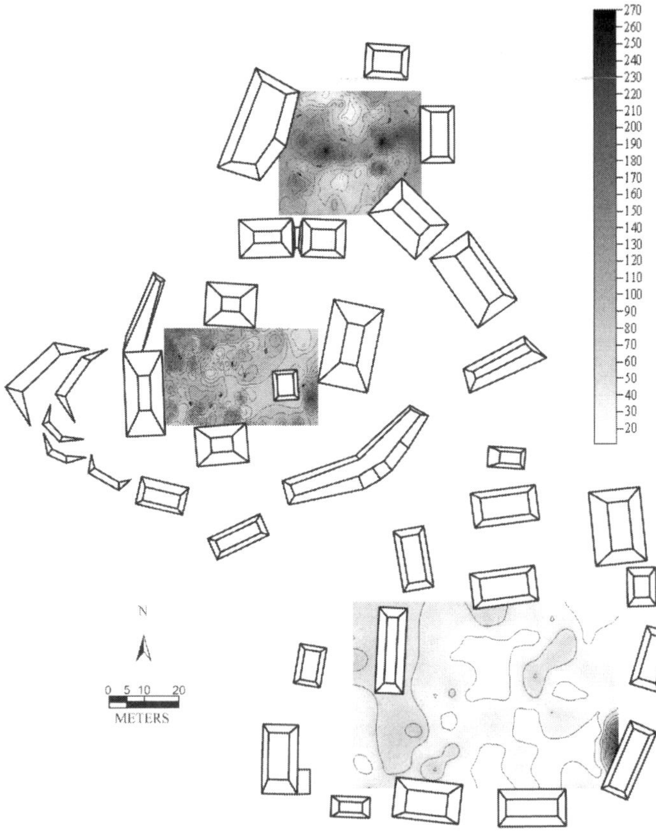

FIGURE 7.2. Kriged image maps overlaid by contour maps showing the distribution of extractable P in ppm (kriging type = point; variogram model = quadratic). Darker hues correspond to higher concentrations.

of the space is differentiated by the west and east areas. In regard to specific elements, concentrations of P, K, Ca, and Mg are patterned across the South Plaza and East Plaza suggesting that some combination of food preparation and consumption, particularly of corn-based food and beverages, may have occurred in these spaces. Groundstone was uncovered from the periphery of both plazas that may have been used to grind corn used in food preparation. The combination of Mg and K may represent the deposition of wood ash from fires used in food preparation. Wells and his colleagues suggest that food preparation and consumption may have taken place across the entire area of the East Plaza, whereas only in certain places within the South Plaza. As mentioned previously, this may have been due to the South Plaza being used by larger groups of people than the East Plaza.

In the North Plaza, concentrations of Ca, Fe, and Sr appear to be patterned; the central and south portions of the space show an enrichment of all three elements in comparison to the northern portion. Other elements, including Ba,

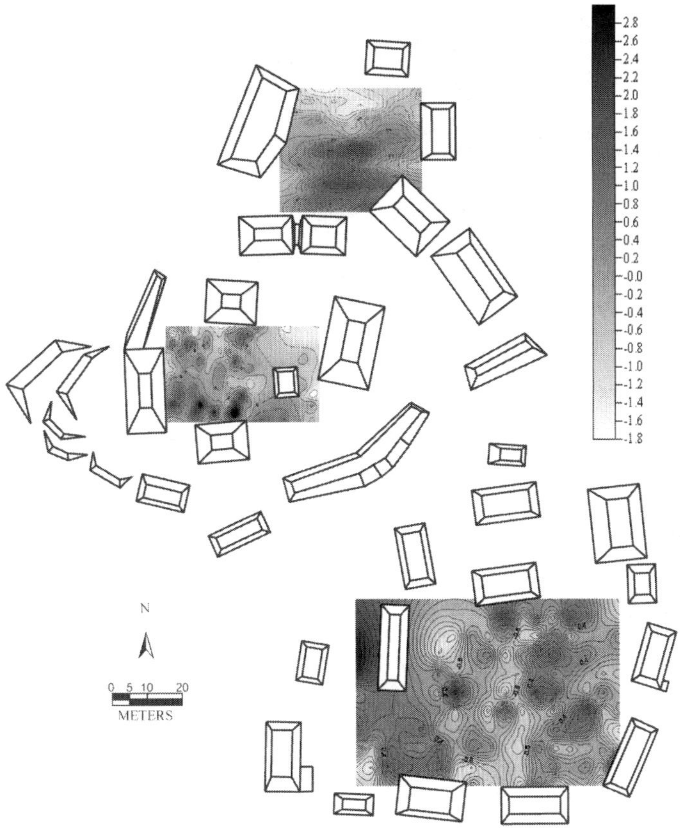

FIGURE 7.3. Kriged image maps overlaid by contour maps showing the distribution of PCA Factor 1 scores (kriging type = point; variogram model = linear). Darker hues correspond to higher concentrations.

Mg, and Mn were distributed rather homogenously. The consistent distribution of Ba and Mn likely indicates that refuse was disposed of outside the plaza space. In contrast to the South Plaza and East Plaza, there does not immediately appear to be evidence of wood ash in specific areas since the dispersion of Mg is homogenous through the space. Interestingly, an enrichment of P occurs across the very center of the plaza (figure 7.2). This pattern is also present, though to a lesser extent, for the distribution of K. These areas overlap with the enrichments of Ca, Fe, and Sr. The combination of P, Fe, Sr, and Ca may indicate that the central portion of the North Plaza was used for the preparation of food and drink that included the processing of corn and agave. This region also corresponds to the middle of both the west and east buildings surrounding the plaza perhaps indicating a connection between these structures.

PCA was conducted separately for each space and showed differences in which elements contributed most to the variation within each space. In the South Plaza, the variance in the results is primarily explained by Mg and Ba

(Factor 1, 60 percent: Mg = 0.95, Ba = 0.63), whereas the variance in the East Plaza is mostly Al, Ba, Mn, and Fe (Factor 1, 77 percent: Al = 0.99, Ba = 0.71, Mn = 0.69, Fe = 0.68) (Wells et al. 2007). In the North Plaza, variation was primarily explained by Ca, Fe, and Sr (Factor 1, 43 percent: Ca = 0.95, Fe = 0.95, Sr = 0.77) (figure 7.3). These results, in conjunction with the spatial distributions and artifact assemblages, suggest that either distinct activities were conducted within each space or a similar range of activities were conducted but in a different capacity.

Discussion

Data suggest that the East Plaza and South Plaza were utilized for similar activities but in a different capacity. The South Plaza was likely used to house large group activities, such as feasting, that occupied the entire area. The data from the East Plaza, on the other hand, suggest that although the space is physically larger, it was utilized by smaller groups. The artifact assemblage from the North Plaza suggests ritual activities were conducted in this space. The same is true of the South Plaza where large effigy censers and large serving vessels were recovered. However, the differences in specific chemical signatures indicated by PCA suggest that there was some degree of functional differentiation between the two plazas. In other words, the activities conducted within each space differed from one another (or the capacity in which similar activities were conducted) in addition to differing from the East Plaza. Does this mean that perhaps Palmarejo had two active ceremonial plazas in use at the same time? Both the North Plaza and the South Plaza appear to be ceremonial, but the exact content of ceremonies and their patterning within the spaces seem to have differed. The North Plaza material is almost exclusively Late Classic, whereas the South Plaza contains artifacts dating to the Late Classic period, but also to earlier time periods, thus supporting that the South Plaza was used before the creation of the North Plaza. However, it is unclear whether there was overlap in the use of these two plazas. It is possible that the use of the South Plaza was abandoned in favor of the North Plaza or that both plazas were used at the same time, perhaps serving as spaces for different types of ceremonies or rituals. Further research may indicate which scenario is more likely.

Conclusion

Overall, this chapter has aimed to show that soil chemistry is an important and valuable tool in the archaeologist's toolkit. In conjunction with information recovered from excavations, soil chemical residue analysis can help researchers better understand activity patterns and loci that may further help us interpret social practices. The combination of excavation and chemical data allows for interpretations about the spaces that would not necessarily have been possible strictly using one line of evidence. This manner of investigation is particularly beneficial when exploring plaza spaces where surfaces were often swept clean after use leaving little material evidence of past activities.

Acknowledgments

I wish to extend my gratitude to Takeshi Inomata and Kenichiro Tsukamoto for inviting me to contribute to this volume as well as helping to guide my concepts into a coherent chapter. Thanks also to Christian Wells and Tatsuya Murakami for their helpful and thoughtful comments on earlier versions of this manuscript. Funding for field work was supported by a grant from the National Geographic Society and the University of South Florida. ICP-MS analysis would not have been possible without the help of Dr. Laure Dussubieux, Department of Anthropology, The Field Museum of Natural History, with funding from the National Science Foundation.

CHAPTER EIGHT

Plazas in Comparative Perspective in South-Central Veracruz from the Classic to the Postclassic Period (AD 300–1350)

Alanna Ossa

Plazas are recognized as important public spaces in Mesoamerica from the Formative period to the present day (Clark 2004; Low 2000). Despite this recognition, they have not often been directly analyzed archaeologically for political and social information. For ancient Veracruz, the studies of plazas have typically been embedded within the study of public space, monumental architecture, and settlement that used mostly architecture as measures of political and social landscapes (Cyphers 1997b; Lunagómez Reyes 2011; Stark and Arnold 1997). Recently, the investigation of plaza space in Mesoamerica has gone beyond the study of architectural plans to space-use focused studies that use plaza dimensions and access points to hypothesize plaza-based activities with political, social, and economic ramifications (Inomata 2006a; Joyce 2004; Moore 1996a). Recent studies, such as Stark's (2011) assessment of ballcourts and their potential use-space and audience in south-central Veracruz, take an experiential approach to public spaces that inspire the current study undertaken here.

Plaza space in Mesoamerica is diverse, varying greatly in size and complexity (Clark 2004), indicating that the data being used to examine these public spaces and its usage requires many different scales of analyses and a firm understanding of local architectural traditions. To evaluate plaza use and purpose in south-central Veracruz, Mexico, I compare the formal construction, average and individual plaza size, access, and settlement context from the Classic (AD 300–900) to the Postclassic (AD 1200–1521) period. My approach also considers a similar scale of analysis by evaluating the relative attraction of plazas and their associated complexes to the proximate residential settlement.

In this study, I begin with a brief overview of the regional comparative background on plazas and plaza-related construction. Next, I introduce the plaza data set from south-central Veracruz using the regional survey and extensive mapping undertaken by the Proyecto Arqueológico La Mixtequilla (PALM) (Stark 1999). For the main analysis, I describe three separate but interrelated measures including area, access, and settlement context. I analyze digitized contour maps and GIS to identify individual plaza size and access points. For the settlement context, I build a Monte Carlo simulation to evaluate both the scale and level of residential associations with monumental complexes that have plazas. I summarize and compare the results of these analyses, identifying significant changes from Classic to Postclassic period plazas in their size, restriction, and settlement context. I argue that these differences are the result of changes in the social, political, and economic use of public space over time. Finally, I discuss the broader implications of evaluating and identifying public spaces within south-central Veracruz and identify future avenues of research.

Concepts and Measures for Evaluating Plaza Space

For the purposes of this study, I define plazas as public space, usually recognized in part by an open space with surrounding monumental architecture (sometimes in formal uniform configurations), and often centrally located within centers. As with Stark's (2011) discussion of ballcourts and their uses, plazas could have served multiple populations. Practice-based approaches to public space stress the experiential aspects of plazas as they relate to relationships among the users. In some interpretations, plazas are used as centralizing mechanisms (Inomata 2006a), where public entrainment and performance supporting political legitimacy is a significant focus. In other interpretations, plazas play a role in social identity with lineages, or other groups of elites, with plaza access identifying the primacy of certain privileged groups over others (Joyce 2004). Pool (2007) examined the differences and similarities among Proto-Classic and Classic complexes at Tres Zapotes (AD 1–600) complexes to identify changing aspects of both top-down and bottom-up political strategizing in construction over time, an approach that can also be applied to evaluate open spaces within south-central Veracruz.

Recent approaches to public spaces in Veracruz have eschewed a solely elite and political organizational approach to consider the competing strategies and overlapping narratives of commoners and elites in understanding the use and creation of public spaces (Inomata 2006a; Pool 2007). I examine three variables to consider these questions, including plaza area, accessibility, and the settlement context. Plaza area can be used to infer how many participants could fit into the area for public events, while the accessibility of plaza space and its configuration can offer insight into ritual narratives and/or social privilege (in the case of restriction) or inclusiveness (if open).

Finally, a major methodological challenge is how one can identify the participation of commoners in the delineation of public space as active agents rather than as a passive audience. I do not have enough contextual domestic assemblages to evaluate the association of monumental architecture and monuments such as stelae with commoner residences, but I can use the settlement context as a line of evidence. Previous research identified that everyone, from elites to commoners, privileged green space (vegetation) and water features within their residence grounds (Stark and Ossa 2007). Every level of Classic period society shared and helped create domestic and public practices involving waterworks and green space. I examine plazas within their settlement context to examine how plaza space was articulated with both residences and monumental architecture.

Regional Background on Plazas

Veracruz is known for its dispersed formal architectural complexes across landscapes, typically interspersed among residential settlements for several square kilometer stretches identified by archaeological survey and reconnaissance (Borstein 2001; Daneels 1997, 2002; Pool 2007; Stark 1999). Previous research has examined the great complexity and variation among formal architectural complexes for many different time periods (Borstein 2001; Covarrubias 2001; Daneels 2002; Inomata 2006a; Stark 1999). For the study region, there are several issues that impact plaza interpretations: multiple period occupations, regionally specific plaza size and layout differences, and varying preservation of monumental constructions within plazas.

Multiple Period Occupations and Construction Phases of Open Space

All of the monumental complexes in south-central Veracruz have antecedent occupation and multiple construction phases. For the Classic period architecture, prior excavations undertaken during the 1940s in Cerro de las Mesas found multiple levels of construction in plazas attached to the "Monument" plaza and the "Stirling" plaza (Drucker 1943:6–11). It is likely that multiple construction phases occurred for all of the plazas analyzed in this study. However, detailed excavation information is not available for most of the monumental complexes within the region. Future plaza-focused research is required in order to evaluate construction records for individual plazas over time. For now, the available evidence allows general comparisons of plazas on a broad chronological time scale, encompassing Classic (including the Late Classic, AD 300–900) and Postclassic (including Middle and Late Postclassic, AD 1200–1521) periods. For this study, I focus on the plan data obtained from the contour maps and GPS footprints to establish a rough "area" measure with which to compare Classic and Postclassic period plazas with the recognition that these could have changed during their use within their respective time periods of several hundred years. Plaza construction over time is not the only factor to consider in assessing public space in Veracruz; analyses of regional variations in plaza areas also offer important insights into how size and access should be assessed.

Relative versus Absolute Plaza Size

Any study of plaza size must also take into account regional patterns of public construction to understand how to interpret the variation among the plazas. Previous research that used settlement pattern data from both south and south-central Veracruz identified regional differences in plaza dimensions between the two areas (Berney 2003). Berney (2003) describes regional differences in plaza dimensions based on measurements taken from the contour maps of architectural complexes produced by major survey projects including the Jamapa-Cotaxtla Basin project (Covarrubias 2001), PALM (Stark 1999), Proyecto Arqueológico Hueyapan (Berney 2003), and Borstein's (2001) survey in the San Juan and lower Coatzacoalcos drainages. Plazas in south-central Veracruz were larger and squarer in shape, possibly reflecting variations in building and using space in plaza activities compared to southern Veracruz (Berney 2003). These differences indicate that there are regional traditions in relative plaza size and shape identified by field measurements, even given differences in field methods and survey techniques.

These data suggest that absolute plaza size may not be the most meaningful measure upon which to base analysis. In other words, the absolute size of a plaza within the PALM survey may not be directly proportional to the amount of people who could fit within the space. Instead, local regional traditions for building these public spaces and their surrounding architecture could be a major determining factor. In my analyses, I use plaza sizes as a relative local measure for assessing the potential for public events in plazas for each time period rather than as an absolute measure directly linked to the population that may have used it. A relative measure is generated by comparing plaza areas for each time period separately within the regional data set.

Temple Platforms and Stone and Clay Monument Associations with Plazas

A related issue concerns the monumental stelae, clay altars, and clay *tableau* (life-size idols) associations with the major plazas of the large centers of Cerro de las Mesas and Azuzules. Based on the remains from all of the major local centers, including Cerro de las Mesas, Zapotal, Azuzules, and Nopiloa, stone and/or clay monuments were recovered from plazas and various large buildings in most cases. Some stelae may be from public areas, some may be from private areas. In some cases the stone monuments had scripts, in others, the surfaces were too eroded to identify any designs, but we may suspect that they were similarly inscribed. In an area like south-central Veracruz, which has no natural source of stone, these monuments represented significant investment in both procuring and processing. Therefore, their association with some of the larger plazas could indicate the relative importance associated with different kinds of public or elite space within the region. For example, in Azuzules, one stela was recovered in the mostly enclosed patio of a monumental structure that may have been an elite residential unit. For this study I do not attempt to evaluate stone monument associations because modern disturbance makes the associations challenging to evaluate.

In addition to stone stelae and sculptures, it is likely that clay or ceramic monuments may have also played an important role in the creation of public and ritual spaces, as indicated by both the Mictlantecuhtli and associated clay idols found within a structure at the Classic period site of Zapotal (primarily Late Classic), located directly north (and adjacent) to the survey area. Another likely clay decorated altar was found by Drucker (1943:7) in Mound 1, located along one side of the Monument Plaza in Cerro de las Mesas. It was too crushed to be properly identified but is probably similar in nature to the one found at Zapotal (Torres Guzmán 1972; Torres Guzmán et al. 1975). There is an association of the large clay idols with public buildings for the Classic period occupation according to PALM data, although a larger regional study has not yet been attempted. Unfortunately, current evidence does not allow the evaluation of stone stelae, sculptures, clay altars, and their associations with plazas.

Regional Factors and Interpretations of Plaza Dimensions

In my interpretation of plaza dimensions, I recognize that current coarse-grained chronological control of plazas could be obscuring changes in plaza size, access, and even usage over time. Plazas were dynamic spaces so the construction and reconstruction of various buildings and monuments both around and within them could make a difference in how one can interpret how public space was being used, and by whom. Evaluating these complex and diachronic processes using only contour maps and residential associations has unique challenges. Although I cannot assess the potential changes and monument constructions of plazas that could be impacting use, I can apply multiple scales of analyses to consider how different groups may have been using them. In the following analyses, I compare plazas at three different scales: individual, aggregate (by time period), and settlement context to capture different social perspectives of this complexity.

South-Central Veracruz Plazas

Intensive settlement pattern research undertaken by the Proyecto Arqueológico La Mixtequilla (PALM) I and II, undertaken by Barbara Stark, form the basis for the following study of plazas and associated monumental complexes (gray space) in the western Papaloapan basin of south-central Veracruz. The topic was inspired by research undertaken by Stark (1999) to assess formal architectural complexes and their role in settlement functions from the intensive survey and contour maps constructed during the PALM projects. The plaza information that I evaluate was mostly obtained from the centers and monumental complexes in a contiguous block of survey, or "main block" of the PALM projects; the main survey block is located in the Blanco delta in south-central Veracruz, just southwest of the modern port city of Veracruz, Mexico (figure 8.1).

These data include the centers and related complexes of Cerro de las Mesas, Azuzules, and Sauce, in addition to minor monumental complexes and potential centers of Mixtequilla, Moral, and so forth. The identification

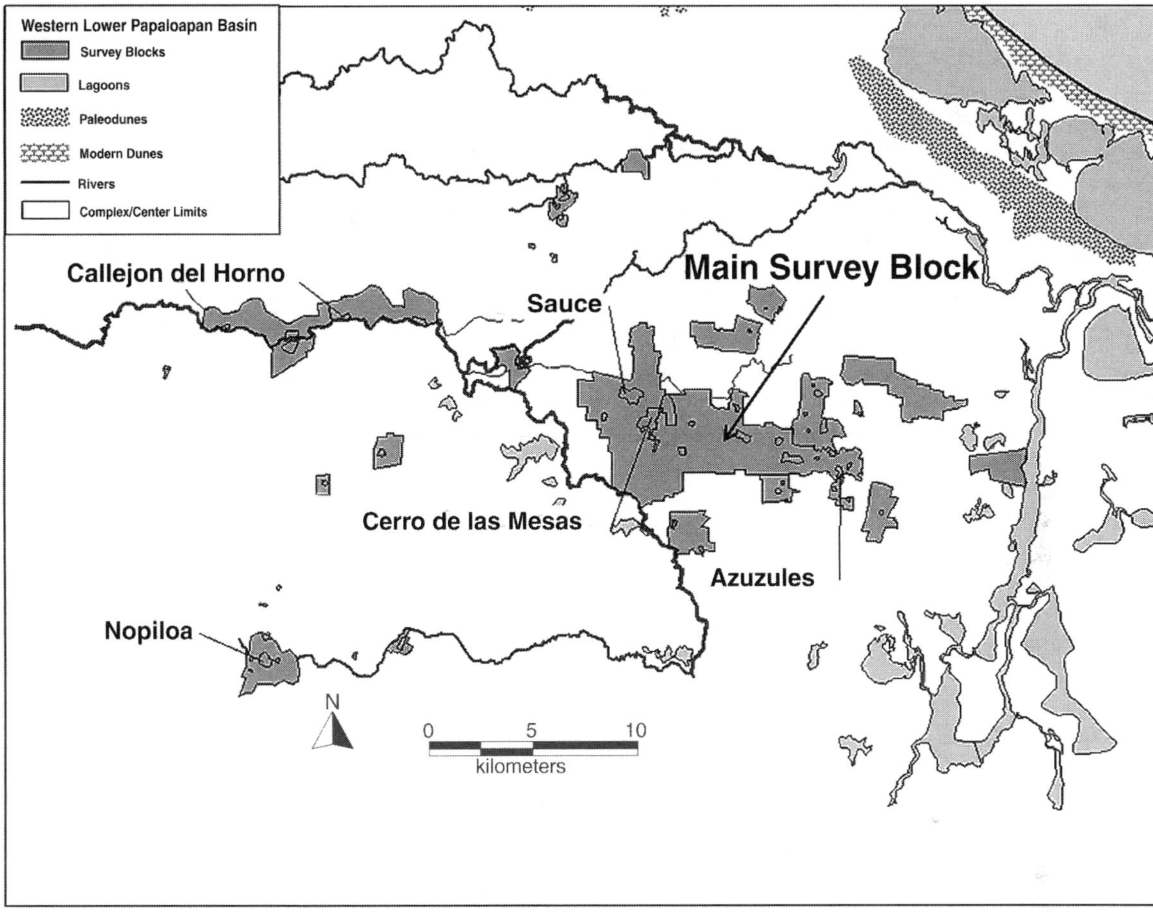

FIGURE 8.1. Map showing major Classic and Postclassic centers within PALM survey blocks in the western lower Papaloapan basin in south-central Veracruz, Mexico.

of centers and their related complexes in the Mixtequilla can be challenging (Stark 1999:221–222) given the dispersed nature of both the settlement and the formal architectural complexes across the survey area. Centers serve as civic-ceremonial loci and likely include some amount of centralized social and economic activities. The densest portions of the formal complexes of Cerro de las Mesas, for example, are easy to identify. Less clear are the roles of associated and spatially more distant formal complexes. In some cases, survey and mapping were limited only to the main block of formal constructions, and did not include outlier formal complexes or settlements. For example, the center of Nopiloa in the Guerengo drainage to the southwest of the main block is used in the plaza size and access analysis; however, Nopiloa is excluded from the settlement attraction analyses as I cannot examine its settlement context fully because the survey did not extend much farther than the immediate environs of the center. I also include the small Late Postclassic center of Callejón del Horno, located in a survey block upriver along the Blanco River, in the size and access analysis because it is the only representative center of that time period found in the region. As with Nopiloa, I do not consider Callejón del Horno in the settlement attraction analysis because the survey did not extend much beyond the immediate environs of the Blanco River (figure 8.1).

In evaluating public space within the PALM study area, I focused on plazas and did not attempt to identify other likely areas of public space because of methodological issues with identifying cultural features in zones that were mapped only using GPS. To evaluate and compare area, access, and settlement context, I used the contour maps created during the PALM project for each of the monumental complexes and centers in combination with the settlement pattern survey data. Contour mapping of the majority of these centers were undertaken by Barbara Stark and Lynette Heller, who kindly allowed me permission to use them in my study. For the Early Classic to the Late Classic period (AD 300–900), this meant identifying plazas by their surrounding suite of buildings that were typically a highly formal arrangement, first identified by Daneels (1997). For the Postclassic period, I used the contour maps to locate the open areas associated with the major public buildings to identify likely plazas and public space. In the following sections, I compare the Classic and Postclassic plazas at the individual, aggregate, and regional settlement scale.

Classic and Postclassic Comparisons

The area of a plaza has been used elsewhere in Mesoamerica to evaluate the potential audience for political and ritual performances (Inomata 2006a:816). When I use the term *plaza size*, I refer to the plaza area as a proxy for overall use space, or the number of people who could fit simultaneously into each plaza space. I recognize that plaza area may not always indicate the amount of people who participated in using this likely public space. Additionally, as stated earlier, there are regional issues in using absolute size as a measure. Therefore, for my study, I compare plaza spaces relative to the study region and for each time period when I discuss potential meanings and uses.

Plaza access, in addition to area, is another measurable way in which one can consider political and social interactions in plaza space. Plazas can serve diverse purposes simultaneously, both as sites for political theater, communal consumption, to settle elite scores, and to create and delineate social divisions. For example, in Joyce's (2004) analysis of changing public space of Monte Albán, he interprets increasing restrictions over time as examples of elite prominence in marking off previously public space for elite use. Admittedly, the elite aspect of restricted access in public space may be difficult to interpret in a case such as south-central Veracruz, where there is virtually no ethnohistoric or art historical representational information to suggest elite annexation of public space. Instead, access restriction may simply be an external side effect of formal layouts of waterworks such as ponds and artificial bajos and ritual space for most Classic period centers (see Daneels 1997; Stark 1999). Additionally, restricted ritual space need not always be interpreted as elite usage; it could also be part of publically accessible ritual space that is restricted to practitioners via stages in a ritual cycle. One can imagine a similar space in a modern

Christian church, where the baptismal font or area is restricted in that most people do not pass through the area unless they are undergoing baptism or participating in this ritual with family members, but baptismal fonts are not restricted to a certain group, per se. Based on these observations, one might distinguish between these kinds of restricted access to public spaces, if one includes settlement context.

In examining the settlement context in relation to plaza space, I evaluate the association of residential settlement and plazas; in this case, the earthen domestic mounds that were mapped in the regional settlement survey. Although it is an indirect measure, I argue that plazas and monumental complexes that attract more residential settlement are more likely to be spaces that were publically used. This allows me to evaluate whether plazas with restricted access were associated with residential settlement. If they are associated, it seems more likely that the restricted access of plaza space was not elite or any other group-based in nature, but may represent increasingly formalized ritual space as one might expect to develop over time.

Plaza Area and Access Comparisons

Classic Period

Many Classic period Veracruz plazas were created with a distinctive selection of buildings in a highly formal arrangement. This pattern was identified by Daneels (1997) as a "standard plan" for south-central Veracruz; these arrangements included a conical mound, typically two elongated mounds, and a ballcourt that enclose a space that is a formal plaza (see example in figure 8.2). There are variations on this theme elsewhere in southern Veracruz, where Pool (2007) identifies a Tres Zapotes variant that is similar to the standard plan except they lack a closing mound on one end. These formal plazas are relatively easy to identify based upon their formal design, and although their sizes varied according to the sizes of the surrounding buildings, there are basic similarities among the variants of the standard plan for the study region.

In comparing the plaza area among the standard plan plazas, most of the Classic period plazas are located within greater Cerro de las Mesas for a total of five identified plaza groups. For the most part, Classic period plazas in Veracruz, with the median value for most of the Classic period plazas at 4,475 sq m, are modest in comparison to the large sizes identified for other parts of Mesoamerica such as the Classic Maya centers (Inomata 2006a) and the great plazas of central Mexico such as Tenochtitlan in the Postclassic period (Berdan 1985) (see figure 8.2). There is some variation in size among the standard plan plazas. Two of the central plazas are not particularly large, including both the Stirling Plaza located on a built-up platform and the so-called Monument Plaza, which had many stone monuments and is directly adjacent to a temple complex mound with a clay altar construction similar to the Mictlantecuhtli complex in Zapotal (Drucker 1943; Stark 2011). The two largest plazas at about 6,000 to 7,000 sq m are found at Azuzules, which has a Late Classic period (AD 600–900) occupation and the complex of Zapotal Sur less than

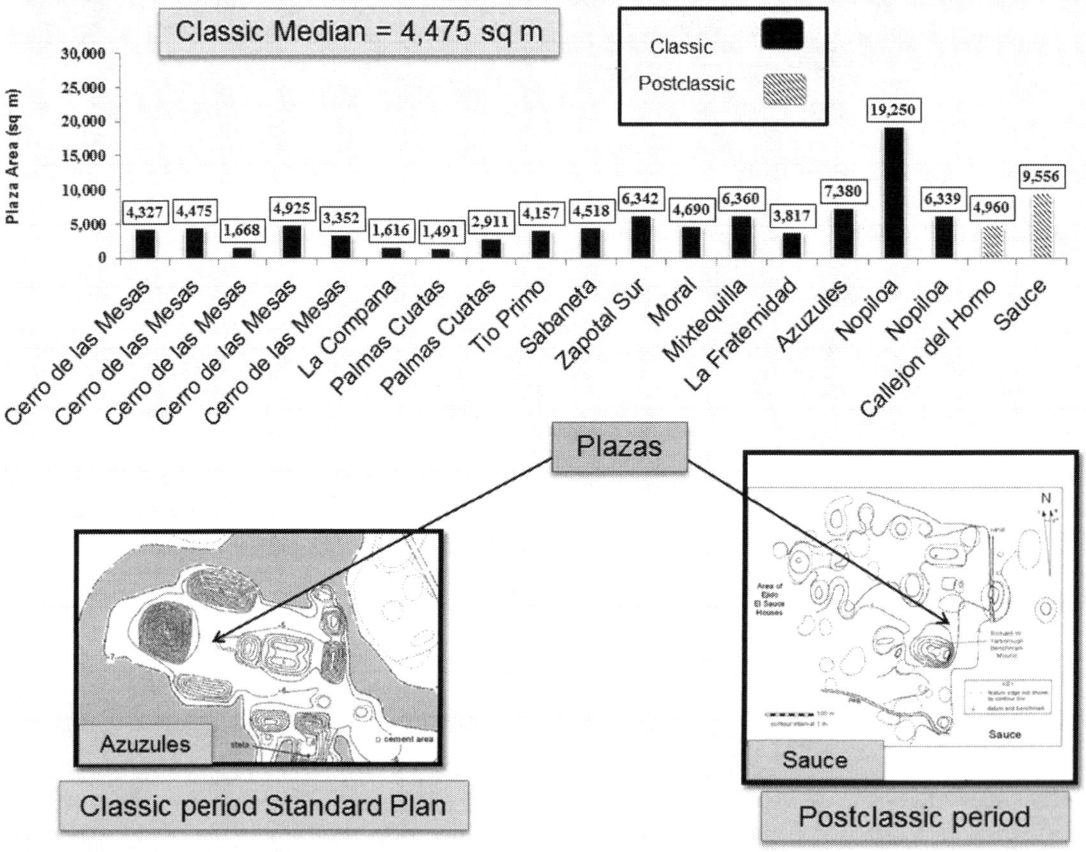

FIGURE 8.2. Chart showing individual plaza areas, an example of a Classic period "standard plan" plaza, and a Postclassic period plaza.

1.5 km away from Cerro de las Mesas, and which also has a Late Classic period occupation, although its construction period is likely Preclassic (Stark 1999). The relatively modest size of most of the Classic period plazas could indicate that their construction was related to the expression of the political claims of different powerful lineages in addition to their potential role in community integration. No single plaza from earlier in the Classic period (not Late Classic) could probably fit the number of people contemporaneously living in the surrounding settlements. The size of these plazas, and their replicative form, with no single plaza really dominating the center of Cerro de las Mesas, suggest that these plazas were used primarily by elite and potentially commoner membership who belonged to units that are smaller than the size of the polity overall, although it is difficult to say for certain. These smaller units of elites and associated commoners could be using many of the plaza groups separately from the whole set of complexes. When one compares total plaza area for each center, the Classic period of Cerro de las Mesas is comparable only to the Late

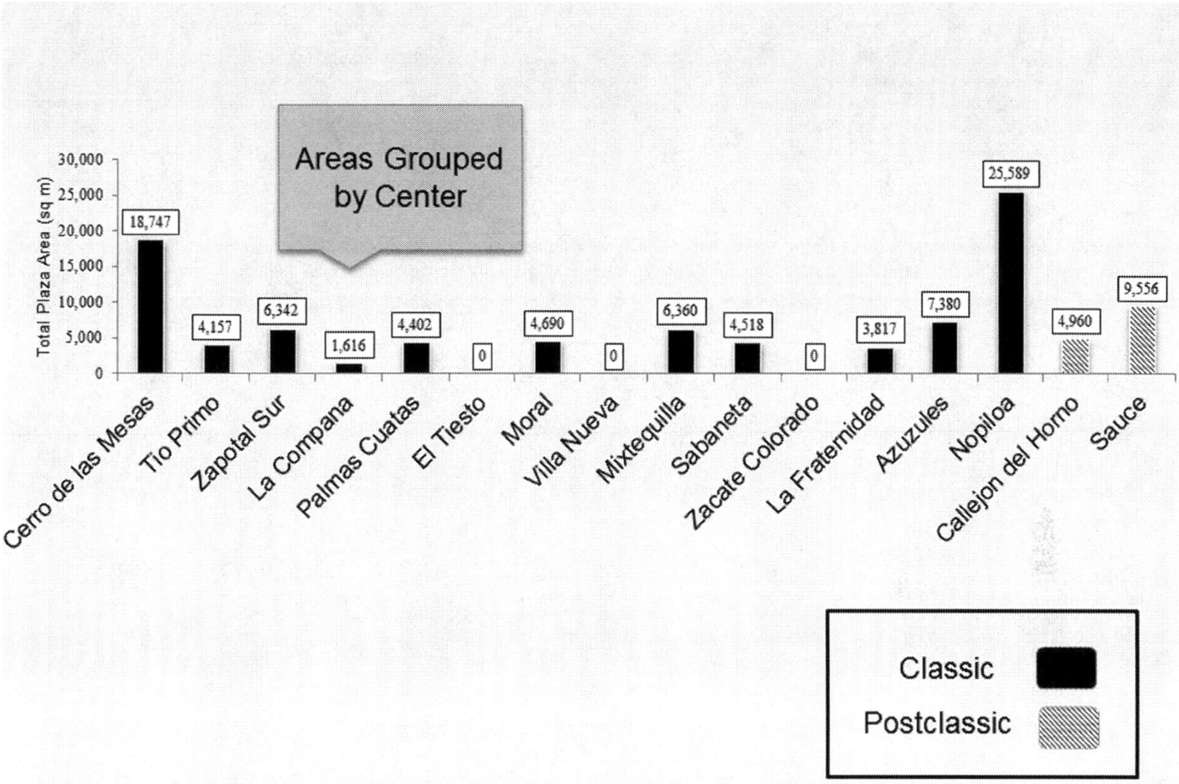

FIGURE 8.3. Chart showing total plaza areas by center and time period.

Classic center plaza spaces of Azuzules and Nopiloa (figure 8.3). This may indicate a shift by the Late Classic toward larger public spaces.

I investigate the role of these spaces at the level of individual plazas by evaluating accessibility to potential audience members whose dwellings were not in the palatial structures close to but not surrounding many of the plaza constructions. Plaza access restriction takes two forms in the Mixtequilla, the accessibility of the surrounding public buildings and the use of waterworks and water features as boundaries encircling plazas. For Cerro de las Mesas, several of the main plaza groups are set apart by waterworks and water features such as formal ponds and bajos that, judging from the ancient river flows, were probably filled with water all year round (and in some cases continue to be so) (Drucker 1943). Stark (1999:211) suggests that chronological shifts may have occurred in artificial pond construction, where they may have changed from being within the center of formal complexes and plazas during the Preclassic to being constructed around the periphery of plazas and formal groups, where they restrict access during the Classic period. Azuzules, dating to the Late Classic, lacks Preclassic pottery and is the most restricted in access (see table 8.1). This pattern is matched by Nopiloa (the other Late Classic center nearby) where most of the public space is surrounded by water (although this may be

TABLE 8.1. Plaza Size Summary, Individual Plaza Access, and Attraction Data for Centers with and without Plazas

Center	Plaza #	Time period	Area (sq m)	Restriction	Water	Buildings	Settlement attraction
Cerro de las Mesas	1	Classic	4,327	Yes	3 sides		750 and greater
Cerro de las Mesas	2	Classic	4,475	Yes	1 side		750 and greater
Cerro de las Mesas	3	Classic	1,668	Yes		Platform access only	750 and greater
Cerro de las Mesas	4	Classic	4,925	Yes	1 side		750 and greater
Cerro de las Mesas	5	Classic	3,352	None			750 and greater
Total Cerro de las Mesas	#1–5		18,747				750 and greater
La Compana	1	Classic	1,616	None			500 m
Palmas Cuatas	1	Classic	1,491	Yes	2 sides		NONE
Palmas Cuatas	2	Classic	2,911	None			NONE
Total Palmas Cuatas	#1–2		4,402				NONE
Tio Primo	1	Classic	4,157	Yes	1 side		500 m
Sabaneta	1	Classic	4,518	None			NONE
Zacate Colorado	0	Classic	N/A				NONE
Zapotal Sur	1	Classic	6,342	None			500 m
El Tiesto	0	Classic	N/A				NONE
Moral	1	Classic	4,690	None			500 m
Villa Nueva	0	Classic	N/A				NONE
Mixtequilla	1	Classic	6,360	Yes	1 side		500 m
La Fraternidad	1	Classic	3,817	Yes	2 sides		500 m
Azuzules	1	Late Classic	7,380	Yes	3 sides		500 m
Nopiloa	1	Late Classic	19,250	Yes	whole area	3 sides	N/A
Nopiloa	2	Late Classic	6,339	Yes	whole area	Platform access only	N/A
Total Nopiloa	#1–2		25,589				N/A
Sauce	1	Postclassic	9,556	None			NONE
Callejon del Horno	1	Postclassic	4,960	None			N/A

the result of modern irrigation, in the past it could simply have been green space filled with vegetation) and the plaza entryways themselves are limited to just two. This finding may indicate that there are temporal changes that supported increasingly elite functions associated with plazas rather than the inclusive public participation of most of the population. Furthermore, a previous study undertaken by Stark and Ossa (2007) indicated that water features and potential green space were associated with all residences within the lower Blanco delta, not just the palatial and public structures. Therefore, the replication of waterworks and green space at monumental and residential scales may indicate communitywide emulation of the social and political functions taking place in plazas, especially by the Late Classic period.

Postclassic

For the Postclassic period, there is a clear break in settlement traditions. The formal planning of the plazas, with recognizable formal groups, and the standard plan and its variants are missing from the corpus. Both of the Postclassic centers considered here, Sauce and Callejon del Horno, have plazas with less obvious boundaries ringing them (such as public buildings). Instead, they are bounded on only one or two sides by large public structures. It is unclear, based on the current evidence, what the administrative function of these structures may be, but they could have held elite residences in addition to public and religious functions. Until they are excavated, it is impossible to know. Besides lacking a formal plan, the ways in which space is controlled and reproduced is also not the same between the two Postclassic centers.

Drucker (1943:7–11) did not find any evidence for the traditional "plaza" group in Middle Postclassic period Sauce (AD 1200–1350), although he identified buildings that he thought were public in character based on their size and construction investments. For Sauce, the Yarborough mound is one of the largest public buildings and has a very flat space along its north side that may be a plaza (Heller 2000:142). The potential Sauce plaza is quite large, at about 9,000 sq m in area, and is one of the largest plazas located in the area (see figure 8.3). Additionally, Sauce's potential plaza, although surrounded by minor buildings, has no obvious restrictions to access (see table 8.1). Another plaza within the Sauce center may have existed around a group of sizeable mounds found within the ejido of Sauce proper; the largest and most promising mound for public architecture has the community's largest church located on top of it (Heller 2000:142, 144). Unfortunately, the heavy disturbance of the modern eijdo settlement makes it impossible to reliably identify this area for dimensions and characteristics.

Callejón del Horno, the only other Postclassic period center identified within PALM, dates to the Late Postclassic period (AD 1350–1521) and is found along the Blanco River, to the northwest of the Sauce center, which it apparently replaces as a primary location during this time period based on pottery evidence (Garraty and Stark 2002). Callejón del Horno, like Sauce, does not have any identifiable plaza group similar to the standard plan model of the prior period. This small center has two conical mounds and a platform

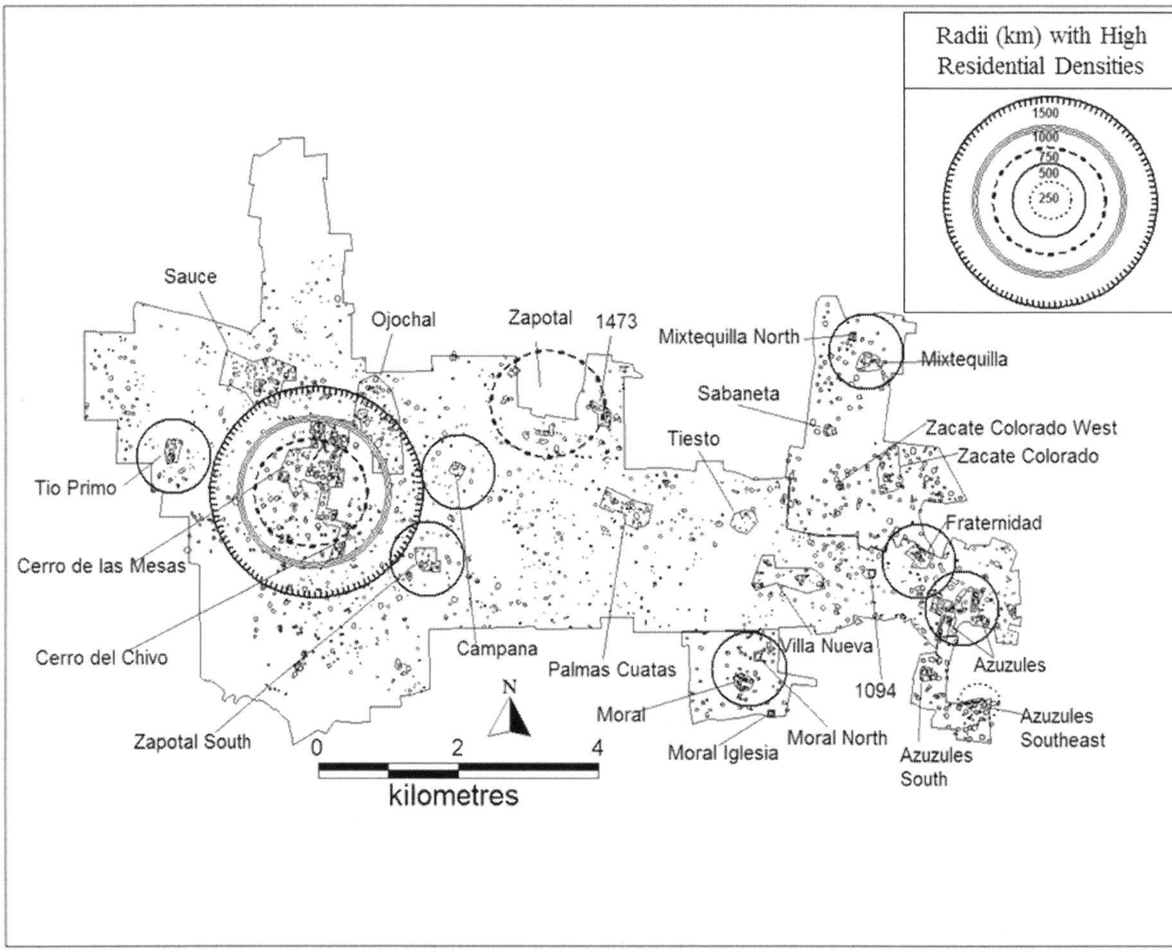

FIGURE 8.4. Simulation results showing the survey area with centers, features, and radii with significant settlement associations identified.

that make up an area of likely public space (to the south) that is similar in size to the Classic period plazas. There are no obvious restrictions in access to the open space associated with this center (see table 8.1).

Generally, Postclassic period plaza areas are much harder to ascertain for the two Postclassic period centers, Sauce and Callejón del Horno; they have less formal construction plans. For Sauce, the potential public space is considerably larger than its associated settlement might indicate (see figures 8.3 and 8.4). For both Postclassic centers, plaza area was identified adjacent to and partly created by the monumental architecture in their core zones. The plaza area in Sauce may be unsurprising given the results of the Sauce Archaeological Project (Ossa 2011) and previous work undertaken by Garraty and Stark (2002) and Heller (2000) suggesting that a marketplace was located somewhere in the center or nearby. This type of economic activity would be consistent with relatively open access that is also observed for Sauce's potential plaza.

However, the activities that may have taken place in this public space remain speculative because no excavation data are available from the plaza except the trenches placed by Drucker (1943) into some of the adjacent public buildings.

Plaza Dimension Discussion

In sum, the plaza dimensional analyses show clear differences between Classic and Postclassic plaza use and conceptualization. Classic period plazas, in many examples, with only one possible entry, exhibit elements of elite expressions of restriction and ritually delineated space that dictated how people had to proceed through these spaces; in many examples, there is only one possible entry. However, these plazas also show a regional scale consistency in terms of water feature association at residential and monumental scales that indicate that a top-down narrative of elite control may be overly simplistic to explain the replication. Classic period public and ritual activities may have become more rigidly formalized over time, with their associated plaza spaces and public areas matching this formalization in their construction and associated waterworks. For the Postclassic period, the few plazas that have been tentatively identified do not have administrative or political functions replicated within their architectural plans in ways that are currently identifiable using the survey data. This lack of replication, combined with their relatively open access and no strong association with water features (although there is an artificial bajo in Sauce), indicates that their use as a form of public entrainment and political expression is not evident using settlement pattern data. At this point, it seems likely that they were a focus of economic activity on the basis of artifact distributions (Garraty and Stark 2002; Heller 2000; Ossa 2011). The size of these two centers, much smaller than the Cerro de las Mesas or Azuzules, is probably also a significant factor. Whatever ritual or economic importance Postclassic public spaces likely had remains relatively obscure in the absence of excavation data for these small centers.

Evaluating Plazas as Settlement Attractors

I undertook a study of the relative attractiveness of monumental architectural groups to residential settlement using a computer program written to assess whether residential features are clustered near complexes. Using a Monte Carlo simulation, I tested the existence of and the scale (if it existed) of settlement associations with monumental architectural groups. Using the empirical residential feature (in this case, earthen mounds) density as a given, I generated random coordinates for these residential features in the same amounts as found in the PALM survey within the main survey block for ten thousand iterations. These simulated results could then be compared to the known empirical spatial patterns of residential features from the survey. My assumption was that a significant departure from random in feature concentrations could be used as a guide to indicate the strength and scale of the attraction of features to formal complexes.

In the simulation, formal complexes remained fixed polygons on the landscape; they were not part of the randomly generated features. Also, all formal complex architecture and its related mound features were not included as part of the "given" feature density of the simulation. I built center polygons in the exact proportions of each center's footprint into the simulation so that the random generation of features would not populate those areas. Raw distances of features to centers were used to measure feature concentration within a range of different radii from each center. Thus, average feature densities around each center were generated for the known empirical data for several different radii and compared to the results of the randomly generated features of the simulation. By comparing the concentrations of features in the empirical data to the simulated data, I was able to evaluate whether the observed settlement attraction was denser around complexes than one might expect due to chance.

The probabilities were calculated as follows: the percentage of runs in which random features around a center reached a density greater than or equal to the empirical densities were the probability that each complex's associated residential features was no greater than the overall feature density for the region. However, the generated probabilities have some flexibility in their interpretation. For example, due to the occurrence of complexes and centers with sizable monumental construction areas, the radii at which large centers are likely to have higher feature densities than random will be the larger radii. In addition, significant departures from random (such as random densities matching empirical densities only about 5 percent of the time), might not adequately account for those complexes whose close proximity to the survey border conflated similarities between empirical and random data due to the boundary effect. In summarizing the results of the simulation, I recognize that there are some boundary problems that may mask patterns of aggregation or segregation of features around centers, for example, Azuzules. Despite these issues, differences were uncovered among the monumental groups. Some were attractive to residences while others were actively disassociated with it, in other words, some monumental complexes had far fewer residences around them than one would expect if the residences were randomly located (figure 8.4). Although I built the simulation specifically to identify which complexes acted as settlement attractors, the simulation framework also allowed me to identify certain complexes as settlement repellants.

Simulation Results

The results of the settlement and plaza association simulation are striking. For the Classic period, some monumental complexes act as settlement attractors while others do not. The associations were deemed to be significant if the empirical densities occurred less than 5 percent of the time (see figure 8.4). Note that for the smaller complexes, the scale at which they are significant decreases after a certain distance. From the results, two interesting patterns emerge for plazas. The monumental complexes that acted as residence attractors also had a formal plaza group in most (but not all) cases (table 8.1). Additionally, complexes that have plazas with restricted access appeared to show stronger residence attraction (table 8.1) for the Classic and Late Classic centers. What do these results mean for our interpretation of general plaza use? It is possible that the more formal plaza groups may have acted as community integrators drawing in associated populations for the Classic period centers. Those Classic period complexes that acted as residence repellents did not have as much obvious public spaces, although they had monumental architecture. Given the stronger association of residential settlement with plazas that had restricted access, it also seems likely that we need not see the restricted access as the result of elite privilege, but that they also offer clues to how plazas created formal and public ritual space that was attractive to all.

Postclassic plazas (and the monumental complexes) showed no attraction to associated residential settlement at any scale. They did not act as repellents either; they were simply not associated with residences in a way that departed from the empirical residence densities. The results of the simulation could show that the scale at which the Postclassic centers acted as integrators is not measurable by closely associated residential mounds.

Conclusions and Future Avenues of Research

The results of the size, accessibility, and settlement context analyses for plazas in south-central Veracruz indicate a clear break in the construction and meaning of public space between the Classic and Postclassic periods. These differences are linked to practices and political differences in the public space represented by most of the plazas. Classic period formal plaza groups have similar areas individually, but large total areas were associated with major centers. There is a shift toward larger plazas in the Late Classic with one main plaza dominating the center (such as Azuzules and Nopiloa) rather than many. There is also support for a shift in waterworks-based restriction to plaza access, supporting increasingly formalized access to ritual space probably beginning in the Classic and reaching full expression in the Late Classic period. However, the settlement context analysis indicates wider participation and emulative processes at work than restricted plaza accessibility alone might suggest. Formal plazas and their monumental complexes acted as attractors to associated residential mounds, even for smaller monumental complexes, and including the Late Classic center of Azuzules. Also, the simulation results indicated that complexes with plazas that had more restrictions on access acted as residential attractors. The key role of plazas in attracting settlement is highlighted by the unexpected findings of complexes that acted as residence repellents. These complexes showed disassociation with residences despite also having water features and monumental architecture, indicating that their lack of formal public spaces is the distinguishing feature. One potential future avenue of research could investigate whether these complexes could have represented elite buildings whose immediate surrounding landholdings were restricted from residences.

Postclassic individual plazas are harder to generalize about since there are so few, but they were large in comparison to their associated settlement. Also, the apparent disappearance of prior plaza groups by the Middle Postclassic period (AD 1200–1350) and the Late Postclassic (AD 1350–1521) could indicate a shift in political use of public spaces linked to new populations and a different political landscape. Plaza access was open, perhaps indicating different uses of public space than in previous periods and is consistent with new populations lacking older local social traditions associated with the formal plaza group. Plazas (and the monumental complexes) showed no attraction to associated residential settlement at any scale, indicating that public community integration took other forms than the formal plaza groups of the prior period.

In summary, the survey and settlement data on plazas for south-central Veracruz indicate their central role in performing integrating and potentially vital functions for the Classic period centers. Postclassic period plazas are much more difficult to interpret politically based on current information, although their economic importance is likely, based on regional economic patterns. Future research targeting plazas that included plaza-based excavations can do much to clarify construction sequences and changes over time, as well as provide more details about how monuments and other architectural features, such as altars, guided the use of public space. Finally, the multiple-scaled approach and Monte Carlo methods used in this study to evaluate individual plazas, aggregate public space, and residential associations with plaza space, offer some new ways of using settlement survey data to infer plaza use and meaning at a regional scale.

Acknowledgments

I am very thankful for the support of my chair, Barbara L. Stark, for the use of the PALM data and use of the considerable fund of PALM contour maps which made this study possible. I would also like to express my gratitude to Lynette Heller, who was responsible for creating and digitizing the contour maps of the PALM projects. I am also grateful to Kenichiro Tsukamoto, who invited me to participate in this project and who was very generous in sharing his insights on plazas. I am thankful for helpful commentary on this research from my mentors and colleagues, including Barbara Stark, Krista Eschbach, Sarah Striker, and Tatsuya Murakami. Finally, the book editors Kenichiro Tsukamoto and Takeshi Inomata, along with two anonymous reviewers, also greatly improved this work and I am grateful for their patience and insight. Any errors or omissions that remain are my own.

PART III

Plazas and Images

CHAPTER NINE

Early Transformations of Monte Albán's Main Plaza and Their Political Implications, 500 BC–AD 200

Javier Urcid and Arthur Joyce

In the field of Mesoamerican studies, the archaeological investigation of political institutions and processes based on the analysis of material culture has been approached from a number of perspectives (Inomata and Tsukamoto, this volume). These include, but are not limited to, the form of architectural units and their distributional patterns (Hirth 1995), performativity (Inomata 2006a), textuality (Sugiyama 1993), and the cultural biographical approach (Ashmore and Sabloff 2002). In this chapter we attempt to combine simultaneously some of these approaches, bearing in mind the ever-present problem of evidentiary scarcity. The nature of our data calls for the detection of patterns, but these are in turn based on deductions that stem from clues (Ginzburg 1980, 1989). We do have relevant data to assume, albeit indirectly, both performative and textuality approaches, but the bulk of the evidence is in the form of actual written texts and visual narratives set in architectural contexts associated with a plaza. As espoused by the cultural biographical approach, we take the inscribed evidence not as invariant signs with an essentialized and universal reading, but as ever-changing symbols whose interpretation was and continues to be contingent on a contextualized semiosis.

Inherent in the architectural design of most Mesoamerican plazas is their dual role as both enabling landscapes (open space) and bounding stages (enclosed space). The first quality bespeaks their multifunctionality and thus their simultaneous and sequential polysemy even within the same life-history; the second quality leads to regimented, controlled, and even restricted access (Tsukamoto, this volume). Given the Mesoamerican quadripartite conception of the cosmos, plazas and their associated buildings materialized the center of such a worldview, and more often than not have evidence of ritual enactments and other performances conducted so as to "center" the world at those paramount axes. Either empty or full, Mesoamerican plazas created novel visual and auditory fields for human perception and must have provided a sense of awe and monumentality, even if the surrounding buildings were not necessarily majestic.[1]

Monte Albán's Main Plaza, which was one of the most formidable plazas of the Mesoamerican world, has been a fertile ground for interpreting how social institutions and ideas were architecturally embodied, and how modifications of the plaza in turn transformed those ideas and institutions (Blanton 1978; Hutson 2002; Joyce 2004, 2009; Winter 2001). More than a century of archaeological research has shown that the urban core of Monte Albán contains complex accretions of building activity; construction sequences are well understood for several buildings within the Main Plaza (Caso et al. 1967; Fahmel 1991; Winter 1994). A major challenge to modeling the dynamic history of the Main Plaza, however, is the difficulty in relating stratigraphically the localized architectural sequences of particular structures. Arguments that the Main Plaza reached a unified scheme as early as the Nisa phase (100 BC to AD 200) are based on the orientation and chronology of the structures now visible around the plaza (Blanton 1978:45; Paddock 1966:111). There is tantalizing evidence, however, of several features beneath the plaza, suggesting a different spatial configuration prior to the beginning of the Common Era.

The constant building and rebuilding episodes that can be attested in the archaeological record create as well the problem of understanding forms of visual communication that were inextricably related to the buildings that faced the plaza or were built within it (also see Cyphers and Murtha, this volume). Orthostats carved with semantic and phonetic writing covered the veneer façades of platforms and buildings so as to render veritable narratives. The jambs and lintels in the entryways to precincts or the columns and inner walls of enclosures were also inscribed so as to convey varied messages. Yet, only a handful of those contexts with writing remained in primary setting by the time modern investigations began. While the constituent elements of numerous dismantled architectural narratives have been found reused in structures built at a later time, certain clues have at times enabled their "virtual" reconstitution (Urcid 2001, 2005, 2011a, 2011b).

In this chapter, we use these clues to develop a preliminary assessment of the early architecture and associated narratives on the Main Plaza and how these architectural, semasiographic, and epigraphic programs were transformed through the first 700 years of urban life, from the settlement's founding circa 500 BC to circa AD 200. Our central question is: what can be inferred in terms of the political life of the city when viewing the history of the Main Plaza as a continuous transformative process (also see Tsukamoto, this volume)? We pay particular attention to key areas of the southern end of the Main Plaza where buildings with grandiose visual displays added to their monumentality. We argue that the creation of such novel landscapes was enmeshed in the political dynamism of the time (also see Inomata, this volume). As part of our argument, we summarize new interpretations that challenge long-held views of

Monte Albán's early architecture and imagery, particularly the meaning of the two major scriptural programs: the so-called "danzantes" of Building L-sub and the "conquest slabs" of Building J (Urcid 1994, 2011a, 2011b).

The Early Configuration of the Main Plaza

Monte Albán was founded circa 500 BC on a previously unoccupied hilltop in the center of the Valley of Oaxaca (Blanton 1978). Archaeological evidence from throughout the Oaxaca Valley indicates that this was a time of political crisis and conflict as well as the development of novel political and religious ideas and practices (Blanton et al. 1999:105–107; Joyce 2000, 2010:128–155; Marcus and Flannery 1996; Spencer and Redmond 2001; Urcid 2011a, 2011b; Winter 2001). One of the first activities carried out at Monte Albán was the construction of the Main Plaza complex, although its early configuration differed significantly from its final layout, which did not become apparent until circa AD 200. Based on indirect evidence, it now seems evident that during the first century of Monte Albán's occupation at least one structure of unknown size and configuration had been built displaying small carved stones with graphic conventions widely deployed at the time in several media throughout Mesoamerica (figure 9.1). One of these blocks (D-18b) was eventually recarved and placed in the façade of Building L-sub so that its earlier imagery was hidden from view.

By the Danibaan phase (550–300 BC), the Main Plaza consisted of an open space delimited by the western row of buildings and much of the eastern half of the massive North Platform (Winter 2001:284–286, fig. 5.4a). The plaza was created by leveling bedrock outcrops and filling in areas to create a flat surface, endeavors that involved considerable resources and labor. Public buildings constructed by circa 400 BC included Building L-sub along the southwestern end of the plaza, whose walls consisted of huge, multiton monoliths many of which displayed carved imagery (Batres 1902:28, Plate V; Caso 1935; Scott 1978a, 1978b). Building IV-sub along the northwestern end of the plaza was a massive platform that included a six-meter-high sloping wall (Acosta 1965:820, fig. 6a–6b). The Danibaan phase version of the North Platform consisted of an enormous architectural complex that encompassed much of the eastern half of the platform's final area and included structures that reached heights of 15 m above the Main Plaza. On top of the North Platform excavations recovered the remains of a temple that included an offering of dozens of fancy grayware serving vessels (Winter 2004:37) that may reference ritual feasting associated with building dedication ceremonies. The structures facing the Main Plaza were constructed of rubble fill quarried locally from the hills around Monte Albán (Winter 1989:42–43). By the Pe phase (300–100 BC), the Main Plaza had seemingly undergone further changes, but these later modifications were still significantly different than the layout of the plaza as we know it today. Some indirect clues suggest the existence at the time of another monumental building whose façade was decorated with finely incised orthostats. Eventually this structure was completely demolished and its inscribed orthostats reused to build three successive versions of Building J. It is this long-dismantled edifice

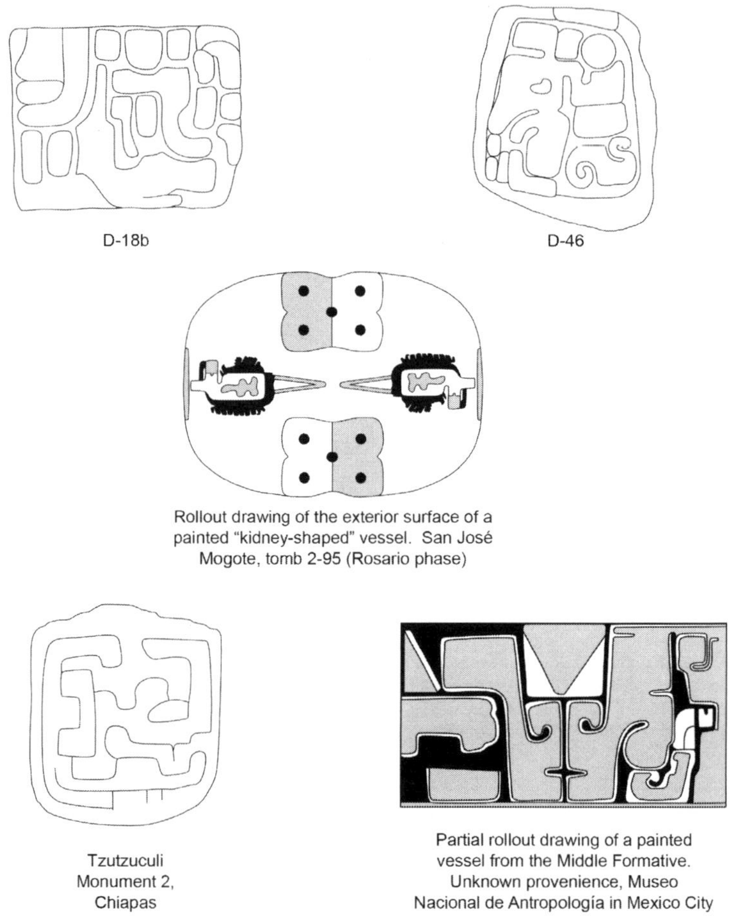

FIGURE 9.1. The earliest known carved blocks from Monte Albán and their comparison with Middle Formative carved and painted materials from other regions of Mesoamerica. Drawing by Elbis Domínguez Covarrubias.

and Building L-sub that formed an important focus of monumental narratives during the earlier life-history of the Main Plaza, and they constitute the core of our analysis.

The Visual Program of Building L-Sub

Of the early buildings around the Main Plaza, Building L-sub constitutes the most daring architectural endeavor of the early inhabitants of the city. Rising 6 m above the Main Plaza, and probably supporting a triad of edifices at the top, Building L-sub made a bold visual statement of community effort and thus identity (figure 9.2). Although previous interpretations view these monuments as victims of human sacrifice (Coe 1962; Flannery and Marcus 1983; Joyce 2000; Marcus 1976; Marcus and Flannery 1996; Winter 1989), we interpret the program as a series of human figures that constituted a sodality organized around age-grades (see Urcid 2011a, 2011b). The young personages represented in the basal façade of Building L-sub were displayed in alternating rows, changing their facing direction so as to render their procession in a boustrophedon sequence that mimicked the ascent through the staircase leading to the upper structures. The presumed upper edifices, in turn, appear to have had their façades covered with depictions of three higher-ranking echelons of the sodality, including individuals wearing cut-shell necklaces, masked personages personifying the rain deity, and a paramount tier of senior adults who seemingly formed a council of elders. All the members of this age-grade organization are shown bleeding from their groins. Parallel to the allusion of self-sacrifice runs another visual trope: that of invoking ancestral spirits for oracular purposes related to warfare. This theme resorts to the pan-Mesoamerican convention of representing ancestors as horizontal figures shown above the living humans that are standing or squatting (figure 9.3). The varied postures of vertical and

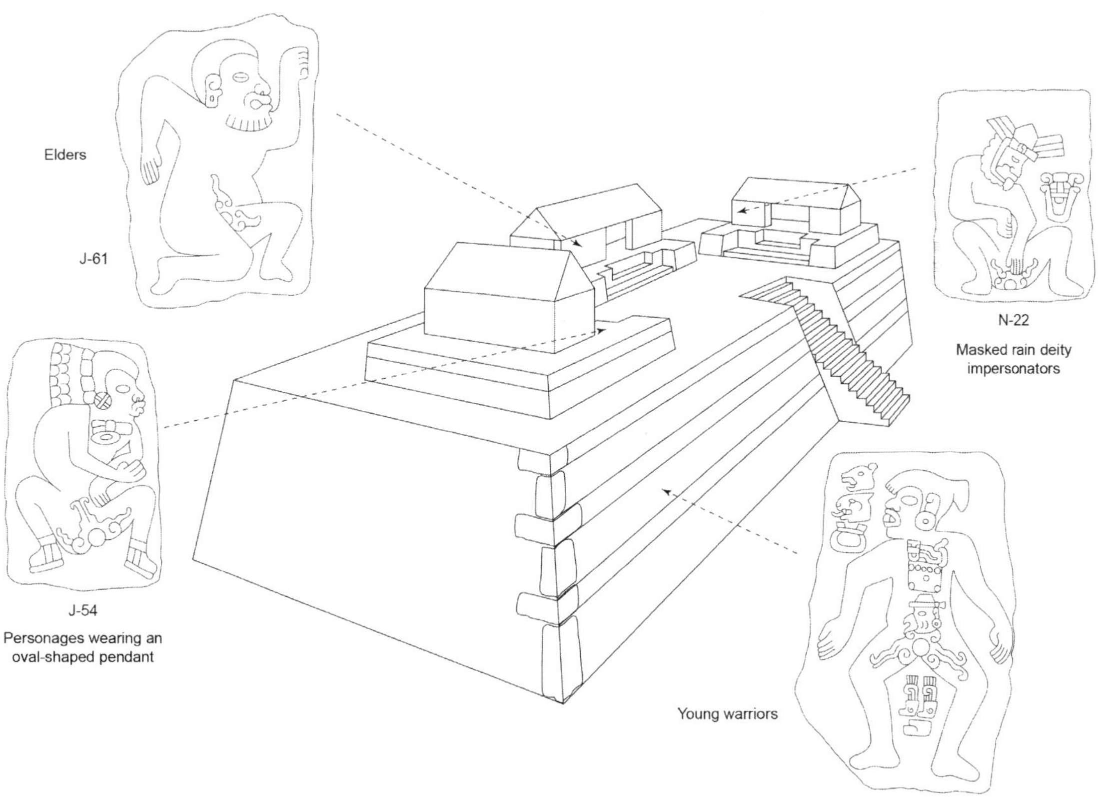

FIGURE 9.2. Hypothetical reconstruction of the grand narrative depicting an age-grade sodality in Building L-sub. Drawing by Elbis Domínguez Covarrubias.

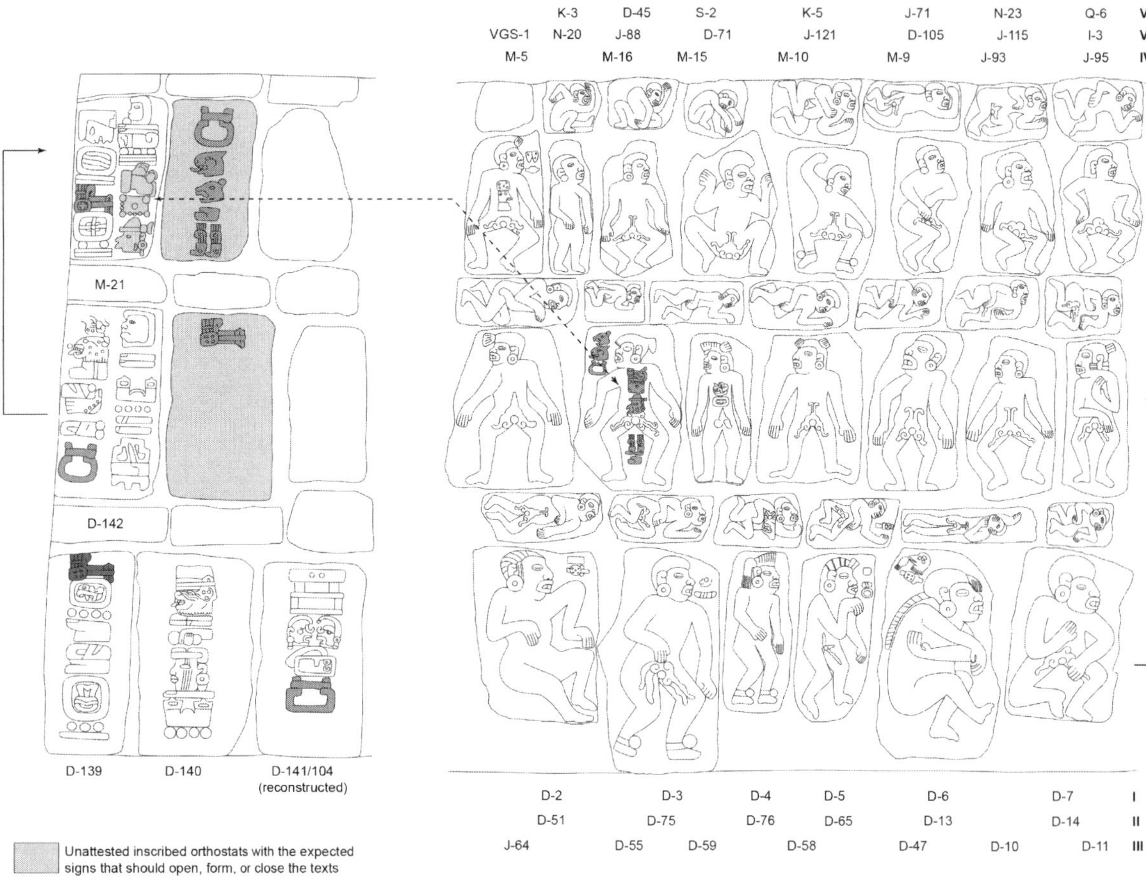

FIGURE 9.3. The texts inscribed in the cornerstones and the theme of living personages (*left*) and ancestral beings (*right*) in the alternating rows of the basal facade of Building L-sub. Drawing by Elbis Domínguez Covarrubias.

horizontal representations imbue the entire narrative with a sense of performance.[2] Some of the rendered figures have brief glyphic captions that convey their names phonetically. This monumental narrative, comprised thus far of nearly 250 carved orthostats, was complemented in the southeast angle of the basal platform with cornerstones carved with texts. These inscriptions, which also read in a boustrophedon sequence from bottom to top, appear to record the enthronement of two, perhaps three rulers throughout a span of forty-eight years, a chronological span rendered by means of Calendar Round dates.

There is a third theme, in addition to veiled references to bleeding of the genitals and ancestral invocation that was seemingly associated with the grand narrative in Building L-sub. Yet, its specific architectural setting within the building remains unknown (figure 9.4a). Four smaller and incomplete orthostats make reference to sacrifice by decapitation. At least three of these (D-78, D-123, and J-112) are accompanied by hieroglyphic captions. The fact that one of the constituent signs in these inscriptions (a budding seed) is repeated suggests that, if the glyph has a nominative value, the stones would only name a single sacrificial victim. A reference to human sacrifice is also found in one of the cornerstones of Building L-sub where—following the statement of enthronement—is a seeming allusion to the defeat and decapitation of an enemy (Figure 9.4b).

By circa 100 BC, the architectural history of Building L-sub became entangled with the life-histories of other buildings. A third modification to the structure involved the construction of a broad staircase that abutted the earlier one (Villagra 1939). The new staircase incorporated several carved stones as steps, which by the time of their incorporation in Building L-sub were battered

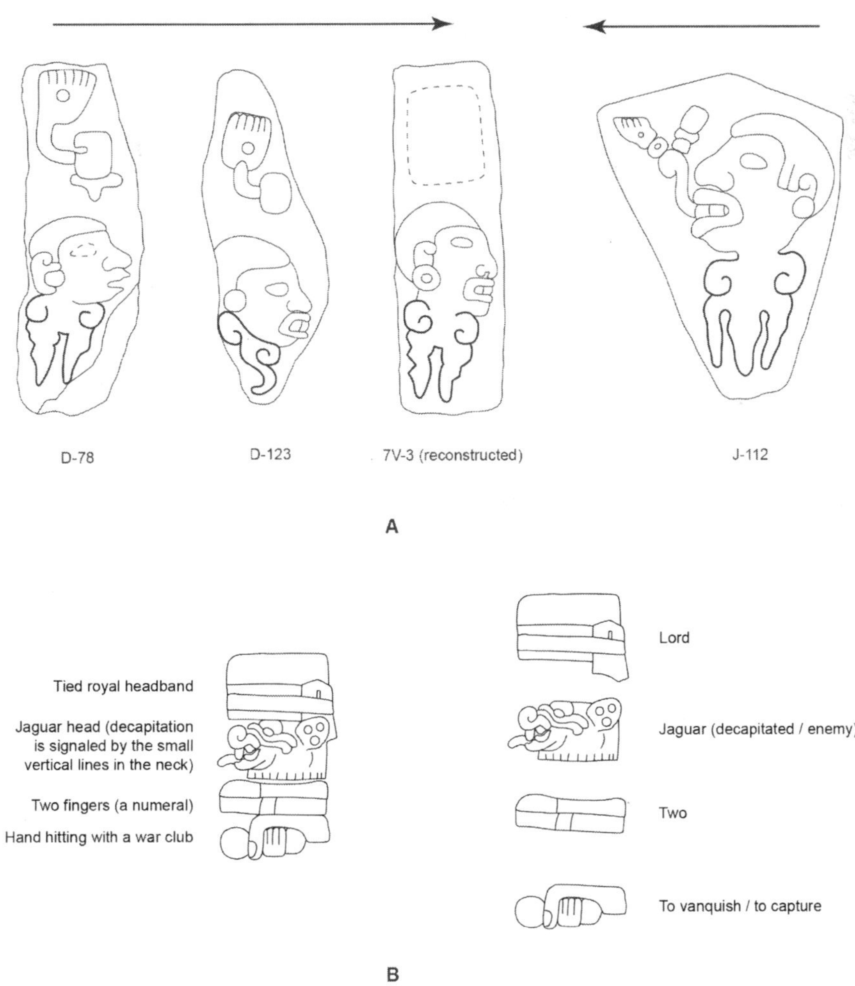

FIGURE 9.4. (a) Monoliths carved with a head and a "blood" glyph; (b) possible logograms in the text carved on stone D-140 that seemingly refer to the conquest and decapitation of a lord named 2 Jaguar. Drawing by Elbis Domínguez Covarrubias.

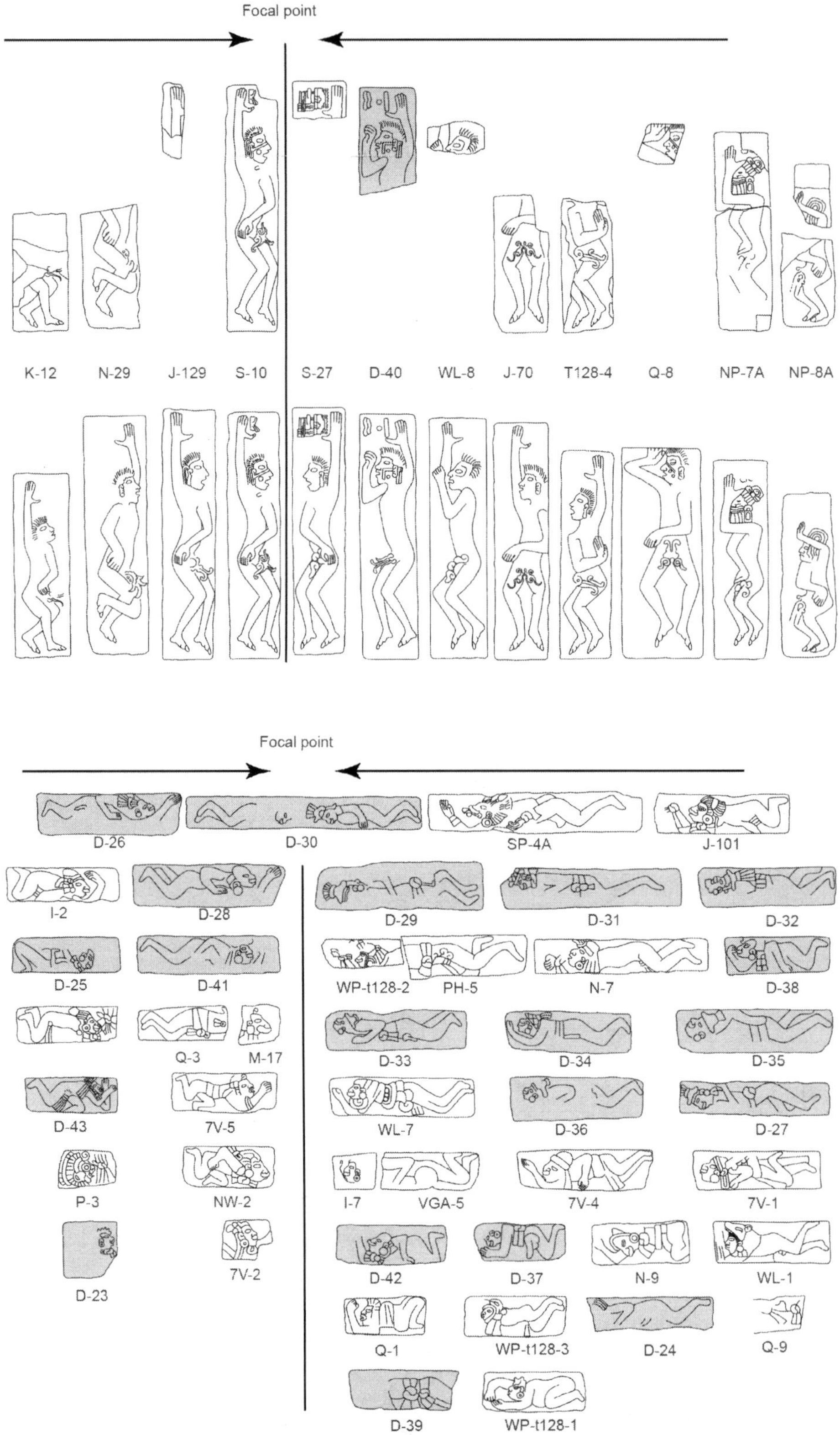

FIGURE 9.5. Carved monoliths from two dismantled architectural programs, some of which (in gray) were reused to build the steps of the broad staircase in front of Building L-sub. Drawing by Elbis Domínguez Covarrubias.

and incomplete, indicating that they came from the dismantling of narratives from other buildings (figure 9.5). While only a few of these carved blocks were reused in the construction of the staircase abutted to Building L-sub, others ended up as construction material in other coeval or later architectural projects. The dismantled narratives originally had similar themes to those in Building L-sub, showing personages engaged in bloodletting or as prone, ancestral figures. There is also some evidence indicating that, in tandem with this modification to Building L-sub, the presumed three structures atop the basal platform were rebuilt and their visual narratives replaced with others bearing almost identical themes as the previous ones.

The life-history of Building L-sub effectively came to an end circa AD 100. Although the structure was still standing at this time, the still extant carved orthostats in the basal facade may have been covered with stucco, just like the carvings re-used as steps in the staircase that was added during the earlier third modification. Much later, probably the middle of the third century AD, the southern half of Building L-sub was dismantled and its northern half covered by a new building (Building L). Thus, many of the carved orthostats in the façade of the basal platform of the building were reused in other coeval architectural projects, including the second of three major modifications to Building J located within the plaza to the east of Building L-sub. In addition to reused monuments from Building L-sub, Building J incorporated dozens of finely carved orthostats that must originally have been part of an earlier graphic program located within a building that was at least partially coeval with Building L-sub.

A Second Visual Program

Building J is unique not only because of its shape and function, but because throughout its three major building episodes, dating respectively to the Tani phase (AD 200–350), the Pitao phase (AD 350–550), and early in the Xoo phase (AD 600–700), the structure—more than any other building at Monte Albán—eventually amassed the largest number of reused inscribed stones (figure 9.6). In terms of spatial configuration and "affective power" accrued by the reuse of by then already ancient stones, the different versions of Building J appear to have acted as ancestor memorials analogous to a series of Classic period quadripartite architectural complexes found at Monte Albán and other sites in the Oaxaca Valley (Lind and Urcid 2010:308–309; Urcid 1995, 2011b:117, fig. 6.5).

But the construction of even the earliest version of Building J benefited in part from the dismantling of what must have been the second grandest of the early architectural narratives from Monte Albán. This narrative, comprised of many finely incised multiton orthostats would have been associated with a building that probably dated to the Pe phase (300–100 BC). The traditional interpretations that the finely incised stones record conquests by the ruling elite of Monte Albán (Caso 1938, 1947), name vanquished towns in the Central Valleys of Oaxaca (Whittaker 1992:12–13), or outline the subjugated territorial limits of the early Zapotec state (Marcus 1976, 1983, 1992) have assumed that the inscribed orthostats were originally related to Building J, and in the case of the last two authors, that Building J had a single construction phase. Again, we

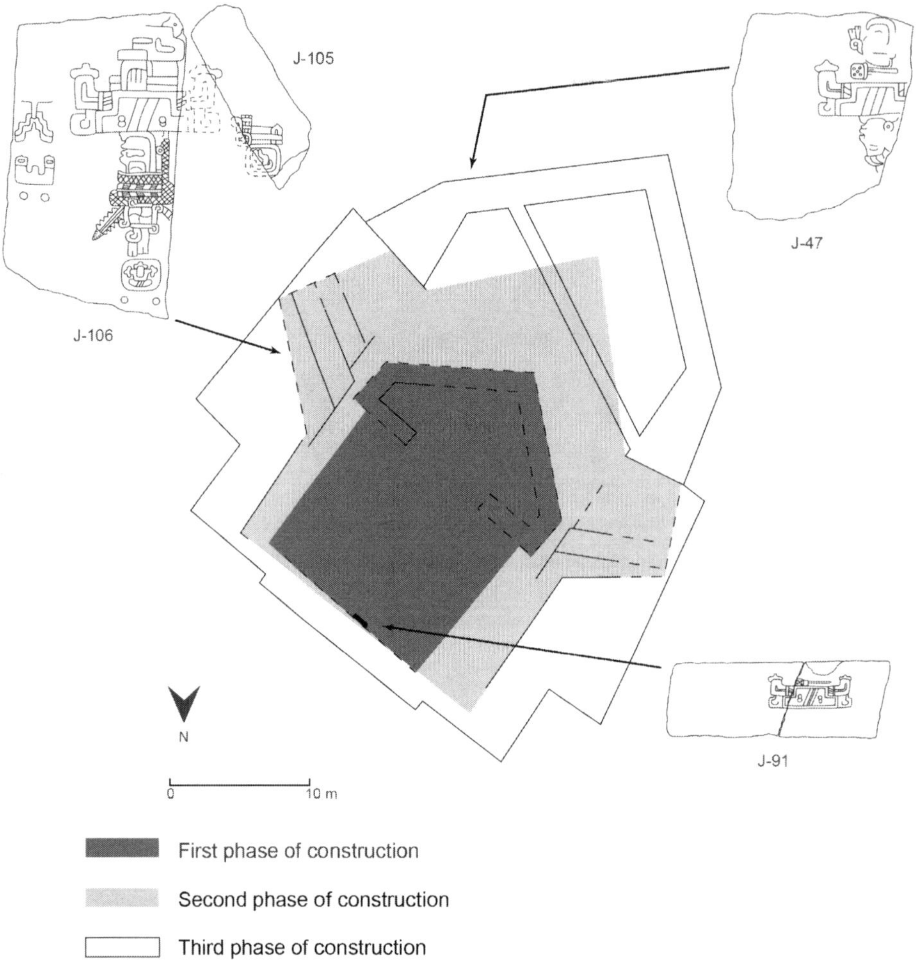

FIGURE 9.6. The three main construction phases of Building J. The finely incised orthostats, many of them already fragmented and eroded, were reused beginning with the first version of the building. Drawing by Elbis Domínguez Covarrubias.

suggest an alternative to these interpretations, positing instead that this second monumental narrative references revered individuals from Monte Albán.[3] We argue that the inscriptions differentially adhered to a glyphic formula that includes, in the center of the composition, a reference to a sector of Monte Albán, graphically rendered as "Hill-diagonal bands-noseplugs" (figure 9.7).[4] Inscribed above this toponymic reference are personal names. Below it appear calendrical names and inverted heads, some with their eyes closed, of those personages whose names bracket the sign "Hill-diagonal bands-noseplugs."

Most "hill" signs in the Zapotec corpus share the diagonal bands, but not the depiction of noseplugs. The latter, together with the sign "hill-diagonal bands" may be a synecdochical recourse meant to be read as "Hill-Lord(s)." The twentieth glyphic day name in the ancient Zapotec calendar (Lord) renders the face of a personage often wearing a noseplug, and these sumptuary goods were of exclusive use by nobles and rulers (cf. Urcid 2001:211–213, 225, 245) (figure 9.8a). In the 1619 and the 1771 versions of the Mapa de Xoxocotlan (Ruiz Cervantes and Sánchez Silva 1997:25; Smith 1973:338, figure 162), the hill with the Main Plaza of Monte Albán is glyphically identified by a tomb door-slab, or a throne, and a feathered oval framing the depiction of a personage with a bird's helmet seated on a throne. The accompanying nahuatl (*teuhtli tepeque*) and mixtec (*yucu ani yya dzoco ñaña*) glosses literally translate, respectively, as "Hill of the Lord" and "Hill of the lords' palaces and tombs" (Jansen 1998:70–72).

The fragment of a monument with a "hill" sign (J-44), carved early in the Pitao phase (circa AD 400) and reused in the second construction phase of Building J, combines as infixes the signs "noseplug" and "heart." Other examples of the hill-heart place name occur in epigraphic contexts that undoubtedly refer to actual rulers from Monte Albán. Given the fact that the imagery of Jaguar-Lords depict them at times devouring hearts (a visual metaphor for sacrifice), the Zapotec name of the fourteenth day (*lache*) in the calendar documented by Córdova (1987 [1578]), a term that literally translates as "heart," could be a metonymy for "jaguar" (figure 9.8b). Thus, the carved monument J-44 seems to conflate the names of the two neighboring hills that in the two versions of the Mapa de Xoxocotlan are identified as "Hill of the Lords" (where the Main Plaza is located) and "Hill of the Jaguar" (the South Platform).[5]

In support of our view that the glyphs carved in the finely incised slabs above the "Hill of the Lords" are anthroponyms rather than toponyms is the fact that some of their constituent signs and combinations (one, two, or three signs at the most) resemble the captions that accompany the depiction of personages

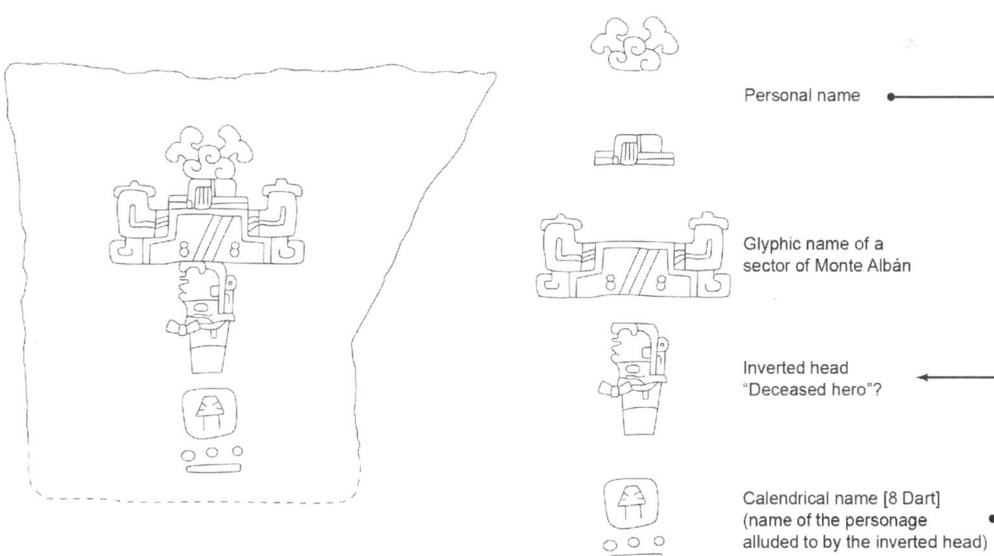

FIGURE 9.7. The central glyphic layout of the finely incised orthostats as rendered in monolith J-7. Drawing by Elbis Domínguez Covarrubias.

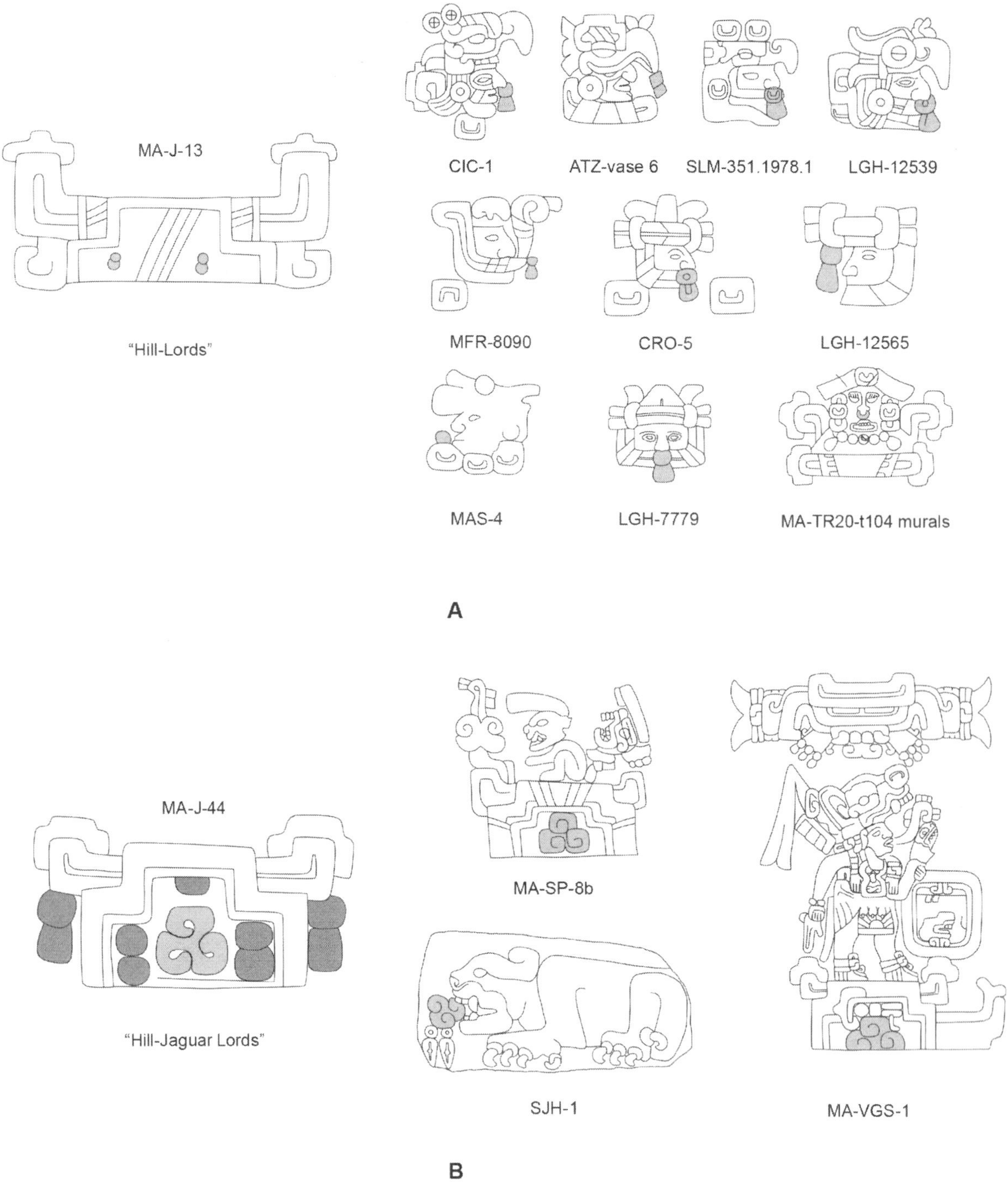

Figure 9.8. Epigraphic evidence used to propose the reading of two toponyms from Monte Albán. (a) The iconicity of noseplugs; (b) the iconicity of the heart sign and other examples of its infixing to the hill glyph. Drawing by Elbis Domínguez Covarrubias.

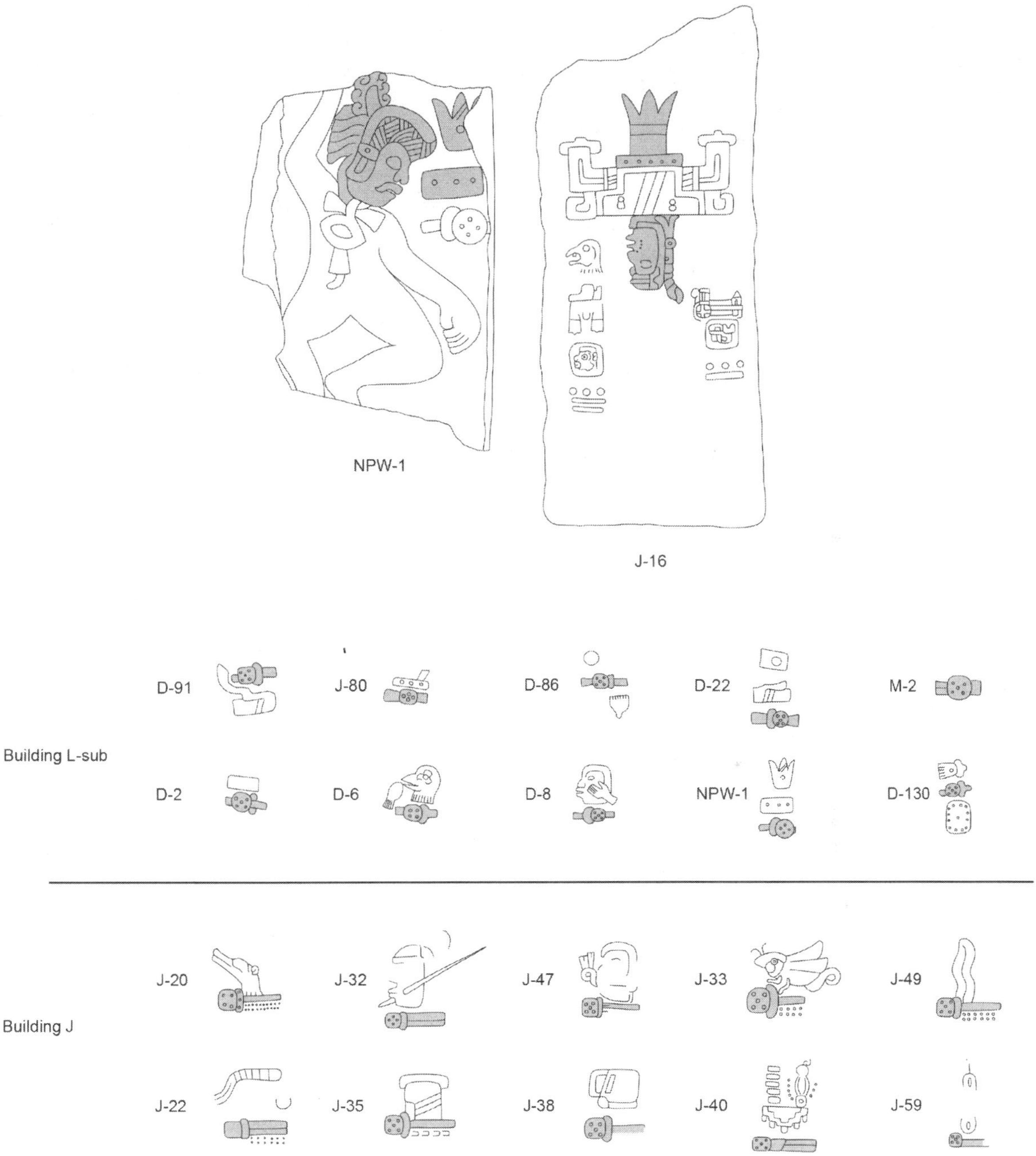

Figure 9.9. The glyphic compounds above the hill sign on the finely incised orthostats resemble in kind and combination the nominative captions that identify the personages in the narrative from Building L-sub (the glyphic compounds shown here share the sign "rattle" and have one more glyphs that vary among the inscriptions). Drawing by Elbis Domínguez Covarrubias.

in the orthostats from Building L-sub (figure 9.9). Given this syntagmatic relation, and as Alfonso Caso argued long ago (1965:940), there is no doubt that the glyphic captions on the carved orthostats from Building L-sub render the personal names of the depicted individuals.

The interpretative work of Caso (1938, 1947) for the remaining portions of the textual format inscribed in the finely incised stones posited that they made reference to dead lords and thus to acts of conquest. Yet, even if one concedes that the semantic value of inverted heads and closed eyes marks the ontological status of being dead, an equally plausible reading that takes into account our previous discussion of anthroponyms and toponyms, could denote "deceased," "fallen hero," or simply "revered ancestor." Categories of inverted heads, which can be made based on their elaborate headdresses (Caso 1947:21–24, 85–90, figs. 51–56), may signal some kind of ranked group identity.

There are good reasons to assume that the narrative comprised of finely incised orthostats formed the façade of a basal platform similar to that of Building L-sub. Such a façade alternated rows of vertically and horizontally placed megaliths, with the size of the former decreasing toward the top of the façade (figure 9.10). Thus, we suggest that this other decorated basal platform and Building L-sub were envisioned as complementary. For instance, the façade of Building L-sub was decorated so that human figures covered the main surface, and texts covered the cornerstones. Our reconstruction reverses this relationship in the hypothesized narrative with finely incised orthostats, namely the cornerstones had figural representations of rulers enacting sacrifice by decapitation, although only one, Monument J-41, is currently known (Urcid and Winter 2003:127) (figure 9.11). The rest of the façade's surface was covered with megaliths carved with texts. Chronologically, the complementarity between the two narratives also implies that they were at least partially coeval, unless the platform with the finely incised orthostats resulted from social memory "in absence" (Connerton 1989, Rowlands 1993:145–146). That is, the building with the finely incised orthostats could have been constructed based on recollections of Building L-sub and its associated narrative after the latter's had been substantially modified by the beginning of the Common Era.

When looking at the pattern of dispersal of carved orthostats in both narratives, there is another binary opposition. Once dismantled, the carved stones from Building L-sub were widely dispersed and reused through time in many construction projects, some of them even outside the Main Plaza (see Urcid 2011a:180, fig. 12). In contrast, the great majority of the known orthostats from the second program were reused in the various rebuildings of Structure J. Only three finely incised slabs or fragments have been found elsewhere, all in nearby buildings such as the South Platform and System M. Such a complementarity between both narratives could imply that one may have been built directly in front of the other, either at the spot where Building J was eventually erected or farther east, under what eventually became Building Q. In fact, limited excavations in the mid-1980s revealed evidence of a structure beneath the plaza and adjacent to the earliest version of Building J, although the architectural configuration and size of that earlier structure was not obtained (Marcus Winter, personal communication 1989).

A

B

Figure 9.10. Portions of the hypothetical reconstructions of the architectural narratives from Monte Albán showing a similar construction technique of alternated vertical and horizontal blocks that decrease in size from bottom to top. (a) Building L-sub; (b) hypothesized platform's facade decorated with finely incised orthostats. Drawing by Elbis Domínguez Covarrubias.

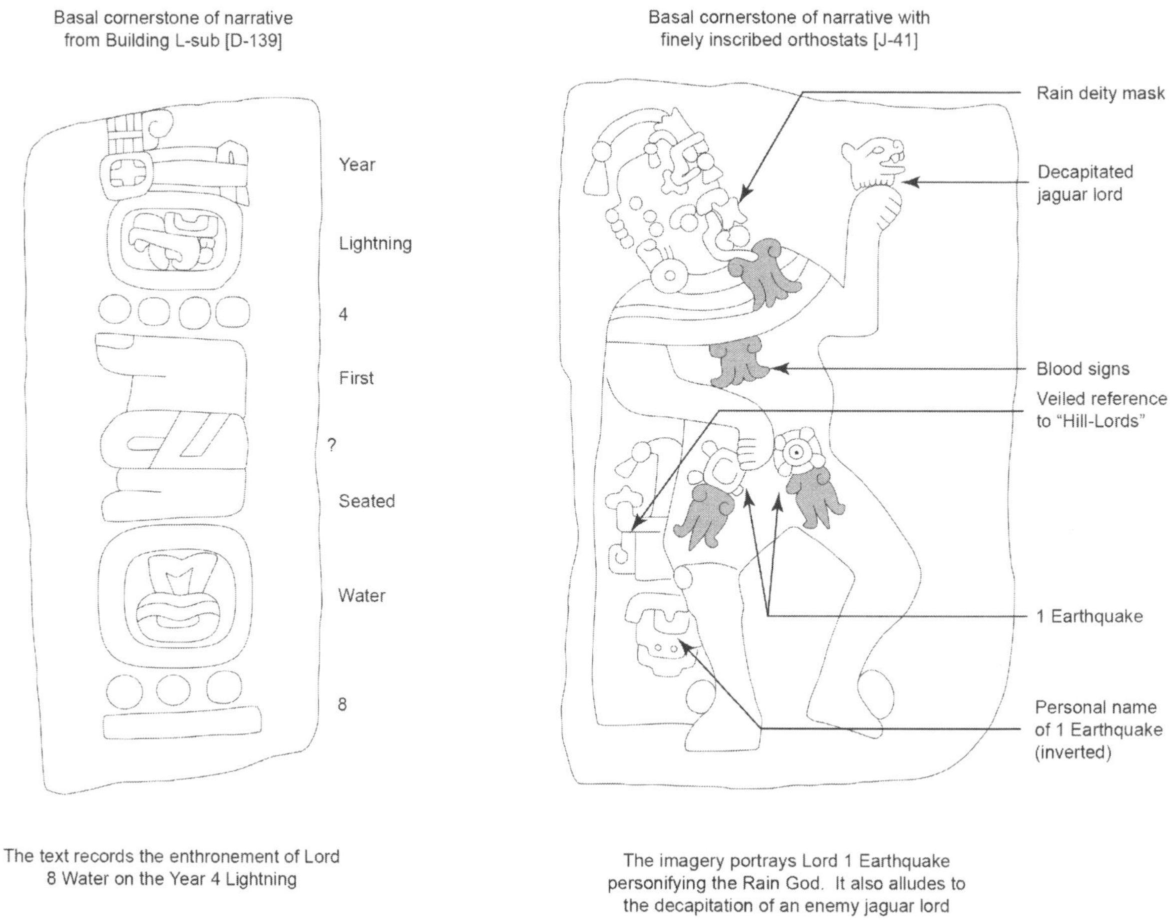

FIGURE 9.11. Reversed complementarity between image and text in the cornerstones of both architectural narratives. Drawing by Elbis Domínguez Covarrubias.

The Political Significance of the Early Visual Programs on the Main Plaza

The architecturally contextualized reading of the two largest early narratives from Monte Albán, presented here, points to a tension between exclusionary and communal forms of authority (Blanton et al. 1996) during the early history of the city. Each narrative includes references to powerful rulers in their cornerstones, which reflects a more exclusionary form of authority. However, the majority of carvings in each narrative represents a more communal vision of authority with an age-grade sodality shown in Building L-sub and ranked groups of possible fallen heroes in the narrative with the finely incised orthostats. Ultimately, both narratives can be thought of as memorials with a focus on the sacred aspects of warfare, including divining the outcome of battles via contact with ancestors, autosacrifice, human sacrifice, and the commemoration of heroes. We disagree with arguments that these monuments make reference to large-scale warfare and territorial conquest, however (see Joyce 2003; Workinger and Joyce 2009).

The Building L-sub program was probably polysemic with different components aimed at different audiences with variable degrees of phonetic and semantic literacy (Urcid 2011a). Sculptures in the east face of Building L-sub would have been visible to large groups of people on the plaza and stressed the ritual and military actions of lower-ranking people. Images of higher-ranking members of the military sodality, including elders and rain god impersonators, were located on buildings on top of the platform, which were probably restricted to higher-status audiences of both prominent commoners and nobles. Archaeological, architectural, semasiographic, and epigraphic data indicate that the early rulers of Monte Albán gained power via the elaboration of an ideology centered on human sacrifice and a primordial covenant between humans and the divine (Joyce 2000, 2004, 2010; Joyce and Winter 1996).

The decision by rulers to commission architectural monuments to bolster community well-being through sacrifice, instead of the self-aggrandizement of paramount and charismatic leaders, suggests that some of the societal uses of early architecture and writing in Oaxaca served the purpose of internal power-building strategies stemming from the potential factionalism of diverse constituencies (Urcid 2011a). These ideological representations would have misrepresented inequalities by promoting group solidarity and identity, the latter being crucial in the context of inter-community conflict and a new way of urban living. The evidence suggests that nobles shared politicoreligious power with communal organizations, which probably included high-ranking commoners as leaders (Joyce 2010:131–146). These two potentially competing forms of authority—communal and noble—carried inherent contradictions and potential points of tension. Evidence from Early and Middle Formative sites suggest that earlier forms of political authority in the Valley of Oaxaca were largely communal with little evidence for powerful rulers until the end of the Middle Formative (Blanton et al. 1999; Joyce 2010). Therefore, during the Late Formative, powerful nobles at Monte Albán could have threatened the traditional authority of communal institutions. In turn, communal authority would have constrained the power of the nobility. The representation of a relatively large council of elders, warriors, and religious specialists on the Building L-sub program includes rain deity impersonators and references to human and autosacrifice. Likewise, hieroglyphic inscriptions and early images of rulers (Monument J-41) also reference rain god impersonation, warfare, and sacrifice. These data suggest that the settings in which hereditary nobles and communal organizations negotiated and contested political authority probably included public rituals and access to special ceremonial roles like diviners, rainmakers, and scribes as well as activities related to the preparation for and conduct of warfare.

The possibility that the two largest earlier narratives from Monte Albán could have been coeval during the Pe phase (300–100 BC) opens the possibility of them being simultaneously the target of a major internal iconoclastic upheaval during the Nisa phase (100 BC–AD 200). This event may have been related to what Blanton (1978:54–56) characterized as a mini-collapse, when Monte Albán saw a reduction in its extent and population, and when major defensive and/or control walls were built. At this time the Building L-sub monumental program was modified by tearing apart some of all of the narrative programs atop the basal platform. The building that originally displayed the finely incised orthostats was also dismantled, and the monuments were later reused in the three major construction phases of Building J. Apparently, other poorly understood narrative programs were also dismantled and a temple on the north end of the North Platform was burned (Winter 1994:15).

Other indications of internal turmoil include the construction of a defensive or monitoring wall around the most vulnerable slopes at Monte Albán as well as the relocation of people behind the wall from outlying parts of the site (O'Brien et al. 1982:207). It has usually been assumed that the wall was constructed to defend against external enemies, but it is also possible that it offered defense against internal factions and was a means of controlling movement into the city. Another indication of conflict comes from an architectural complex termed the Conjunto PNLP on the northwestern end of the Main Plaza. By the Nisa phase (100 BC–AD 200), the Conjunto PNLP acted as a control point for entry onto the Main Plaza (Martínez López and Markens 2004). The recovery of twenty-seven projectile points in the Conjunto PNLP suggests that coercive force was used to monitor access to the plaza.[6]

The destruction of the narrative programs at Monte Albán by dismantling structures, covering up carved stones, and breaking others to use as construction fill points to a major societal upheaval. Monte Albán eventually recovered from this upheaval, although inter-community conflict continued to play an important role in the social dynamics of the Central Valleys during the Classic period (Joyce 2010; Lind and Urcid 2010). Yet, from then on, more exclusionary forms of government prevailed, as attested by subsequent architectural narratives that memorialize the identity and deeds of singular historical figures.

Notes

1. We take the position that plazas and their surrounding buildings are a profitable unit of analysis. By focusing only on the open, flat spaces within larger architectural aggregates, one runs the risk of decontextualizing the way such bounded spaces were construed and used.

2. The features that commonly have been mustered in support of interpreting the human figures as depictions of sacrificial victims, such as the (1) closed eyes, (2) open mouths, (3) contorted body positions, (4) nakedness of the figures, and (5) signs indicative of mutilation, and specifically castration, are alternatively explained in this reinterpretation by assuming that (1) Mesoamerican modes of representation were capable of rendering varied states of being (e.g., closed eyes and open mouths as indexing pain or trance from self-bleeding penitence); (2) the representations of the human body were not meant to be realistic (i.e., if the figures were intended to be shown naked, why the omission of nipples and navels? [although the state of being mostly naked could be accounted for in terms of allowing the self-sacrificial blood to spill onto the floor and not

on the garments]); and (3) a comparative assessment of Mesoamerican semasiography indicates that usually when mutilation of body parts is referenced, both severed parts are shown (e.g., torso/decapitated head). Furthermore, we are unaware, either in prehispanic indigenous sources or in native/European colonial documents, of explicit references to castration as a treatment of prisoners of war. The perception that the human figures were rendered "contorted" stems to a large extent from viewing the carved stones in their nonprimary contexts. The heuristic and partial reconstruction of the façade of Building L-sub based on available evidence strongly suggests that the intent was to imbue the human figure with a sense of movement (see Urcid 2011a:182–183, figs. 13, 14). Ultimately, construing the bodily positions of the figures as contorted derives from an etic, even ethnocentric, perception of representational modes different from ours.

3. Other challengers to the traditional interpretation of "conquest slabs" include Buigues (1993:83, 108), who views the slabs as depicting "the earth monster [the hill glyph] swallowing dead rulers [the inverted heads]," and Carter (2006:78, 96–98) who posits that the textual format in the slabs "reads as so-and-so (a named individual) was at the mountain (Monte Albán) on such-and-such a date." Buigues and Carter, however, take for granted that the primary context of the finely incised orthostats was Building J.

4. Whittaker (1980:150–151) originally suggested the reading of this sign as "Taniquiecache" (Hill of the Precious Stone), a proposal that involves creating a linguistic term based on the direct, iconic interpretation of the signs. It also assumes—contrary to seventeenth- and eighteenth-century cartographic evidence—that Monte Albán was designated in ancient times by a single, all-encompassing name.

5. The naming of the southern sector of Monte Albán as "Hill-Jaguar" in the Mapa of Xoxocotlan may have originated from decoupling metonymically a single ancient name (Hill-Lords) for the Main Plaza. Another possibility is that by the early seventeenth century, the probable exposure of Monument SP-1, which depicts a jaguar-lord and was embedded in the northeast corner of the South Platform (see Urcid 2001:319, fig. 5.30), motivated the naming of the southern sector of Monte Albán as "Hill-Jaguar."

6. Although there has been much debate involving whether the open space of the Main Plaza could have been used for staging marketplace exchanges on a rotational basis, we agree with Blanton (1978:63–64) that throughout its history the Main Plaza was mostly secluded for the high-ranking elites and probably only accessible to the general public during important ceremonies. Blanton's (1978:85–87) survey of Monte Albán detected a large open space (area 16) on the northeast slope of the main hill bounded by major mounded groups on terraces 278, 1306, and 938 (N5E8 and N5E7) that could have better served as the stage for a daily marketplace in the city.

CHAPTER TEN

Plazas and Patios of the Feathered Serpent

William M. Ringle

Rites of investiture are critical opportunities for demonstrating, or at least simulating, the orderly and legitimate transfer of power. Sanctioned by precedent and often by a state religion, and incorporating symbols and ritual objects of the highest importance, they are moments of peak political drama for which a substantial audience is required. Although such rituals often have a hidden, esoteric component, as classic rites of passage it is almost inconceivable that they might dispense with revealed stages during which the newly invested lord emerges to the acclaim of his or her subjects. For while such ceremonies mark the assumption of a new and often divine social persona by the ruler himself, they also reflect the reincorporation of the entire body politic into the new political order, who are thus necessary participants in the drama.

Plazas and patios must therefore be central to the search for arenas of investiture among the cityscapes of ancient Mesoamerica. In the search for such spaces, crowd capacity, restrictions of entry and visibility, and associated architecture are all important considerations (e.g., Inomata 2006a; Inomata and Tsukamoto, this volume), but without associated iconographic or textual evidence, definitive identification is often difficult. This chapter suggests that in several of the cities that can be plausibly identified as Tollans,[1] architecture, iconography, and the largest plaza spaces were consistently associated in ways that suggest they were places of investiture. Given the ravages of time, the evolution of ceremonial practices, and their incorporation of local ideologies, it is not to be expected that Toltec investiture ceremonies were everywhere identical. Nevertheless, I argue that these ceremonies find plausible parallels among the investiture rituals for which we have textual information, primarily from the Basin of Mexico, Tlaxcala, and Puebla. Enough evidence survives to suggest an evolving complex of investiture practices that began in the Early Classic period and persisted until the Conquest.

Of course, such spaces were not reserved solely for rites of investiture. We know from historical accounts, for instance, that the Temple of Huitzilopochtli of the Templo Mayor was a station in Mexica rites of accession, but also played a role in numerous other state and calendrical rituals. The plaza connecting the many temples of the Sacred Precinct undoubtedly served an even broader set of ceremonies. Thus, this account makes no claim to exclusivity, but is rather an attempt to provide some specificity to the often rather broad interpretations we are forced to make concerning the functions of ancient architectural spaces. It is an overview of a longer study being prepared on Toltec investiture, which will provide fuller contexts for these rites.

Linguistic Evidence

Among Nahuatl speakers, two roots refer to formal open spaces. *Tianquiztli/tianquizco* is defined as both "plaza" and "market" in the dictionaries, reflecting a broader Mesoamerican calque since *k'iuik* in Yucatec Maya and Mixtec *yahui* also share both meanings. The more relevant root, defined most often as "patio," is *ithualli*, with orthographic or dialect variants such as *ytvalli* or *itoali*. This root seems to refer specifically to enclosed open spaces and so was incorporated into references to courtyards, atriums, and household patios (as will be seen, investiture rites seem to pointedly connect these semantic domains). *Teuitoalco/teoithualco*, for example, referred to the patio or courtyard of a temple where dances or festivities might be held. Sahagún (1979:61) refers to the area in front of the Templo Mayor as *in jitoalco vitzilopuchtli*, probably the front patio surrounded by serpents, the true *coatepantli* according to López Luján and López Austin (2011). But it also seems to have been used for spaces we might consider plazas, since in the *Primeros Memoriales*, Sahagún lists *ytvalli* as one of the components of a ceremonial center (Sahagún 1979:119–120). Since *ytvalli* is not there attached to a specific temple and is followed by general precinct features (*covatenamitl*, "wall of snakes" and *teuquiyaoatl*, "sacred portals"), the term here seems to refer to the entire ceremonial precinct. Such precincts were of course frequently enclosed, as for example the broad platforms defining Tenochtitlan's Sacred Precinct and the Ciudadela of Teotihuacan, whose similarity was recently remarked upon by López Luján and López Austin (2011:67).

As the term designating the patios of house compounds, *ithualli* was extended metaphorically to include kinship relations. Thus, *cemithualtin*, literally "those of a single patio," is defined as "family" by Siméon (1988:78). It is interesting that this, rather than the house, was the architectural metaphor of choice, suggesting that the open common space between houses, the locus of daily socializing, visual contact, and task performance, was thought to better reflect the social bonds holding a household together. We can therefore perhaps see why it was also applied to public plaza spaces, as the locus of those activities binding the *altepetl* together through spectacle. It is also worth noting in this respect that *ithualli* is derived from *italli*, the verb "to see" (Karttunen 1983:107), suggesting the fundamental importance of visual communication in such places.

Interestingly, a Mixtec account from the 1560s relates that the first act of a new royal pair on taking possession of the palace of Yucundaa (Teposcolula) was to seat themselves on a mat in the main patio before the assembled nobles (Terraciano 2000:17). They then proceeded to repeat this act in each of the main buildings of the compound, but the patio seating was first and most significant. This supports the notion that the patio was viewed as the axis about which the household revolved, but also connects that space with rituals of political appropriation.

Investiture among the Nahuas of Central Mexico

To return to the connection between plazas and investiture, three sets of descriptions describe the coronations of the *tlahtoque* of Tenochtitlan. One group, derived from the so-called *Crónica X* and represented by the works of Durán and Tezozomoc, provides accounts of the successive coronations of Tenochtitlan monarchs from the reign of Axayacatl onward. Another group instead offers a generalized description of these ceremonies. These texts parallel, and may be derived from, a chapter in Motolinia's *Memoriales* (1970:chap. 10); other authors of this group include Torquemada, Zorita, las Casas, and Muñoz Camargo. Finally, Sahagún's (1979:chap. 18) account is also generalized, but includes details not available in the others (see Townsend 1987 for a useful overview).

Motolinia's account, and those that are cognate to it, are then followed by a description of rites involving the investiture of the *teteuctin*, the members of the highest rank of the nobility, except that these describe ceremonies practiced by the Nahua groups of the tramontane kingdoms, especially Tlaxcala, Cholula, and Huexotzinco. These rites are also described independently by Mendoza in an early-sixteenth-century text (Carrasco 1966). Finally, another very important account of similar events in Cholula can be found in the *Relación de Cholula* (de Rojas 1927 [1579]). Comparison of these accounts reveals broad similarities among the Nahua nations of Central Mexico, as well as strong parallels between the rites for *tlahtoque* and *teteuctin*, the latter probably explicable by the fact that the *tlatoani* was selected from the ranks of the *teteuctin*. With regard to the former, I concur with Carrasco (1966) that regional parallels reflect the fact that these were "Toltec" rituals, at least as they were construed by the leaders of the late prehispanic horizon.

Sahagún tells us (1979:61–62) that following the secret selection of the *tlahtoani* by a council of elders, all the princes assembled in the courtyard (*jitoalco*) of the Temple of Huitzilopochtli to learn who among them had been chosen. The initiate was then grabbed from the assembled candidates by priests and "before them, all the people beheld him," underscoring the importance of public visual proclamation from the very outset of these rites (Sahagún 1979:62). After clothing him in simple garments, the initiate was then whisked up the stairs of the pyramid to offer incense to the image of Huitzilopochtli (see also Durán 1994:296). According to Sahagún, four lords newly selected as his inner council accompanied him to the temple, similarly clad. "And all the common folk stood looking up at him. Trumpets were sounded; the shell trumpets were blown" (296). It was at this point, according to Durán and Motolinia, that his nose was pierced for insertion of a jade jewel, a trait of Toltec origin.

This account finds archaeological support in that the only true feathered serpents around the base of the Templo Mayor terminate the balustrades of the stairway leading to the temple of Huitzilopochtli, unlike the balustrade serpents leading to the Tlaloc temple (López Luján and López Austin 2011:66). As will be seen, feathered serpent balustrades characterize a number of the temples where rites of investiture were conducted, demonstrating that whatever other attributes it had, the feathered serpent was fundamentally associated with rulership. Here that is symbolized by the mat motifs embedded above the serpents' eyes (figure 10.1a).[2] This is actually a very old motif; vessels from Teotihuacan make explicit the connection between feathered serpents, mat signs, and headdresses of office (figure 10.1b). This association of the feathered serpent and headdresses of office provides another key to identifying the location of investitures.

Then followed a hidden phase in the rites, during which the initiate and his companions were cloistered in a place called the *tlacochcalco* or *tlacatecco* for four days to do penance, pray, and perform autosacrifice. The four days having elapsed, the new ruler and his councilors emerged and left for home. At the palace a sumptuous feast was prepared to which rulers from near and far were invited. Much dancing and eating took place, as well as the presentation of costly gifts to the attendees. This, however, was but a prelude to a military campaign whose purpose was to demonstrate the mettle of the new ruler. On its successful outcome, imperial largesse was further demonstrated by the distribution of capes, breech clouts, and other marks of royal favor.

Sahagún's account only briefly mentions the postwar events, but Durán's (1994) account of the coronations of Tizoc, Ahuitzotl, and Moctecuhzoma II indicates that the actual enthronement only occurred at this point, on Cipactli, the first day of the ritual cycle.[3] On his return from war, the king was received at the chief temple. In the case of Moctecuhzoma, his coronation was performed by the kings of Texcoco and Tacuba, and by the high priest (Durán 1994:406). Pitch was applied to his body, and he was presented with the diadem and garments of office. He then seated himself on the Divine Seat, and captives were brought out for sacrifice. Afterward, he repaired to his palace, and it was at this point that the major feast was held, four days of feasting, dancing, and sacrifices to which friend and foe alike were invited. Thus, two plaza or patio spaces were involved in such ceremonies: the plaza in front of the Templo Mayor, where the ruler was first made known to his peers and probably the citizenry as well, and then the courtyard or patio of his palace, where he hosted feasts for his fellow nobles. Sahagún (1979:64) tells us specifically that following his descent from his four-day fast, the *tlahtoani* was conveyed *in tecpan itoalco*, "to the courtyard of the palace," perhaps again a reflection of the central symbolic importance of such spaces to residences at all levels of the social spectrum.

A final description of coronation, in this case of Topiltzin Quetzalcoatl himself, is given in a brief fragment by Alva Ixtlilxóchitl (1985:I:387): "They seated him on a throne (*icpal*) and placed a blue mantle on him, and he fasted for four days, during which he was shut off and could not communicate with anyone, and his vassals awaited him and there they received him as lord." The clear

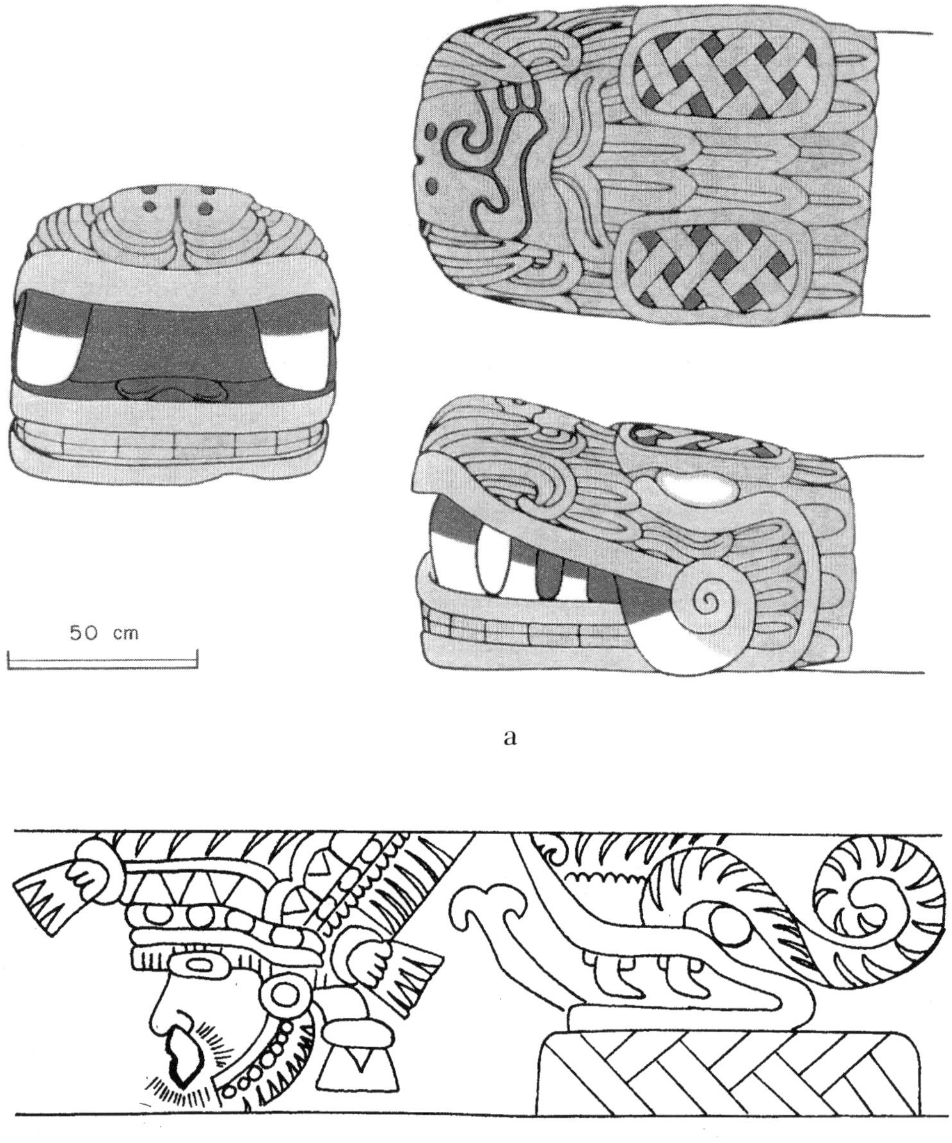

FIGURE 10.1. (a) Serpent head at the base of the balustrade of the Huitizilopochtli temple, Templo Mayor. Note mat (*petate*) element over eye. Courtesy of the Proyecto Templo Mayor; (b) tripod vessel scene, Teotihuacan (von Winning 1987: Capítulo X:fig. 3b). Note conjunction of a headdress of office, feathered serpent, and petate.

parallels with the imperial coronations described by Sahagún and Motolinia support the contention that such rituals consciously emulated Toltec precedents, at least as they were then understood.

Such ceremonies not only celebrated the *tlahtoani* of Tenochtitlan, for as Motolinia states:

> The lords of the provinces or towns who were the immediate subjects of Mexico, went there [to the Temple of Huitzilopochtli] to be confirmed in their titles, after the first men of the provinces had chosen them; and with some nobles they made the same ceremonies like those described herein at the top of temple, and with others at the base at the foot of the stairs. (Motolinia 1970:chap. 10)

The base of the stairs probably refers either to the open *itoalco* there or to the two buildings that delimited it and contained benches with processional friezes on their interior (Beyer 1955; López Austin and López Luján 2009:310–313). Similarly, de Rojas (1927 [1579]) states that "all the priests and governors of this New Spain" were confirmed in office at Cholula and that officials would accompany the new lord home to authenticate his new position.[4]

As mentioned, such ceremonies also involved the tramontane *teteuctin* (Carrasco 1966; Motolinia 1970:chap. 11). These rites shared several features with *tlahtoque* rites, but also incorporated the added dimension of the initiate's home barrio. The initial step for the prospective *tecutli* was to accumulate sufficient goods for payment to the priests of the main temple. This could take months or more, and required the combined efforts of all his supporters, since the *tecutli* was the head of a substantial "house" with dependent commoners and lesser nobles (Carrasco 1966; Lockhart 1992). Thus, the payment was not simply personal, but came from the entire lordly estate and marked its fealty to the center. Once this was amassed, the prospective *tecutli*, like the *tlahtoani*, ascended the main pyramid where he was ritually stripped and his nose perforated with eagle or jaguar bones for the insertion of a nose plug. Like the *tlahtoani*, he and some of his supporters were sequestered for four days, during which they performed penance and kindled a new fire. Completing this, he was given the name Nacxitl, an epithet of Quetzalcoatl.

The initiate then returned home to begin gathering another large payment, part of which went again to the priesthood but part of which was to finance the feast culminating his initiation. Ritually, the initiate performed a series of acts mirroring those conducted on the principal pyramid, but now in his home barrio. He kindled another new fire and again sequestered himself, after which he carried the "idol" associated with the barrio to its local temple. The future lord and his kinsmen went to this altar or temple, danced, and made offerings to this deity. Once these preparations were completed, he hosted a great feast for the high priests and important nobles, in which many presents were given out. After bathing and committing autosacrifice, he returned for a second time to the main temple, he had the red and white headband of lordship placed upon his head, as well as the two-feather ornament and other new garments. This headband was the Tlaxcalan equivalent of the *xiuhuitzolli*, the crown worn by *teteuctin* (Nicholson 1967). He then descended and returned home to great fanfare as a fully invested *tecutli*.

In addition to drawing parallels between the *tlahtoani* and the *tecutli*, both invested by "Toltec" rites through the agency of the feathered serpent, these ceremonies seem designed to call attention to the hidden affinities between the plazas of the center and those of the home, between the *teoithualli* and the *ithualli* of the *tecpan* or *teccalli*. The noble was first selected and proclaimed in the central plaza, but it was at his residence that he performed his first paradigmatic acts of rulership, those of providing food, clothing, and finery for his subjects in the culminating feast. These rites are thus as much about the burdens and obligations of rulership as they are about the prerogatives of rank, as is clear from some of the orations to which the initiate was subjected. Investiture involves not only the assumption of power, but also self-mortification, the loss of previous identify, and, in the case of the *tecutli*, actual payments in acknowledgment of the primacy of the center.

A few archaeological expectations can therefore be framed for analogues to such rites elsewhere and earlier in time. First, the plazas involved should be focused on the structures associated with accession and sufficiently ample to accommodate large crowds. The feathered serpent should be prominent on the specific buildings and in those open spaces associated with accession, often to the exclusion of other areas. The pyramids, in particular, should show specific iconographic similarities, although as will be seen, pyramids were in some cases of lesser importance. Houses and plazas might be expected to figure prominently in both the iconography and archaeology of investiture, as might connections between the main and barrio temples in the case of the *teteuctin* confirmation. Evidence for processions of nobles, feasting, sequestration of the initiate, often with several other individuals, and associated rites of penitence and autosacrifice are also important clues.

Finally, pairing or duality might be expected among some of these traits. Lockhart (1992:25–26) has remarked upon the "tendency toward dualism" of the prehispanic Nahua groups of Central Mexico. The dual temples surmounting the principal pyramids of Tenayuca, Tlatilolco, and Tenochtitlan are frequently interpreted as expressions of ideological or economic duality (Broda 1987; Hirth 2000:220; Matos Moctezuma 1987:194; Smith 2008) or unity in duality (López Austin and López Luján 2009:475–479), but ethnohistorical sources point to duality of office as another possible dimension (Ringle 2004). Space does not permit a full treatment of this point, but certainly this was the case with the dual rulership of the *tlaquiach* and *aquiach* in Cholula, both of whom were members of the Quetzalcoatl priesthood.

Teotihuacan

In their influential study of the iconography of the Feathered Serpent Pyramid (FSP) (see figure 10.2), López Austin, López Luján, and Sugiyama (1991) identified the second head on the façade of the FSP as a headdress of Cipactli, the monster from whom the earth was born and the first day of the Sacred Calendar, and concluded that the pyramid was essentially "a temple dedicated

Figure 10.2. Detail, façade of the Feathered Serpent Pyramid (Temple of Quetzalcoatl), Ciudadela, Teotihuacan (photograph by author).

to the passage of time" (103). With the identification of the second head on the façade as a headdress, coupled with the unearthing of hundreds of sacrificial burials around and under the FSP, interpretation increasingly favored militarism and rulership (e.g., Sugiyama 1989, 2004, 2005; Taube 1992). Yet discussion has been largely confined to the pyramid; the complex as a whole continues to be identified as either a palace or a temple (see, however, Murakami, this volume).

That themes of rulership and militarism are central to the FSP can hardly be doubted, but I suggest they must be understood within the larger function of the Ciudadela (figure 10.3). Both internal and comparative evidence indicates that the Ciudadela was the arena where the nobility of Teotihuacan and its tributaries were confirmed in office, at least for several centuries. The Ciudadela is one of the largest public spaces along the Street of the Dead, the area within the Great Compound directly across the way being its only rival. As Cowgill (1983) recognized, the plaza within the enclosure could have held almost the entire adult population of Teotihuacan. In considering whether the Ciudadela could have been the royal palace of Teotihuacan's paramount, he grappled with

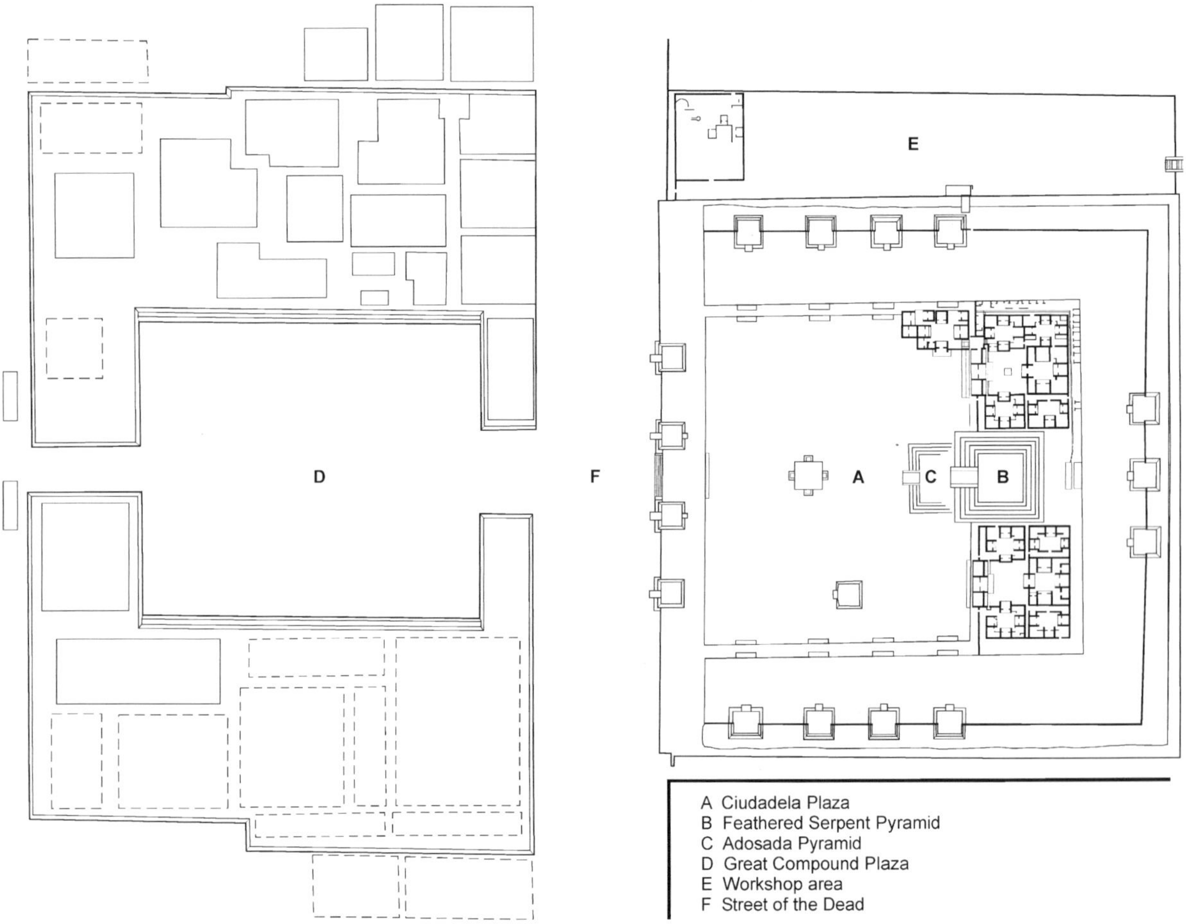

FIGURE 10.3. Detail map of Teotihuacan showing the relative positions of the Ciudadela and the Great Platform (redrawn from Map 1: Archaeological and Topographical, 1:10,000, Millon et al. 1973 and Cabrera Castro 1993).

the problem of why there were so few rooms in the two compounds flanking the FSP and why their floor plans had remained virtually unmodified for several hundred years, whereas palaces are usually subject to continual remodeling and expansion, or even abandonment. The question of why a palace would require such a vast open plaza was left unasked, however. Although Cowgill came to no firm conclusion regarding function, one possibility he favored was that the Ciudadela began as a palace and then became a "frozen" symbol of state power, while the actual palaces migrated around the city according to the particular dynasty in power. Yet clearly the Ciudadela could have provided the stage for the great state ceremonies of investiture, emphasizing precisely those themes that were the duties of the nobility: militarism, rulership, and ritual leadership.

The Ciudadela and the FSP were both built at about the same time, and so were likely the result of a single unified vision. Rattray (2001:371) dates construction of the Great Platform surrounding the compound to the Miccaotli and Early Tlamimilolpa phases,[5] while Sugiyama (2004, 2005) favors a date of around AD 150–200 for the FSP dedicatory burials and the commencement of construction of the pyramid. About AD 350, the Adosada pyramid was built against the front of the FSP, an act that Sugiyama (1998b) interprets as a termination ritual. However, the Ciudadela as a whole continued to be utilized and modified until Metepec times (Rattray 2001:387, 393, 401), suggesting its continued relevance to the city. Certainly the feathered serpent continued to be a popular theme of Teotihuacan murals until its collapse.

The Ciudadela is also one of the most formally organized public spaces, and the fact that the FSP faces along the central axis of the Great Compound across the Street of the Dead is surely significant. This formality extends to the fifteen symmetrically placed temples along the Great Platform and to the virtually identical "palaces" on either side of the FSP (figure 10.3). Although these compounds appear to be somewhat later constructions, during the Early and Late Tlamimilolpa phases, they are nevertheless early in the history of apartment compound construction at Teotihuacan. Yet excavations revealed that their floor plans remained invariant for centuries (Jarquín Pacheco and Martínez Vargas 1982:123), leading to Cowgill's questions regarding function.

The strongest reason for considering the Ciudadela as the locus of investiture is of course the sculpture of the FSP. This platform is unique at Teotihuacan in being completely covered with stone sculpture.[6] Like the principal pyramids of Tenochtitlan, Xochicalco, Tenayuca, and Chichén Itzá, feathered serpents adorn the balustrades of the FSP (figure 10.2), and like many other feathered serpent pyramids, it faced west. Interpretation of the FSP as the point of investiture also permits a fuller understanding of why headdresses occur on the bodies of feathered serpents. Although they could simply be general allusions to themes of militarism and warfare, in keeping with the pyramid as a "frozen symbol," in my view they refer specifically to the *placing* of such headdresses through the agency of the feathered serpent. As noted by Sugiyama (1989), the feathered serpent is paired with a number of headdress types elsewhere at the site. These varied pairings are a strong argument against interpretation of the FSP as a "temple to time" or to specific deities; a more parsimonious explanation is to see such headdress-feathered serpent pairings as references to specific offices and ranks within Teotihuacan. Feathered serpents here and elsewhere provide a path; as balustrades, by framing the passages between rooms, or along the edges of benches or walls. They also transform, as the many examples of warriors issuing from the maws of feathered serpents attest. Thus, the feathered serpent forms the common denominator behind the investiture of a number of noble ranks or offices within the network of ancient Tollans.

Feathered serpents also bind and enclose, most famously on the *coatepantli* of Tenochtitlan, and the border around the Gran Nivelación of Chichén Itzá (Pérez de Heredia Puente 2010:194). Although no iconography has survived, the Great Platform surrounding the plaza of the Ciudadela performs similarly, creating an interior "sunken" space. Kristan-Graham (2007) has noted the significance of sunken patios in the ceremonial spaces of northern Mesoamerica and suggested that the Ciudadela might be one source for this tradition. Symbolically, the enclosed patio may represent the watery world, as the secondary imagery of the FSP frieze might suggest, from which rises the primordial Coatepetl. This does little to explain the fifteen temple platforms symmetrically arrayed along the Great Platform, though, which seemingly have little to do with either cosmogonic symbolism or any function the Ciudadela may have had as a palace. Instead there may again be a political dimension to its symbolism. By analogy with the *Codex Mendoza*, in which temples represent *altepetls*, and the *Mapa Quinatzin*, where glyphs representing Texcoco's subject polities are arranged in a rectangle around the palace, these temples may represent Teotihuacan's tributaries, enclosing and defining the plaza. The plaza, in turn, may thus symbolize the common space of the polity as a whole. The symmetrical arrangement of the temples suggests that they represent an abstract conception of the state, rather than particular subject polities. As for the "palaces" flanking the pyramid, the "majority of the architectonic elements combined with the severe rigidity of its floor plan, fortify the hypothesis that it was a center of basically religious functions, whose occupants possibly received as tribute sumptuary items and sustenance" (Jarquín Pacheco and Martínez Vargas 1982:123). Modifying Millon's (1976:237) argument that these housed twin rulers, they may instead have lodged a dual priesthood ancestral to the Quetzalcoatl priests who oversaw investitures at Cholula and perhaps at other Tollans in subsequent times. Perhaps some of the rooms also served as places of penitence and fasting, similar to the *tlacochcalco* of the Nahuas.

As mentioned earlier, Nahua investiture rites seemed to establish a complementary affinity between the *teoithualli* and the *ithualli* of the *tecpan* or *teccalli*, a correspondence that I believe can also be seen at Teotihuacan. In the search for the royal patio at the time of the Ciudadela, Millon's (1973:20, 1976:236) suggestion that the Great Compound (figure 10.3, G) may have housed the administrative apparatus of the city merits reconsideration. This compound supported a number of apartment complexes on its two halves, bounding an enormous central patio larger than that of the Ciudadela. As mentioned, the midline of this compound continues directly east to the FSP and notably, when walls were constructed between the temples of the Ciudadela in the Late Xolalpan period, the western wing was kept free of such obstructions (Rattray 2001:393), suggesting the sight line was important. The Great Compound has also been interpreted as the main market of the city, probably because of heavy Xolalpan-Metepec deposits (Rattray 2001:401) and its large open patio, but perhaps by this time the royal residence had moved northward to other complexes along the Street of the Dead, as Cowgill (1983) suggested.

With regard to the peripheries and the lesser nobility, descriptions of Toltec investiture among the later highland Guatemalan groups describe a variety of objects and emblems presented to the initiates following their confirmation (e.g., the *Popol Vuh*, Tedlock 1985:204). I suggest that insignias and prestations may also reflect the involvement of the nobility resident in Teotihuacan's apartment compounds in Toltec investiture rites. Sugiyama's (1998a) suggestive discussion of theater censers outlines one line of evidence. During excavations of the Ciudadela, a large workshop dedicated to the manufacture of mold-made theater censer components was discovered in an enclosure along its north side. Significant quantities were also discovered within the North Palace. Although hand-built theater censers are an Early Tlamimilolpa innovation, mold-made theater censers appear during the Late Tlamimilolpa phase (Rattray 2001:373, 377). Although thus postdating construction of the FSP, Sugiyama believes theater censers were products of a state-run manufactory.

As Berlo (1980) and Sugiyama (1998a) note, the iconography of theater censers concern warriors, and each censer could be individualized by the addition of selected *adornos*. Berlo also makes the point that the frames that often surround the head or body of the warrior are architectural. This is particularly clear with some of the Esquintla censers, where the frames are clearly houses or temples. In my view this point is central to their symbolism, for at Teotihuacan theater censers of known provenience overwhelmingly derive from apartment compounds, sometimes from beneath house floors but often from the main patios of apartment compounds. When they accompany burials, it is almost always of high-status males. Although typically identified as founders or lineage heads, at least in a number of cases they may have been the Teotihuacan equivalents of Toltec *teteuctin*, the theater censers being either heirlooms from their investiture or produced at the Ciudadela on the occasion of their burial. Burial 8 from Oztoyahualco is an example of such a mortuary context: a young adult male, he was by far the richest of the compound and had been buried in a pit in Patio 2 with a dismantled theater censer depicting a standing warrior (Manzanilla 2004:137). The fact that he was young makes it unlikely he was a lineage head or a founder, but he may well have been a young *tecutli*. Burials 1 and 10 of Zacuala (Séjourné 1959:fig. 35; Sempowski and Spence 1994:60, 64) both contained theater censers, and Burial 10 seems to have been placed in a patio, judging from Séjourné's profile.

Theater censers not accompanying burials may instead have been used to dedicate a compound as a lordly one by marking its most important communal space. An example of the latter would be fragments of at least two censers Linné (1934:48, 112–113) found beneath the central altar of the main patio of Xolalpan. These fragments, which include a butterfly nosepiece, clearly indicate a warrior was at its center. An interesting example combining both aspects was Burial 4 from Tlamimilolpa, a Late Xolalpan adult male burial placed in a courtyard (Room 1). The floor under the burial, the first of the series, sealed four fragmentary theater censers that had been ritually arranged when the patio floor was laid down (Linné 1942:172). Burial 4 was sealed by the subsequent floor. His grave contained two obsidian human effigies (the only examples from Tlamimilolpa) and laurel leaf obsidian points, objects perhaps distinctive to his rank. Perhaps it was he who was responsible for the initial designation of the courtyard group as a Toltec house and then, upon his death, he was placed at the center of the patio with further marks of his rank.

Other objects might signal similar connections. From the pretheater censer period, Burial 57 of the Tlajinga compound was buried in a patio beneath an altar and was one of the richest and earliest excavated (Storey 1992:97, table 4.4). Among other objects, excavation indicated he "was wrapped or clothed in a garment that had approximately 4,000 olivella shells sewn on it. On the skull was an elaborate headdress consisting of four shell disks, two carved in the form of coiled rattlesnakes and two shell filigree disks" (Storey 1992:97). The olivella-covered garment recalls the later *xicolli* tunic of Tula Toltecs, Itza, and Mexica investitures, while the serpent "goggles" recall the gold disks pulled from the Great Cenote of Chichén Itzá and those worn by the "effigy" of the Lower Temple of the Jaguars (who also had a pair of plain rings in his forehead). These and other objects suggest that the equivalent of *tecutli* investitures were also practiced in Early Classic Teotihuacan. In fact, their multiplicity may have been a contributing factor to the repetitive and "faceless" aspect of its iconography, leading some to doubt the existence of a central leadership (e.g., Pasztory 1997).

Xochicalco

The Plaza Ceremonial (or Principal) of Xochicalco very likely provided the corresponding arena for investitures at Xochicalco (figure 10.4). The Cerro Xochicalco is by far the most densely settled of the hilltops comprising the urban zone, and the Plaza Ceremonial was the largest and most elevated of the several plazas along its slopes (Hirth 2000:227–228). The plaza is further set off from surrounding construction by high terrace façades, restricting access to the zone of highest ritual and residential importance. Hirth also notes that it was the only plaza not connected to other districts by paved causeways, and that access was confined to two stairways. He further suggests that the Plaza Central to the south probably provided for public ritual on a regular basis, leaving the summit dedicated to elite ceremonies. Ballcourts, which seem to be intimately involved with Epiclassic accession rites, were located a relatively short distance away to the north and east.

The tendency toward dualism is evident in the bilaterally symmetric floor plans of many of the principal structures, such as the Pirámide de las Estelas and the Acrópolis, but less well appreciated is that this included the Pirámide de las Serpientes Emplumadas (PSE) as well, for just to its north is the poorly preserved Pirámide Gemela (PG). The Proyecto Xochicalco trenched both structures, revealing that the PG had a virtually identical orientation and dimensions to its neighbor, though it was apparently decorated with murals rather than stone friezes (González Crespo et al. 2008:132). The two faced west, as do the FSP and many of the serpent temples at Chichén Itzá. Both structures also had substructures, though these differed in form. Radiocarbon samples taken from the infill of these earlier buildings just prior to construction of the PSE and PG indicate they were some of the earliest buildings built in the ceremonial core, the PSE date being the oldest and the PG the third oldest at cal AD 635–669 and AD 664–723 respectively (González Crespo et al. 2008:fig. 9). Although physically separate, the two pyramids indicate the antiquity of the twin-temple group; another slightly later example can be found at Tula Chico (Mastache et al. 2002:71–76).

Like the FSP of Teotihuacan, the PSE was the only structure at Xochicalco to have been covered by sculptural friezes, and like it, was entered via a feathered serpent stairway. The friezes of both prominently feature the feathered serpent and symbols of rulership (figure 10.5). Smith (2000), in her stimulating

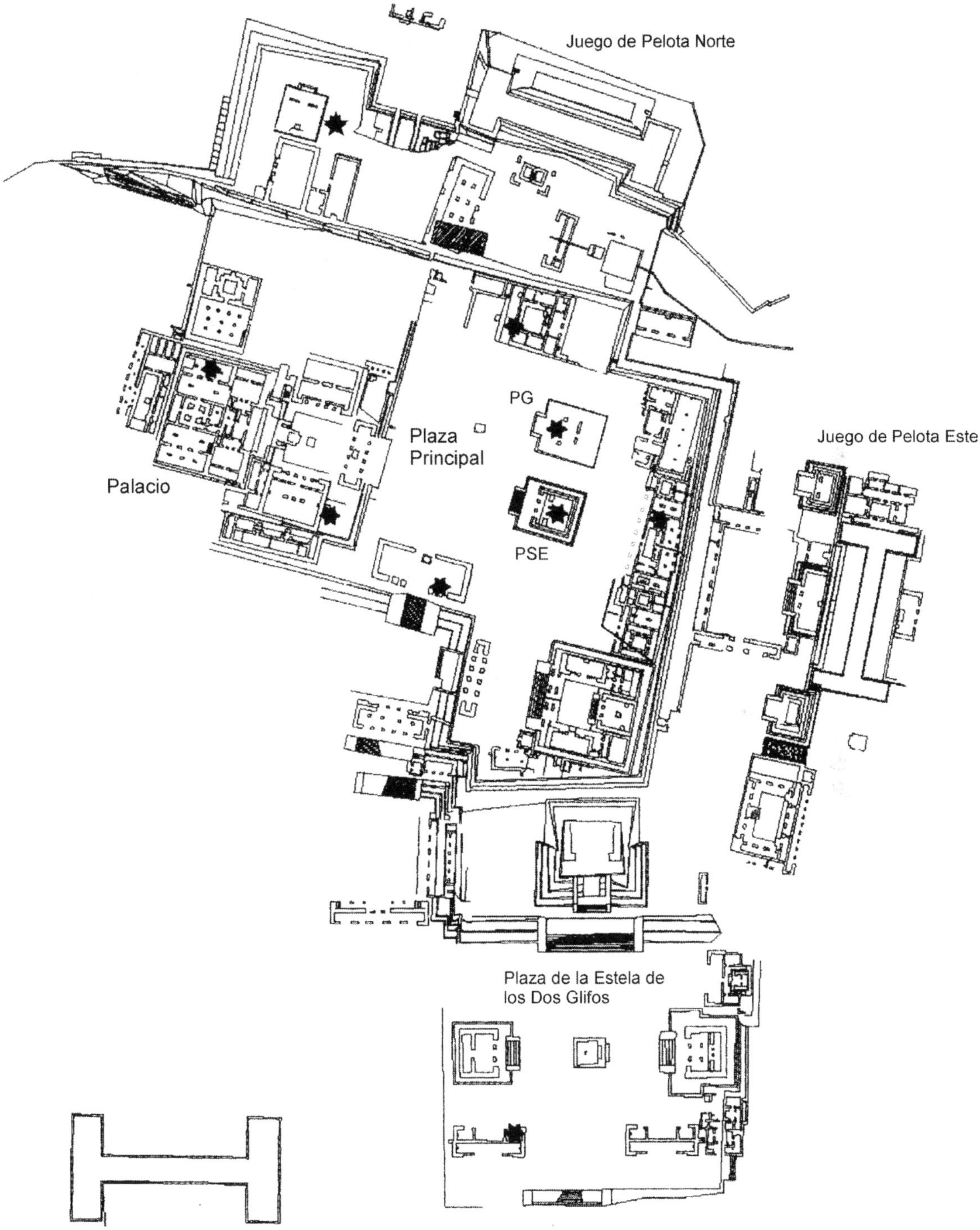

Figure 10.4. Map of the Plaza Principal/Ceremonial, Xochicalco (González Crespo et al. 2008: fig. 7).

study of the PSE sculptures, argues that they display political and military themes, rather than religious or nature symbolism. Although not hazarding a precise function, she seems to suggest that the building served as a memorial. In her view, the basal *taluds* (figure 10.5c) represent the watery underworld, with the figures on its back being "royal predecessors who have assumed the identity of, or who have been equated with, the Feathered Serpent" (Smith 2000:79). These are in essence ancestors, members of the "spiritual realm" floating around the feathered serpents. The *tablero* frieze (figure 10.5b), she argues, is a record of tribute and military conquest, with the seated warriors offering submission and tribute to Xochicalco's rulers. Following Hirth (1989), a repeated motif of a circle divided in quarters next to an open mouth with teeth exposed is interpreted as the "consumption of tribute or something precious" (Smith 2000:71). Finally, she argues that the *talud* of the superstructure (figure 10.5a), consisting of a series of seated (and some standing) warriors, perhaps represents members of Xochicalco's eagle and coyote military orders (Smith 2000:78), though she does not speculate further as to their precise purpose.

While agreeing with her general points regarding militarism and political authority, I believe that, like the FSP, these should be subsumed within the larger theme of investiture. First, the *tablero* frieze depicts several seated figures clad identically, even with regard to their headdresses, the usual place where individuality was marked in Mesoamerica. These headdresses have an embedded A-O trapeze-ray motif above a band with small circles, and each of the figures wears circular goggles. Both are markers usually associated with Teotihuacan's legacy, and I believe mark them as local or regional nobles of a particular rank or caste. But most telling to the conquest interpretation is that none of these figures are armed or in a posture of submission; instead each proffers an incense bag, or in the case of the four at the center of the rear façade, pots of some sort.

As for the glyph preceding each figure, it is unlikely they represent verbs since Central Mexican texts chiefly represent toponyms, dates, and names, while actions are represented pictorially. Also, the order of the texts is probably [variable glyph]:[quartered circle]:[mouth with teeth]. Following Berlo (1989:28, 33), the first is probably a specific toponym, but the two following glyphs probably indicate the type of place, much as the burning temples do for the toponyms in the first section of the *Codex Mendoza*. If Nahuatl was spoken at Xochicalco, a possible interpretation of the final sign is *-tlan*, which means "teeth" but is also a common grammatical suffix to indicate "place." It would therefore be a typical example of Nahuatl rebus sign formation. The quartered circle is less clear, but possibly refers to the four quadrants of the ideal community, the circle itself representing the community or perhaps the central plaza as a metaphor for that community.[7]

In my view, the incense bags indicate the seated figures belong to a priestly caste, or perhaps underscore the ritual duties of the nobility. (Those with pots may refer to the festivities associated with investiture.) They are not foreigners, but instead represent the communities or noble estates forming the Xochicalco polity. This group contrasts with the seated "procession" of warriors above them on the *talud* of the superstructure. They too are costumed identically

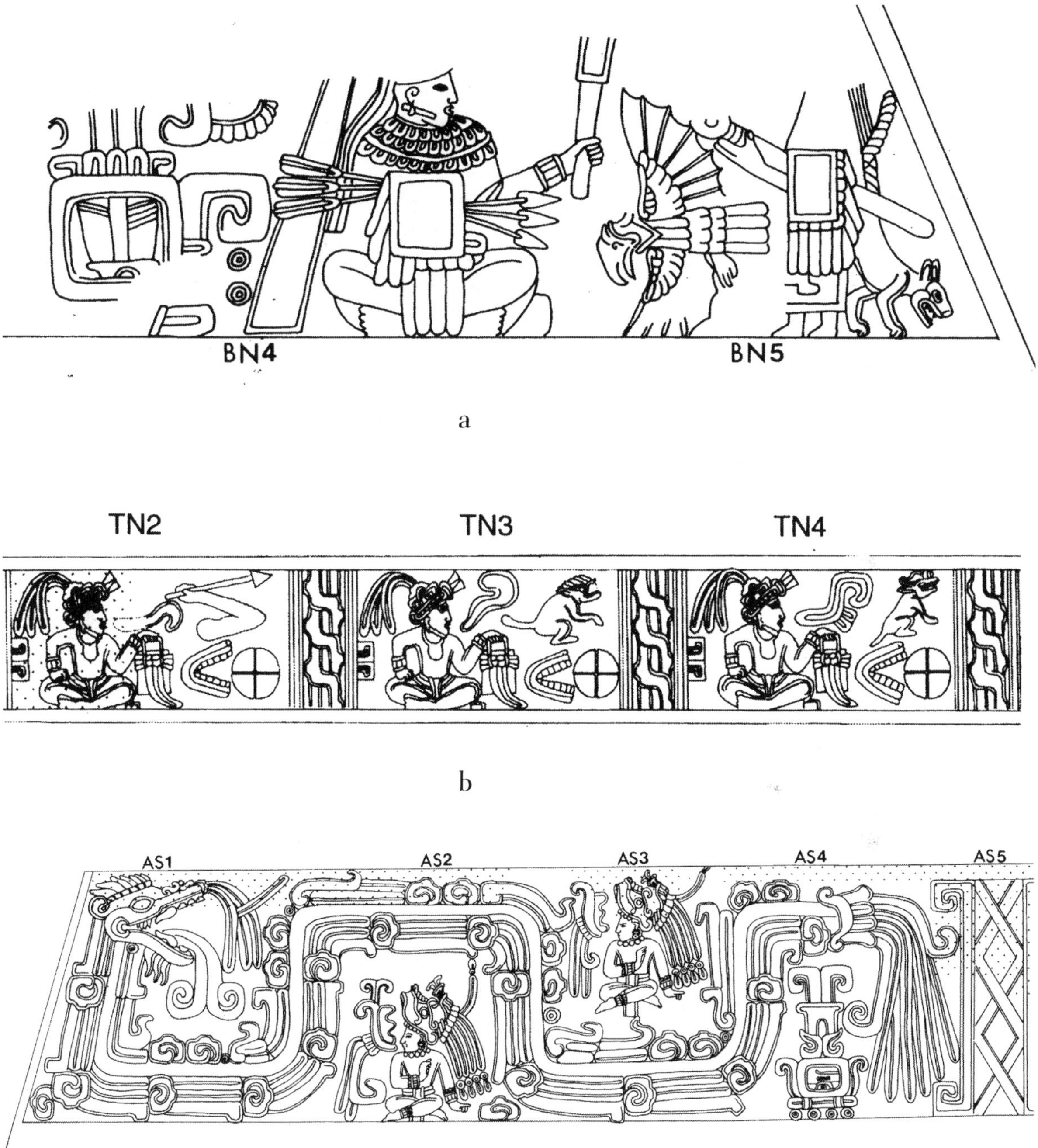

FIGURE 10.5. Details of the sculptural friezes of the Pirámide de la Serpiente Emplumada, Xochicalco. (a) Portion of the frieze of seated warriors from the upper northern *talud*; (b) portion of the frieze of seated priests or nobles on the northern *tablero*; (c) portion of the frieze of the lower southern *talud* (all from Smith 1988:fig. 1).

and carry darts, shields, and (probably) atlatls, but instead of toponyms, most seem to be associated with a large day-sign cartouche. Here I believe Smith to be correct in seeing them as representatives of the Xochicalco warrior sodality, with the caveat that their posture is one of attendance, not aggression. The important point to note is the contrast between this procession and that of the seated "priests" on the *tablero* below, both of whom encircle and bind the building. This same contrast of processional groups appears on two benches of the Temple of the Chac Mool, on the accession scene from the North Temple of the Great Ballcourt at Chichén Itzá (Ringle 2004; Wren 1994), and on the contrasting façades of the Nunnery at Uxmal (Ringle 2012), where I believe they depict two of the constituent "estates" of most Toltec polities. Thus, like the Ciudadela, the PSE is also a three-dimensional model of Xochicalco's political structure.

With regard to the *talud* along the base of the building, to my mind the figures are less ancestors than they are images of initiates: they are in essence full-figure forms of the headdress-on-feathered serpent so common at Teotihuacan (Ringle 2004). As Smith (2000) notes, the seated figures are very plainly clad in a loincloth, simple anklets and wristlets, and a necklace. All wear identical headdresses, not what one would expect of a series of portraits of past rulers. It makes more sense to see these as initiates stripped of their finery and poised to be conveyed by the feathered serpent to their new offices, represented in part by the mat signs that delimit each feathered serpent. Their helmets are not images of the feathered serpent, as Smith argued, but are instead akin to the war serpent headdress at Teotihuacan and to the similar headdress of the "hombre-pajaro-serpiente" complex (Taube 1992).

Although the residences of Xochicalco are at present insufficiently known to trace ties to individual *teteuctin* equivalents, the affinity between the plaza of investiture and the palace patio seems clear from the layout of the hilltop. The second oldest radiocarbon date came from the Acrópolis, a large palace structure forming the west side of this plaza (González Crespo et al. 2008:fig. 9). As mentioned, the palace has a highly symmetric floor plan,[8] and the PSE faces directly along the midline of this building from across the plaza, much as the FSP is oriented along the midline of the Great Compound. Palace and pyramid may well have been part of the same early construction event as Xochicalco established itself as a regional Tollan, providing strong spatial and temporal connections between the residence of the ruler(s) and the temples where they received their power. In addition to Teotihuacan, this pattern can also be seen later at Uxmal with the simultaneous construction of the Palace of the Governors and the Nunnery Quadrangle (Kowalski 1987; Ringle 2012).

Chichén Itzá

The dynamic between the central plaza of investiture and the patios of residential compounds is also reflected at Chichén Itzá, indicating that Toltec influence there extended beyond those resident in the site center. I will not rehearse previous arguments (Ringle 2004, 2009; Ringle and Bey 2009; Wren

1994) that several of the structures of the Gran Nivelación (Great Terrace) served as stations in rites of investiture, probably culminating in the ascent of the Castillo, but here I would like to briefly discuss the Lower Temple of the Jaguars. This small structure at the back of the Great Ballcourt faced east onto the Gran Nivelación. Indeed, it may be one of the earliest buildings still visible on this vast plaza. The central motif of the rear wall (figure 10.6), directly behind the jaguar throne, is the famous image of a feathered serpent rearing behind a strangely costumed figure. This figure, who has rings around his eyes and on his forehead and was clearly of central importance to the ritual life of the city, stands behind a hamper, facing two figures carrying large multicolor woven bags.

This is thus yet another example of a serpent bearing the headdress of high office, in this case the *xiuhuitzolli*, the peaked diadem worn by Mexica emperors. The *xiuhuitzolli* had a much broader distribution, however, as can be seen in the *Codex Mendoza,* where it is worn by a number of high officials and where it also serves as a glyph for *tecutli* (Berdan and Anawalt 1997:187, ff.17v, 18r). Mexica processional scenes also depict multiple instances of individuals wearing the crown (Beyer 1955). This is abundantly confirmed by recent excavations in the Casa de las Aguilas, where over 40 percent of the 201 bench figures wear the *xiuhuitzolli* (López Luján 2006:114). Processional scenes from Chichén Itzá also demonstrate that the peaked diadem could be worn by subroyal nobles: on the back wall of the Lower Temple of the Jaguars, two prominent individuals wear the crown (D9, C11), as do about 25 percent of the figures on the benches of the Temple of the Warriors and the Mercado.

The scene depicted in the Lower Temple of the Jaguars recalls the presentation of gifts and offerings by *teteuctin* candidates to the central leadership, as mentioned by Motolinia and de Rojas. A jaguar throne at its entrance, one of only a few at Chichén Itzá, may mark the spot where the paramount or high priest sat to receive these payments. The initiate, possibly the figure behind the strangely clad figure, is accompanied by figures in a variety of costumes, though few bear typical Toltec insignias. These may be his dependents from his home barrio or community. A further piece of support is that the rear frieze of this temple shows strong compositional parallels to the rear wall of the North Temple of the Great Ballcourt. The top registers of both center on figures with sun attributes seated on a jaguar throne placed within either a sun disk or a circular frame of feathered serpents and flanked by rows of Toltec warriors. Below are rows of nobles, many with Toltec insignia, followed at the bottom by processions of warriors in a variety of costumes. These scenes contrast at their centers, however: in the Lower Temple of the Jaguars, the subject is tribute presentation, but in the North Temple, the subject seems to be donning a *xicolli* tunic (Wren 1994),[9] one of the garments also presented to Nahua initiates in the Late Postclassic. Thus, the presence of the *xiuhuitzolli* on the feathered serpent, the presentation of offerings or tribute, and the deliberate compositional contrast with the donning of the *xicolli* all suggest that the Lower Temple of the Jaguars was an early station in the rites of investiture carried out on the Gran Nivelación and that such rites involved the local equivalents of *teteuctin,* as well as paramounts.

FIGURE 10.6. Detail, rear wall of the Lower Temple of the Jaguars, Chichén Itzá (Maudslay 1895–1902: plate 49).

Some sense of how this played out beyond the Gran Nivelación can be seen in the changes that outlying plaza groups experienced during the transition to the full Toltec manifestation (figure 10.7). We now have excavation information on one such group, the Grupo de la Serie Inicial, thanks to the work of Peter Schmidt (2005, 2007; see also Pérez de Heredia Puente 2010), and a much fuller picture of the organization of the *sacbe* system and the outlying groups they connect, owing to a survey conducted by Rafael Cobos (2003a, 2003b; Cobos and Winemiller 2001) and by Francisco Pérez Ruiz of Schmidt's project. It is clear that the progressive development of the Toltec arrangement was marked by the greater prominence and significant reorganization of outlying elite residential groups (Cobos 2003a; Ringle and Bey 2009). Most evident are the changes during the Modified Florescent stage of the city, when existing elite residential groups, set on large terraces usually connected to the site center by sacbes, were modified by the addition of an architectural complex consisting of a temple, an altar, and a gallery-patio or patio building, sometimes with the addition of a ballcourt. At the same time, new groups consisting of only these new forms were constructed around the peripheries of the city (Cobos 2003a, 2003b). Insofar as architecture is any guide, the introduction of temples, ballcourts, and gallery-patio structures, as well as the expansion of the sacbe system, reflect a new strategy of binding groups to the site core.

The regularity and comprehensiveness of such modifications indicate they were almost certainly the result of central directives regarding the reorganization of the nobility according to the new political ideology. Although we have little detailed architectural information outside of the Carnegie survey area, virtually all the reported group temples have warrior imagery, some sort of feathered serpent decoration (either balustrades, columns, or moldings), and a similar floor plan. They were in effect miniatures of the temples on the Great Terrace, a similarity that suggests they were part of an integrated network of *tecutli* rituals similar to those connecting the *teccalli* temples of Tlaxcala with the central temples. Similarly, the ballcourt and gallery-patio structures were miniatures of those ringing the Gran Nivelación.

Although information is again limited, it is intriguing that certain basal terraces (plazas) also share this pattern. The platforms of the Grupo de la Serie Inicial (figure 10.7a), the Grupo de las Bóvedas, the Grupo del Extremo Este (figure 10.7b), and the Grupo del Chultun (partially) are edged by low walls, which suggest a parallelism with those surrounding the Gran Nivelación and more broadly with the concept of the *ithualli* as an enclosed space. At Chichén Itzá, this parallelism is made literal by the physical linking of the two by means of *sacbes*. The latter may even have been conceptualized as extensions of plaza space, since the enclosure walls around the Gran Nivelación also extended up the edges of Sacbe 1.

Some iconographic support for this argument can be found in the procession scenes at Chichén Itzá. Some, such as the reliefs of the Lower Temple of the Jaguars, the North Temple, and the Temple of the Wall Panels, are large tableaux involving multiple registers, but another genre decorates the lower portions of benches in both serpent temples and gallery-patio structures, with close counterparts at Tula and Tenochtitlan. Where preserved, two lines of nobles usually converge on a sacrificial vessel or a *zacatapayolli*, almost always

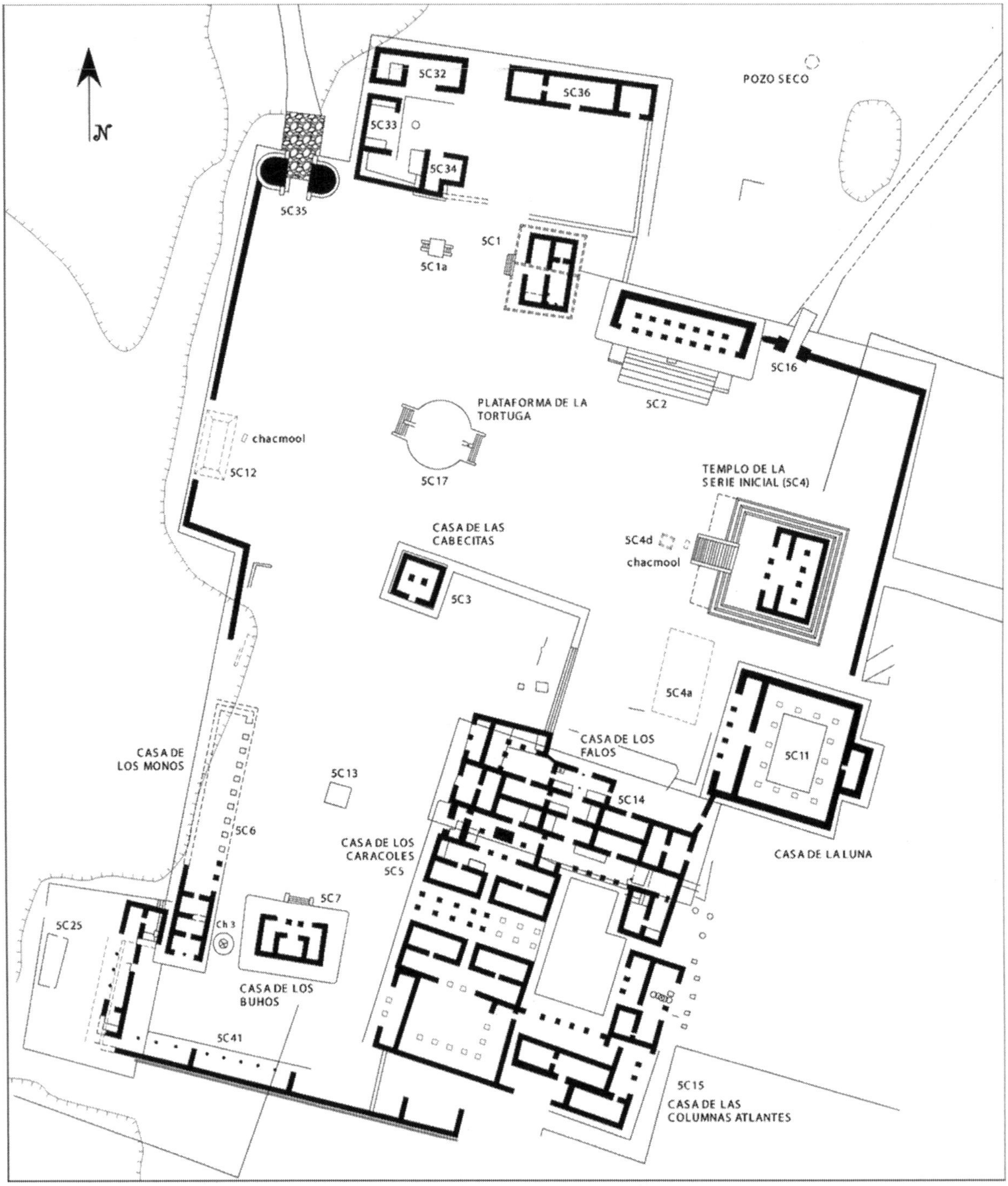
N
5C32
5C36
POZO SECO
5C33
5C34
5C35
5C1
5C1a
5C16
5C2
PLATAFORMA DE LA TORTUGA
chacmool
5C12
5C17
TEMPLO DE LA SERIE INICIAL (5C4)
CASA DE LAS CABECITAS
5C4d
chacmool
5C3
5C4a
CASA DE LOS FALOS
5C11
CASA DE LOS MONOS
5C13
5C14
5C6
CASA DE LOS CARACOLES 5C5
CASA DE LA LUNA
5C7
5C25
Ch 3
CASA DE LOS BUHOS
5C41
5C15
CASA DE LAS COLUMNAS ATLANTES

a

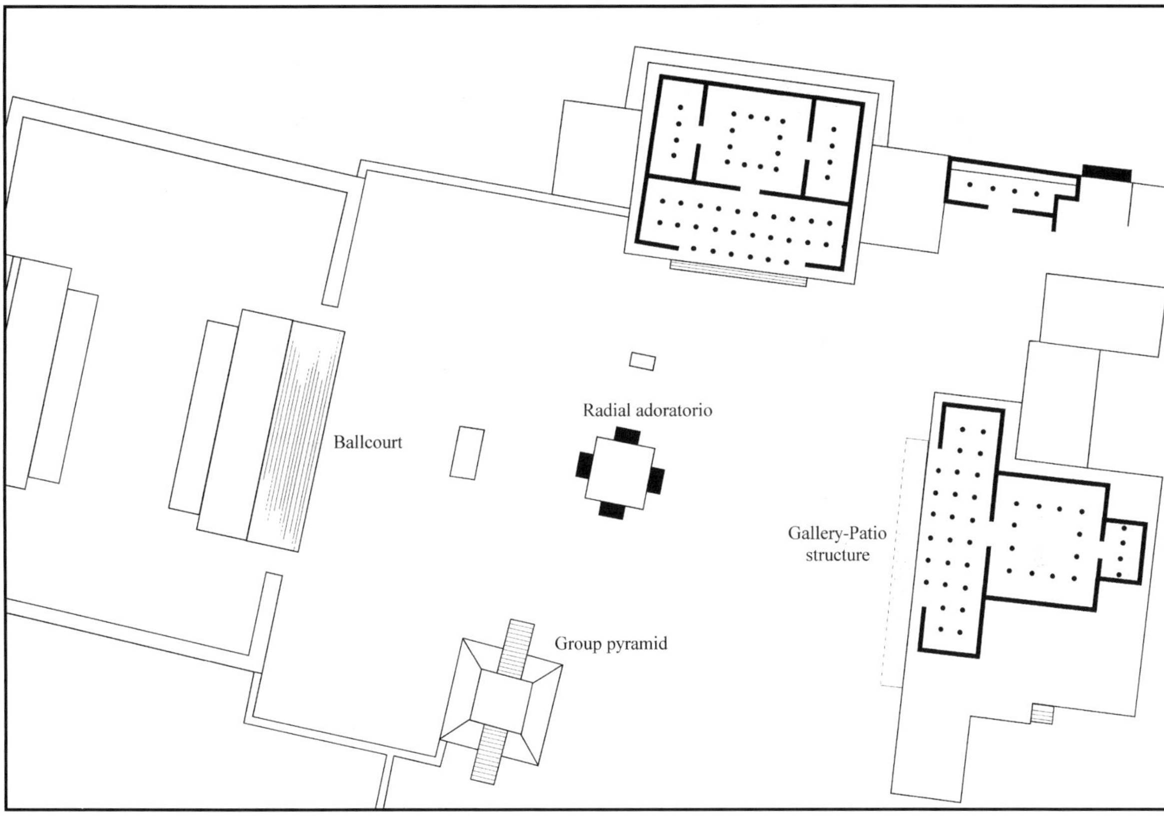

b

FIGURE 10.7. Outlying elite compounds, Chichén Itzá. (a) The Grupo de la Serie Inicial (redrawn from Schmidt 2005); (b) the Grupo del Extremo Este (redrawn from Cobos 2003a:fig. 5).

placed beneath the midpoint of a throne-like extension to the benches, equating the event depicted with whoever sat above. In the site center, these have been found associated with the Temple of the Warriors and the Mercado,[10] the largest of the gallery-patio structures, but the central portion of one such relief was found associated with Structure 5C11, the gallery-patio of the Grupo de la Serie Inicial (Schmidt 2005). What is interesting is that very similar conventions apply to all of them, including costume. In each a figure in a cap is one of the pair facing the central sacrificial object; often the opposing figure wears the *xiuhuitzolli*. This cap, blue where color is recorded, also has the two-feather *aztaxelli* ornament affixed. These may have had something to do with the founding of outlying compounds, as I favor, but whatever ceremony was being recorded, it was carried out in similar ways with similar ranks and in similar places in both the center and in the outlying noble compounds. That these processions were Toltec rituals is indicated by Mexica reliefs, such as the Centro Mercantil stone, as well as benches from the Casa de las Aguilas and the Templo Mayor. These show individuals in very similar costumes, including caps and *xiuhuitzollis*, while other costume details make it clear that these are archaized portraits of Tula Toltecs (López Luján and López Austin 2009:403–411). Presumably warriors seated on these benches were thus undergoing rites strongly influenced by this historical tradition.

Concluding Remarks

Much as humble architectural symbols such as the house could be telescoped to ever-broader levels of social integration, the above discussion argues for a similar metaphorical affinity between household patios and the civic plazas of the *altepetl* (or its equivalent). Were we able to elicit how the ancient residents of the cities discussed above regarded these open paved architectural spaces, I suspect that their answers would reflect the semantic domain associated with *ithualli* rather than *tianquiztli*. That is, I suspect their perceptions would emphasize the common bounded nature of such spaces, rather than the divisions between sacred and secular, or public and private, that contribute to our distinction between patio and plaza. At the highest level, this affinity was manifested in the link between the ceremonial precinct and the palace patio, but investiture rituals indicate these were also seen as like-in-kind to the patios of certain nonroyal nobles.

What, then, was being enclosed? A number of ethnohistorians (Chance 2000; Hicks 2009; Lockhart 1992; Terraciano 2000) concur that the house, in Levi-Strauss's (1987) sense of the term,[11] provides a useful means of characterizing social organization among a variety of highland communities at the time of the Conquest. The enclosed or raised residential patio may therefore have served to define the noble "house" in this extended sense, that is, not simply the lordly residence, but additional structures involved with the administration of the noble house as well, including places of gathering, temples, shrines, and so forth. Historically, I would argue, this commonality had its roots in the Toltec tradition forming the basis of their political organization, a key aspect of which was the empowerment of a broad spectrum of the nobility.[12] In addition to being warriors, such nobles directed large landed estates, or, as I argue, apartment compounds in the case of Teotihuacan. As the leaders of the fundamental residential divisions below the level of the polity itself, it was natural to symbolically equate the *teoithualli* with the *ithualli*, the *teocalli* with the *teccalli*, and the investiture of the *tlahtoani* and the *tecutli*. Abundant evidence indicates the symbolic use of the physical house in a similar fashion, but that is another project. But in any event, it suggests a somewhat different response to the question of who the Toltecs were. While variously understood as a people, a nation, or an ideology, they were also a noble stratum; Toltecs from the time of Teotihuacan onward were in some fundamental way the *teteuctin* of their time, as is made clear by the feathered serpent rearing above the assembled nobility in the frieze of the Lower Temple of the Jaguars.

Notes

1. By this is meant cities following a political ideology first defined at Teotihuacan and then widely disseminated after its fall. Tula Xicocotitlan was only one of these centers, thus Toltec as used here refers to a broader and longer lasting tradition.

2. Several FS sculptures in the Aztec gallery of the Museo Nacional de Antropología also have mat panels. The serpent balustrades on the side of the Tlaloc temple have neither feathers nor mat motifs, but are marked with two circles, references either to Tlaloc's goggles or to the two circles worn in the headdresses of gods and warriors associated with Toltec themes.

3. This perhaps suggests that the Cipactli head on the façade of the Feathered Serpent Pyramid at Teotihuacan refers not to time in the abstract ("a temple dedicated to the passage of time," López Austin, López Luján, and Sugiyama 1991:103), but to time as mediated through the ruler and his office.

4. Somewhat similar claims were made for Chichén Itzá in the *Relación de Tekanto y Tipikan* and the *Relación de Izamal y Santa María* (Garza 1983:I), though there framed in terms of tribute.

5. The approximate spans of the Miccaoltli and succeeding Tlamimilolpa phases are AD 150–200 and AD 200–350. Estimates of the final two phases differ slightly, with Sugiyama (2005) favoring AD 350–500 for the Xolalpan and AD 500–600 for the Metepec phases, while Rattray (2001:fig. 1b) dates the end of the Xolalpan to AD 550 and the Metepec phase from AD 550–650.

6. Other structures have façade sculptures, but none apparently to the extent of the FSP. A considerable quantity of sculpture lies along the base of the Pyramid of the Sun, for instance, but given the depredations to its exterior, it is impossible to know how much of it was originally covered by sculpture.

7. Berlo (1989:33) identifies the mouth glyph as the Mixtec locative prefix *a-*, rather surprisingly in that she quotes (1989:28) a previous suggested reading of *-tlan*. In my view, the ordering of the signs makes it more likely that the mouth served as a suffix. Her figures 5 and 10 show several examples in which a mouth with a full set of teeth was used to represent *-tlan*, even though other cases use just a tooth or two.

Berlo (1989:28) notes the use of the quartered circle and mouth compound at Cacaxtla to represent what is probably another toponym. Here there is only a single "variable" element, a bleeding heart, and since it is repeated five times, it most likely refers to Cacaxtla itself. This casts further doubt on the "consumption/tribute" argument, as it is unlikely that Cacaxtla would refer to itself in that fashion.

The quartered circle serves as the fifth day name on Zapotec monuments and also forms part of the Zapotec year sign, represented graphically as a headdress (Caso 1932:figs. 7, 8). It also ornaments (twice) the staff of office held by the ruler on Monte Alban Stela 1. A quartered circle forms the toponym for Pochtlan, where it seems to serve as a variant for *tianquiztli* (López Luján and Olmedo 2009:fig. 6f). It can also be seen on the façade of the Temple of the Warriors, Chichén Itzá, where it seems to be a back mirror, though these have a small central circle.

8. Excavations completed after González Crespo et al. (2008) revealed that a building very similar in floor plan to the palace was constructed just to its north, further reinforcing this "tendency toward dualism." This structure can be seen in the most recent Google Earth images.

9. Wren (1994:28) suggests the Lower Temple of the Jaguars served as the equivalent of the Mexica *tlacochcalco* or "house of fasting," but in my view (Ringle 2009), the Upper Temple of the Jaguars had that function.

10. The central figure of the Mercado procession is a single triumphant eagle warrior.

11. Lévi-Strauss (1982:174) defined the house as a "corporate body holding an estate made up of both material and immaterial wealth, which perpetuates itself through the transmission of its name, its goods, and its titles down a real or imaginary line, considered legitimate as long as this continuity can express itself in the language of kinship [descent] or of affinity [alliance] and, most often, of both."

12. I do not argue that this notion of the house was applicable solely to Toltec societies (see, for example, Joyce and Gillespie 2000, for other applications). I am also aware of Watanabe's (2004) critique of the concept. However, the house seems to be of fundamental importance for several of the societies who adopted Toltec ideology.

CHAPTER ELEVEN

Plaza, Atrium, and Maya Social Memory in Sixteenth-Century Itzmal

AMARA SOLARI

> After the high mass he brought a cross, newly made and for this purpose, and brought it in procession in all of the church's patio and he carried it, singing the litany, to the site and . . . he put by his own hands three rocks at the base of the cross as a symbol of the possession that he has taken.
>
> —Friar Tomé de Aragon to the crown, 1573, Archivo General de Indias

In August 1573 two Franciscan friars, Gregorio de Fuente Ovejuna and Hernando Sopuerta slowly made their way across the eastern expanse of the Yucatan Peninsula. Despite nearly four decades of colonization effort, this region of the province remained marginally Christianized, in Spanish eyes a wholly uncivilized corner of their expanding territory in New Spain. Beyond sustaining traditional Maya settlement patterns, in this region the indigenous population continued to venerate ancient deities, using ritual structures and associated plazas that did not adhere to Spanish notions of architecture appropriate for Christian worship. The Franciscans set out to change this, to recongregate the Maya population in Spanish-style towns organized around a central church and plaza. Selecting the peninsula's more eastern territory, the island of Cozumel, which had functioned as a pilgrimage destination for centuries, the friars began their ill-fated mission (Roys et al. 1940:7–8).[1] On October 3, the missionaries entered a sleepy island village of under two hundred souls, apparently with little ado. Six days later, on October 9, the friars performed the first mass for the Maya villagers, the account of which is quoted in the epigraph.

They then recount performing a possession ceremony, a procession, occurring in what they refer to as the "patio" of the "church," carrying a wooden cross to "all [its] parts." The friar then planted the cross in the middle of the plaza, signifying the colonization of pagan space for that of the Spanish *Dios* and by extension, the Spanish Crown as God's earthly representative.

This short anecdote, which surely echoes hundreds of evangelical experiences, highlights the ways in which open civic spaces of the built urban environment, plazas, or "patios," to use the Hispanized term, were the primary stages of the initial and then sustained Spanish-Indian colonial interaction.[2] In this chapter, I analyze plaza-like spaces and their associated ritual, arguing that in an ironic twist, introduced Catholic rites that were preformed in quadrilateral spaces can actually be understood as providing Maya populations with opportunities for resistance to the colonial regime. While archaeological excavations have yet to reveal how Maya populations conceived of these spaces, colonial archival sources, such as that quoted above, can be mined to show how the Maya population of the northern lowlands associated plaza rituals with transformation, the marking of temporal and social shifts.

In the following pages, I closely analyze detailed ethnographic accounts recorded by the now infamous Friar Diego de Landa in a manuscript known today as the *Relación de las cosas de Yucatán* (Restall and Chuchiak 2002).[3] In his rendering of two quadrilateral rites, it becomes clear that the Maya understood that during ritualized activation, plaza spaces became linked with past events, such as primordial cosmogenesis. In the Colonial period, friars such as Landa invented new forms of plaza rites, performed primarily in church atriums. To analyze this shift I look to the monastic complex of San Antonio de Padua in Itzmal (now called Izamal), designed by Landa himself, to offer a reading of Maya conceptions of Catholic rites. As the best-preserved mission church of the early Colonial period, this structure houses material evidence of the choreographed use of its atrium space, primarily in the form of painted walls and embedded Pre-Columbian finished stones. This evidence reveals a continuity of religious function of public quadrilateral spaces. Via the similarity of structured choreography, during ceremonies such as the Franciscan Ritual of the Five Wounds, Maya social memory was activated and built upon, allowing performance in plazas to function as a way of maintaining indigenous agency, even when clouded or concealed by the veil of Catholicism.

To do so it is first necessary to expand our traditional understanding of plaza spaces to include all open quadrilateral spaces surrounded by a built environment, either of domestic or ceremonial architecture. This allows for the consideration of nonelite civic spaces, such as village plazas and even domestic areas, spaces typically ignored due to their lack of material remains. In the northern Maya lowlands, at the time of Spanish contact, ceremonial cores were defined by a few low lying platforms, the summits of which hosted rather humble small chapels or corbel vaulted domestic structures. Given that there was no masonry church in Cozumel in 1573, the "church" to which the friars refer was undoubtedly a humble pole and thatch structure, erected on top of one of the village's diminutive mounds. The "patio" then, by extension, was the Maya village's central plaza, a space that for centuries surely hosted a veritable suite of ritualized public events.

I argue below that the semantics associated with Pre-Columbian plazas were transferred in the early Colonial period to a newly introduced quadrilateral space that was similarly monumental in scale: the church atrium. Like their Pre-Columbian predecessors, atriums fronted the most sacred religious structure in a colonial town, the Catholic church, abutted the actual plazas of colonial urban plans, and functioned as the primary stage for community religious events. Moreover, the designed choreography of Catholic processional rites appears to have fortuitously replicated those of the precontact ritual tradition, opening up the possibility of Catholic rites as spaces of indigenous appropriation in the early colonial world.[4]

Landa's Ethnohistorical Accounts of Quadrilateral Ritual Spaces

Friar Diego de Landa arrived in the Yucatan in 1549, as one of four new recruits delivered to aid in the drastically understaffed evangelical effort of his Franciscan order. He was assigned to the more experienced Friar Lorenzo de Bienvenida, and the two were charged with establishing a mission center in the area ruled by the Ah Kin Chel patriline. They selected the site of Itzmal as a base due to its impressive Pre-Columbian ruins (figure 11.1), which Friar Bienvenida recognized as an expedient aspect of building the new monastery.[5] While Itzmal had been inhabited from the Late Preclassic period, its material remains largely dated to the Early Classic, during which it was one of the largest urban centers in the northern Maya lowlands. The ceremonial core consisted of four immense mounds, clustered around the negative space of a monumental plaza. Extant sculpture, such as the monumental stucco masks that adorned the southern side of the Kabul pyramid, was also visible with its iconography linking this center to those of the southern Maya lowlands (figure 11.2). This resemblence of similar forms from lowland sites such as Cerros, Uaxactún, and Tikal suggests Itzmal's participation in a similar and mutually informing aesthetic system. By the mid-sixteenth century, however, Itzmal's political and economic glory had faded, but the site's religious importance remained intact; the site functioned as a pilgrimage center to Itzamnaaj, the Maya deity of healing and sacred knowledge. When the Franciscans established their mission, the mostly ruined city was still inhabited by a handful of religious specialists attending to pilgrims who wished to come into contact with the site's numinous powers.

On August 6, the Franciscans mounted the largest of Itzmal's monumental structures, what today is known as the Kinich Kak Moo, constructed a temporary church out of perishable materials, and recited the first mass. In a seeming supernatural moment, a large gust of wind swept through the Yucatec plain, crashing the humble church to the plaza below. The friars then moved their operational base to the summit of the mound that graced the southern side of the plaza, the Ppap Hol Chac. This mound featured architectural spaces that lent to the friars' missionary project and thus remained relatively unworked for the next four years. During this time, Landa left Itzmal, venturing into the primarily uncontacted zone of central Yucatan. It was during these years

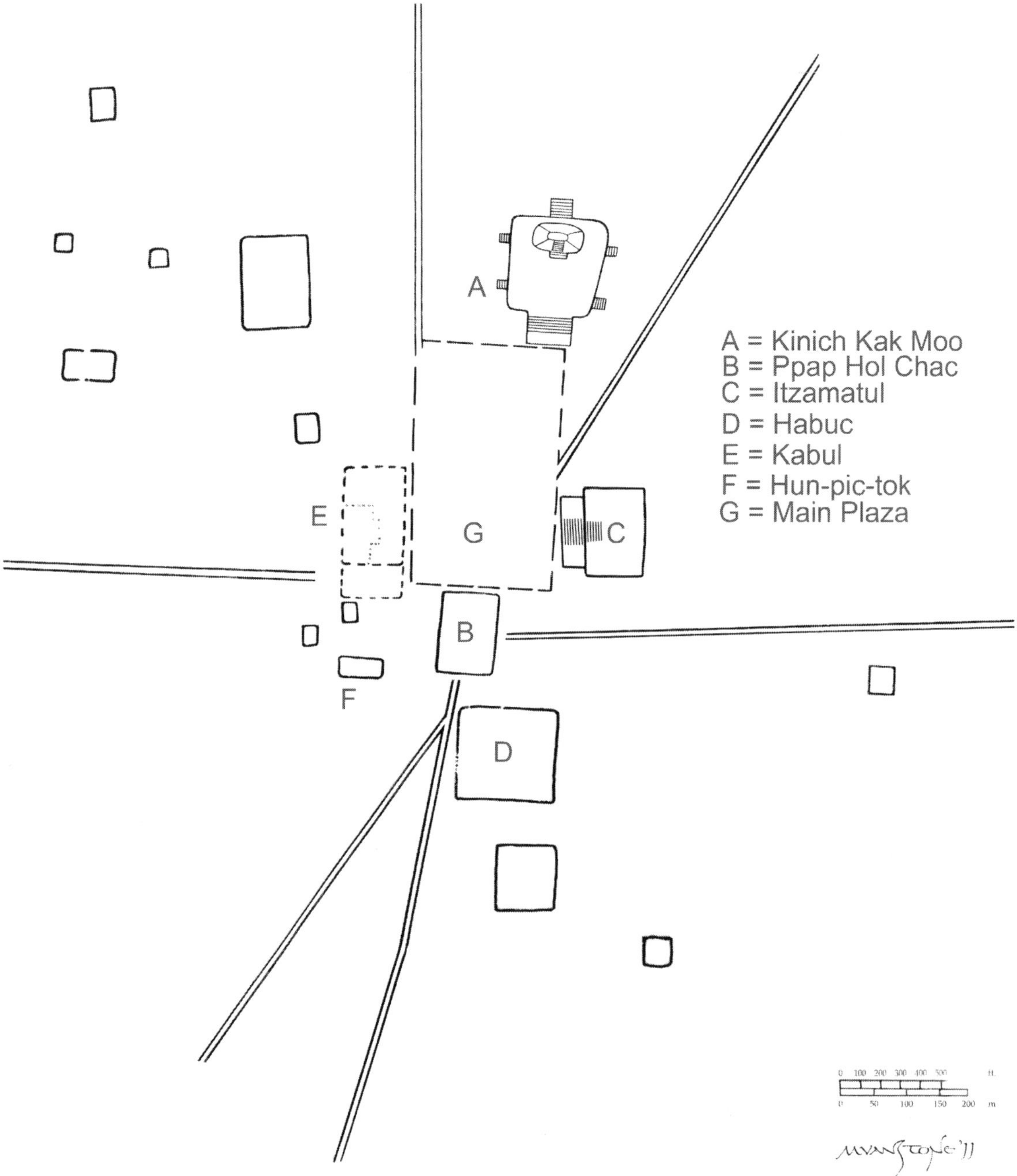

FIGURE 11.1. Plan of the Pre-Columbian city of Itzmal. Drawn by Mark Van Stone.

FIGURE 11.2. Photograph of a monumental sculpture (now destroyed) that adorned the upper terrace of the Kabul pyramid. Photograph by Désiré Charnay.

that Landa must have had firsthand contact with many of the region's ruling families, perhaps most significantly with the Cocoms of the kingdom based at Sotuta. After being summoned back to Spain, following the now infamous events of 1562, Landa recorded a plethora of ethnographic data, presumably garnered during this time period, but never with the initial intent of preserving accounts of Maya lifeways. Regardless, in the absence of a Florentine codex-like commissioned project, Landa's writings remain the most detailed colonial account of Yucatec Maya cultural practices in existence today.

As a religious man, Landa found particular relevance in Maya ceremonial life, although like his contemporary Friar Bernardino de Sahagún in central Mexico, his motives were probably aligned with his missionary goals of first identifying and then eliminating practices he deemed idolatrous. Regardless of his motivations, Landa recounted various forms of Maya ritual in sumptuous detail, allowing for a unique vision into the now lost world of ephemeral ritual moments. Without drawing definitive differences, Landa described two primary forms of Maya ritual life, those of personal endeavor associated with long distance pilgrimage, and those enacted at the community level within civic space. This chapter is concerned with the latter class of ritual, for they featured village-level, quadrilateral spaces that replicated the more monumental plaza spaces of Maya lowland sites.

While scholars of the Classic Maya have attempted to correlate architectural remains with probable ritual circuits, the modern restructuring of many Postclassic Yucatec towns makes such a methodology difficult (Reese-Taylor 2002;

Newsome 2001).[6] As such, the words of sixteenth-century chroniclers have to be relied upon to illuminate Pre-Columbian practices. In Postclassic Yucatan, the singularly predominant ritual format, that of quadrilateral circumambulation in a counterclockwise course, appears to have defined localized public ritual. During these ritual performances participants either physically delineated or kinetically mapped a square-shaped ritual stage through counterclockwise circumambulation around the four cardinal directions (Gossen 1974; Restall 1997; Vogt 1976).[7] Landa's *Relación* recounts many examples of this form, presumably witnessed firsthand during his time in Sotuta, but I discuss only two. Matthew Restall has also observed a similar pattern in his discussion of early colonial Maya land titles. For a further discussion on the graphic implications of this tradition on colonial Maya cartography, see Solari (2010).

I begin with a ritual that Friar Landa mistakenly terms "baptism," which is more appropriately understood as a coming of age ritual. The Franciscan relates that when parents of children between the ages of three and twelve determined their offspring ready to undergo this social transformation, they informed the community's *ah-kin* of their intentions. After a period of three days of bodily ritual preparation, which including fasting from food and sexual relations, the rite was directed by the ah-kin, the sponsoring fathers, and four community elders whom Landa refers to as "chaces." Transpiring in the town's central communal area, the plaza, the ritual space was prepared by further physically and thus spiritually demarcating it from that of the mundane community. According to the Franciscan:

> they placed four little stools in the four corners of the patio, on which sat the four chacs with a large cord strung one to the other, in this way they kept the children inside or outside of the cord, the fathers who had fasted then passed over the cord to enter the circuit. Later, or before, they had placed in the middle of the circuit another little stool where the priest sat with a brazier, a little bit of ground maize and a little bit of incense, and they placed these in the brazier. (Landa 1996:93)

To Landa's Eurocentric eyes, this process ensured that the "demonio" was removed from the ritual stage, but to the Maya participants, this series of actions clearly had larger cosmological significance. Once delineated, the children went through a series of ritual prescriptions, including the removal of accoutrements they had donned since birth, the anointing of their bodies, and finally their first act of sacrifice, offering corn kernels to the flames of the central brazier. While these pithy ethnographical details deserve more attention than space allows here, what is intriguing for the purpose of this study is that in the Yucatec example the rectilinear ritual stage is clearly intended to map a cosmogram. In Maya conceptions of the universe, there were actually five world directions, the cardinal directions and also the center, defined by the central point of the square-shaped terrestrial realm (Mathews and Garber 2004). The four deity impersonators sitting in the world directions defined the shape of the cosmos, visually delineating the microcosm of the ritual stage by holding the dividing cord between them. The presence of the ah-kin in the center of the square further emphasized the cosmogram. Conceptually, it was at this center point where a connection between the levels of the universe was established, and thus it was the most appropriate point for the ah-kin, as the community's mediator between the mundane and the divine.

Due to the fact that chac impersonators embodied the anchoring points of the cosmogram, they also granted a myth-historical aspect to the spatial scheme. Each of chac's four aspects was linked to a specific direction of the cosmos and a particular color. As such, the chacs were directly associated with the *Bakabob* of the Postclassic. According to Landa:

> They were four brothers, those put by God when he created the world, at the four parts of it, supporting the sky so that it wouldn't fall down. . . . They assigned each one of these names and signaled with them the part of the world where God had put them, holding the sky, and they applied to them one of the four cardinal directions and the area where they are. And they pointed out the miserable or happy events that they said had happened during the year of each of them. (Landa 1996:115)

With the presence of the four chacob/Bakabob, the coming of age ritual's stage provided a spatial and temporal context mirroring that described in creation accounts. The ritual's actors established and further reified the ideal form of the world, as dictated by the deities, due to the physical presence of primordial actors responsible for the cosmos's maintenance.

Coming of age rituals traditionally function as public acknowledgment of a vast change in the composition of the corporate body as the society's disparate age grades are augmented. Within this Maya ritual form, the sacred acts of the deities are replicated, providing divine validation for the social alteration completed by the ritual act. Thus, the reenactment of the primordial event of creation is a stabilizing act. It fuses cosmic space and time with that of the living community and, in the process, restructures and solidifies the composition of the corporate body.

An additional ritual description furnished by Landa also evinces this ritualized commensurability of cosmic and historical time, the annual Maya New Year ceremonies. Landa's description of this ceremony's four variants is so detailed that, like the coming of age ritual, he most likely witnessed these events firsthand.[8] Traditionally, it has been assumed that Landa's descriptions detailed the New Year rituals as commencing on the preceding year's first day of Uayeb, but Taube has convincingly argued that Landa's accounts actually correspond to the Uayeb period of each named yearbearer (Taube 1988:277). The New Year's rites commenced during the *tolk'in*'s terminal and portentous "month," Uayeb, which lasted only five days. Due to the mathematical principles particular to the *haab*'s divisional form (the contributing values of eighteen and twenty) the solar year could only begin on one of four days from the tzolk'in calendar, Cauac, Kan, Muluc, or Ix.[9] The Maya imbued these days, like all days of the tzolk'in, with particular characteristics, associated with specific colors, trees, deities, and cardinal directions. Specifically, the day Kan registered the south and yellow, Muluc the east and red, Ix the north and white, and finally

Cauac, the west and black. Termed the "yearbearers," the personality of the day that inaugurated the New Year foreshadowed the events that were destined to transpire in the next 365 days (Vail 2009:60–61).

In the interest of space and due to structural variances between all four yearbearer rites, I will describe in detail only that which commemorated the ending of Kan years and began at the beginning of Uayeb.[10] On the first day of Uayeb, a hollow ceramic vessel representing the year's patron deity, Kan u Uayeyab, was produced. Community leaders carried this image to the town entrance located nearest to the yearbearer's directional association, the south. Here, Kan u Uayeyab inhabited one of two facing altars, confronting the yearbearer statue positioned at its post since the onset of the previous year, the Chac u Uayeyab of the preceding Cauac year. After sweeping and adorning the road leading to the town's southern entrance, priests incensed the Kan u Uayeyab with forty-nine grains of ground corn and copal and sacrificed a turkey as an offering. Meanwhile, religious leaders transported an additional statue, Bolon Dzacab, to the home of the festivity's sponsor, located in the town's center, where the deity was placed on an altar. The Kan u Uayeyab was then processed to the sponsor's house where it was positioned next to Bolon Dzacab. Once inside, townspeople offered food and drink to the two deities and elite men performed autosacrifice, smearing their drawn blood on a stone called *kanal acantun*. When the five days of Uayeb terminated, these men carried Bolon Dzacab to the town's most important religious temple. Simultaneously, others transported the Kan u Uayeyab to the town's eastern entrance, the direction associated with the impending Muluc year. The New Year ceremonies ended with an animal sacrifice (Landa 1996:117).

Three hundred and sixty days later, with the onset of the Muluc year Uayeb month, the New Year celebrations for the following year, Ix, commenced. Artists created another hollow clay image of the new yearbearer, Chac u Uayeyab, and carried it to the eastern entrance of town, on the altar facing Kan u Uayeyab. Like the Kan year, Muluc years had an additional patron deity, Kinich Ahau, whom participants transported to the house of the Muluc sponsor. At the eastern entrance, religious leaders again incensed Chac u Uayeyab, but for Muluc years, the prescription was slightly altered; fifty-three grains of ground corn and incense were burned and they again offered a headless turkey. Thereafter, the priests placed Chac u Uayeyab on a standard and carried it to the patron's home to be reunited with Kinich Ahau. This New Year ritual called for dances that community members performed on the town's eastern road en route to the sponsor's house. Again, men and some boys engaged in autosacrifice, applying the blood to a stone called *chac acantun*. On the last day of Uayeb, townspeople carried Kinich Ahau to the temple, like Bolon Dzacab of the previous year, and Chac u Uayeyab took up his appropriate residence at the northern entrance of town, the direction associated with the Ix yearbearer.

The Chac u Uayeyab remained at the northern entrance for the 360 days of the Ix year and on the first day of Uayeb it was joined by the yearbearer of Cauac years, Sac u Uayeyab. The Ix New Year ceremonies approximate those of the Kan and Muluc years, the only difference being that the patron deity was Itzamnaaj. After community members completed the incensing and blood sacrifices in the patron's home, they carried Itzamnaaj to the temple and Sac u

Uayeyab inhabited one of the two altars erected at the city's western entrance. After 360 days passed and the Ix year's Uayeb began, the Cauac yearbearer, Ek u Uayeyab, joined Sac u Uayeyab. Repeating the ritual prescription, the *ah-kinob* carried this yearbearer to the house of the ceremony's sponsor where they reunited it with the year's additional patron, Uac Mitun Ahau. After the five days passed, Uac Mitun Ahau was carried to the town's temple and Ek u Uayeyab took its place at the western entrance. When 360 days transpired, the cycle began again.

When the ritual circuit is charted, as evidenced in Landa's account, two patterns emerge. The first is that a counterclockwise course was adopted, taking four years to complete a single rotation around the four world directions of the microcosmic town plan.[11] In the Uayeb rite, time was solidly anchored to specific loci in the local urban landscape. Thus, history and space were conflated; the passage of time dramatically inscribed the cityscape, functioning as the organizing principle of the human landscape.[12] Second, in its directional associations and ceremonial processional pattern, the New Year ritual corresponds to Maya perceptions of the cosmos' creation. This notion of time as a spatial model of urban planning mirrors, on a local level (the microcosm), conceptions of the shape of the macrocosm. The zenith path of the sun determined the shape of the universe's terrestrial plane. The arches the sun creates on summer and winter solstice determines the universe's northern and southern edges. Within the microcosm of the city, human actors and individual yearbearer statues performed the same organizing function as the sun for the entirety of the cosmos. In the course of its enactment, this highly choreographed ceremony creates the idealized Maya urban plan, described during foundation rituals, and in the process weds community identity with the origin and continuation of the universe.[13] Therefore, the circumambulation of the yearbearers around the political boundaries of the community served to reenact the shape of the cosmos and its creation, and thus the subsequent production of the social body during an annual rite of renewal and its four-year completed cycle.

In accordance with this primordial mapping for civic ritual, Paul Connerton (1989) notes that the rhetoric of rituals that reenact (or merely substantiate) moments of creation uses the metaphorical present, not the past, creating the illusion that mundane time is suspended (43). He goes on to argue that since reenactments of past events depend on prescribed bodily behavior (such as a defined and repeated quadrilateral and counterclockwise structure) to be rhetorically persuasive, the past becomes effective and meaningful because the present population is still capable of performing it. In the Maya world, when a community delineated the shape of their cosmos in the context of a coming of age ritual or during the Uayeb rites, the local population reenacted the deities' creative acts. The square-sided space of plazas activated primordial events, placing the community within the moment of creation and reifying the corporate body and associated community identity. They effectively restructured the corporate body during times of social and temporal change, defining local communities as a distinct "self" and thereby cementing community cohesion via divine validation. In the following section, we will see how this spatial ideology of rectilinear ritual stages continued in the Colonial period, albeit put to a drastically divergent sacred function.

Itzmal's San Antonio de Padua Monastery

After his wanderings in the Yucatec *monte*, Landa was recalled to Itzmal to take residence as the mission's primary friar. In the intervening years his predecessor, Friar Bienvenida, had done little to establish a permanent monastery. With the assistance of architect turned Franciscan friar, Friar Juan de Mérida, Landa designed and then constructed the monastic complex that would be cited as a mark against the Franciscan order due to its opulence (figure 11.3).[14] Construction began in 1552 and, using forced indigenous labor, lasted nearly ten years.

Unlike most of the religious structures in Yucatan, San Antonio de Padua was conceived of in its final form, its architects always intending it to consist of a masonry nave, double-storied cloister, open chapel, and, of course, a monumental atrium (figure 11.3).[15] The sixteenth-century monastery remains remarkably intact, with only the later colonial additions of a *camarín* at the eastern side of the nave, an additional cloister, atrium arcades, and a clock tower to alter Landa and Mérida's original vision. Due to shifting aesthetic values in the eighteenth century, the monastery's original murals of the mid-sixteenth and early seventeenth century were covered with whitewash. During a recent reconstruction project, this extensive visual culture was revealed, allowing it to be interpreted within the context of early colonial ritual.

Like all monasteries of the sixteenth century, the open space of Itzmal's atrium functioned as the colonial town's center, hosting the primary activities associated with ideological colonization including catechism, baptism, and a suite of Catholic rites. Like their Pre-Columbian precedents, little evidence exists for the exact ritualized use of this space; Spanish friars are strangely silent on the topic. However, the material evidence does allow for the elucidation of particular routes, and iconographic details suggest when particular Catholic rites were enacted.

The four-sided space of the atrium was used as a processional route, with a counterclockwise course being the common pathway for orchestrated movements. While numerous rites that used this choreography surely existed, I will focus on just one, the Ritual of the Five Wounds. Although European in origin, the mendicants of the New World adapted its kinetic format in the first years of the American evangelical program in Mexico City, transforming it into a quadrilateral circumambulation. The New World Ritual of the Five Wounds so perfectly adheres to the physical limitations of colonial atriums that the architectural design and the ritual performance are in a dialectical relationship—the rite appears as an organic outgrowth of the ritual space. It seems that the adaptation of the rite was not accidental, the Franciscan order augmented this ritual as a means to replicate indigenous understandings of the sacred by creating a ceremonial procession that mirrored ideologies of place-making and cosmogenesis.

On Good Friday, congregations gathered in monastic cemeteries and performed the Crucifixion, nailing an articulated Christ statue crucified to a cross. On the following day, participants performed the Descent and removed the Christ statue under the observation of Joseph, Nicodemus, Mary, and John the Baptist, in accordance with biblical doctrine. Directly following the Descent, the Ritual of the Five Wounds began by the transporting of the Christ statue

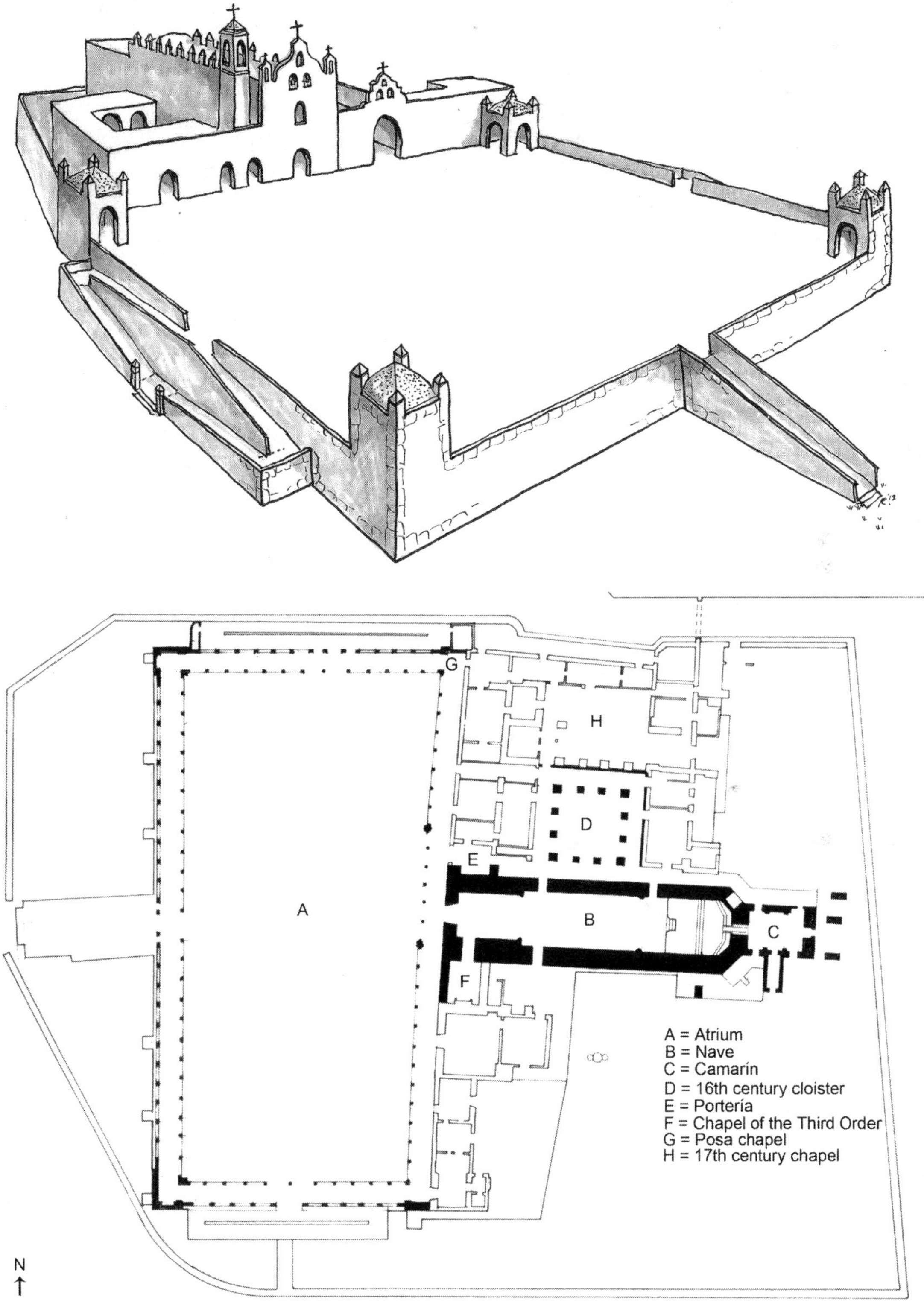

FIGURE 11.3. Drawing of San Antonio de Padua, as it would have appeared in 1562 upon completion. Drawn by Matthew Restall. Plan of the San Antonio de Padua Monastery, Itzmal, Yucatan. Photograph from the Hal Box and Logan Wagner Collection of Mexican Architecture and Urban Design. Courtesy of the School of Architecture Visual Resources Collection, The University of Texas at Austin.

into the nave of the church and ambulating toward the eastern altarpiece. Here, participants deposited Christ's body directly on the altar and the priest orated a sermon honoring the first of Christ's five wounds. With the sermon complete, the procession then recommenced and participants lifted Christ's body, processing along the south side of the nave, toward the church's main entrance in the western façade. Once outside, the procession immediately turned right, walked along the mission's façade, and paused at the first of the atrium's four *posa* chapels, located in the northeast corner of the patio. Participants deposited Christ's body on a small altar situated against the posa's northern wall and the priest gave another sermon honoring Christ's second wound.

Evidence for this route is provided at Itzmal by the extant murals located on the northern wall of this northeastern posa chapel.[16] Included in this later mural cycle is a diminutive image painted on the north wall of the northeast posa chapel. Like the façade murals, this painting likely covers a nearly identical sixteenth-century version. Following the structure provided by the chapel's *testera*, the painting represents an arched form, completed in shades of blue and red, outlined with a heavy black line (figure 11.4). The arch is divided into square-shaped registers by parallel lines that are placed perpendicular to the framing lines of the arch. Within each square frame a single image is registered. Only the left half of the arch has been amply preserved to allow for analysis, but it is clear that the mural represents a stylized *arma christi*, detailing the instruments used against Christ during the Passion. Moving up from the bottom left jamb of the arch, the nails, cloak, die, rooster, and ladder are all clearly visible. The presence of the arma christi in this grid-like architectural context suggests its didactic purpose in Passion rituals, such as the Ritual of the Five Wounds.[17]

The procession then walked the length of the atrium's northern wall, pausing in the northwest posa for the sermon. Next, the southwest and then southeast posas were visited completing the last two wounds.[18] Having appropriately venerated the Five Wounds, the participants turned left and processed the western façade of the monastery until they reached the *portería*, the antechamber leading from the atrium to the cloister. Once inside, the congregation began the next rite, the Deposition, by interring Christ in a sepulcher located in one of the cloister's deep testera niches.[19]

The formal similarity between this Catholic rite and Pre-Columbian quadrilateral rituals, such as those discussed above, would have clearly resonated with the indigenous population. Catholic rituals enacted within the Itzmal atrium actually referenced, capitalized on, and directly responded to the Pre-Columbian function of similarly shaped spaces. As such, the Ritual of the Five Wounds, and others that utilized this ritual design, stands as an example of what Eleanor Wake (2010), in reference to Pre-Columbian religious traditions, has recently termed "framing rituals," rites that create "a ritual arena to which the sacred could be called or enticed, in which its presence could be indulged, albeit for only a fleeting moment" (46). The Ritual of the Five Wounds was performed during the moment of the Passion that was inherently conceived of in liminal terms. Between the time of the crucifixion and burial, the death of Jesus and his Resurrection on the third day, the course of Christian history was inevitably in question. Liturgical reenactment of these events during Holy Week

Figure 11.4. Detail of the arma christi mural located in the northern wall of the northeastern posa chapel. Photograph by author.

FIGURE 11.5. Embedded stone in the western entry to the monumental plaza, looking into the atrium at the façade of the church. Photograph by Emily Burns.

produced similar conceptions as the body of the dead Messiah who had yet to be spiritually transfigured was physically processed along a prescribed circuit.

To the Maya participant, during this moment of crisis, to ensure the continuance of cosmic time, the deity was processed to the sides of the world, re-enacting moments of community foundation and cosmogenesis. The Ritual of the Five Wounds fused Christian biography with architectural design as the narrative of Christ's Passion is formulaically grafted onto monastic architecture. Pre-Columbian history was continually referenced as well, since finished stones—which certainly came from the Ppal Hol Chac's Postclassic renovations—were embedded within this processional pathway (figure 11.5). This animated the landscape of the atrium, and as the quadrilateral microcosm of the universe, the entirety of the cosmos as well. As such, the narrative of the Ritual of the Five Wounds parallels the Uayeb ritual in both form and function: both are performed during calendrical moments of transition. Moreover, both the Pre-Columbian and Catholic examples illustrated above strove to emit the same emotive response that was surely prompted by so many Pre-Columbian rituals: the collective focus of feeling and experience that defined community memory, and therefore identity.[20]

Conclusion

This chapter has attempted to show that for the colonial Maya (and presumably the generations who preceded them), public ceremonial spaces were produced via their repeated ritual activation, orchestrated movements that served to wed contemporary lived reality with that of primordial cosmogenesis. The detailed ethnographic accounts left by Friar Landa, among others, give voice to the often silent material remains of ancient Maya four-sided spaces. The Franciscan's description alludes to the full symbolism of the supposed negative space of plaza spaces; rather than being vacant vessels that merely hosted ephemeral public rites, these embedded spaces were, in fact, repositories for memories of the past, both on the cosmic and communal level. In their resonation of Maya modes of place-making, colonial atria appropriated this civic function in the early years of the evangelical project, allowing seemingly fully indoctrinated Maya neophytes to define their emerging colonial identity via the continual reification of social memory.

Notes

1. The island had been inhabited for centuries and, since the midcentury conquest of western Yucatan, had technically been granted as an encomienda and its population had suffered under excessive tribute payment. In fact, it was the encomendero's abusive treatment of the Maya population that prompted the governor in Yucatan to launch a more systematic conversion effort and send the two friars (Roys et al. 1940:7–8).

2. One only has to recall the two meetings of the Conquest, that of the Mexica ruler, Moctecuhzoma II, and Hernando Cortes in 1519, and that of the Inca ruler, Atahualpa, and Francisco Pizarro in 1532 to be reminded of the primacy of plazas during moments

of initial cultural interaction. In addition to textual accounts of these historical events, later colonial art work, primarily in the form of panel paintings and large-scale biombos, served to reify the social memory of conquest by depicting these pivotal moments within plaza spaces.

3. Although scholars have tended to treat Landa's *Relación* as a completed narrative text, Restall and Chuchiak have shown that the manuscript is actually a collection of documents, excerpted from a long-lost larger work, that lacks a central narrative or overall cohesion.

4. In a similar vein, Setha Low (1995) has argued that colonial plazas, as deeply contested spaces derived from a multitude of cultural factors, cannot be merely deemed an "instrument of colonial domination and control." Rather, they "retain architectural, spatial, and physical elements from both traditions, such that the issues of conquest and resistance are symbolically encoded in its architecture" (759). More recently, Logan Wagner, Hal Box, and Susan Kline Morehead (2013) have followed a similar line of argmuentation, drawing a cultural parallel between ancient Mesoamerican plaza spaces and the town plazas and atria of the colonial period.

5. Writing to the Crown in 1548, Friar Bienvenida explained that in 1541 the Spanish conquerors of the province had selected the Maya town of Tiho as the site of their colonial capital, Mérida, because "of the superb buildings that were already there" (*Cartas de Indias* 1877:71).

6. Although we can never assume a direct correlation between the spatialized behavioral intentions of urban designers and the eventual use of architectural spaces, Kathryn Reese Taylor has convincingly argued that Preclassic and Classic period (250 BCE–CE 1000) Maya city planners designed monumental civic centers according to their use as ritual sites. From this material evidence she has created a typology of three rituals that defined urban Classic Maya religious life: circumambulatory rituals, where architectural markers are processed in a counterclockwise direction; banner processions, performed to link the periphery of cities to the civic center; and processions from the base to the summit of a mountain, either real or symbolically constructed. Elizabeth Newsome's investigations of the Classic Maya city of Copán have also shed light on ancient urban ritual practices, here in direct correlation to the life of a Copán ruler, Waxaklahuun U Baah K'awiil, and his monumental stelae that he erected in the city's Great Plaza. Due to the high level of archaeological preservation, it may also be possible to ascertain probable ritual circuits for Yucatec cities of the early Postclassic period, such as Chichén Itzá, Uxmal, and Mayapán, among others.

7. Intriguingly, this ritual route is still widely utilized among modern Maya groups. For the Maya of Zinacanteco, Evon Z. Vogt (1976) explains, "if the ritual is enclosing a sacred space, as occurs in completing a ceremonial circuit, the direction taken is almost always counterclockwise" (42).

8. It is also possible, but not provable, that Landa may have been working from a Maya codex (Taube 1988:274). In addition to Landa's account, archaeological evidence at Santa Rita Corozal in Belize also elucidates Uayeb practices. Chase's (1985) investigations have revealed cache patterns aligned to directional associations that appear to represent Uayeb ritual events. In particular, Chase has found figurative clay effigies that are iconographically related to the deities of the various yearbearers.

9. Interestingly, Classic period inscriptions relay that during this earlier moment of Maya history different days commenced the New Year, suggesting a systematic shift in calendrical calculations in the Postclassic (Chase 1985:224).

10. Other scholars have summarized these complicated ritual events and analyzed Landa's description in comparison to indigenous textual and pictorial sources. (See Bill et al. 2000; Chase 1985; Taube1988.) These ritual events are also known from their visual and textual description in the Madrid Codex (pp. 34–37) and the Dresden Codex (pp. 25–28) and a variant may also be referenced in the colonial "Ritual of the Bacabs" (Coe 1965; Vail 2009).

11. Michael Coe (1965) has argued that Uayeb rites fulfilled a purely political function of office rotation whereby the selected principal was chosen to preside over the coming year (105–106).

12. This spatial/temporal ideology is also graphically depicted on pages 75 and 76 of the Madrid Codex (Vail 2009:76–77).

13. Gary H. Gossen (1974), working with contemporary Chamula communities, has witnessed a similar ritual pathway, observing that this particular kinetic pattern is actually "the horizontal equivalent of the sun's daily vertical path across the heavens from east to west . . . this horizontal transformation allows [ritual participants] to 'move as the sun moves,' thereby restating symbolically both the temporal and spatial cycles for which the sun is responsible" (32–33).

14. Bishop Francisco de Toral, in a letter to the Spanish crown, remarked that the monastery "is a fine thing to see and it's scandal to permit it, for surely St. Francis condemns it in his Rule" (Scholes and Adams 1938:71).

15. Craig A. Hanson (1995) has established a developmental sequence for Yucatec mission churches.

16. Susan Verdi Webster (1997) has done a close iconographic analysis of the extant architectural sculpture and murals in the monastery of Huejotzingo in central Mexico to determine the most common pathway of this Franciscan rite. For discussion of the Izamal murals in the context of Maya concepts of space and the Franciscan missionary project, see Solari 2013, chap. 6, and in the broader context of the history of the apocalypse, see Restall and Solari 2011:95–98.

17. Depictions of the arma christi were among the most common visual didactic tools utilized in the New World evangelical campaign. In addition to being a subject of mural cycles, this iconography appeared on atrium crosses of central Mexico and small-scale prints representing the Mass of St. Gregory (Edgerton 2001:67).

18. This processional circuit composed of a quadrilateral form interrupted by scripted pauses at defined loci emphasized by structural or sculptural artworks has many precedents in the Pre-Columbian world. The most clearly articulated case has been made for stelae rituals in the ceremonial plazas of Preclassic and Classic Maya cities, where large-scale sculptural reliefs provided ritual pauses for processional routes. It is believed that these sculptures functioned as altars for the deposition of offerings, as ritual stages, or as backdrops for narrative performances referenced in the sculptures' visual imagery (Guernsey Kappleman 2001).

19. Jeanette Favrot Peterson has also found ample evidence that mendicants and indigenous neophytes alike utilized the interior spaces of cloisters for counterclockwise processional and liturgical activities (Peterson, 1993).

20. Inga Clendinnen (1990) has argued that the ability to structure identical emotive responses was the defining characteristic of Pre-Columbian ritual events and was often produced during formulaic ritual actions such as fasting and ritualized intoxication that ensured participants had similar responses.

PART IV

Commentary

CHAPTER TWELVE

Ancient Plazas

Spaces of Inquiry in Mesoamerica and Beyond

JERRY D. MOORE

The city where I live—Long Beach, California—was incorporated in the late nineteenth century, when an orthogonal grid was surveyed and superimposed on the beachside bluffs and low hills, the floodplains and wetlands of this portion of southern California. This region's prehistory dates to before circa 9000 BP, and at contact the area was occupied by the Garbrileño-Tongva who had established dozens of villages across the coastal plain. Founded in the late eighteenth century, Spanish missions flanked the area, to the north at San Gabriel (established AD 1771) and to the south at San Juan Capistrano (1776). The south-facing, wave-protected coast at the mouth of the Los Angeles River became the major port for the Pueblo de los Angeles, established in 1781 about 40 km to the north, which in turn was the western terminus of the Santa Fe Trail. Under Spanish rule the well-watered grasslands between the Pueblo de Los Angeles and its port were divided into land grants of large ranchos with vast herds of livestock, a process that continued in the Mexican period and resulting in a landscape vividly described in Richard Henry Dana's (1840) *Two Years Before the Mast*, as "a fine plane country, filled with herds of cattle." After California's statehood in 1850, these ranchos increasingly were held by Anglo-American landowners and development companies, who began to establish new towns and cities. After several less-than-successful efforts at city-building, the City of Long Beach was established in 1897.[1]

And when the city was laid out, a plaza was at its core.

The founders of Long Beach were uninspired urban planners. Apparently unaware and certainly uninfluenced by the innovations of Fredrick Law Olmstead and Calvert Vaux, who planned New York's Central Park and the intriguingly linear "Emerald Necklace," which linked Boston's various open spaces

FIGURE 12.1. Lincoln Park, Long Beach, California, postcard circa 1930–37. Photograph by author.

into a sinuous chain of parks. Long Beach's founding fathers simply plotted an open city block at the corner of Pacific Avenue and Broadway Street and named it Pacific Park.

Bounded by major thoroughfares, the plaza's perimeter has remained stable, although its names, uses, and meanings have not. In 1915, the local chapter of the Veterans of the Civil War installed a cannon and a statue of Abraham Lincoln to commemorate the end of America's bloodiest conflict, and the plaza was renamed Lincoln Park. A Carnegie Library opened in 1909, was destroyed by fire in 1970, and was demolished in 1973. The core of the park was landscaped with palms, flower beds, sidewalks, and benches, a tranquil center in a normally tranquil city.

In March 1933 a massive earthquake of magnitude 6.5 hit Long Beach and adjacent regions, the most destructive earthquake ever recorded in Southern California. Lincoln Park and all of the other parks in the city were converted into emergency centers where makeshift kitchens fed the survivors and homeless residents were sheltered under large military tents. Today, decades later, Lincoln Park is again occupied by the homeless, but by permanent street people not temporary refugees. Lincoln Park was the center of public protests in 2011, as the Occupy Movement established an encampment, inevitably leading to arrests and controversy. In 2012, as I write this, the homeless rest on the

FIGURE 12.2. Outdoor kitchen and food lines, Lincoln Park, in aftermath of 1933 earthquake. Photograph reproduced by permission, Historical Society of Long Beach.

green in the mild winter sun, dogs and their owners scamper in the dog park (built in 2009), and Long Beach citizens debate renovations of the plaza.

When Long Beach was first laid out and Pacific Park was planted in the heart of this urban space, no one could have imagined the variations in forms, functions, and human activities that would occur in this open space. Yet, these are exactly the classes of variations we attempt to understand when we presume to explore the archaeology of plazas.

* * *

As Inomata and Tsukamoto state in the opening lines of the introduction to this volume, "Plazas are focal points of Mesoamerican public life. Throughout Mesoamerican history, plazas have been essential components of the site layouts of cities, towns, and even small villages." More broadly, plazas and other constructed open spaces are among the most commonly encountered elements in the built environment in the ancient world and pose significant challenges for archaeological analysis.

It is a privilege to comment on the chapters in this very intriguing volume, and I do so as an Andean archaeologist who has tried to develop more explicit methods for understanding ancient architecture, including plazas (Moore

1992, 1996a, 1996b, 2005a). First, as an Andeanist, I have been struck by the differences in the degrees of variation in monumental architecture in Mesoamerica and the Andes. It has seemed to me that, speaking in very broad terms, Mesoamerica exhibits greater continuities in monumental architecture than are seen in the Andes, where there are marked discontinuities in form, scale, and presumed social functions in monumental architecture, including in plazas (e.g., Moore 1996a, 2004). In the following comments, I will emphasize the evidence for continuities and discontinuities in Mesoamerican plazas as discussed by specific authors. Second, I have argued that archaeological approaches to architecture are underdeveloped, and I contend that we need to apply testable methods in analyses of the built environment; therefore, I will discuss selected chapters in this collection in terms of their methodological strengths and applications. I conclude with some observations about differences between Mesoamerican and Andean plazas and with a call for a broader comparative inquiry into these important places in human settlements.

Continuities and Variations in Mesoamerican Plazas

The chapters in this volume explore varying aspects of plazas as recurrent spaces in Mesoamerican sites. Inomata (chapter 1) describes an intriguing case of anchored variations expressed by plaza rebuilding at Ceibal, events that spanned twelve centuries of the Preclassic period. Beginning in the early Middle Preclassic, Ceibal's plaza was a significant focus of social effort, as the inhabitants scraped the soils to carve a flat surface in the natural marl, excavations punctuated by votive offerings of greenstone celts. This was followed by more than fourteen layers of plaza reconstruction with additional offerings—shifting from greenstone celts to ceramic vessels and sacrificed humans—covered by layers of fill and capped by finished floors. Two points in Inomata's article are particularly noteworthy. First, the volume of plaza construction was significant from the earliest part of the sequence, peaking in the late Middle Preclassic (as measured by estimates of annual volume of construction), and tapering off during the Late–Terminal Classic. Inomata writes that "the construction of plazas and public gatherings that took place there offered a central mechanism through which a new community was constituted." Second, significantly more earth was moved to construct Ceibal's central plaza than to erect the surrounding pyramids. Inomata's analysis underscores the fundamental importance of plazas in Mesoamerica, a recurrent point in this volume.

For example, Cyphers and Murtha (chapter 4) summarize data from extensive coring program that documented the changing modifications enacted by the Olmec and post-Olmec occupants at San Lorenzo and by natural erosion at the site. In addition, Cyphers and Murtha observe that open space on San Lorenzo's central plateau was transformed from a very large (68,750 m^2) and amorphous space at 1600 cal BC into a large (62,500 m^2) quadrangular space in 1100 cal BC that included a more restricted 10,000 m^2 plaza flanked by prestigious structures and colossal stone heads. Arguing that these changing configurations of open space reflect "mechanisms of exclusion and inclusion" in which "the former acted to increase social distance and the latter for social integration," Cyphers and Murtha tentatively conclude that these variations in San Lorenzo's plazas express "the complex interplay between ideas and/or agency and the political theaters in which they were performed."

A fascinating example of continuities in plaza as ritual spaces is found in Amara Solari's rich discussion of plaza, ritual, and cosmology in sixteenth-century Yucatan (chapter 11). Drawing on ethnohistoric sources and architectural analyses, Solari discusses the formal similarities of Pre-Columbian and Catholic rites that occurred in four-sided spaces, such as plazas and atria. She writes, "In the Maya world, when a community delineated the shape of their cosmos in the context of a coming of age ritual or during the Uayeb rites, the local population reenacted the deities' creative acts. The square-sided space of plazas activated primordial events, placing the community within the moment of creation and reifying the corporate body and associated community identity. They effectively restructured the corporate body during times of social upheaval, defining local communities as a 'self' distinct and thereby cementing community cohesion via divine validation." After the conquest, the Franciscan order modified the Ritual of the Five Wounds, which commemorates the Crucifixion, converting it into a circumambulatory rite that "so perfectly adheres to the physical limitations of colonial atriums that the architectural design and the ritual performance are in a dialectical relationship—the rite appears as an organic outgrowth of the ritual space." Solari suggests that "the Franciscan order augmented this ritual as a means to replicate indigenous understandings of the sacred by creating a ceremonial procession that mirrored native ideologies of place-making and cosmogenesis," yet another example of the significance of plazas in the Mesoamerican world—which all the chapters in this volume clearly document.

Another exploration of variation is provided by Marijke Stoll (chapter 5), who discusses the role of plazas in various phases in the Mixteca Alta. She notes that the small size of most plazas, in part reflects the mountainous terrain and hillside and piedmont locations of settlements, but also the possibility "that ceremonies and other ritual practices were perhaps intimate affairs involving only select groups or members of the communities." While this seems quite possible—and none of the Mixteca Alta plazas approach Ceibal or San Lorenzo in size—there are specific sites in her data set that seem disproportionately large given the population estimates for the associated settlements. While the sites with the largest estimated populations have plazas that could not accommodate all the residents, there are several sites—often with estimated populations of fewer than one hundred residents—that have plazas which could have held twice to ten times that number of people. More interesting, one site, TLA-TLA-TLA-1, with an estimated population of seventy-five residents had three plazas, any one of which could hold the entire community. While Stoll may be correct in her emphasis on the use of small spaces for nuanced and intimate rituals, these exceptional cases from the Mixteca Alta would profit from further discussion and analysis.

A similar issue is glossed over in the chapter by Liendo Saturado, López Mejía, and Campiani (chapter 6) in their examination of Classic Maya centers in Chiapas, Mexico. Analyzing the regional roles of Palenque and Chinikihá, the authors suggest that these settlements—along with Piedras Negras—were the principal centers of autonomous political entities, an indisputable conclusion given the concentration of monumental architecture at these sites. They propose "that residents living in discrete settlements in their respective regional sector might have attended regularly their immediate major site during significant gatherings." Turning to the problem of plazas and the resident population of a site, all the sites in their samples have plazas that could easily contain the entire community and the authors cite a strong positive correlation between estimated population and plaza size (table 6.1). But interestingly, the most populated sites with the largest plazas—Palenque and Chinikihá—actually have a *proportionately lower plaza capacity* than some of the smaller settlements, 135 percent and 184 percent respectively. For example, the smallest sites—Xupá and La Providencia, with estimated populations of seventy-eight and eighty-four people respectively—have plazas large enough to hold more than 1,200 percent—1,905 percent of their populations. This would seem the inverse of what the authors suggest: if the centers of Palenque and Chinikihá were drawing subjects from satellite communities to major gatherings, then why do the smaller sites have such disproportionately large plazas? This issue warrants further investigation.

Kara Rothenberg (chapter 7) reports on the analysis of soil chemistry of three open spaces at the Late Classic site of Palmarejo, Honduras. This is an intriguing and detailed study unfortunately marred by a simple dichotomy between "residential" and "ceremonial" activities. Rothenberg analyzed 297 soil samples systematically collected from the North Plaza at Palmarejo and compared these samples to two other spaces: "South Plaza identified as a civic-ceremonial plaza" and "East Plaza as an elite residential patio." South Plaza and East Plaza at Palmarejo initially were characterized based on artifactual assemblages (e.g., incensarios and serving vessels vs. utilitarian wares), and subsequent analyses by E. Christian Wells et al. provided comparative data regarding the chemical elements from these areas. Rothenberg contrasts her results from the North Plaza against these two comparative sets. Essentially, the chemical analyses indicate high concentrations of calcium and strontium across all three spaces, although there are variations in other chemical elements and in the spatial concentrations within the three spaces. None of these variations, however, neatly fits the dichotomy between residential and ceremonial activities, which should not be a surprise given the significance of maize in Mesoamerican subsistence, social life, and religion. Further, it seems possible that the presence of these chemical elements were the result of repeated short-term practices—such as drying maize cobs on the hard-packed surface of plazas and patios—that were secondary to the "purpose" of these open spaces as viewed from this dichotomy.

In a delightfully cautious study, Alanna Ossa (chapter 8) examines three dimensions of plazas—area, accessibility, and settlement context—at Classic and Postclassic sites in south-central Veracruz. In contrast to the vast plazas of Lowland Maya sites, the Classic period plazas were relatively modest, formalized settings for public ceremonies and ritual that probably served social groupings smaller than the overall polity. Further, access to these plazas was restricted by the construction water features or encircled by public buildings. In the Postclassic this changed: plazas became larger, open, and somewhat ill-defined, and were perhaps used as marketplaces. Moving to a second analytical plane, Ossa compares the settlement contexts of plazas, observing that Classic period sites that served as regional centers were also those with more formal plazas. Attracting people from surrounding communities, these Classic period centers served to integrate broader sociopolitical networks.

As demonstrated in these chapters, the Mesoamerican plaza, which might seem a straightforward and inert plane, simply a space where buildings did not occur, in fact turns out to be highly variable and profoundly constructed. The case studies document the varying emphases on construction efforts, scale, boundedness, functions, formality, and inclusiveness. In light of such clear cases of variation in Mesoamerican plazas, there is some reason to consider additional methods that we could apply to our analyses.

Methodological Issues in the Study of Mesoamerican Plaza

Obviously, all the chapters in this book apply "methods" to the study of Mesoamerican plazas, but several give special emphasis to methodological issues. For example, Murakami (chapter 2) provided a valuable analysis of the changing configurations of plazas and courtyards at Teotihuacan. From its diverse initial architectural traditions, Teotihuacan underwent major urban renewal at ca. AD 250–300 and thereafter as it became a city of 100,000. A simple analysis of size variations (table 2.1) indicate four classes of open spaces: civic-ceremonial plazas, administrative/residential plazas, courtyards in elite apartment compounds, and courtyards in commoner apartment compounds. In turn these different spaces, Murakami argues, "can be conceptualized as a frame for diverse activities and experiences . . . [within which] multiple group identities, as a house member, a member of an ethnic group, a member of a neighborhood, a member of other institutions, and a member of the polity, were negotiated and were reaffirmed or transformed, thereby creating overlapping and sometimes contradicting urban communities." This strikes me as a plausible hypothesis awaiting other lines of evidence. For example, what is the evidence for continuity in houses? Did these residential units contain evidence of a corporate existence?

Drawing on his research at El Palmar, a Classic Maya center in southeastern Campeche, Tsukamoto (chapter 3) discusses the multiplictity of plazas in Mayan sites, including the large plazas in the core of settlements and the smaller spaces found throughout settlements. At El Palmar, the initial plazas—the Central Plaza and Plaza H—were constructed in the course of a century during the Late Preclassic (300 BC–AD 250). In the Middle Classic period (AD 400–600), four large plazas were established in El Palmar's urban landscape, roughly quadrupling the amount of open space at the site. Not all these plazas were equivalent in access and visibility: during the Middle Classic, two plazas (the Great Plaza and Plaza E) were accessible and visible spaces perhaps used for mass spectacles, one plaza (Plaza G) was restricted in access and visibility, and the fourth plaza (the K'awiil Plaza) may have served as a node for ritual processions. This all seems relatively straightforward, reasonably inferred from the architecture of these plazas. Less obvious are some of the inferences that Tsukamoto derives from these spaces, such as his contention that during the Middle Classic, "ritual knowledge exhibited on the plazas would have become a resource for ruling elites to create ideological power for defining the relationship between people and deities, elites and nonelites, and among elites" or that the dramatic increase in plaza space reflected "social anxieties that resulted from the hegemonic extension of the Tikal and Kaan dynasties, motivated people to engage in cooperative activities, in turn providing critical opportunities for negotiating and claiming power relations and group identities in the process of creating a politywide identity. Simultaneously, mass spectacles at the Great Plaza and Plaza E might have served to release such social anxieties." Either of these are plausible hypotheses; neither of these are proven.

Issues of interpretation are acknowledged and addressed in Urcid and Joyce's (chapter 9) examination of the Main Plaza at Monte Albán, which, as "one of the most formidable plazas of the Mesoamerican world, has been a fertile ground for interpreting how social institutions and ideas were architecturally embodied, and how modifications of the plaza in turn transformed those ideas and institutions." These scholars shift our analytical focus from the "plaza as space" to "plaza as exhibit gallery" surrounded by narratives sculpted in stone. In their analysis of the visual program at Building L-sub, Urcid and Joyce investigate "the most daring architectural endeavor of the early inhabitants" of Monte Albán: a six-meter-tall façade in which alternating rows of orthostats depict a progression of personages that the authors interpret as reflecting a sodality based on age-grades. Beginning at the lowest row, the reliefs progress from youngest members to elders, alternating rows in a procession that signal an ascent to the highest levels occupied by elites and individuals depicting rain deities. Marking the ascension of two or possibly three rulers, the visual program connected the present and the ancestral, alluded to human sacrifice, and denoted the divine requisite of blood that flows from each of the participants' genitals. Urcid and Joyce provide an equally nuanced analysis of the visual program at Monte Albán's Building J, where the carved orthostats "render the personal names of the depicted individuals" showing "early images of rulers [and] also reference rain god impersonation, warfare, and sacrifice." Arguing from these different motifs, the authors suggest that different messages were conveyed to different audiences, for example noting:

> The Building L-sub program was probably polysemic with different components aimed at different audiences. . . . Sculptures in the east face of Building L-sub would have been visible to large groups of people on the plaza and stressed the ritual and military actions of lower-ranking people. Images of higher-ranking members of the military sodality, including elders and rain god impersonators, were located on buildings on top of the platform, which were probably restricted to higher-status audiences of both prominent commoners and nobles. (Urcid and Joyce, chapter 9)

This would seem to be a perfect situation for the application of ideas about proxemics and communication as articulated by Edward T. Hall and others, and as applied by Stoll in this volume. The issue of visibility of these visual programs at Monte Albán could be complemented by an analysis of legibility of the iconography. Were these complex symbols designed to be read or simply seen and noted? To deploy Sherry Ortner's (1973) still-useful distinctions, did the different programs incorporate "key symbols" and if so did these fulfill "summarizing" or "elaborating" functions when gazed upon by the ancient occupants of Monte Albán?

Eschewing methodological approaches concerning the spatial and experiential properties of plazas, which he claims are flawed "without associated iconographic or textual evidence," William Ringle (chapter 10) engages in a wide-ranging search for parallels and analogies between sites in the Basin of Mexico, Tlaxcala, Puebla, and the Yucatan and concludes that plazas were spaces for investiture from the Early Classic period until the Spanish Conquest. A very important hypothesis emerges from Ringle's paper, that is, that plazas were imbued with the value of being a common, bounded space shared by a recognized social group. As reflected in the Nahuatl *cemithuatlin* or "those of a single patio," Ringle notes, "It is interesting that this, rather than the house, was the architectural metaphor of choice, suggesting the open common space between houses, the locus of daily socializing, visual contact, and task performance, was thought to better reflect the social bonds holding a household together." In rituals of investiture, the residential plaza became ideologically transformed into a model of the entire polity. Ringle observes that "glyphs representing Texcoco's subject polities are arranged as a rectangle about the palace, these temples may represent Teotihuacan's tributaries, enclosing and defining the plaza. The plaza, in turn, may thus symbolize the common space of the polity as a whole. The symmetrical arrangement of the temples suggests that they represent an abstract conception of the state, rather than particular subject polities." While I would argue that Ringle's methods pose epistemological problems of their own, his hypothesis is intriguing on two levels. First, it bolsters Inomata's discussion of plaza creation and group identity at Ceibal as well as Murakami's observations about plazas and varying social memberships at Teotihuacan. Second, the notion of public plazas as residential plazas "writ large" would seem to diverge from the exclusionary spaces discussed by Cyphers and Murtha at San Lorenzo, by Urcid and Joyce at Monte Albán, and by Ossa for the Classic Period in south-central Veracruz. If this difference is true, what might it imply? This could be a very useful line for future investigations, as other scholars examine the varied implications of such variations.

Plazas as Spaces for Comparative Inquiry

Often lacking the formal properties, features, and artifactual assemblages that allow us to determine the functions and valences of other architectural spaces, plazas may be something of an archaeological Rorschach test in which we perceive patterns in the past that may or may not actually be there. This is not to suggest that the archaeology of plazas is impossible, but rather that it requires careful and explicit approaches, which are exemplified by many of the chapters in this volume.

I hope that this volume is the first in a series of wide-ranging archaeological investigations into plazas, as there are cross-cultural variations in the social functions of these unroofed but constructed spaces that a regional focus may overlook. Although the studies in this volume document specific variations in plazas, as an Andeanist I am struck by the continuities exhibited by these components of Mesoamerican built environments. Based on my study of changes in Andean urban patterns, I think that a much broader array of open/unroofed architectural spaces were used by different cultural traditions in the prehispanic Andes than seen in ancient Mesoamerica. A thorough review is beyond the scope of this discussion, but a few examples illustrate my point. Along the coast of Peru in the Initial Period (ca. 3000–1000 BC) large plazas were constructed whose principal axes intersect with the staircases and peaks of large mounds at sites like Salinas de Chao, Pampa de las Llamas-Moxeke, Sechin Alto, Las Aldas, Garagay, and Huaca de los Reyes (see Moore 1996a:34–47; 2005a); this plaza form was abandoned after ca. 1000–500 BC. Open sunken circular courts were a prominent architectural form between ca. 3000–500 BC in the Peruvian coast and highlands, but not thereafter. In the Titicaca basin, a rectangular sunken courtyard form appeared during the Middle Formative, ca. 800–200 BC (Cohen 2010a, 2010b), was incorporated into Tiwanaku religious architecture (Goldstein 1993; Stanish 2003), but disappeared from view. The walled plazas within Chimú royal compounds (ca. AD 900–1470) were fundamentally different from the large open plazas at the core of many Inca settlements (ca. AD 1300–1550), varying in size, visibility, and social meanings (Moore 2003, 2004).

I raise this difference between plazas in Mesoamerica and in the Andes in order to ask, What do these variations imply about plazas and power in Mesoamerica and the Andes? If we recognize, following Eric Wolf, that structural power refers to "the power manifest in relationships that not only operates within settings and domains but also organizes and orchestrates the settings themselves, and that specifies the direction and distribution of energy flows" (Wolf 1999:5), it seems obvious that at some fundamental level, plazas are reflections of structural power (Moore 2005b). Whether we consider the intensive reconstructions of plazas at Ceibal, the multiplicity of open spaces at El Palmar, the reconfigurations of open areas at San Lorenzo, or the iconographies of investiture across Mesoamerica, these and every other plaza discussed in every chapter of this volume are reflections of structural power. As Wolf argued, structural power is deployed in two directions; it has empirical effects in the real world—mobilizing social labor, controlling resources—and it is engaged in the world of symbols and ideas. Allocation and connotation are intertwined, and that is clearly evident in plazas and the built environment.

Informed by Wolf's notion of structural power, a comparative study of plazas in Mesoamerica and the Andes could lead to a provocative suite of inquiries: Why were there apparently more sustained continuities in Mesoamerican plazas and the built environment and what does this imply about the ideologies of power? Were there marked differences in the potential audiences and political messages conveyed in open spaces at different times? Do variations in accessibility and exclusion correlate with other media that express power relations, such as monumental sculpture, ceramic styles, or esoteric objects? A comparative study could explore these and many other fruitful lines of inquiry.

Moving beyond these two regions, it would be very useful to incorporate comparative examples of plazas from prehistoric North America and elsewhere. For example, Pauketat and Alt (2005:228) have discussed the creation of marker posts and woodhenges at Cahokia, where the practice of placing large upright posts in the middle of open courtyards surrounded by dwellings was elaborated into a large public event in which "cavernous post pits were dug by hand in order to set monumentally large posts" exemplifying the "ways in which quotidian construction practices were scaled up at Cahokia." Turning to a very different region and cultural tradition, Fleisher and Wynne-Jones (2010, 2012) have explored the creation of and social meanings of open spaces in ancient Swahili towns, investigations that explicitly address constructions and open spaces. A broader, more inclusive perspective could contribute new insights into the archaeology of plazas and ancient built environments in Mesoamerica and beyond. Additional case studies and inquiries could readily complement the studies presented in the chapters of this present volume, leading to a broader archaeological perspective of plazas—these important, but often overlooked spaces that sit at the core of so many cultural traditions and human settlements, including in the city where I live.

Note

1. Mesoamericanists might be interested to learn that Long Beach was the boyhood home of the American archaeologist, Gordon Willey (1913–2002) who had such an impact on Mesoamerican archaeology.

REFERENCES

Acosta, Jorge R. 1964. *El Palacio del Quetzalpapalotl*. Instituto Nacional de Antropología e Historia, Mexico City.

———. 1965. Preclassic and Classic Architecture of Oaxaca. In *Handbook of Middle American Indians*, vol. 3: *Archaeology of Southern Mesoamerica*, pt. 2, edited by Robert Wauchope and Gordon R. Willey, pp. 814–836. University of Texas Press, Austin.

Adams, Richard E. W. 1971. *The Ceramics of Altar de Sacrificios*. Papers of the Peabody Museum of Archaeology and Ethnology Vol. 63, No. 1. Harvard University Press, Cambridge, Massachusetts.

Agamben, Giorgio. 1998. *Homo Sacer: Sovereign Power and Bare Life*. Stanford University Press, Stanford, CA.

Agrinier, Pierre. 2000. *Mound 27 and the Middle Preclassic Period at Mirador, Chiapas, Mexico*. Papers of the New World Archaeological Foundation, no. 58. Brigham Young University, Provo, Utah.

Aimers, James J., and Prudence M. Rice. 2006. Astronomy, Ritual, and the Interpretation of Maya "E-Group" Architectural Assemblages. *Ancient Mesoamerica* 17(1):79–96.

Aldenderfer, Mark. 1993. Ritual, Hierarchy, and Change in Foraging Societies. *Journal of Anthropological Archaeology* 12:1–40.

———. 2012. Envisioning a Pragmatic Approach to Archaeology of Religion. In *Beyond Belief*, edited by Yorke M. Rowan, pp. 22–36. Archaeological Papers of the American Anthropological Association Vol. 21, No. 1.

Alonso, Ana M. 2005. Sovereignty, the Spatial Politics of Security, and Gender: Looking North and South from the US–Mexico Border. In *State Formation: Anthropological Perspectives*, edited by Christian Krohn-Hansen and Knut G. Nustad, pp. 27–52. Pluto Press, London.

Alva Ixtlilxóchitl, Fernando de. 1985. *Obras Históricas*. 2 vols. Universidad Nacional Autónoma de México, Mexico City.

Anaya, Hernández Armando. 2001. *Site Interaction and Political Geography in the Upper Usumacinta Region during the Late Classic: A GIS Approach*. Hadrian Books. BAR International Series 994, Oxford.

Anaya, Hernández Armando, L. Williams-Beck, and S. P. Guenter. 2011. Alianzas efímeras y fronteras fluctuantes: La organización política del alto Usumacinta durante el Clásico Tardío. In *El despliegue del poder entre los mayas: Nuevos estudios sobre la organización política*, edited by Ana Luisa Izquierdo, pp. 123–150. Instituto de Investigaciones Filológicas, Centro de Estudios Mayas, Universidad Nacional Autónoma de México, Mexico City.

Anderson, Benedict. 2006. *Imagined Communities: Reflections on the Origin and Spread of Nationalism*. Revised Edition. Verso, London and New York.

Andrews V., E. Wyllys, George J. Bey III, and Christopher Gunn. 2008. Rethinking the Early Ceramic History of the Northern Maya Lowlands: New Evidence and Interpretations. Paper presented at the annual meeting of the Society for American Archaeology, Vancouver.

Angulo V., Jorge. 1987. Nuevas consideraciones sobre los llamados conjuntos departamentales, especialmente Tetitla. In *Teotihuacán: Nuevos datos, nuevas síntesis, nuevos problemas*, edited by Emily McClung de Tapia and Evelyn C. Rattray, pp. 275–315. Instituto de Investigaciones Antropológicas, Serie Antropológica 72. Universidad Nacional Autónoma de México, Mexico City.

———. 2007. Early Teotihuacan and Its Government. In *The Political Economy of Ancient Mesoamerica: Transformations during the Formative and Classic Period*, edited by Vernon L. Scarborough and John E. Clark, pp. 83–99. University of New Mexico Press, Albuquerque.

Anselmetti, Flavio S., David A. Hodell, Daniel Ariztegui, Mark Brenner, and Michael F. Rosenmeier. 2007. Quantification of Soil Erosion Rates Related to Ancient Maya Deforestation. *Geology* 35(10):915–918.

Ashmore, Wendy. 1981. Some Issues of Method and Theory in Lowland Maya Settlement Archaeology. In *Lowland Maya Settlement Patterns*, edited by Wendy Ashmore, pp. 37–69. University of New Mexico Press, Albuquerque.

———. 1991. Site Planning and Concepts of Directionality among the Ancient Maya. *Latin American Antiquity* 2(3):199–226.

Ashmore, Wendy, and Jeremy A. Sabloff. 2002. Spatial Orders in Maya Civic Plans. *Latin American Antiquity* 13(2):201–215.

———. 2003. Interpreting Ancient Maya Civic Plans: Reply to Smith. *Latin American Antiquity* 14(2):229–236.

Austin, John L. 1975. *How to Do Things with Words*. 2nd ed. Harvard University Press, Cambridge, MA.

Bachand, Bruce R. 2007. The Pre-Classic Ceramic Sequence of Punta de Chimino, Petén, Guatemala. *Mayab* (19):5–26.

———. 2011. Chiapa de Corzo: Rise of Zoque Capital in the Heart of Mesoamerica. *Popular Archaeology* 3. http://popular-archaeology.com/issue/june-2011/article/chiapa-de-corzo-rise-of-a-zoque-capital-in-the-heart-of-mesoamerica. Accessed June 2011.

Bachand, Bruce R., Lynneth S. Lowe, and Emiliano Gallaga Murieta. 2008. Un reencuentro con Chiapa de Corzo: Rescatando y aumentando los datos de un centro mayor Mesoamericano. Paper presented at the Simposio de Arqueologia Guatemalteca.

Bakhtin, Mikhail. 1984. *Rabelais and His World*. Translated by Hélène Iswolsky. Indiana University Press, Bloomington.

Balkansky, Andrew K. 1998a. Origin and Collapse of Complex Societies in Oaxaca (Mexico): Evaluating the Era from 1965 to Present. *Journal of World Prehistory* 15(1):211–255.

———. 1998b. Urbanism and Early State Formation in the Huamelulpan Valley of Southern Mexico. *Latin American Antiquity* 9(1):37–67.

Balkansky, Andrew K., Stephen A. Kowalewski, Veronica Perez Rodriguez, et al. 2000. Archaeological Survey in the Mixteca Alta of Oaxaca, Mexico. *Journal of Field Archaeology* 27(4):365–389.

Balkansky, Andrew K., Verónica Pérez Rodríguez, and Stephen A. Kowalewski. 2004. Monte Negro and the Urban Revolution in Oaxaca, Mexico. *Latin American Antiquity* 15(1):33–60.

Barba, Luis. 1986. La química en el estudio de áreas de actividad. In *Análisis de unidades habitacionales mesoamericanas y sus áreas de actividad*, edited by Linda Manzanilla, pp. 21–39. Instituto de Investigaciones Antropológicas, Universidad Nacional Autónoma de México, Mexico City.

———. 1990. El análisis químico de pisos de unidades habitacionales para determinar sus áreasde actividad. In *Etnoarqueología coloquio Bosch Gimpera 1988*, edited by Mari Carmen Serra Puche, pp. 177–200. Instituto de Investigaciones Antropológicas, Universidad Nacional Autónoma de México, Mexico City.

Barba, Luis, and Gregorio Bello. 1978. Análisis de fosfatos en el piso de una casa habitada actualmente. *Notas Antropológicas* 1:188–193.

Barba, Luis, and Pierre Denis. 1984. Actividades humanas y análisis químico de los suelos: El caso de Osumacinta Viejo, Chiapas. *Memorias de la XVII Mesa Redonda de la Sociedad Mexicana de Antropología* 2:263–277.

Barba, Luis, and Agustin Ortiz Butrón. 1992. Análisis químico de pisos de ocupación: Un caso etnográfico en Tlaxcala, México. *Latin American Antiquity* 3:63–82.

Barba, Luis, Fabienne de Pierrebourg, Claudia Trejo, Augustin Ortiz Butrón, and Karl Link. 1995. Activites humaines refletees dans les sols s'unites d'habitation contemporaine et prehispanique de Yucatán (Mexique): Etudes chimiques, ethnoarchéologiques et archéologiques. *Revue d'Archéométrie* 19:79–95.

Barnhart, Edwin. 2001. The Palenque Mapping Project: Settlement and Urbanism at an Ancient Maya City. PhD dissertation, University of Texas, Austin.

Barrett, John C., and Ilhong Ko. 2009. A Phenomenology of Landscape: A Crisis in British Landscape Archaeology? *Journal of Social Archaeology* 9:275–294.

Batres, Leopoldo. 1902. *Exploraciones en Monte Albán*. Inspección y Conservación de Monumentos Arqueológicos de la República Mexicana. Gante St. Press, Mexico.

Bell, Catherine M. 1992. *Ritual Theory, Ritual Practice*. Oxford University Press, New York.

Bellas, Monica Lynn. 1997. The Body in the Mixtec Codices: Birth, Purification, Transformation and Death. PhD dissertation, University of California, Riverside.

Bender, Barbara. 1992. Theorizing Landscape, and the Prehistoric Landscapes of Stonehenge. *Man* 27:735–755.

Berdan, Frances F. 1985. Markets in the Economy of Aztec Mexico. In *Markets and Marketing*, edited by Stuart Plattner, pp. 339–368. University Press of America, Lanham, MD.

Berdan, Frances F., and Patricia Rieff Anawalt. 1997. *The Essential Codex Mendoza*. University of California Press, Berkeley.

Berlo, Jane C. 1980. Teotihuacan Art Abroad: A Study of Metropolitan Style and Provincial Transformation in Incensario Workshops. PhD dissertation, 2 vols., Yale University, New Haven, CT.

———. 1989. Early Writing in Central Mexico: In Tlilli, In Tlapalli before A.D. 1000. In *Mesoamerica after the Decline of Teotihuacan, A.D. 700–900*, edited by Richard A. Diehl and Janet C. Berlo, pp. 19–48. Dumbarton Oaks, Washington, DC.

Berney, Christine. 2003. Interaction, Emulation, and Socio-political Relations: Patterning of Civic-Ceremonial Complexes in the Gulf Lowlands. Unpublished manuscript, School of Human Evolution and Social Change. Arizona State University, Tempe.

Beverido Pereau, Francisco. 1970. San Lorenzo Tenochtitlán y la Civilización Olmeca. Master's thesis, Facultad de Antropología. Universidad Veracruzana, Xalapa.

Beyer, Hermann. 1955. La "Procesión de los Señores," decoración del primer teocalli de piedra en México Tenochtitlan. *El México antiguo* 8:1–42.

Bill, Cassandra R., Christine L. Hernández, and Victoria R. Bricker. 2000. The Relationship between Early Colonial Maya New Year's Ceremonies and Some Almanacs in the *Madrid Codex*. *Ancient Mesoamerica* 11(2):149–168.

Blake, Emma. 2006. Space, Spatiality and Archaeology. In *A Companion to Social Archaeology*, edited by Lynn Meskell and Robert Preucel, pp. 231–254. Blackwell, Oxford.

Blanton, Richard E. 1978. *Monte Alban: Settlement Patterns at the Ancient Zapotec Capital*. Academic Press, New York.

Blanton, Richard E., Gary M. Feinman, Stephen A. Kowalewski, and Linda M. Nicholas. 1999. *Ancient Oaxaca*. Cambridge University Press, Cambridge.

Blanton, Richard E., Gary M. Feinman, Stephen A. Kowalewski, and Peter N. Peregrine. 1996. A Dual-Processual Theory for the Evolution of Mesoamerican Civilization. *Current Anthropology* 37 (1):1–14.

Bloch, Maurice. 1989. *Ritual, History, and Power: Selected Papers in Anthropology*. London Schools of Economics, Monographs on Social Anthropology 58. Athlone, London.

Blomster, Jeffrey P. 1998. Context, Cult, and Early Formative Period Public Ritual in the Mixteca Alta. *Ancient Mesoamerica* 9(2):309–326.

Blucher, Darlena K. 1971. Late Preclassic Cultures in the Valley of Mexico: Pre-Urban Teotihuacan. PhD dissertation, Brandeis University, Waltham, MA.

Borstein, Joshua. 2001. Tripping over Colossal Heads: Settlement Patterns and Population Development in the Upland Olmec Heartland. PhD dissertation, Pennsylvania State University, College Station.

Bourdieu, Pierre. 1977. *Outline of a Theory of Practice*. Translated by R. Nice. Cambridge University Press, Cambridge, UK.

Bradley, Richard. 1991. Ritual, Time and History. *World Archaeology* 23:209–219.

———. 2003. A Life Less Ordinary: The Ritualization of the Domestic Sphere in Later Prehistoric Europe. *Cambridge Archaeological Journal* 13:5–23.

Brenner, Mark, David A. Hodell, Jason H. Curtis, Michael F. Rosenmeier, Flavio S. Anselmetti, and Daniel Ariztegui. 2003. Paleolimnological Approaches for Inferring Past Climate in the Maya Region: Recent Advances and Methodological Limitations. In *Lowland Maya Area: Three Millennia at the Human-Wildland Interface*, edited by Arturo Gómez-Pompa, Michael A. Allen, Scott L. Fedick, and Juan J. Jiménez-Osornio, pp. 45–76. Haworth Press, Binghamton, NY.

Broda, Johanna. 1987. Templo Mayor as Ritual Space. In *The Great Temple of Tenochtitlan*, edited by Johanna Broda, David Carrasco, and Eduardo Matos Moctezuma, pp. 61–123. University of California Press, Berkeley.

Brück, Joanna. 1999. Ritual and Rationality: Some Problems of Interpretation in Europe. *European Journal of Archaeology* 2:313–344.

Brüggeman, Jürgen K., and Marie-Areti Hers. 1970. Exploraciones arqueológicas en San Lorenzo Tenochtitlán. *Boletín del INAH* 39:18–23. Instituto Nacional de Antropología e Historia, Mexico City.

Buigues, Santiago V. 1993. Archaeology and Iconography of Monte Alban's Mound J (Mexico). Master's thesis, University of Calgary, Calgary.

Butler, Judith. 1993. *Bodies That Matter: On the Discursive Limits of "Sex."* Routledge, New York.

Byland, Bruce E., and John M. D. Pohl. 1994. *In the Realm of 8 Deer: The Archaeology of the Mixtec Codices*. University of Oklahoma Press, Norman.

Cabrera Castro, Rubén. 1993. Human Sacrifice at the Temple of the Feathered Serpent: Recent Discoveries at Teotihuacan. In *Teotihuacan: Art from the City of the Gods*, edited by Kathleen Berrin and Esther Pasztory, pp. 100–107. Thames and Hudson, New York.

Cabrera C., Rubén, and Sergio Gómez Chávez. 2008. La Ventilla: A Model for a Barrio in the Urban Structure of Teotihuacan. In *Urbanism in Mesoamerica*, vol. 2, edited by Alba Guadalupe Mastache, Robert H. Cobean, Angel García Cook, and Kenneth G. Hirth, pp. 37–83. INAH and Pennsylvania State University, Mexico City and University Park.

Campiani, Arianna, Atasta Flores Esquivel, and Javier López Mejía. 2011. Topografía y espacio: El caso de Chinikihá, Chiapas, México. Paper presented at XXV Simposio de Investigaciones Arqueológicas en Guatemala. Guatemala City, Guatemala.

Carrasco, Pedro. 1966. Documentos sobre el rango de *tecuhtli* entre los Nahuas tramontanos. *Tlalocan* 5(2):133–160.

Cartas de Indias. 1877. vol. 11. Imprenta de Manuel G. Hernandez, Madrid.

Carter, Nicholas. 2006. New Approaches to the "Emblem" Monuments of Structure J at Monte Albán, Oaxaca, Mexico. Master's thesis, University of Texas at Austin, Austin.

Caso, Alfonso. 1932. Reading the Riddle of Ancient Jewels. *Natural History* 32:464–480.

———. 1935. *Las exploraciones en Monte Albán, temporada 1934–35*. Instituto Panamericano de Geografía e Historía, Publicación 18, Mexico City.

———. 1938. *Exploraciones en Oaxaca, quinta y sexta temporadas 1936–1937*. Instituto Panamericano de Geografía e Historia, Publicación 34, Mexico City.

———. 1947. Calendario y escritura de las antiguas culturas de Monte Albán. *Obras completas de Miguel Othón de Mendizábal* 1:116–143.

———. 1965. Zapotec Writing and Calendar. In *Handbook of Middle American Indians*, vol. 3, edited by Gordon R. Willey, pp. 931–947. University of Texas Press, Austin.

Caso, Alfonso, Ignacio Bernal, and Jorge R. Acosta. 1967. *La cerámica de Monte Albán*. Memorias del Instituto Nacional de Antropología e Historia No. 13, Mexico City.

Cavanagh, W. G., S. Hirst, and C. D. Litton. 1988. Soil Phosphate, Site Boundaries, and Change Point Analysis. *Journal of Field Archaeology* 15:67–83.

Chance, John K. 2000. The Noble House in Colonial Puebla, Mexico: Descent, Inheritance, and the Nahua Tradition. *American Anthropologist* 102:485–502.

Chase, Arlen F., and Diane Z. Chase. 1995. External Impetus, Internal Synthesis, and Standardization: E-Group Assemblages and the Crystallization of Classic Maya Society in the Southern Lowlands. In *Emergence of Lowland Maya Civilization: The Transition from the Preclassic to the Early Classic*, vol. 8, edited by Nikolai Grube, pp. 87–101. Acta Mesoamericana. Verlag Anton Saurwein, Möckmühl, Germany.

Chase, Diane Z. 1985. Between Earth and Sky: Idols, Images and Postclassic Cosmology. In *Fifth Palenque Round Table*, edited by Merle G. Robertson and Virginia M. Fields, pp. 223–234. Pre-Columbian Art Research Institute, San Francisco, CA.

Cheetham, David T. 1995. Reconstruction of the Formative Period Site Core of Cahal Pech, Belize. In *Belize Valley Preclassic Maya Project: Report on the 1995 Field Season*, edited by Paul F. Healy and Jaime J. Awe, pp. 1–33. Occasional Papers in Anthropology, No. 12. Trent University, Peterborough, Ontario.

Ciudad Real, Antonio de. 1976. *Tratado curioso y docto de las grandezas de la Nueva España: Relación breve y verdadera de algunas cosas de las muchas que sucedieron al padre fray Alonso Ponce en las provincias de la Nueva España siendo comisario general de aquellas partes*. 2 vols. Instituto de Investigaciones Históricas, Universidad Nacional Autónoma de México, Mexico City.

Ciudad Ruiz, Andrés, María Josefa Iglesias Ponce de León, and Miguel Sorroche Cuerva (editors). 2010. *El ritual en el mundo maya: De lo privado a lo público*. Sociedad Española de Estudios Mayas, Madrid.

Clark, John E. 2004. Mesoamerica Goes Public: Early Ceremonial Centers, Leaders, and Communities. In *Mesoamerican Achaeology*, edited by Julia A. Hendon and Rosemary A. Joyce, pp. 43–72. Blackwell, Malden, MA.

Clark, John E., and David Cheetham. 2002. Mesoamerica's Tribal Foundations. In *Archaeology of Tribal Societies*, edited by W. A. Parkinson, pp. 278–339. International Monographs in Prehistory Vol. 15. Ann Arbor, MI.

Clark, John E., and Richard D. Hansen. 2001. Architecture of Early Kingship: Comparative Perspectives on the Origins of the Maya Royal Court. In *Royal Courts of the Ancient Maya*, vol. 2: *Data and Case Studies*, edited by Takeshi Inomata and Stephen D. Houston, pp. 1–45. Westview Press, Boulder, CO.

Clayton, Sarah. 2009. Ritual Diversity and Social Identities: A Study of Mortuary Behaviors at Teotihuacan. PhD dissertation, Arizona State University, Tempe.

Clendinnen, Inga. 1990. Ways to the Sacred. *History and Anthropology* 5:105–141.

Coben, Laerence S., and Takeshi Inomata. 2006. Behind the Scenes: Producing the Performance. In *Archaeology of Performance: Theaters of Power, Community, and Politics*, edited by Takeshi Inomata and Lawrence S. Coben, pp. 3–7. Alta Mira Press, Oxford.

Cobos Palma, Rafael. 2003a. Ancient Community Form and Social Complexity at Chichen Itza, Yucatan. In *El Urbanismo en Mesoamérica; Urbanism in Mesoamerica*, vol. 1, edited by William T. Sanders, Alba G. Mastache, and Robert H. Cobean, pp. 451–472. Instituto Nacional de Antropología e Historia/Pennsylvania State University, Mexico City.

———. 2003b. *The Settlement Patterns of Chichen Itza, Yucatan, Mexico*. PhD dissertation, Tulane University, New Orleans, LA.

Cobos Palma, Rafael, and Terance L. Winemiller. 2001. The Late and Terminal Classic-Period Causeway Systems of Chichen Itza, Yucatan, Mexico. *Ancient Mesoamerica* 12(2):283–291.

Coe, Michael D. 1962. *Mexico*. Praeger, New York.

———. 1965. A Model of Ancient Community Structure in the Maya Lowlands. *Southwestern Journal of Anthropology* 21(2):97–114.

Coe, Michael D., and Richard A. Diehl. 1980. *In the Land of the Olmec*. University of Texas Press, Austin.

Coggins, Clemecy. 1967. Palaces and Planning of Ceremonial Centers in the Southern Maya Lowlands. Unpublished manuscript. Tozzer Library, Peabody Museum, Harvard University, Cambridge, MA.

Cohen, Amanda. 2010a. Ritual and Architecture in the Titicaca Basin: The Development of the Sunken Court Complex in the Formative Period. PhD dissertation, University of California, Los Angeles.

———. 2010b. Ritualization in Early Village Society: The Case of the Lake Titicaca Basin Formative. In *Becoming Villagers: Comparing Early Village Societies*, edited by Matthew S. Bandy and Jake R. Fox, pp. 81–99. University of Arizona Press, Tucson.

Connerton, Paul. 1989. *How Societies Remember*. Cambridge University Press, Cambridge.

Conolly, James, and Mark Lake. 2006. *Geographical Information Systems in Archaeology*. Cambridge University Press, Cambridge, UK.

Cook de Leonard, Carmen. 1957. Proyecto del CIAM en Teotihuacan: Excavaciones en la Plaza 1 "Tres Palos," Teotihuacan. *Boletín del Centro de Investigaciones Antropológicas de México*, núm. 4.

Cooper, Matthew. 1993. Access to the Waterfront: Transformations of Meaning on the Tront Lakeshore. In *The Cultural Meaning of Urban Space*, edited by Robert Rotenberg and Gary McDonogh, pp. 157–171. Bergin & Garvey, Westport, CT.

Córdova, Fray Juan de. 1987 [1578]. *Arte en lengua Çapoteca*. Pedro Balli, Mexico. Introduction by Nicolás León. Imprenta del Gobierno, Morelia.

Covarrubias, Elba Domínguez. 2001. Larquitectura monumental del periodo Clasico en el sur de Veracruz: Un enfoque regional. Tesis de Licenciatura, Departmento de Antropología, Universidad de las Americas, Puebla, Mexico.

Cowgill, George L. 1983. Rulership and the Ciudadela: Political Inferences from Teotihuacan Architecture. In *Civilization in the Ancient Americas: Essays in Honor of Gordon R. Willey*, edited by Richard M. Leventhal and Alan L. Kolata, pp. 313–343. University of New Mexico Press and Peabody Museum of Archaeology and Ethnology, Cambridge, MA.

———. 1997. State and Society at Teotihuacan, Mexico. *Annual Review of Anthropology* 26:129–161.

———. 2000. The Central Mexican Highlands from the Rise of Teotihuacan to the Decline of Tula. In *The Cambridge History of the Native Peoples of the Americas*. Vol. 2: Mesoamerica, Pt. 1, edited by Richard E. W. Adams and Murdo J. MacLeod, pp. 250–317. Cambridge University Press, Cambridge, UK.

———. 2003. Teotihuacan: Cosmic Glories and Mundane Needs. In *The Social Construction of Ancient Cities*, edited by Monica L. Smith, pp. 37–55. Smithsonian Institution Press, Washington, DC.

———. 2008. Teotihuacan as an Urban Place. In *Urbanism in Mesoamerica*, vol. 2, edited by lba Guadalupe Mastache, Robert H. Cobean, Angel García Cook, and Kenneth G. Hirth, pp. 85–112. INAH and Pennsylvania State University, Mexico City and University Park.

Croissier, Michelle M. 2007. *The Zapotec Presence at Teotihuacan, Mexico: Political Ethnicity and Domestic Identity*. PhD dissertation, University of Illinois at Urbana-Champaign, Urbana.

Cyphers, Ann. 1993. Escenas Escultóricas Olmecas. *Antropológicas* 6:47–52. Mexico: Instituto de Investigaciones Antropológicas, Universidad Nacional Autónoma de México, Mexico City.

———. 1994. Olmec Sculpture. *National Geographic Research and Exploration* 10(3): 294–305.

———. 1997a. El contexto social de monumentos en San Lorenzo. In *Población, subsistencia y medio ambiente en San Lorenzo Tenochtitlán*, edited by Ann Cyphers, pp. 163–194. Instituto de Investigaciones Antropológicas, Universidad Nacional Autónoma de México, Mexico City.

———. 1997b. Olmec Architecture at San Lorenzo. In *Olmec to Aztec: Settlement Patterns in the Ancient Gulf Lowlands*, edited by Barbara L. Stark and Philip J. Arnold Stark III, pp. 96–114. University of Arizona Press, Tucson.

———. 1999. From Stone to Symbols: Olmec Art in Social Context at San Lorenzo Tenochtitlán. In *Social Patterns in Pre-Classic Mesoamerica*, edited by David C. Grove and Rosemary A. Joyce, pp. 155–181. Dumbarton Oaks, Washington, DC.

———. 2004a. Escultura monumental olmeca: Temas y contextos. In *Acercarse y Mirar, Homenaje a Beatriz de la Fuente*, edited by María Teresa Uriarte and Leticia Staines, pp. 51–74. Instituto de Investigaciones Estéticas, Universidad Nacional Autónoma de México, Mexico City.

———. 2004b. *Escultura Olmeca de San Lorenzo Tenochtitlán*. Instituto de Investigaciones Antropológicas, Universidad Nacional Autónoma de Mexico and the Coordinación de Humanidades, Mexico City.

———. 2012. *Las bellas teorías y los terribles hechos: Controversias sobre los Olmecas del preclásico inferior.* Instituto de Investigaciones Antropológicas, Universidad Nacional Autónoma de México, Mexico City.

Cyphers, Ann, and Judith Zurita Noguera. 2006. A Land That Tastes of Water. In *Precolumbian Water Management: Ideology, Ritual and Power*, edited by Lisa Lucero and Barbara Fash, pp. 33–50. University of Arizona Press, Tucson.

Cyphers, Ann, Alejandro Hernández, Marisol Varela, and Lilia Grégor. 2006. Cosmological and Sociopolitical Synergy in Preclassic Architectural Precincts. In *Precolumbian Water Management: Ideology, Ritual and Power*, edited by Lisa Lucero and Barbara Fash, pp. 17–32. University of Arizona Press, Tucson.

Cyphers, Ann, Timothy Murtha, Joshua Borstein, Judith Zurita-Noguera, Roberto Lunagómez, Stacey Symonds, Gerardo Jiménez, Mario Arturo Ortiz, and José Manuel Figueroa. 2007–2008. Arqueología digital en la primera capital olmeca, San Lorenzo. *Thule* 22–25:121–144. Centro Studi Americanistici "Circolo Amerindiano," Perugia, Italia.

Cyphers, Ann, Timothy Murtha, Judith Zurita Noguera, Gerardo Jiménez, Elvia Hernández Guevara, Brizio Martínez Gracia, Virginia Arieta Baizabal, Roberto Lunagómez, Joshua Borstein, Stacey Symonds, Mario Arturo Ortiz, and José Manuel Figueroa. In press. *Atlas digital de la zona arqueológica de San Lorenzo, Veracruz.* Instituto de Investigaciones Antropológicas, Universidad Nacional Autónoma de México, Mexico City.

Dahlgren, Barbo. 1966. *La Mixteca: Su cultura e historia prehispanicas*. 2nd ed. Universidad Nacional Autónoma de México, Mexico City.

Dahlin, Bruce H., Christopher T. Jensen, Richard E. Terry, David R. Wright, and Timothy Beach. 2007. In Search of an Ancient Maya Market. *Latin American Antiquity* 18(4):363–384.

Daneels, Annick. 1997. Settlement History in the Lower Cotaxtla Basin. In *Olmec to Aztec: Settlement Patterns in the Ancient Gulf Lowlands*, edited by Barbara L. Stark and Philip J. Arnold III, pp. 206–252. University of Arizona Press, Tucson.

———. 2002. El patrón de asentamiento del periodo Clásico en la Cuenca baja del Río Cotaxtla, Arqueología, Universidad Nacional Autónoma de México, Mexico City.

Davis-Salazar, Karla L., E. Christian Wells, and Jose E. Moreno-Cortés. 2007. Balancing Archaeological Responsibilities and Community Commitments: A Case from Honduras. *Journal of Field Archaeology* 32:196–205.

De Certeau, Michel. 1984. *The Practice of Everyday Life.* Translated by Steven Rendall. University of California Press, Berkeley.

DeMarrais, Elizabeth, Luis Jaime Castillo, and Timothy Earle. 1996. Ideology, Materialization, and Power Strategies. *Current Anthropology* 37(1):15–31.

DeMers, Michael N. 2009. *GIS for Dummies*. Wiley, Indianapolis, IN.

de Rojas, Gabriel. 1927 [1579]. Relación de Cholula. *Revista Méxicana de estudios históricos* 1: Apéndice:158–169.

Derrida, Jack. 1977. Signature, Event, Context. *Glyph* 1:172–197.

Dornan, Jennifer L. 2004. Beyond Belief: Religious Experience, Ritual, and Cultural Neuro-Phenomenology in the Interpretation of Past Religious Systems. *Cambridge Archaeological Journal* 14:25–36.

Drucker, Phillip. 1943. *Ceramic Stratigraphy at Cerro de las Mesas, Veracruz, Mexico*. Smithsonian Institution, Bureau of American Ethnography, Bulletin 141. Smithsonian Institution Press, Washington, DC.

———. 1952. *La Venta, Tabasco: A Study of Olmec Ceramics and Art*. Bureau of American Ethnology Bulletin Vol. 153. Smithsonian Institution, Washington, DC.

Drucker, Philip, Robert F. Heizer, and Robert H. Squier. 1959. *Excavations at La Venta, Tabasco*. Bureau of American Ethnology Bulletin Vol. 170. Smithsonian Institution, Washington, DC.

Duncan, James S. 1985. Individual Action and Political Power: A Structuration Perspective. In *The Future of Geography and Geography in the Future*, edited by Ronald J. Johnston, pp. 174–189. Methuen, London.

Dunning, Nicholas, Timothy Beach, and David Rue. 1997. The Paleoecology and Ancient Settlement of the Petexbatun Region, Guatemala. *Ancient Mesoamerica* 8(2):255–266.

Durán, Fray Diego. 1994. *The History of the Indies of New Spain*. University of Oklahoma Press, Norman.

Edgerton, Samuel Y. 2001. *Theaters of Conversion: Religious Architecture and Indian Artisans in Colonial Mexico*. University of New Mexico Press, Albuquerque.

Eliade, Mircea. 1978. *A History of Religious Ideas*. Vols. 1–3. Chicago University Press, Chicago.

Elson, M. Christina. 2006. Intermediate Elites and the Political Landscape of the Early Zapotec State. In *Intermediate Elites in Pre-Columbian States*, edited by Christina M. Elson and R. Alan Covey, pp. 44–67. University of Arizona Press, Tucson.

Esparza Olguin, Octavio, and Kenichiro Tsukamoto. 2011. Espacios de la escenografía ritual. In *Los Mayas: Voces de piedra*, edited by Alejandra Martínes and Maria Elena de la Vega, pp. 393–399. Ámbar Diseño, Mexico City, Mexico.

Estrada-Belli, Francisco. 2006. Lightning Sky, Rain, and the Maize God: The Ideology of Preclassic Maya Rulers at Cival, Peten, Guatemala. *Ancient Mesoamerica* 17(1):57–78.

———. 2011. *The First Maya Civilization: Ritual and Power before the Classic Period*. Routledge, London.

Estrada-Belli, Francisco, and Gair Tourtellot. 2005. Classic Ritualized Landscape at La Milpa, Belize. *Art for Archaeology's Sake: Material Culture and Style across the Disciplines: Proceeding of the Thirty-third Annual Conference of the Archaeological Association* 33:217–227.

Fahmel Beyer, Bernd. 1991. *La arquitectura de Monte Albán*. Instituto de Investigaciones Antropológicas. Universidad Nacional Autónoma de México, Mexico City.

Farriss, Nancy M. 1984. *Maya Society under Colonial Rule: The Collective Enterprise for Survival*. Princeton University Press, Princeton, NJ.

Fernández, Fabián G., Richard E. Terry, Takeshi Inomata, and Markus Eberl. 2002. An Ethnoarchaeological Study of Chemical Residues in the Floors and Soils of Q'eqchi Maya Houses at Las Pozas, Guatemala. *Geoarchaeology* 17:487–519.

Finsten, Laura, Stephen A. Kowalewski, Charlotte A. Smith, Mark D. Borland, and Richard D. Garvin. 1996. Circular Architecture and Symbolic Boundaries in the Mixtec Sierra, Oaxaca. *Ancient Mesoamerica* 7(1):19–35.

Flannery, Kent V. 1976. Contextual Analysis of Ritual Paraphernalia from Formative Oaxaca. In *The Early Mesoamerican Village*, edited by Kent V. Flannery, pp. 333–345. Academic Press, New York.

Flannery, Kent V., and Joyce Marcus. 1976. Evolution of the Public Building in Formative Oaxaca. In *Cultural Change and Continuity*, pp. 205–222. Academic Press, New York.

———. 1983. The Earliest Public Buildings, Tombs, and Monuments of Monte Albán. In *The Cloud People: Divergent Evolution of the Zapotec and Mixtec Civilizations*, edited by Kent V. Flannery and Joyce Marcus, pp. 87–91. Academic Press, New York.

Fleisher, Jeffrey, and Stephanie Wynne-Jones. 2010. Archaeological Investigations at Songo Mnara, Tanzania: Urban Space, Social Memory and Materiality on the 15th- and 16th-century Southern Swahili Coast. Preliminary Report Submitted to the Department of Antiquities, Republic of Tanzania.

———. 2012. Finding Meaning in Ancient Swahili Spatial Practices. *African Archaeological Review* 29:171–207.

Fleming, Andrew. 2005. Megaliths and Post-Modernism: The Case of Wales. *Antiquity* 79:921–932.

Flores Esquivel, Atasta. 2011. Centros cívico ceremoniales menores o "sitios de orden secundario" en la región de Palenque. Características y Componentes. In *B'aakal arqueología de la región de Palenque, Chiapas, México, temporadas 1996–2006*, edited by Rodrigo Liendo Stuardo, pp. 35–48. Paris Monographs in American Archaeology 26. BAR International Series 2203, Oxford.

Forde, Jamie E. 2002. Ideology, Identity, and Icons: A Study of Mixtec Polychrome Pottery from Late Postclassic Yucu Dzaa (Tututepec), Oaxaca, Mexico. Master's thesis, University of Colorado, Boulder.

Foucault, Michel. 1977. *Discipline and Punish: The Birth of the Prison*. Translated by Alan Sheridan. Vintage, New York.

———. 1982. The Subject and Power. *Critical Inquiry* 8:777–795.

———. 1984. Space, Knowledge, and Power. In *The Foucault Reader*, edited by Paul Rabinow, pp. 239–256. Pantheon, New York.

———. 2007. *Security, Territory, Population: Lecture at the Collège de France 1977–1978*. Translated by G. Burchell. Palgrave Macmillan, London.

Freidel, David A., Héctor L. Escobedo, and Stanley P. Guenter. 2007. A Crossroads of Conquerors: Waka' and Gordon Willey's "Rehearsal for the Collapse" Hypothesis. In *Gordon R. Willey and American Archaeology: Contemporary Perspectives*, edited by William L. Fash and Jeremy A. Sabloff, pp. 187–208. University of Oklahoma Press, Norman.

Furst, Jill L. M. 1990. Rulership and Ritual: Myth and the Origin of Political Authority in Mixtec Pictorial Manuscripts. In *Circumpacifica I, Mittel-und Südamerika* Vol. 1, edited by Thomas S. Barthel and Bruno Illius, pp. 123–141. Peter Lang, Frankfurt am Main.

Garraty, Christopher P., and Barbara L. Stark. 2002. Imperial and Social Relations in Postclassic South-Central Veracruz, Mexico. *Latin American Antiquity* 13(1):3–33.

Garza, Mercedes de la. 1983. *Relaciones histórico-geográficas de la gobernación de Yucatán: Mérida, Valladolid y Tabasco*. Instituto de Investigaciones Filológicas, Centro de Estudios Mayas, Fuentes para el Estudio de la Cultura Maya, 2 vols. Universidad Nacional Autónoma de México, Mexico City.

Geertz, Clifford. 1980. *Negara: The Theatre State in Nineteenth-Century Bali*. Princeton University Press, Princeton, NJ.

Giddens, Anthony. 1979. *Central Problems in Social Theory: Action, Structure, and Contradiction in Social Analysis*. University of California, Berkeley.

———. 1984. *The Constitution of Society: Outline of the Theory of Structuration*. University of California Press, Berkeley.

Gillespie, Susan D. 2000. Rethinking Ancient Maya Social Organization: Replacing "Lineage" with "House." *American Anthropologist* 102:467–484.

———. 2008. History in Practice: Ritual Deposition at La Venta Complex A. In *Memory Work: Archaeologies of Material Practice*, edited by Barbara J. Mills and William H. Walker, pp. 109–136. School of Advanced Research Press, Santa Fe.

Ginzburg, Carlo. 1980. Morelli, Freud, and Sherlock Holmes: Clues and Scientific Method. *History Workshop Journal* 9:5–36.

———. 1989. *Clues, Myths, and the Historical Method*. Translated by John and Anne Tedeschi. John Hopkins University Press, Baltimore, MD.

Goldstein, Paul. 1993. Tiwanaku Temples and State Expansion: A Tiwanaku Sunken-Court Temple in Moquegua, Peru. *Latin American Antiquity* 4(1):22–47.

Gómez Chávez, Sergio. 2000. *La Ventilla: Un barrio de la antigua ciudad de Teotihuacán*. Tesis de licenciatura. Escuela Nacional de Antropología e Historia, Mexico City.

González Crespo, Norberto, Silvia Garza Tarazona, Beatriz Palavicini Beltrán, and Claudia Alvarado León. 2008. La cronología de Xochicalco. *Arqueología* 37 (segunda época):123–139.

González Lauck, Rebecca. 1996. La Venta: An Olmec Capital. In *Olmec Art of Ancient Mexico*, edited by Elizabeth P. Benson and Beatriz de la Fuente, pp. 73–81. National Gallery of Art, Washington, DC.

Gose, Peter. 1996. Oracles, Divine Kingship, and Political Representation in the Inka State. *Ethnohistory* 43(1):1–32.

Gossen, Gary. 1974. *Chamulas in the World of the Sun: Time and Space in a Maya Oral Tradition*. Harvard University Press, Cambridge, MA.

Graham, John A. 1990. *Excavations at Seibal, Department of Peten, Guatemala: Monumental Sculpture and Hieroglyphic Inscriptions*. Memoirs of the Peabody Museum of Archaeology and Ethnology Vol. 14, No. 1. Gordon R. Willey, series editor. Harvard University Press, Cambridge, MA.

Grove, David C. 1997. Public Monuments and Sacred Mountains: Observations on Three Formative Period Sacred Landscapes. In *Social Patterns in Pre-classic Mesoamerica*, edited by David C. Grove and Rosemary A. Joyce, pp. 255–300. Dumbarton Oaks, Washington, DC.

Grube, Nikolai. 2008. Monumentos esculpidos: Epigrafía e iconografía. In *Reconocimiento arqueológico en el sureste del estado de Campeche, México: 1996–2005*, edited by Ivan Šprajc, pp. 177–231. Paris Monographs in American Archaeology Vol. 19. BAR International Series 1742, Oxford.

Guernsey Kappleman, Julia. 2001. Sacred Geography at Izapa and the Performance of Rulership. In *Landscape and Power in Ancient Mesoamerica*, edited by Rex Koontz, Kathryn Reese–Taylor, and Annabeth Headrick, pp. 81–111. Westview Press, Boulder, CO.

Hall, Edward T. 1968. Proxemics. *Current Anthropology* 9(2):83–95.

———. 1972. Silent Assumptions in Social Communication. In *People and Buildings*, edited by Robert Gutman, pp. 131–151. Basic Books, New York.

———. 1990 [1966]. *The Hidden Dimension*. Anchor Books, New York.

———. 2003. Proxemics. In *The Anthropology of Space and Place: Locating Culture*, edited by Setha M. Low and Denise Lawrence-Zúñiga, pp. 51–73. Blackwell, Malden, MA.

Hamann, Byron. 2002. The Social Life of Pre-Sunrise Things: Indigenous Mesoamerican Archaeology. *Current Anthropology* 43(3):351–382.

Hammond, Norman. 1991. Inside the Black Box: Defining Maya Polity. In *Classic Maya Political History*, edited by T. Patrick Culbert, pp. 253–284. Cambridge University Press, Cambridge.

Hammond, Norman, Juliette Cartwright Gerhardt, and Sara Donaghey. 1991. Stratigraphy and Chronology in the Reconstruction of Preclassic Developments at Cuello. In *Cuello: An Early Maya Community in Belize*, edited by Norman Hammond, pp. 23–60. Cambridge University Press, Cambridge.

Hansen, Richard D. 1998. Continuity and Disjunction: The Pre-Classic Antecedents of Classic Maya Architecture. In *Function and Meaning in Classic Maya Architecture*, edited by Stephen D. Houston, pp. 49–122. Dumbarton Oaks Research Library and Collection, Washington, DC.

Hanson, Craig A. 1995. The Hispanic Horizon in Yucatan: A Model of Franciscan Missionization. *Ancient Mesoamerica* 6(1):15–28.

Hawken, James R. 2007. Socio-Natural Landscapes in the Palmarejo Valley, Honduras. Master's thesis, University of South Florida, Tampa.

Headrick, Annabeth. 2001. Merging Myth and Politics: The Three Temple Complex at Teotihuacan. In *Landscape and Power in Ancient Mesoamerica*, edited by Rex Koontz, Kathryn Reese-Taylor, and Annabeth Headrick, pp. 169–195. Westview Press, Boulder, CO.

———. 2007. *The Teotihuacan Trinity: The Sociopolitical Structure of an Ancient Mesoamerican City*. University of Texas Press, Austin.

Healy, Paul F., David Cheetham, Terry G. Powis, and Jaime J. Awe. 2004. Cahal Pech: The Middle Formative Period. In *The Ancient Maya of the Belize Valley: Half a Century of Archaeological Research*, edited by James Garber, pp. 103–124. University Press of Florida, Gainesville.

Heller, Lynette. 2000. Postclassic Obsidian Workshop Debris from El Sauce, Veracruz, Mexico. *Mexicon* 22:139–146.

Henderson, John S. 1977. The Valley de Naco: Ethnohistory and Archaeology in Northwestern Honduras. *Ethnohistory* 24(4):363–377.

Henderson, John S., Ilene Sterns, Anthony Wonderley, and Patricia A. Urban. 1979. Archaeological Investigations in the Valle de Naco, Northwestern Honduras: A Preliminary Report. *Journal of Field Archaeology* 6(2):169–192.

Hicks, Frederic. 2009. Land and Succession in the Indigenous Noble Houses of Sixteenth-Century Tlaxcala. *Ethnohistory* 56:569–588.

Hillier, Bill, and Julienne Hanson.1984. *The Social Logic of Space*. Cambridge University Press, Cambridge.

Hirsch, Eric. 1995. Introduction: Landscape: Between Place and Space. In *The Anthropology of Landscape: Perspectives on Place and Space*, edited by Eric Hirsch and Michael O'Hanlon, pp. 1–30. Clarendon Press, Oxford.

Hirsch, Eric, and Michael O'Hanlon. 1995. *The Anthropology of Landscape: Perspective on Place and Space*. Oxford University Press, Oxford.

Hirth, Kenneth G. 1989. Militarism and Social Organization at Xochicalco, Morelos. In *Mesoamerica after the Decline of Teotihuacan,* A.D. *700–900*, edited by Richard A. Diehl and Janet C. Berlo, pp. 69–82. Dumbarton Oaks, Washington, DC.

———. 1995. Urbanism, Militarism, and Architectural Design: An Analysis of Epiclassic Sociopolitical Structure at Xochicalco. *Ancient Mesoamerica* 6(2):237–250.

———. 2000. *Ancient Urbanism at Xochicalco: The Evolution and Organization of a Prehispanic Society, Archaeological Research at Xochicalco: 1*. University of Utah Press, Salt Lake City.

Hirth, Kenneth G. (editor). 2000. *Archaeological Research at Xochicalco: 2. The Xochicalco Mapping Project*. University of Utah Press, Salt Lake City.

Hobsbawm, Eric, and Terrence Ranger (editors). 1983. *The Invention of Tradition*. Cambridge University Press, Cambridge.

Holland, Dorothy, William Lachicote Jr., Debra Skinner, and Carole Cain. 2001 [1998]. *Identity and Agency in Cultural Worlds*. Harvard University Press, Cambridge, MA.

Holley, George R., Rinita A. Dalan, and Philip A. Smith. 1993. Investigations in the Cahokia Site Grand Plaza. *American Antiquity* 58(2):306–319.

Holliday, V. T. 2004. *Soils in Archeological Research*. Oxford University Press, New York.

Holstein, James. 1989. *The Modernist City: An Anthropological Critique of Brasilia*. University of Chicago Press, Chicago.

Houston, Stephen D. 1998. Classic Maya Depictions of the Built Environment. In *Function and Meaning in Classic Maya Architecture*, edited by Stephen D. Houston, pp. 333–372. Dumbarton Oaks, Washington, DC.

Hruby, Zachary X. 2007. Ritualized Chipped-Stone Production at Piedras Negras, Guatemala. In *Rethinking Craft Specialization in Complex Societies: Archaeological Analyses of the Social Meaning of Production*, edited by Zachary X. Hruby and Rowan K. Flad, pp. 68–87. Archaeological Papers of the American Anthropological Association, no. 17. Arlington, VA.

Hutson, Scott R. 2002. Built Space and Bad Subjects: Domination and Resistance at Monte Albán, Oaxaca, Mexico. *Journal of Social Archaeology* 2:53–80.

Inomata, Takeshi. 2006a. Plazas, Performers, and Spectators: Political Theaters of Classic Maya. *Current Anthropology* 47(5):805–842.

———. 2006b. Politics and Theatricality in Maya Society. In *Archaeology of Performance: Theaters of Power, Community, and Politics*, edited by Takeshi Inomata and Lawrence Coben, pp. 187–222. Altamira Press, Lanham, MD.

———. In press. War, Violence, and Society in the Maya Lowlands. In *Embattled Bodies, Embattled Places: War in Pre-Columbian America*, edited by Andrew K. Scherer and John W. Verano. Dumbarton Oaks Research Library and Collection, Washington, DC.

Inomata, Takeshi, and Lawrence S. Coben. 2006. Overture: An Invitation to the Archaeological Theater. In *Archaeology of Performance: Theaters of Power, Community, and Politics*, edited by Takeshi Inomata and Lawrence S. Coben, pp. 11–44. AltaMira Press, Oxford.

Inomata, Takeshi, and Stephen Houston. 2001. Opening the Royal Maya Court. In *Royal Courts of the Ancient Maya, Volume 1: Theory, Comparison, and Synthesis*, edited by Takeshi Inomata and Stephen Houston, pp. 3–23. Westview Press, Boulder, CO.

Inomata, Takeshi, Daniela Triadan, and Otto Rodrigo Román. 2010. La transformación y continuidad de ritos durante el período preclásico en Ceibal, Guatemala. In *El ritual en el mundo Maya: De lo privado a lo público*, edited by Andrés Ciudad Ruiz, Iglesias Ponce de León, María Josefa, and Miguel Sorroche, pp. 29–48. Sociedad Española de Estudios Mayas, Madrid.

Inomata, Takeshi, Daniela Triadan, Kazuo Aoyama, Victor Castillo, and Hitoshi Yonenobu. 2013. Early Ceremonial Constructions at Ceibal, Guatemala, and the Origins of Lowland Maya Civilization. *Science* 340(6131):467–471.

Islebe, Gerald A., Henry Hooghiemstra, Mark Brenner, Jason H. Curtis, and David A. Hodell. 1996. A Holocene Vegetation History from Lowland Guatemala. *The Holocene* 6:265–271.

Jansen, Maarten. 1998. Monte Albán y Zaachila en los códices Mixtecos. In *The Shadow of Monte Albán: Politics and Historiography in Postclassic Oaxaca, Mexico*, edited by Maarten Jansen, Peter Kröfges, and Michel R. Oudijk, pp. 67–121. Research School of Asian, African and Amerindian Studies, Leiden University, Leiden.

———. 1990. The Search for History in Mixtec Codices. *Ancient Mesoamerica* 1(1):99–112.

Jansen, Martin. 1982. *Huisi Taci, estudio interpretativo de un libro mixteco antiguo: Codex Vindobonensis Mexicanus I*. Centrum voor Studie en Documentatie van Latijns Amerika, Amsterdam.

Janusek, John Wayne. 2004. *Identity and Power in the Ancient Andes: Tiwanaku Cities through Time*. Routledge, New York.

Jarquín Pacheco, Ana Maria, and Enrique Martínez Vargas. 1982. Las excavaciones en el conjunto 1D. In *Memoria del proyecto arqueológico Teotihuacan 80–82, volumen 1*, edited by Ruben Cabrera Castro, Rodriquez G. Ignacio, and Morelos G. Noel, pp. 89–126. Colección Científica 132. Instituto Nacional de Antropología e Historia, Mexico City.

Johnston, Kevin. 2006. Preclassic Maya Occupation of the Itzan Escarpment, Lower Río de La Pasión, Petén, Guatemala. *Ancient Mesoamerica* 17(2):177–201.

Johnson, Matthew H. 2012. Phenomenological Approaches in Landscape Archaeology. *Annual Review of Anthropology* 41:269–284.

Jones, Andy. 2005. Lives in Fragments? Personhood and the European Neolithic. *Journal of Social Archaeology* 5:193–224.

Joyce, Arthur A. 2000. The Founding of Monte Albán: Sacred Propositions and Social Practices. In *Agency in Archaeology*, edited by Marcia-Anne Dobres and John Robb, pp. 71–91. Routledge, London.

———. 2003. Imperialism in Pre-Aztec Mesoamerica: Monte Albán, Teotihuacan, and the Lower Río Verde Valley. In *Ancient Mesoamerica Warfare*, edited by M. Kathryn Brown and Travis M. Stanton, pp. 49–72. Alta Mira Press, Walnut Creek, CA.

———. 2004. Sacred Space and Social Relations in the Valley of Oaxaca. In *Mesoamerican Archaeology, Theory and Practice*, edited by Julia A. Hendon and Rosemary A. Joyce, pp. 192–216. Blackwell, Malden, MA.

———. 2009. The Main Plaza of Monte Albán: A Life History of Place. In *The Archaeology of Meaningful Places*, edited by Brenda Bowser and María Nieves Zedeño, pp. 32–52. University of Utah Press, Salt Lake City.

———. 2010. *Mixtecs, Zapotecs, and Chatinos: Ancient Peoples of Southern Mexico*. Wiley-Blackwell, Malden, MA.

Joyce, Arthur A., and E. T. Weller. 2007. Commoner Rituals, Resistance, and the Classic-to-Postclassic Transition. In *Commoner Ritual and Ideology in Ancient*

Mesoamerica, edited by Nancy Gonlin and Jon C. Lohse, pp. 141–182. University Press of Colorado, Boulder.

Joyce, Arthur, and Marcus Winter. 1996. Ideology, Power, and Urban Society in Pre-Hispanic Oaxaca. *Current Anthropology* 37(1):33–47.

Joyce, Arthur A., Andrew G. Workinger, Byron Hamann, et al. 2004. Lord 8 Deer "Jaguar Claw" and the Land of the Sky: The Archaeology and History of Tututepec. *Latin American Antiquity* 15(3):273–297.

Joyce, Rosemary A. 2003. Concrete Memories: Fragments of the Past in the Classic Maya Present (500–1000 A.D.). In *Archaeologies of Memory*, edited by Ruth M. Van Dyke and Susan E. Alcock, pp. 104–125. Blackwell, Malden, MA.

Joyce, Rosemary A., and Susan D. Gillespie. 2000. *Beyond Kinship: Social and Material Reproduction in House Societies*. University of Pennsylvania Press, Philadelphia.

Karttunen, Frances. 1983. *An Analytical Dictionary of Nahuatl*. University of Texas Press, Austin.

Kertzer, David I. 1988. *Ritual, Politics, and Power*. Yale University Press, New Haven, CT.

King, Mark B. 1990. Poetics and Metaphor in Mixtec Writing. *Ancient Mesoamerica* 1(1):141–151.

Knapp, A. Barnard, and Wendy Ashmore. 1999. Archaeological Landscapes. In *Archaeologies of Landscape: Constructed, Conceptualized, Ideational*, edited by Cynthia Kristan-Graham, pp. 1–30. Blackwell, Malden, MA.

Kolb, Michael J. 1994. Monumentality and the Rise of Religious Authority in Precontact Hawai'i. *Current Anthropology* 35(5):521–547.

Kowalski, Jeff Karl. 1987. *The House of the Governor*. University of Oklahoma Press, Norman.

Kowalski, Jeff Karl, and Cynthia Kristan-Graham (editors). 2007. *Twin Tollans: Chichén Itzá, Tula and the Epiclassic to Early Postclassic Mesoamerican World*. Dumbarton Oaks, Washington, DC.

Kowalewski, Stephen A., Andrew K. Balkansky, Laura R. Stiver, and Verónica Pérez Rodríguez. 2009. *Origins of the Ñuu: Archaeology in the Mixteca Alta, Mexico*. University Press of Colorado, Boulder.

Kristan-Graham, Cynthia. 2007. Structuring Identity at Tula: The Design and Symbolism of Colonnaded Halls and Sunken Spaces. In *Twin Tollans: Chichén Itzá, Tula and the Epiclassic to Early Postclassic Mesoamerican World*, edited by Jeff K. Kowalski and Cynthia Kristan-Graham, pp. 531–577. Dumbarton Oaks, Washington, DC.

Landa, Diego de. 1996. *Relación de las cosas de Yucatán*, edited by Miguel Rivera Dorado. Dastin, S.L., Madrid.

Laporte, Juan Pedro, and Vilma Fialko. 1995. Un reencuentro con Mundo Perdido, Tikal, Guatemala. *Ancient Mesoamerica* 6(1):41–94.

Laporte, Juan Pedro, and Juan Antonio Valdés (editors). 1993. *Tikal y Uaxactún en el preclásico*. Universidad Nacional Autónoma de México, Mexico City.

Leach, Edmund R. 1954. *The Political Systems of Highland Burma, A Study of Kachin Social Structure*. Athlone Press, London.

Lefebvre, Henri. 1991. *The Production of Space*. Translated by Donald Nicholson-Smith. Editions Anthropos, Malden, MA.

Lejarazu, Manuel Hermann. 2007. Símbolos de poder: Un análisis comparativo entre la iconografía del clásico Maya y los códices Mixtecos. *Estudios de cultura maya* 30:79–106.

———. 2008. Rituals of Power in the Mixtec Codices. *Latin American Indian Literatures Journal* 24(2):125–150.

Leve, Lauren. 2011. Identity. *Current Anthropology* 52(4):513–535.

Lévi-Strauss, Claude. 1982. *The Way of the Masks*. Douglas & McIntyre, Vancouver.

———. 1987. The Concept of "House." In *Anthropology and Myth: Lectures, 1951–1982*, pp. 151–152. Basil Blackwell, London.

Liendo Stuardo, Rodrigo. 2002. The Organization of Agricultural Production at a Classic Maya Center: Settlement Patterns in the Palenque Region, Chiapas, Mexico. University of Pittsburgh and Instituto Nacional de Antropología e Historia, Pittsburgh.

———. 2003. Access Patterns in Maya Royal Precincts. In *Maya Palaces and Elite Residences*, edited by Jessica Joyce Christie, pp. 184–203. University of Texas Press, Austin.

———. 2011. *B'aakal Arqueología de la Región de Palenque, Chiapas, México, Temporadas 1996–2006*, edited by Rodrigo Liendo Stuardo. Paris Monographs in American Archaeology 26. BAR International Series 2203, Oxford.

Lind, Michael, and Javier Urcid. 2010. *The Lords of Lambityeco: Political Evolution in the Valley of Oaxaca during the Xoo Phase*. University Press of Colorado, Boulder.

Linné, Sigvald. 1934. *Archaeological Research at Teotihuacan, Mexico*. The Ethnographical Museum of Sweden, n.s. 1, Stockholm.

———. 1942. *Mexican Highland Cultures: Archaeological Researches at Teotihuacan, Calpulalpan, and Chalchicomula in 1934–35*. The Ethnographical Museum of Sweden, n.s. 7, Stockholm.

Lockhart, James. 1992. *Nahuas after the Conquest: A Social and Cultural History of the Indians of Central Mexico, Sixteenth through Eighteenth Centuries*. Stanford University Press, Stanford, CA.

Lohse, Jon C. 2010. Archaic Origins of the Lowland Maya. *Latin American Antiquity* 21(3):312–352.

Looper, Matthew G. 2001. Dance Performances at Quirigua. In *Landscape and Power in Ancient Mesoamerica*, edited by Rex Koontz, Kathryn Reese-Taylor, and Annabeth Headrick, pp. 113–136. Westview Press, Boulder, CO.

———. 2009. *To Be Like Gods: Dance in Ancient Maya Civilization*. University of Texas Press, Austin.

López Austin, Alfredo, and Leonardo López Luján. 2009. *Monte Sagrado—Templo Mayor*. Instituto Nacional de Antropología e Historia/Universidad Autónoma de México, Mexico City.

López Austin, Alfredo, Leonardo López Luján, and Saburo Sugiyama. 1991. The Temple of Quetzalcoatl at Teotihuacan: Its Possible Ideological Significance. *Ancient Mesoamerica* 2(1):93–105.

López Bravo, Roberto, Javier López Mejía, and Benito Venegas Durán. 2003. Del Motiepá al Picota: La primera temporada del Proyecto Crecimiento Urbano de la antigua ciudad de Palenque (PCU). In *Lakamhá* (9):10–15.

———. 2004. Del Motiepá al Murciélagos: La segunda temporada de campo del Proyecto. Crecimiento Urbano de la antigua ciudad de Palenque. In *Lakamhá* (13):8–12.

López Luján, Leonardo. 2006. *La Casa de las Águilas*. Fondo de Cultura Económica/CONACULTA, Mexico City.

López Luján, Leonardo, and Alfredo López Austin. 2009. The Mexica in Tula and Tula in Mexico-Tenochtitlan. In *Art of Urbanism: How Mesoamerican Kingdoms*

Represented Themselves in Architecture and Imagery, edited by William L. Fash and Leonardo López Luján, pp. 384–422. Dumbarton Oaks Research Library and Collection, Washington, DC.

———. 2011. El *coatepantli* de Tenochtitlan; historia de un malentendido. *Arqueología Mexicana* 19(111):64–71.

López Luján, Leonardo, and Bertina Olmedo. 2009. Los monolitos del mercado y el glifo tianquiztli. *Arqueología Mexicana* 17(101):18–21.

López Mejía, Javier. 2005. *Los grupos arquitectónicos de palenque: Una propuesta de análisis*. Tesis de Licenciatura, Escuela Nacional de Antropología e Historia, Mexico City.

Love, Michael W. 1999. Ideology, Material Culture, and Daily Practice in Pre-Classic Mesoamerica: A Pacific Coast Perspective. In *Social Patterns in Pre-Classic Meosamerica*, edited by David C. Grove and Rosemary A. Joyce, pp. 127–153. National Gallery of Art, Washington DC.

Low, Setha M. 1995. Indigenous Architecture and the Spanish American Plaza in Mesoamerica and the Caribbean. *American Anthropologist* 97(4):748–762.

———. 2000. *On the Plaza: The Politics of Public Space and Culture*. University of Texas Press, Austin.

Low, Setha M., and Denise Lawrence-Zúñiga. 2003. Locating Culture. In *The Anthropology of Space and Place: Locating Culture*, edited by Setha M. Low and Denise Lawrence-Zúñiga, pp. 1–47. Blackwell, Malden, MA.

Lowe, Gareth W. 1960. *Excavations at Chiapa de Corzo, Chiapas, Mexico*. Papers of the New World Archaeological Foundation, no. 8 to 11, Brigham Young University, Provo, Utah.

———. 1981. Olmec Horizon Defined in Mound 20, San Isidro, Chiapas. In *The Olmec and Their Neighbors*, edited by Michael D. Coe and David Grove, pp. 231–256. Dumbarton Oaks Research Library and Collection, Washington, DC.

Lowe, Lynneth. 2012. Chiapa de Corzo y su arqueología a la luz de las investigaciones actuales. In *XXV Simposio de Investigaciones Arqueológicas en Guatemala, 2011*, edited by Bárbara Arroyo, Lorena Paiz, and Héctor Mejía, pp. 285–292. Ministerio de Cultura y Deportes, Instituto de Antropología e Historia, and Asociación Tikal, Guatemala City.

Lucero, Lisa J. 2003. The Politics of Ritual: The Emergence of Classic Maya Rulers. *Current Anthropology* 44(4):523–558.

Lunagómez Reyes, Roberto. 2011. *Los patrones arquitectónicos prehispánicos del sur de Veracruz: Epoca Clásica*. Universidad Veracruzana, Xalapa, Mexico.

Lynch, Kevin. 2000 [1960]. *The Image of the City*. Massachusetts Institute of Technology and the President and Fellows of Harvard College, Cambridge, MA.

Mack, Alexandra. 2004. One Landscape, Many Experiences: Differing Perspectives of the Temple Districts of Vijayanagara. *Journal of Archaeological Method and Theory* 11(1):59–81.

Maler, Teobert. 1901. *Researches in the Central Portion of the Usumacintla Valley*. Harvard University, Memoirs of the Peabody Museum of American Archaeology and Ethnology Vol. 2, No. 1, Cambridge, MA.

Mann, Michael. 1984. The Autonomous Power of the State: Its Origins, Mechanisms and Results. *European Journal of Sociology* 25:185–213.

Manzanilla, Linda. 2002. Living with the Ancestors and Offering to the Gods: Domestic Ritual at Teotihuacan. In *Domestic Ritual in Ancient Mesoamerica*, edited by Patricia

Plunket, pp. 43–52. Monograph 46, the Cotsen Institute of Archaeology, University of California, Los Angeles.

———. 2004. Social Identity and Daily Life at Classic Teotihuacan. In *Mesoamerican Archaeology: Theory and Practice*, edited by Julia A. Hendon and Rosemary A. Joyce, pp. 124–147. Blackwell, Oxford.

———. 2006. Estados corporativos arcaicos. Organizaciones de excepción en escenarios excluyentes. *Cuicuilco* 13(36):13–45.

———. 2009. Corporate Life in Apartment and Barrio Compounds at Teotihuacan, Central Mexico: Craft Specialization, Hierarchy, and Ethnicity. In *Domestic Life in Prehispanic Capitals: A Study of Specialization, Hierarchy, and Ethnicity*, edited by Linda R. Manzanilla and Claude Chapdelaine, pp. 21–42. Memoirs of the Museum of Anthropology Vol. 7, No. 46, University of Michigan, Ann Arbor.

Marcus, Joyce. 1976. The Iconography of Militarism at Monte Albán and Neighboring Sites in the Valley of Oaxaca. In *Origins of Religious Art and Iconography in Preclassic Mesoamerica*, edited by Henry Nicholson, pp. 125–139. UCLA Latin American Center Publications, Los Angeles.

———. 1983. The Conquest Slabs of Building J, Monte Albán. In *The Cloud People: Divergent Evolution of the Zapotec and Mixtec Civilizations*, edited by Kent V. Flannery and Joyce Marcus, pp. 106–108. Academic Press, New York.

———. 1992. *Mesoamerican Writing Systems*. Princeton University Press, Princeton, NJ.

Marcus, Joyce, and Kent V. Flannery. 1994. Ancient Zapotec Ritual and Religion: An Application of the Direct Historical Approach. In *The Ancient Mind: Elements of Cognitive Archaeology*, edited by Colin Renfrew and Ezra B. Zubrow, pp. 55–74. University of Cambridge Press, Cambridge.

———. 1996. *Zapotec Civilization*. Thames and Hudson, London.

Marcus, Joyce, Kent V. Flannery, and Ronald Spores. 1983. The Cultural Legacy of the Oaxacan Preceramic. In *The Cloud People: Divergent Evolution of the Zapotecs and Mixtecs*, edited by Kent V. Flannery and Joyce Marcus, pp. 36–39. Academic Press, New York.

Martin, Simon, and Nikolai Grube. 2008. *Chronicle of the Maya Kings and Queens: Deciphering the Dynasties of the Ancient Maya*. 2nd ed. Thames and Hudson, London.

Martínez López, Cira, and Robert Markens. 2004. Análisis de la función político-económico del conjunto Plataforma Norte lado poniente de la Plaza Principal de Monte Albán. In *Estructuras políticas en el Oaxaca antiguo*, edited by Nelly M. Robles García, pp. 75–99. Instituto Nacional de Antropología e Historia, Mexico City.

Masson, Marilyn A., and Heather Orr. 1999. The Writing on the Wall: Political Representation and Sacred Geography at Monte Albán. In *The Sowing and the Dawning: Termination, Dedication, and Transformation in the Archaeological and Ethnographic Record of Mesoamerica*, edited by Shirley B. Mock, pp. 165–175. University of New Mexico Press, Albuquerque.

Mastache, Alba Guadalupe, Robert H. Cobean, and Dan M. Healan. 2002. *Ancient Tollan: Tula and the Toltec Heartland*. University Press of Colorado, Boulder.

Mathews, Jennifer P., and James F. Garber. 2004. Models of Cosmic Order: Physical Expression of Sacred Space among the Ancient Maya. *Ancient Mesoamerica* 15(1):49–59.

Matos Moctezuma, Eduardo. 1987. Symbolism of the Templo Mayor. In *The Aztec Templo Mayor*, edited by Elizabeth H. Boone, pp. 185–209. Dumbarton Oaks, Washington, DC.

Maudslay, Alfred P. 1895–1902. *Biologia Centrali-Americana. Archaeology*, vol. 3: Plates, edited by F. Duncan Godman and Osbert Salvin. R. H. Porter and Dulau, London.

McAnany, Patricia A. 2004. Domiciles and Construction Histories. In *K'axob: Ritual, Work, and Family in an Ancient Maya Village*, edited by Patricia A. McAnany, pp. 23–62. Monumenta Archaeologica 22. Cotsen Institute of Archaeology, University of California, Los Angeles.

McAnany, Patricia A., and Sandra L. López Varela. 1999. Re-creating the Formative Maya Village of K'axob: Chronology, Ceramic Complexes, and Ancestors in Architectural Context. *Ancient Mesoamerica* 10(1):147–168.

Middleton, William D., and T. Douglas Price. 1996. Identification of Activity Areas by Multi-Elemental Characterization of Sediments from Modern and Archaeological House Floors Using Inductively Coupled Plasma–Atomic Emission Spectroscopy. *Journal of Archaeological Science* 23:673–687.

Miller, Mary Ellen. 1986. *The Murals of Bonampak*. Princeton University Press, Princeton, NJ.

Millon, René. 1973. *The Teotihuacan Map: Part One: Text. Urbanization at Teotihuacán, Mexico*, vol. 1, edited by René Millon. University of Texas Press, Austin.

———. 1976. Social Relations in Ancient Teotihuacan. In *The Valley of Mexico: Studies in Pre-Hispanic Ecology and Society*, edited by Eric R. Wolf, pp. 205–248. University of New Mexico Press, Albuquerque.

———. 1981. Teotihuacan: City, State, and Civilization. In *Supplement to the Handbook of Middle American Indians, vol. 1: Archaeology*, edited by Victoria Bricker and Jeremy A. Sabloff, pp. 198–243. University of Texas Press, Austin.

———. 1993. The Place Where Time Began: An Archaeologist's Interpretation of What Happened in Teotihuacan History. In *Teotihuacan: Art from the City of the Gods*, edited by Kathleen Berrin and Esther Pasztory, pp. 17–43. Thames and Hudson and the Fine Arts Museums of San Francisco, San Francisco.

Millon, René, R. Bruce Drewitt, and James A. Bennyhoff. 1965. The Pyramid of the Sun at Teotihuacan: 1959 Investigations. *Transactions of the American Philosophical Society* 55 (pt. 6), Philadelphia, PA.

Millon, René, R. Bruce Drewitt, and George L. Cowgill. 1973b. *The Teotihuacan Map: Part Two: Maps. Urbanization at Teotihuacán, Mexico*, vol. 1, edited by René Millon. University of Texas Press, Austin.

Mills, Barbara J. 2007. Performing the Feast: Visual Display and Suprahousehold Commensalism in the Puebloan Southwest. *American Antiquity* 72(2):210–239.

Mills, Barbara J., and William H. Walker. 2008a. Introduction: Memory, Materiality, and Depositional Practice. In *Memory Work: Archaeologies of Material Practices*, edited by Barbara J. Mills and William H. Walker, pp. 3–23. School for Advanced Research Press, Santa Fe, NM.

———. 2008b. *Memory Work: Archaeologies of Material Practices*. School for Advanced Research Press, Santa Fe, NM.

Monaghan, John. 1990. Performance and the Structure of the Mixtec Codices. *Ancient Mesoamerica* 1(1):133–140.

———. 1995. *The Covenants with Earth and Rain: Exchange, Sacrifice, and Revelation in Mixtec Sociality*. University of Oklahoma Press, Norman.

———. 1998. Dedication: Ritual or Production. In *The Sowing and the Dawning: Termination, Dedication, and Transformation in the Archaeological and Ethnographic Record of Mesoamerica*, edited by Shirley Boteler Mock, pp. 47–52. University of New Mexico Press, Albuquerque.

Moore, Jerry D. 1992. Pattern and Meaning in Prehistoric Peruvian Architecture: The Architecture of Social Control in the Chimú State. *Latin American Antiquity* 3:95–113.

———. 1995. The Archaeology of Dual Organization in Andean South America: A Theoretical Review and Case Study. *Latin American Antiquity* 6(2):165–181.

———. 1996a.The Archaeology of Plazas and the Proxemics of Ritual, Three Andean Traditions. *American Anthropologist* 98(4):789–802.

———. 1996b. *Architecture and Power in the Ancient Andes: The Archaeology of Public Buildings*. Cambridge University Press, Cambridge.

———. 2003. *Life behind Walls: Patterns in the Urban Landscape on the Prehistoric North Coast of Peru. The Social Construction of Ancient Cities*. Smithsonian Books, Washington, DC.

———. 2004. The Social Basis of Sacred Spaces in the Prehispanic Andes: Ritual Landscapes of the Dead in Chimú and Inka Societies. *Journal of Archaeological Method and Theory* 11(1):83–124.

———. 2005a. *Cultural Landscapes in the Prehispanic Andes: Archaeologies of Place*. University Press of Florida, Gainesville.

———. 2005b. Power and Practice in the Prehispanic Andes: Final Comments. In *Power and Authority in the Prehispanic Andes*, edited by Christina Conlee, Dennis Ogburn, and Kevin Vaughn, pp. 261–274. Archaeological Papers of the American Anthropological Association Vol. 14(1).

———. 2010. Making a Huaca: Memory and Praxis in Prehispanic Far Northern Peru. *Journal of Social Archaeology* 10:398–422.

Morelos García, Noel. 1993. *Proceso de producción de espacios y estructuras en Teotihuacan*. Instituto Nacional de Antropología e Historia, Mexico City.

Motolinia, Fray Toribio. 1970. *Memoriales e historia de los indios de la Nueva España*, edited by Fidel de Lejaraza. Biblioteca de Autores Españoles Vol. 240. Ediciones Atlas, Madrid.

Munn, Nancy D. 1996. Excluded Spaces: The Figure in the Australian Aboriginal Landscape. *Critical Inquiry* 22:446–465.

———. 2003. Excluded Spaces: The Figure in the Australian Aboriginal Landscape. In *The Anthropology of Space and Place: Locating Culture*, edited by Setha M. Low and Denise Lawrence-Zúñiga, pp. 92–109. Blackwell, Malden, MA.

Munson, Jessica. 2012. Building on the Past: Temple Histories and Communities of Practice at Caobal, Petén, Guatemala. PhD dissertation, University of Arizona, Tucson.

Murakami, Tatsuya. 2010. Power Relations and Urban Landscape Formation: A Study of Construction Labor and Resources at Teotihuacan. PhD dissertation. Arizona State University, Tempe.

Newsome, Elizabeth A. 2001. *Trees of Paradise and Pillars of the World: The Serial Stela Cycle of '18–Rabbit–God K,' King of Copan*. University of Texas Press, Austin.

Nicholson, Henry B. 1967. A "Royal Headband" of the Tlaxcalteca. *Revista Mexicana de Estudios Antropológicos* 21:71–106.

O'Brien, Michael J., Roger D. Mason, Dennis E. Lewarch, and James A. Neely. 1982. *A Late Formative Irrigation Settlement below Monte Albán: Survey and Excavation on the Xoxocotlán Piedmont, Oaxaca, Mexico*. Institute of Latin American Studies. The University of Texas, Austin.

Ortner, Sherry. 1973. Key Symbols. *American Anthropologist* 75(5):1338–1346.

———. 1984. Theory in Anthropology since the Sixties. *Comparative Studies in Society and History* 26(1):126–166.

Ossa, Alanna. 2011. Given, Borrowed, Bought, Stolen: Exchange and Economic Organization in Postclassic Sauce and Its Hinterland in Veracruz, Mexico. PhD dissertation, Arizona State University, Tempe.

Paddock, John. 1966. Oaxaca in Ancient Mesoamerica. In *Ancient Oaxaca: Discoveries in Mexican Archaeology and History*, edited by John Paddock, pp. 83–240. Stanford University Press, Stanford, CA.

Pasztory, Esther. 1997. *Teotihuacán: An Experiment in Living*. University of Oklahoma Press, Norman.

Pauketat, Timothy R. 2000. The Tragedy of the Commoners. In *Agency in Archaeology*, edited by Marcia-Anne Dobres and John E. Robb, pp. 113–129. Routledge, New York.

———. 2001. Practice and History in Archaeology. *Anthropological Theory* 1(1):73–98.

Pauketat, Timothy R., and Susan M. Alt. 2005. Agency in a Postmold? Physicality and the Archaeology of Culture-Making. *Journal of Archaeological Method and Theory* 12(3):213–236.

Pérez de Heredia Puente, Eduardo José. 2010. Ceramic Contexts and Chronology at Chichen Itza, Yucatan, Mexico. PhD dissertation, La Trobe University, Bundoora, Australia.

Pérez Rodríguez, Verónica. 2003. Household Intensification and Agrarian States: Excavations of Houses and Terraced Fields in a Mixtec Cacicazgo. PhD dissertation, University of Georgia, Athens.

———. 2006. States and Households: The Social Organization of Terrace Agriculture in Postclassic Mixteca Alta, Oaxaca, Mexico. *Latin American Antiquity* 17(1):3–22.

Peterson, Jeanette Favrot. 1993. *The Paradise Garden Murals of Malinalco: Utopia and Empire in Sixteenth-Century Mexico*. University of Texas Press, Austin.

Pluckhahn, Thomas J. 2009. Plazas y mercados en la mixteca alta prehispáncica. In *Bases de la complejidad social en Oaxaca: Memoria de la cuarta mesa redonda de Monte Albán*, edited by Nelly M. Robles García, 277–293. Instituto Nacional de Antropología e Historia, Mexico City.

Plunket, Patricia (editor). 2002. *Domestic Ritual in Ancient Mesoamerica*. Monograph 46. Cotsen Institute of Archaeology, University of California, Los Angeles.

Pohl, John M. D. 1984. The Earth Lords: Politics and Symbolism of the Mixtec Codices. PhD dissertation, University of California, Los Angeles.

———. 1994. *The Politics of Symbolism in the Mixtec Codices*. Vanderbilt University Press, Nashville.

———. 2003a. Creation Stories, Hero Cults, and Alliance Building: Confederacies of Central and Southern Mexico. In *The Postclassic Mesoamerican World*, edited by Michael E. Smith and Frances F. Berdan, pp. 61–66. University of Utah Press, Salt Lake City.

———. 2003b. Ritual Ideology and Commerce in the Southern Mexican Highlands. In *The Postclassic Mesoamerican World*, edited by Michael E. Smith and Frances F. Berdan, pp. 172–177. University of Utah Press, Salt Lake City.

———. 2003c. Royal Marriage and Confederacy Building among the Eastern Nahuas, Mixtecs, and Zapotecs. In *The Postclassic Mesoamerican World*, edited by Michael E. Smith and Frances F. Berdan, pp. 243–248. University of Utah Press, Salt Lake City.

Pohl, John M. D., and Bruce E. Byland. 1990. Mixtec Landscape Perception and Archaeological Settlement Patterns. *Ancient Mesoamerica* 1(1):113–131.

Pohl, John, M. D., John Monaghan, and Laura R. Stiver. 1997. Religion, Economy, and Factionalism in Mixtec Boundary Zones. In *Códices y documentos sobre México. Segundo simposio.* Vol 1, edited by S. Rueda Smithers, C. Vega Sosa, and R. Martínez Bracas, pp. 205–232. INAH and Consejo Nacional para la Cultura y las Artes, Mexico City.

Pohl, Mary D., Kevin O. Pope, John G. Jones, John S. Jacob, Dolores R. Piperno, Susan D. deFrance, David L. Lentz, John A. Gifford, Marie E. Danforth, and J. Kathryn Josserand. 1996. Early Agriculture in the Maya Lowlands. *Latin American Antiquity* 4:355–372.

Pool, Christopher A. 2007. Architectural Plans, Factionalism, and the Proto-Classic-Classic Transition at Tres Zapotes. In *Cultural Currents in Classic Veracruz*, edited by Philip J. Arnold III and Christopher A. Pool, pp. 121–158. Dumbarton Oaks, Washington, DC.

Porter, James. 1989. Olmec Colossal Heads as Recarved Thrones: "Mutilation," Revolution, and Recarving. *RES: Anthropology and Aesthetics* 17/18:23–30.

Preucel, Robert W. 2006. *Archaeological Semiotics*. Blackwell, Malden, MA.

Preucel, Robert W., and Alexander Bauer. 2001. Archaeological Pragmatics. *Norwegian Archaeological Review* 34:85–96.

Proskouriakoff, Tatiana. 1950. *A Study of Classic Maya Sculpture*. Classic Maya Sculpture. Carnegie Institution of Washington, Washington, DC.

Rabinow, Paul. 1989. *French Modern: Norms and Forms of Missionary and Didactic Pathos*. MIT Press, Cambridge, MA.

———. 2003. Ordonnance, Discipline, Regulation: Some Reflections on Urbanism. In *The Anthropology of Space and Place: Locating Culture*, edited by Setha M. Low and Denise Lawrence-Zúñiga, pp. 353–362. Blackwell, Oxford.

Rattray, Evelyn C. 1987. Los barrios foráneos de Teotihuacan. In *Teotihuacán: Nuevos datos, nuevas síntesis, nuevos problemas*, edited by Emily McClung de Tapia and Evelyn C. Rattray, pp. 243–273. Instituto de Investigaciones Antropológicas, Serie Antropológica 72. Universidad Nacional Autónoma de México, Mexico City.

———. 2001. *Teotihuacan: Cerámica, cronología y tendencias culturales/Ceramics, chronology, and cultural trends*. Arqueología de México. Instituto Nacional de Antropología e Historia/University of Pittsburgh, Mexico City and Pittsburgh.

Reese-Taylor, Kathryn. 2002. Ritual Circuits in Maya Civic Center Designs. In *Heart of Creation: The Mesoamerican World and the Legacy of Linda Schele*, edited by Andrea Stone, pp. 143–165. University of Alabama Press, Tuscaloossa.

Restall, Matthew. 1997. *The Maya World: Yucatec Culture and Society, 1550–1850*. Stanford University Press, Stanford, CA.

———. 2001. The People of the Patio: Ethnohistorical Evidence of Yucatec Maya Royal Courts. In *Royal Courts of the Ancient Maya, Vol. 2: Data and Cane Studies*, edited by Takeshi Inomata and Stephen D. Houston, pp. 335–390. Westview Press, Boulder, CO.

Restall, Matthew, and John F. Chuchiak IV. 2002. A Reevaluation of the Authenticity of Fray Diego de Landa's *Relación de las Cosas de Yucatán*. *Ethnohistory* 49(3):651–69.

Restall, Mathew, and Amara Solari. 2011. *2012 and the End of the World: The Western Roots of the Maya Apocalypse*. Rowman and Littlefield, Lanham, MD.

Richardson, Miles. 2003. Being-in-the-Market versus Being-in-the-Plaza: Material Culture and the Construction of Social Reality in Spanish America. In *The Anthropology of Space and Place: Locating Culture*, edited by Setha M. Low and Denise Lawrence-Zúñiga, pp. 74–91. Blackwell, Malden, MA.

Ricketson, Oliver Garrison, and Edith Bayles Ricketson. 1937. *Uaxactun, Guatemala. Group E-1926–1931.*Carnegie Institution of Washington Publication Vol. 477. Carnegie Institution of Washington, Washington, DC.

Ringle, William M. 1985. The Settlement Patterns of Komchen, Yucatan, Mexico. PhD dissertation, Tulane University, New Orleans.

———. 2004. On the Political Organization of Chichen Itza. *Ancient Mesoamerica* 15(2):167–218.

———. 2009. The Art of War: Imagery of the Upper Temple of the Jaguars, Chichen Itza. *Ancient Mesoamerica* 20(1):15–44.

———. 2012. The Nunnery Quadrangle of Uxmal. In *The Ancient Maya of Mexico: Reinterpreting the Past of the Northern Maya Lowlands*, edited by Geoff Braswell, pp. 189–226. Equinox Press, London.

Ringle, William M., and E. Wyllys Andrews V. 1988. Formative Residences at Komchen, Yucatan, Mexico. In *Household and Community in the Mesoamerican Past*, edited by Richard Wilk and Wendy Ashmore, pp. 171–197. University of New Mexico Press, Albuquerque.

Ringle, William M., and George J. Bey III. 2001. Post-Classic and Terminal Classic Courts of the Northern Maya Lowlands. In *Royal Courts of the Ancient Maya, Volume 2: Data and Case Study*, edited by Takeshi Inomata and Stephen D. Houston, pp. 266–307. Westview Press, Boulder, CO.

———. 2009. The Face of the Itzas. In *The Art of Urbanism: How Mesoamerican Kingdoms Represented Themselves in Architecture and Imagery*, edited by William L. Fash and Leonardo Lopez Lujan, pp. 329–383. Dumbarton Oaks, Washington, DC.

Robb, John E. 1998. The Archaeology of Symbols. *Annual Review of Anthropology* 27:329–346

Robertson, Ian. 2001. Mapping the Social Landscape of an Early Urban Center: Socio-Spatial Variation in Teotihuacan. PhD dissertation, Arizona State University, Tempe.

———. 2008. "Insubstantial" Residential Structures at Teotihuacán, México. FAMSI Report (http://www.famsi.org/reports/06103/index.html). Accessed April 16, 2010.

Robin, Cynthia. 2002. Outside of Houses: The Practices of Everyday Life at Chan Ñohol, Belize. *Journal of Social Archaeology* 2:245–268.

Rosenmeier, Michael F., David A. Hodell, Mark Brenner, Jason H. Curtis, and Thomas P. Guilderson. 2002. A 4000-Year Lacustrine Record of Environmental Change in the Southern Maya Lowlands, Petén, Guatemala. *Quaternary Research* 57:183–190.

Rosenswig, Robert M. 2011. An Early Mesoamerican Archipelago of Complexity. In *Early Mesoamerican Social Transformations: Archaic and Formative Lifeways in the Soconusco Region*, edited by Richard G. Lesure, pp. 242–271. University of California Press, Berkeley.

Rothenberg, Kara A. 2010. Multi-Elemental Chemical Analysis of Anthropogenic Soils as a Tool for Examining Spatial Use Patterns at Prehispanic Palmarejo, Northwest Honduras. Master's thesis, University of South Florida, Tampa.

Rowlands, Michael. 1993. The Role of Memory in the Transmission of Culture. *World Archaeology* 25(2):141–151.

Roys, Ralph L., France V. Scholes, and Eleanor B. Adams. 1940. Report and Census of the Indians of Cozumel, 1570. *Contributions to American Anthropology and History* 6:1–30.

Ruiz Cervantes, Francisco José, and Carlos Sánchez Silva. 1997. *La ciudad de Oaxaca a través de sus planos*. Instituto Oaxaqueño de las Culturas. Patronato Amigos de Oaxaca, and Municipio de la Ciudad de Oaxaca. Oaxaca de Juárez.

Sabloff, Jeremy A. 1975. *Excavations at Seibal, Department of Peten, Guatemala: Ceramics*. Memoirs of the Peabody Museum of Archaeology and Ethnology Vol. 13, No. 2. Gordon R. Willey, series editor. Harvard University, Cambridge, MA.

Sabloff, Jeremy, and John Henderson. 1993. *Lowland Maya Civilization in the Eighth Century A.D.: A Symposium at Dumbarton Oaks, October 7 and 8, 1989*. Dumbarton Oaks Research Library and Collection, Washington, DC.

Sahagún, Fray Bernardino de. 1979. *Florentine Codex: General History of the Things of New Spain: Book 8—Kings and Lords*. Monographs of the School of American Research, No. 14. The School of American Research and the University of Utah, Sante Fe.

Sahagún, Fray Bernardino de. 1997 *Primeros Memoriales: Paleography of Nahuatl Text and English Translation*, edited by Thelma D. Sullivan. University of Oklahoma Press, Norman.

Sanchez, Julia L. 2005. Ancient Maya Royal Strategies: Creating Power and Identity through Art. *Ancient Mesoamerica* 16(2):261–275.

Sanders, William T., and David Webster. 1988. The Mesoamerican Urban Tradition. *American Anthropologist* 90:521–546.

Schachner, Gregson. 2001. Ritual Control and Transformation in Middle-Range Societies: An Example from the American Southwest. *Journal of Anthropological Archaeology* 20:168–194.

Schechner, Richard. 1985. Points of Contact between Anthropological and Theatrical Thought. In *Between Theater*, pp. 3–33. University of Arizona Press, Tucson.

Schele, Linda, and Peter Mathews. 1998. *The Code of Kings: The Language of Seven Sacred Maya Temples and Tombs*. Scribner, New York.

Schmidt, Peter J. 2005. Proyecto Chichen Itza: Informe de actividades julio de 1999 a diciembre de 2002. Report submitted to the Instituto Nacional de Antropología e Historia, Mexico City.

———. 2007. Birds, Ceramics, and Cacao: New Excavations at Chichén Itzá, Yucatan. In *Twin Tollans: Chichén Itzá, Tula and the Epiclassic to Early Postclassic Mesoamerican World*, edited by Jeff K. Kowalski and Cynthia Kristan-Graham, pp. 151–203. Dumbarton Oaks, Washington, DC.

Scholes, France V., and Eleanor B. Adams (editors). 1938. *Don Diego Quijada, alcalde mayor de Yucatan, 1561–1565. Documentos sacados de los archivos de España*. Antigua Librería Robredo de José Porrúa e Hijos, Mexico.

Schortman, Edward M., and Patricia A. Urban. 1994. Living on the Edge: Core/Periphery Relations in Ancient Southeastern Mesoamerica. *Current Anthropology* 35:401–430.

———. 1996. Actions at a Distance, Impacts at Home: Prestige Good Theory and a Pre-Columbian Polity in Southeastern Mesoamerica. In *Pre-Columbian World Systems*, edited by P. N. Peregrine and G. M. Feinman, pp. 97–114. Prehistory Press, Madison, WI.

Schortman, Edward M., Patricia A. Urban, and Marne Ausec. 2001. Politics with Style: Identity Formation in Prehispanic Southeastern Mesoamerica. *American Anthropologist* 103:312–330.

Scott, James C. 1990. *Domination and the Arts of Resistance: Hidden Transcript*. Yale University Press, New Haven, CT.

———. 1998. *Seeing Like a State: How Certain Schemes to Improve the Human Condition Have Failed*. Yale University Press, New Haven, CT.

Scott, John F. 1978a. *The Danzantes of Monte Albán. Part I: Text*. Dumbarton Oaks, Studies in Pre-Columbian Art and Archaeology no. 19, Washington, DC.

———. 1978b. *The Danzantes of Monte Albán. Part II: Catalogue*. Dumbarton Oaks, Studies in Pre-Columbian Art and Archaeology no. 19, Washington, DC.

Séjourné, Laurette. 1959. *Un palacio en la ciudad de los dioses [Teotihuacan]*. Instituto Nacional de Antropología e Historia, Mexico City.

Sempowski, Martha L., and Michael W. Spence. 1994. *Mortuary Practices and Skeletal Remains at Teotihuacan. Urbanization at Teotihuacan, Mexico*, vol. 3, edited by René Millon. University of Utah Press, Salt Lake City.

Shore, Bradd. 1996. *Culture in Mind: Cognition, Culture, and the Problem of Meaning*. Oxford University Press, New York.

Siméon, Rémi. 1988. *Diccionario de la lengua Nahuatl o Mexicana*. Siglo Veintiuno, Mexico City.

Smith, Adam T. 2003. *The Political Landscape: Constellations of Authority in Early Complex Polities*. University of California Press, Berkeley.

Smith, A. Ledyard. 1982. *Excavations at Seibal, Department of Peten, Guatemala: Major Architecture and Caches*. Memoirs of the Peabody Museum of Archaeology and Ethnology Vol. 15, No. 1. Gordon R. Willey, series editor. Harvard University, Cambridge, MA.

Smith, Mary Elizabeth. 1973. *Picture Writing from Ancient Southern Mexico: Mixtec Place Signs and Maps*. University of Oklahoma Press, Norman.

Smith, Michael E. 2008. *Aztec City-State Capitals*. University Press of Florida, Gainesville.

Smith, Virginia G. 1988. The Iconography of Power at Xochicalco, Morelos. PhD dissertation, University of Kentucky, Lexington.

———. 2000. Iconography of Power at Xochicalco: The Pyramid of the Plumed Serpent. In *Archaeological Research at Xochicalco: 2. The Xochicalco Mapping Project*, edited by Kenneth Hirth, pp. 57–82. University of Utah Press, Salt Lake City.

Solari, Amara. 2010. Circles of Creation: The "Invention" of Maya Cartography in Early Colonial Yucatan, *The Art Bulletin* 42(3):154–168.

———. 2013. *Maya Ideologies of the Sacred: The Transfiguration of Space in Colonial Yucatan*. University of Texas Press, Austin.

Spence, Michael W. 1992. Tlailotlacan, a Zapotec Enclave in Teotihuacan. In *Art, Ideology, and the City of Teotihuacan*, edited by Janet C. Berlo, pp. 59–88. Dumbarton Oaks, Washington, DC.

Spencer, Charles S., and Elsa M. Redmond. 2001. Multilevel Selection and Political Evolution in the Valley of Oaxaca, 500–100 B.C. *Journal of Anthropological Archaeology* 20:195–229.

Spores, Ronald M. 1967. *The Mixtec Kings and Their People*. University of Oklahoma Press, Norman.

———. 1974. Marital Alliance in the Political Integration of Mixtec Kingdoms. *American Anthropologist* 76(2):297–311.

Stanish, Charles. 2003. *Ancient Titicaca: The Evolution of Complex Society in Southern Peru and Northern Bolivia*. University of Texas Press, Austin.

Stark, Barbara L. 1999. Formal Architectural Complexes in South-Central Veracruz, Mexico: A Capital Zone? *Journal of Field Archaeology* 26:197–225.

———. 2011. Canchas de la Mixtequilla. Paper presented at the Primer Coloquio Temas Selectos del Centro-Sur de Veracruz: El Juego de Pelota, Casa del Campesino, Villa Emiliano Zapata (antes El Carrizal), Veracruz.

Stark, Barbara L., and Philip J. Arnold III. 1997. Introduction to the Archaeology of the Gulf Lowlands. In *Olmec to Aztec: Settlement Patterns in the Ancient Gulf Lowlands*, edited by Barbara L. Stark and Philip J. Arnold III, pp. 3–32. University of Arizona Press, Tucson.

Stark, Barbara L., and Alanna Ossa. 2007. Ancient Settlement, Urban Gardening, and Environment in the Gulf Lowlands of Mexico. *Latin American Antiquity* 18(4):385–406.

Stirling, Matthew W. 1943. *Stone Monuments of Southern Mexico*. Bureau of American Ethnology Bulletin Vol. 138. Smithsonian Institution, Washington, DC.

———. 1947. On the Trail of La Venta Man. *National Geographic Magazine* 91:137–172.

Storey, Rebecca. 1992. *Life and Death in the Ancient City of Teotihuacan: A Modern Paleodemographic Synthesis*. University of Alabama Press, Tuscaloosa.

Strauss, Claudia, and Naomi Quinn. 1997. *A Cognitive Theory of Cultural Meaning*. Publications of the Society for Psychological Anthropology Vol. 9. Cambridge University Press, Cambridge.

Stuart, David. 1989. Hieroglyphs on Maya Vessels. In *The Maya Vase Book: A Corpus of Rollout Photographs of Maya Vases*, vol. 1, edited by Justin Kerr, pp. 149–160. Kerr Associates, New York.

———. 2000. "The Arrival of Strangers": Teotihuacan and Tollan in Classic Maya History. In *Mesoamerica's Classic Heritage: From Teotihuacan to the Aztecs*, edited by David Carrasco, Lindsay Jones, and Scott Sessions, pp. 465–513. Colorado University Press, Niwot.

Sugiyama, Saburo. 1989. Iconographic Interpretations of the Temple of Quetzalcoatl at Teotihuacan. *Mexicon* 11(4):68–74.

———. 1993. Worldview Materialized in Teotihuacán, Mexico. *Latin American Antiquity* 4(2):103–129.

———. 1998a. Archaeology and Iconography of Theater-Type Censers: Official Military Emblems from the Ciudadela? *Teotihuacan Notes* I:2. Electronic document, http://archaeology.asu.edu/teo/notes/SS/noteI_2SS.htm. Accessed February 28, 2012.

———. 1998b. Termination Programs and Prehispanic Looting at the Feathered Serpent Pyramid in Teotihuacan, Mexico. In *The Sowing and the Dawning: Termination, Dedication, and Transformation in the Archaeological and Ethnographic Record of Mesoamerica*, edited by Shirley B. Mock, pp. 146–164. University of New Mexico Press, Albuquerque.

———. 2004. Governance and Policy at Classic Teotihuacan. In *Mesoamerican Archaeology: Theory and Practice*, edited by Julia A. Hendon and Rosemary A. Joyce, pp. 97–123. Blackwell, Oxford.

———. 2005. *Human Sacrifice, Militarism, and Rulership: Materialization of State Ideology at the Feathered Serpent Pyramid, Teotihuacan*. Cambridge University Press, Cambridge.

Sugiyama, Saburo, and Rubén Cabrera C. 2007. The Moon Pyramid Project and the Teotihuacan Polity: A Brief Summary of the 1998–2004 Excavations. *Ancient Mesoamerica* 18(1):109–125.

Swenson, Edward R. 2008. The "Disjunctive Approach" to the Archaeological Analysis of Ritual Politics. In *Religion, Archaeology, and the Material World*, edited by Lars Fogelin, pp. 237–260. Center for Archaeological Investigations, Southern Illinois University, Carbondale.

Symonds, Stacey, Ann Cyphers, and Roberto Lunagómez. 2002. *Asentamiento Prehispánico en San Lorenzo Tenochtitlán*. Instituto de Investigaciones Antropológicas, Universidad Nacional Autónoma de México, Mexico City.

Taube, Karl. 1988. The Ancient Yucatec New Year Festival: The Liminal Period in Maya Ritual and Cosmology. PhD dissertation, Yale University, New Haven, CT.

———. 1989. Ritual Humor in Classic Maya Religion. In *Word and Image in Maya Culture*, edited by William F. Hanks and Don S. Rice, pp. 351–382. University of Utah Press, Salt Lake City.

———. 1992. The Temple of Quetzalcoatl and the Cult of Sacred War at Teotihuacan. *RES: Anthropology and Aesthetics* 21:53–87.

Tedlock, Dennis. 1985. *Popol Vuh: The Definitive Edition of the Mayan Book of the Dawn of Life and the Glories of Gods and Kings*. Simon and Schuster, New York.

Terraciano, Kevin. 2000. The Colonial Mixtec Community. *Hispanic American Historical Review* 80:1–42.

———. 2004. *The Mixtecs of Colonial Oaxaca: Nudzahui History, Sixteenth through Eighteenth Centuries*. Stanford University Press, Stanford, CA.

Terry, Richard E., Fabian G. Fernández, J. Jacob Parnell, and Takeshi Inomata. 2004. The Story in the Floors: Chemical Signatures of Ancient and Modern Maya Activities at Aguateca, Guatemala. *Journal of Archaeological Science* 31:1237–1250.

Thomas, Julian. 1996. *Time, Culture, and Identity: An Interpretative Archaeology*. Routledge, London.

Tilley, Christopher Y. 2004. *The Materiality of Stone*. Berg, Oxford.

Torres Guzmán, Manuel. 1972. Hallazgos en el Zapotal, Veracruz: Informe preliminar (segunda temporada). *Boletin del Instituto Nacional de Antropologia e Historia* Epoca 2(2):3–8.

Torres Guzmán, Manuel, Marco Antonio Reyes, and Jaime Ortega. 1975. Proyecto Zapotal, Veracruz. In *Balance y perspectiva de la antropología en Mesoamérica*, vol. 1, pp. 232–329. XII Mesa Redonda, Sociedad Mexicana de Antropología, Mexico City.

Tourtellot, Gair, III. 1988. *Excavations at Seibal, Department of Peten, Guatemala: Peripheral Survey and Excavation, Settlement and Community Patterns*. Memoirs of the Peabody Museum of Archaeology and Ethnology Vol. 16. Gordon R. Willey, series editor. Harvard University, Cambridge, MA.

Tourtellot, Gair, III, and Norman Hammond. 2007. Serendipity at Seibal: Gordon Willey in the Pasión Valley. In *Gordon R. Willey and American Archaeology*, edited by Jeremy A. Sabloff and William L. Fash, pp. 126–140. University of Oklahoma Press, Norman.

Townsend, Richard F. 1987. Coronation at Tenochtitlan. In *The Aztec Templo Mayor*, edited by Elizabeth H. Boone, pp. 371–409. Dumbarton Oaks, Washington, DC.

Tozzer, Alfred M. 1941. *Landa's Relación de las Cosas de Yucatan*. Papers of the Peabody Museum of Archaeology and Ethnology, No. 18, Harvard University, Cambridge.

Tsukada, Matsuo 1966. The Pollen Sequence. In *The History of Laguna Petenxil*, edited by Ursula Cowgill and George Hutchinson, pp. 63–66. Memoirs of the Connecticut Academy of Sciences Vol. 17. Connecticut Academy of Sciences, Hartford.

Tsukamoto, Kenichiro. 2009. Power and Urban Spaces in Classic Maya Society. Master's thesis, University of Arizona, Tucson.

Tsukamoto, Kenichiro, and Javier López Camacho (editors). 2010. *Proyecto Arqueológico El Palmar: Urbanización del espacio social en las tierras bajas mayas. Informe de la segunda temporada de campo 2009*. Instituto Nacional de Antropología e Historia, Mexico City.

Tsukamoto, Kenichiro, and Javier López Camacho (editors). 2011. *Proyecto Arqueológico El Palmar: Urbanización del espacio social en las tierras bajas mayas. Informe de la tercera temporada de campo 2010–2011*. Instituto Nacional de Antropología e Historia, Mexico City.

Tsukamoto, Kenichiro, Hirokazu Kotegawa, and Luz Evelia Campaña Valenzuela. 2012. Secuencia constructiva de las plazas en el grupo principal de El Palmar, Campeche, México. *Estudios de Cultura Maya* 39:13–30.

Tsukamoto, Kenichiro, and Octavio Q. Esparza Olguín. In press. Ajpach' Waal: The Hieroglyphic Stairway at the Guzmán Group of El Palmar, Campeche, Mexico. In *Maya Archaeology III*, edited by Charles Golden, Stephen D. Houston, and Joel Skidmore. Precolumbian Mesoweb Press, San Francisco, CA.

Turner, Victor. 1969. *The Ritual Process: Structure and Anti-structure*. Aldine Transaction, New Brunswick, NJ.

———. 1972. *The Ritual Process*. Cornell University Press, Ithaca.

———. 1982. *From Ritual to Theatre*. Performing Arts Journal Publications, New York.

Urban, Patricia A. 1986. Precolumbian Settlement in the Naco Valley, Northwestern Honduras. In *The Southeast Maya Periphery*, edited by Patricia A. Urban and Edward M. Schortman, pp. 275–295. University of Texas Press, Austin.

———. 1993. Naco Valley. In *Pottery of Prehistoric Honduras*, edited by John S. Henderson and Marilyn Beaudry-Corbett, pp. 30–63. Institute of Archaeology, Los Angeles.

Urcid, Javier. 1994. Mound J at Monte Albán and Zapotec Political Geography during Period II (200 B.C.–A.D. 200). Paper presented at the 59th Annual Meeting of the Society for American Archaeology, Anaheim, CA.

———. 1995. A Peculiar Stone with Zapotec Hieroglyphic Inscriptions. *Mexicon* 17(5):87–92.

———. 2001. *Zapotec Hieroglyphic Writing*. Dumbarton Oaks Studies in Pre-Columbian Art and Archaeology 34, Washington, DC.

———. 2005. *The Zapotec Scribal Tradition: Knowledge, Memory, and Society in Ancient Oaxaca*. Foundation for the Advancement of Mesoamerican Studies Inc., Coral Gables, FL. http://www.famsi.org/zapotecwriting/.

———. 2011a. Los Oráculos y la Guerra: El papel de las narrativas pictóricas en el desarrollo temprano de Monte Albán (500 A.C.–200 D.C.). In *Monte Albán en la encrucijada regional y disciplinaria: Memoria de la quinta Mesa Redonda de Monte Albán*, edited by Nelly M. Robles García and Ángel Rivera Guzmán, pp. 163–240. Instituto Nacional de Antropología e Historia, Mexico City.

———. 2011b. The Written Surface as a Cultural Code: A Comparative Perspective of Scribal Traditions from Southwestern Mesoamerica. In *Their Way of Writing: Scripts, Signs, and Pictographies in Pre-Columbian America*, edited by Elizabeth Hill Boone and Gary Urton, pp. 111–148. Dumbarton Oaks, Washington DC.

Urcid, Javier, and Marcus Winter. 2003. Nuevas variantes glíficas zapotecas. *Mexicon*. 25(5):123–128.

Vail, Gabrielle. 2009. Yearbearer Rituals and Prognostications in the Maya Codices and Landa's *Relación de las cosas de Yucatán*. In *Text and Context: Yucatec Maya Literature in a Diachronic Perspective*, edited by Antje Gunsenheimer, Tsubasa Okoshi

Harada, and John F. Chuchiak, pp. 53–82. Bonner Amerikanistische Studien, Institut für Altamerikanistik und Ethnologie, Universität Bonn, Bonn.

Van Dyke, Ruth M., and Susan E. Alcock. 2003. Archaeologies of Memory: An Introduction. In *Archaeologies of Memory*, edited by Ruth M. Van Dyke and Susan E. Alcock, pp. 1–13. Blackwell, Malden, MA.

Vaughan, Hague H., Edward S. Deevy, and Samuel E. Garrett-Jones. 1985. Pollen Stratigraphy of Two Cores from the Peten Lake District. In *Prehistoric Lowland Maya Environment and Subsistence Economy*, edited by Mary D. Pohl, pp. 73–90. Memoirs of the Peabody Museum of American Archaeology and Ethnology Vol. 77. Harvard University, Cambridge, MA.

Villagra, Agustín. 1939. Los Danzantes. Piedras grabadas del Montículo L, Monte Albán, Oaxaca. *Congreso Internacional de Americanistas* 27:143–158. Mexico.

Vogt, Evon Z. 1969. *Zinacantan: A Maya Community in the Highlands of Chiapas*. The Belknap Press of Harvard University Press, Cambridge, MA.

———. 1976. *Tortillas for the Gods: A Symbolic Analysis of Zinacantecan Rituals*. Harvard University Press, Cambridge.

von Winning, Hasso. 1987. *La iconografía de Teotihuacán; los dioses y los signos*. 2 vols., Estudios y Fuentes del Arte en Mexicano, 47. Universidad Nacional Autónoma de México, Mexico City.

Wagner, Logan, Hal Box, and Susan Kline Morehead. 2013. *Ancient Origins of the Mexican Plaza: From Primordial Sea to Public Space*. University of Texas Press, Austin.

Wahl, David, Roger Byrne, Thomas Schreiner, and Richard Hansen. 2006. Holocene Vegetation Change in the Northern Peten and Its Implications for Maya Prehistory. *Quaternary Research* 65:380–389.

Wake, Eleanor. 2010. *Framing the Sacred: The Indian Churches of Early Colonial Mexico*. University of Oklahoma Press, Norman.

Walker, William H. 2002. Stratigraphy and Practical Reason. *American Anthropologist* 104:159–177.

Watanabe, John M. 2004. Some Models in a Muddle: Lineage and House in Classic Maya Social Organization. *Ancient Mesoamerica* 15(1):159–166.

Webster, David. 2001. Spatial Dimension of Maya Courtly Life: Problems and Issues. In *Royal Courts of the Ancient Maya*, vol. 1, edited by Takeshi Inomata and Stephen D. Houston, pp.130–168. Westview Press, Boulder, CO.

Webster, Susan Verdi. 1997. Art, Ritual, and Confraternities in Sixteenth-Century New Spain. *Anales del Insituto de Investigaciones Estéticas* 70:5–43.

Wells, Christian E. 2003. Artisans, Chiefs, and Feasts: Classic Period Social Dynamics at El Coyote, Honduras. PhD dissertation, Arizona State University, Tempe.

———. 2004. Investigating Activity Patterns in Prehispanic Plazas: Weak Acid-Extraction ICP-AES Analysis of Anthrosols at Classic Period El Coyote, Northwestern Honduras. *Archaeometry* 46:67–84.

———. 2006. Cultural Soilscapes. In *Function of Soils for Human Societies and the Environment*, edited by Emmanuel Frossard, Windfried E. H. Blum, and Benno P. Warkentin, pp. 125–132. Geological Society, London.

Wells, E. Christian, and Richard E. Terry. 2007a. Introduction. *Geoarchaeology* 22 (3):285–290.

———. 2007b. Introduction. *Geoarchaeology* 22(4):387–390.

Wells, E. Christian, Karla L. Davis-Salazar, and David D. Kuehn. 2013. Soilscape Legacies: Historical and Emerging Consequences of Socioecological Interactions in Honduras. In *Soils, Climate and Society: Archaeological Investigations in Ancient America*, edited by John D. Wingard and Sue E. Hayes, pp. 21–60. University Press of Colorado, Boulder.

Wells, E. Christian, Claire Novotny, and James R. Hawken. 2007. Quantitative Modeling of Soil Chemical Data from Inductively Coupled Plasma—Optical Emission Spectroscopy Reveals Evidence for Cooking and Eating in Ancient Mesoamerican Plazas. In *Archaeological Chemistry: Analytical Techniques and Archaeological Interpretation* (A.C.S. Symposium Series #968), edited by Michael D. Glascock, Robert J. Speakman, and Rachel S. Popelka-Filcoff, pp. 210–230. Oxford University Press, New York.

Wells, E. Christian, Richard E. Terry, J. Jacob Parnell, Perry J. Hardin, Mark W. Jackson, and Stephen D. Houston. 2000. Chemical Analyses of Ancient Anthrosols in Residential Areas at Piedras Negras, Guatemala. *Journal of Archaeological Sciences* 27:449–462.

Wells, E. Christian, and Patricia A. Urban. 2002. An Ethnoarchaeological Perspective on the Material and Chemical Residues of Communal Feasting at El Coyote, Northwest Honduras. In *Materials Issues in Art and Archaeology VI*, edited by J. R. Vandiver, Martha Goodway, and Jennifer L. Mass, pp. 193–198. Materials Research Society, Warrendale, PA.

Wernke, Steven A. 2006. The Politics of Community and Inka Statecraft in the Colca Valley, Peru. *Latin American Antiquity* 17(2):177–208.

Wheatley, David, and Mark Gillings. 2002. *Spatial Technology and Archaeology: The Archaeological Applications of GIS*. Taylor and Francis, London.

Whittaker, Gordon. 1980. The Hieroglyphs from Monte Albán. PhD dissertation, Yale University, New Haven, CT.

———. 1992. The Zapotec Writing System. In *Supplement to the Handbook of Middle American Indians: Epigraphy*, vol. 5, edited by Victoria R. Bricker, pp. 5–19. University of Texas Press, Austin.

Widmer, Randolph J. 1987. The Evolution of Form and Function in a Teotihuacan Apartment Compound. In *Teotihuacán: Nuevos datos, nuevas síntesis, nuevos problemas*, edited by Emily McClung de Tapia and Evelyn C. Rattray, pp. 317–368. Instituto de Investigaciones Antropológicas, Serie Antropológica 72. Universidad Nacional Autónoma de México, Mexico City.

Willey, Gordon R. 1978. *Excavations at Seibal, Department of Peten, Guatemala: Artifacts*. Memoirs of the Peabody Museum of Archaeology and Ethnology Vol. 14, No. 1. Gordon R. Willey, series editor. Harvard University, Cambridge, MA.

———. 1990. *Excavations at Seibal, Department of Peten, Guatemala: General Summary and Conclusions*. Memoirs of the Peabody Museum of Archaeology and Ethnology Vol. 17, No. 4. Gordon R. Willey, series editor. Harvard University, Cambridge, MA.

Willey, Gordon R., A. Ledyard Smith, Gair Tourtellot III, and Ian Graham. 1975. *Excavations at Seibal, Department of Peten, Guatemala: Introduction: The Site and its Setting*. Memoirs of the Peabody Museum of Archaeology and Ethnology Vol. 13, No. 1. Gordon R. Willey, series editor. Harvard University, Cambridge, MA.

Williams, Robert Lloyd. 2009. Codex Zouche-Nuttall, Pages 1–41: Narrative Structure, Contents, and Chronologies. PhD dissertation, University of Texas, Austin.

Winter, Marcus. 1989. *Oaxaca: The Archaeological Record*. Minutiae Mexicana, Mexico City.

———. 1994. El Proyecto Especial Monte Albán 1992–1994: Antecedentes, intervenciones y perspectivas. In *Monte Albán: Estudios recientes*, edited by Marcus Winter, pp. 1–24. Contribución No. 2 del Proyecto Especial Monte Albán 1992–1994, Oaxaca.

———. 2001. Palacios, templos y 1300 años de vida urbana en Monte Albán. In *Reconstruyendo la ciudad Maya: El urbanismo en las sociedades antiguas*, edited by Andrés Ciudad Ruíz, María Josefa Iglesia Ponce de Léon, and María del Carmen Martínez, pp. 253–301. Sociedad Española de Estudios Mayas, Madrid.

———. 2004. Monte Albán: Su organización e impacto político. In *Estructuras políticas en el Oaxaca antiguo*, edited by Nelly M. Robles García, pp. 27–59. Instituto Nacional de Antropología e Historia, Mexico City.

Wolf, Eric. 1999. *Envisioning Power: Ideologies of Dominance and Crisis*. University of California Press, Berkeley.

Workinger, Andrew, and Arthur A. Joyce. 2009. Reconsidering Warfare in Formative Period Oaxaca. In *Blood and Beauty: Organized Violence in the Art and Archaeology of Mesoamerica and Central America*, edited by Heather Orr and Rex Koontz, pp. 3–38. Cotsen Institute of Archaeology Press, Los Angeles, CA.

Wren, Linnea. 1994. Ceremonialism in the Reliefs of the North Temple, Chichén Itzá. In *Seventh Palenque Round Table, 1989*, edited by Virginia Miller and Merle Greene Robertson, pp. 25–31. Pre-Columbian Art Research Institute, San Francisco, CA.

Yaeger, Jason. 2003. Untangling the Ties That Bind: The City, the Courtryside, and the Nature of Maya Urbanism at Xunantunich, Belize. In *The Social Construction of Ancient Cities*, edited by Monica L. Smith, pp. 121–155. Smithsonian Books, Washington, DC.

Zalaquett Rock, Francisca. 2011. Representaciones públicas en el Grupo Norte de Palenque. In *Representaciones y espacios públicos en el área maya: Un estudio interdisciplinario*, edited by Rodrigo Liendo Stuardo and Francisca Zalaquett Rock, pp. 197–214. Universidad Nacional Autónoma de México, Mexico City.

Zender, Marc. 2011. Thoughts on the Inscriptions of Cahal Pech, Belize. Paper presented at the 5th Annual Maya at the Playa Conference, Flagler County, Florida, October 6–9.

Zurita, Judith, and Ann Cyphers. 2008. El context arqueológico de un monumento Olmeca. Poster presentation in the Congreso Interno del Instituto de Investigaciones Antropológicas, Universidad Nacional Autónoma de México, October 7–10. Mexico City.

CONTRIBUTORS

Arianna Campiani is an architect and a PhD candidate in architecture at the National Autonomous University of Mexico. She is interested in prehispanic Maya architecture focusing on the study of city design and urban form. In 2003 and 2004 she worked in the Rio La Venta Archaeological Project, directed by Thomas Lee and Davide Domenci, and from 2005 to 2007 in the Xoclán Archaeological Project, directed by Josep Ligorred. Since 2008 she has collaborated with Rodrigo Liendo Stuardo in the Archaeological Project of Political Interaction of Lordship in Palenque—the Chinikihá Archaeological Project as part of the topography team and is responsible for the study of the urban and architectonic characteristics of the explored sites.

Ann Cyphers received her PhD from the National Autonomous University of Mexico (UNAM) in 1987. She is a senior research scientist at the Institute for Anthropological Research-UNAM in Mexico City and has conducted research in Mesoamerica at the sites of Chalcatzingo, Xochicalco, San Lorenzo Tenochtitlán, and Laguna de los Cerros with a specific focus on the Preclassic period and the Olmec culture.

Takeshi Inomata is a professor of anthropology at the University of Arizona. He has been conducting investigations at the Maya sites of Aguateca and Ceibal, Guatemala. His publications include: *Burned Palaces and Elite Residences of Aguateca: Excavations and Ceramics* (coedited with Daniela Triadan, 2010), *The Classic Maya* (coauthored with Stephen Houston, 2009), and *Archaeology of Performance: Theaters of Power, Community, and Politics* (coedited with Lawrence Coben, 2006).

Arthur Joyce is a professor of anthropology at the University of Colorado, Boulder. He received his PhD from Rutgers University in 1991. Since 1986, he has conducted interdisciplinary archaeological and paleoenvironmental research in Oaxaca, particularly on issues of power, political dynamics, landscape, and ecology. He is the author of *Mixtecs, Zapotecs, and Chatinos: Ancient Peoples of Southern Mexico* (2010) and *Arqueología de la costa de Oaxaca: Asentamientos del periodo Formativo en el valle del Río Verde inferior* (with M. Winter and R. G. Mueller, 1998) and editor of *Polity and Ecology in Formative Period Coastal Oaxaca* (2013). His publications also include "The Main Plaza of Monte Albán: A Life History of Place" (in *The Archaeology of Meaningful Places* edited by B. Bowser and N. Zedeño, 2009) and "Theorizing Urbanism in Ancient

Mesoamerica" (*Ancient Mesoamerica*, 2009). He has held research fellowships from the American Museum of Natural History (1992–93), Dumbarton Oaks (1999), and the American Council of Learned Societies (2006).

Rodrigo Liendo Stuardo is a researcher at the Institute of Anthropological Investigations at the National Autonomous University of Mexico. With a PhD from the University of Pittsburgh, he has carried on several projects in the Palenque region, Mexico, and currently directs the Chinikihá Archaeological Project. His main research concerns deal with the study of ancient Maya settlements, community organization, and urbanism in Mesoamerica.

Javier López Mejía is a Master's candidate in anthropology at the National Autonomous University of Mexico. He received a Licentiate in archaeology from the National School of Anthropology and History (ENAH) in 2005. He has held administrative positions and has been an instructor at ENAH and UNAM. He participated in several archaeological projects conducted in the states of Hidalgo, Chihuahua, Veracruz, and Chiapas in Mexico. Currently, his research field is in the Classic Maya centers of the Usumacinta region, Chiapas. Since 2002, he has collaborated with Rodrigo Liendo Stuardo in the Archaeological Project of Political Interaction of Lordship in Palenque and most recently in the Chinikihá Archaeological Project. His research interests include spatial analyses using GIS and cartographic modeling, political organization, power relations, and economy.

Jerry D. Moore is professor of anthropology at California State University, Dominguez Hills. His research focuses on cultural landscapes, the archaeology of architecture, and human adaptations on the north coast of Peru and northern Baja California. His research has been supported by the National Science Foundation, the National Geographic Society, the Wenner-Gren Foundation for Anthropological Research, the Getty Research Institute, and other agencies and foundations. He is the author of *Architecture and Power in the Prehispanic Andes: The Archaeology of Public Buildings* (1996), *Cultural Landscapes in the Prehispanic Andes: Archaeologies of Place* (2005), *The Prehistory of Home* (2012), *Visions of Culture: An Introduction to Anthropological Theories and Theorists* (2012), twenty-three peer-reviewed articles and book chapters, and sixty-seven professional papers. His book, *A Prehistory of South America: Cultural Diversity on the Least Known Continent* is forthcoming in 2014.

Tatsuya Murakami received his PhD from Arizona State University and is currently an assistant professor at the Department of Anthropology of Tulane University. His research focuses on the materiality of power relations among different social segments as expressed in labor and material resources in Central Mexico. His research is especially concerned with developing a set of concepts and methodologies to discern the complex social landscapes of power based on practice-based and multidisciplinary approaches, including the application of archaeometric methods. He has conducted construction experiments, materials analysis of lime plaster and cut stone blocks, and an analysis of lapidary objects (especially greenstone) at Teotihuacan. He is currently codirecting an archaeological project with Shigeru Kabata (Universidad de las Américas-Puebla) at the Formative site of Tlalancaleca, Puebla, Mexico, which is investigating sociopolitical dynamics in a prestate society and broader regional processes leading to state formation at Teotihuacan.

Timothy Murtha is an anthropological archaeologist with twenty years of field research experience in Mesoamerica, North America, and Northern Europe. His primary research focuses on historic and prehistoric settlement ecology, agrarian settlement patterns, as well as household and landscape archaeology. With an emphasis on environmental anthropology, Murtha's work leverages advanced geospatial technologies, such as GIS, remote sensing and coupled human-environmental modeling. He is an associate professor in the Stuckeman School of Architecture and Landscape Architecture at Penn State University.

Alanna Ossa was the visiting scholar at the Center for Comparative Archaeology at the University of Pittsburgh in 2011–12. She received her PhD in anthropology from Arizona State University in 2011. Her research interests include the social dynamics driving exchange and their intersection with economic cycles of development and collapse. She is currently developing analytical concepts, as well as quantitative and spatial analyses using computer simulations to evaluate social and economic landscapes, and comparative methods for differentiating exchange systems such as markets, gift-giving, and so forth. Her field research is in south-central Veracruz, Mexico, studying economic changes during periods of political transition in the Preclassic (600 BC–AD 300), Late Classic (AD 600–900), and the Middle Postclassic (AD 1200–1350).

William M. Ringle received his PhD in anthropology from Tulane University and currently chairs the department of anthropology at Davidson College. He has codirected projects at Ek Balam and its environs (with George Bey) and for the past eleven years in the Bolonchen District of the Puuc Hills (with Tomás Gallareta Negrón and George Bey), where his work has focused on the urban organization of Kiuic and Huntichmul. Currently he is working in the adjacent Yaxhom Valley of the Puuc Hills. His research interests include political organization, urbanism, writing systems, and iconography. Methodologically, he is interested in computer applications in settlement studies, including CAD, GIS, remote sensing, and laser scanning techniques.

Kara A. Rothenberg is a PhD candidate in the department of anthropology at the University of South Florida. She has participated in archaeological projects in Mexico, Honduras, and Belize since 2007. Her research interests include household- and community-level archaeology, microscale activity analysis using soil chemistry, geoarchaeology, spatial analysis, and quantitative modeling. She is currently conducting research on relationships and shared practices among Terminal Classic households at Actuncan, Belize.

Amara Solari is an assistant professor of art history and anthropology at the Pennsylvania State University. Her research focuses on processes of cultural, visual, and theological interchange between Spanish settlers of New Spain and indigenous groups, primarily the Maya of the Yucatan peninsula. Using the translation of Mayan language texts and extant visual culture, she elucidates how indigenous conceptions of space, landscape, and history influenced the reception and efficacy of the Franciscan evangelical campaign. In addition to having articles appear in *The Art Bulletin*, *Terrae Incognita*, and *Ethnohistory*, she published, with Matthew Restall, *2012 and the End of the World: The Western Roots of the Maya Apocalypse* (2011). Her first monograph, *Maya Ideologies of the Sacred: The Transfiguration of Space in Colonial Yucatan*, was published in 2013.

Marijke Stoll is a graduate student and PhD candidate in archaeology at the University of Arizona's School of Anthropology. She received her Bachelor's degree in anthropology and her Master's in the social sciences from the University of Chicago. Her research interests include ritual and religion, landscape, complex society, the Mesoamerican ballgame, and understanding the relationships between culture, ritual architecture, and spatiality. Though she has worked in Peru, Guatemala, and Mexico, her geographical interests lie in Mesoamerica, particularly in the state of Oaxaca where she has carried out the majority of her fieldwork. Currently she is preparing for the fieldwork stage of her dissertation research, which will focus on newly discovered ballcourts in the Nejapa region of Oaxaca. She currently lives in Oaxaca and can often be found in the capital's Zócalo watching people as they move about and interact in the plaza space. Several publications are forthcoming.

Kenichiro Tsukamoto is a PhD candidate in anthropology at the University of Arizona. He has participated in archaeological projects in Mexico, Guatemala, and Japan, and since 2007 he has been the codirector of the El Palmar Archaeological Project: Urbanization of Social Space in the Maya Lowlands with Javier López Camacho (Escuela Nacional de Antropología e Historia). His research focuses on power and ideological relations, ritual performance, social change, and spatial organization. His methodological approaches include spatial analyses, epigraphic studies, technological analyses, and petrographic microscopy. He received a junior fellowship from Dumbarton Oaks (2012–13).

Javier Urcid is an associate professor of anthropology at Brandeis University. He received his PhD from Yale University in 1992. His interests include the study of ancient scripts, archaeological approaches to political systems, the social dimensions of mortuary practices, and the ritual treatment of human remains. He is the author of *Zapotec Hieroglyphic Writing* (2001) and *The Lords of Lambityeco: Political Evolution in the Valley of Oaxaca during the Xoo Phase* (with Michael D. Lind, 2010). Other publications include "The Written Surface as a Cultural Code" (in *Their Way of Writing*, edited by E. Boone and G. Urton, 2011) and "El Sacrificio Humano en el Suroeste de Mesoamérica" (in *Nuevas Perspectivas sobre el Sacrificio Humano entre los Mexicas*, edited by L. López Luján and G. Olivier, 2010). He has held research fellowships from Dumbarton Oaks (1990), and the Center for the Advanced Study in the Visual Arts, National Gallery of Art (1998).

INDEX